THE ETERNAL PRESENT

Also by Andrea Wells Miller

Facing Codependence, Pia Mellody, with Andrea Wells Miller and J. Keith Miller (HarperCollins)

Breaking Free, Pia Mellody and Andrea Wells Miller (HarperCollins)

Facing Love Addiction, Pia Mellody, with Andrea Wells Miller and J. Keith Miller (HarperCollins)

A Choir Director's Handbook, compiled and edited by Andrea Wells Miller (Word Books)

The Single Experience, Keith Miller and Andrea Wells Miller

BodyCare, Andrea Wells Miller (Word Books)

Recovering Connections, Richard D. Grant, Jr., Ph.D. and Andrea Wells Miller (HarperCollins)

THE ETERNAL PRESENT

Andrea Wells Miller, Editor

A Crossroad Book
The Crossroad Publishing Company
New York

Unless otherwise indicated, Scripture quotations are taken from the Holy Bible, NEW INTERNATIONAL VERSION®. Copyright © 1973, 1978, 1984 International Bible Society. All rights reserved throughout the world. Used by permission of International Bible Society.

Scripture from the New Revised Standard Version Bible, copyright © 1989 by the Division of Christian Education of the National Council of the Churches of Christ in the U.S.A., and used by permission.

Scripture from the Revised Standard Version of the Bible, copyrighted 1946, 1952, 1971, 1973 by the Division of Christian Education of the National Council of the Churches of Christ in the U.S.A., and used by permission.

Scripture from the Jerusalem Bible, copyright © 1966 by Darton, Longman & Todd, Ltd. and Doubleday & Company, Inc.

Scripture from The Message Copyright © 1993, 1994, 1995, 1996, 2000, 2001, 2002. Used by permission of the NavPress Publishing Group."

Scripture from the New King James Version, copyright © 1982 by Thomas Nelson, Inc. Used by permission. All rights reserved.

Scripture from The New Testament in Modern English, Revised Edition, Copyright © J. B. Phillips 1958, 1960, 1972. Used by permission of the Macmillan Publishing Company.

Scripture from the New American Bible copyright © 1991, 1986, 1970 by the Confraternity of Christian Doctrine, 3211 Fourth Street, N.E., Washington, D.C. 20017-1194. All rights reserved.

The Crossroad Publishing Company
www.crossroadpublishing.com

Copyright © 2003 by Andrea Wells Miller

All rights reserved. No part of this book may be reproduced, stored in a retrieval system, or transmitted, in any form or by any means, electronic, mechanical, photocopying, recording, or otherwise, without the written permission of The Crossroad Publishing Company.

The text type is 10/12 Cheltenham. Display type is Cheltenham Handtooled, Copperplate, and Caslon Antique.

Printed in the United States of America

Library of Congress Cataloging-in-Publication Data
The eternal present / Andrea Wells Miller, editor.
   p. cm.
   Includes indexes.
   ISBN 0-8245-2112-9
   1. Devotional calendars. I. Miller, Andrea Wells. II. Title.
BV4810.E74 2003
242'.2–dc21
                                      2003003521

CONTENTS

Publisher's Note
7

JANUARY
9

FEBRUARY
41

MARCH
73

APRIL
107

MAY
140

JUNE
172

JULY
204

AUGUST
236

SEPTEMBER
271

OCTOBER
304

NOVEMBER
338

DECEMBER
368

Permissions
398

About the Contributors
404

Acknowledgments
406

Scripture Index
407

Author Index
412

PUBLISHER'S NOTE

Lectio Divina. A new phrase to the eyes and hears of many Protestants. It was certainly a new and strange phrase to me, a former fundamentalist, former evangelical Presbyterian, now charismatic Episcopalian who is seeking to become friends with God, Jesus, and the Holy Spirit. Divine Reading. Lectio Divina. What does that phrase really mean? And how is it different from the well-known "devotional" reading that many of us practiced as a part of our daily Christian lives? Actually the difference is striking and important.

In the early 1970s I was a student at Fuller Theological Seminary. In one class I unexpectedly encountered a skill that profoundly shaped my understanding of the role of the Scripture in the church. The class was "Public Reading of Scripture" taught by the late film and stage actor John Holland. When John would stride up to the pulpit in his home church, Hollywood Presbyterian, to read the Bible passage for that Sunday morning, all breathing seemed to stop. His ability, as a gifted orator and actor, to read the Scripture with power, meaning, and drama surprised us students every time. He demonstrated the same skill in our class.

We all secretly wished we had his ability and skill. And we tried. Sometimes, in our videotaped presentations, we would ascend to that place of power and meaning and our untrained voices would serve us well, even if just for a few seconds. But it would only last a few seconds. We could not perform in that way which I now realize took John a whole lifetime of skilled practice to accomplish. But we were all changed nonetheless. Now we knew how the Scriptures should be read, and why. For the meaning. For the power. And whenever I am asked today to read the Scripture in church I descend to my library and read the prescribed passage out loud over and over again, searching for the meaning, searching for the power, searching even for the drama. Then when I stand behind the lector pulpit on a Sunday morning, I try my best to speak the words of the Bible with faith, humility, openness, and wonder, even with a little drama. So what has this to do with divine reading?

First, it means that we (or each of us individually) read the Scripture as if it were a public act. Start by allowing me to encourage you to read the Scripture passages at the beginning of each of these devotional entries aloud. Maybe more than once. Think about how your voice adds meaning to the words. Think about how the words mean more to you when you hear them, as others would hear them. Then read the entry again at least once aloud, knowing that in this way our Divine Friend is speaking to us. In the words of Jesus, "I no longer call you servants, but friends." In this way we enter into the ancient practice of Lectio Divina, "which is letting our Divine Friend speak to us through his inspired and inspiring Word" as M. Basil Pennington says. We hear and read, not just in a private way but as a part of the community that constitutes the kingdom of God.

Father Pennington, a Benedictine, also says in his book *Lectio Divina,* "The tradition of the lectio is certainly one of the most ancient in the Church.... Hearing this Good News is one of the most essential acts of our being. Receiving the Word is receiving God in a most human way: Friend to friend, sharing what is inmost.... When we receive the Word as word, we communicate at deeper, more fully human levels, opening the way to the divine communication that brings us into the communication within the Trinity of the Father and the Son in Holy Spirit. It is a communion beyond words because we have become one with the Word."

The goal of the Lectio Divina is to incorporate the Scripture into our innermost being and have it transform us. This is the second dimension of Lectio Divina. Too often our goal in reading Scripture or a devotion, like the entries in this marvelous book, is sentimentality. But sentimentality has no power to change us, to remake us in the image of Christ. If we hear and speak the Word, however, and do it as a part of our public experience it begins to work on our inner self in ways that are mysterious and powerful. This is why the monastic communities chant the Psalter in a never ending cycle of repetition and prayer, always an act of community. Then the powerful Word begins to seep deep into our souls and transform us from within.

Over the years as I have walked along with friends who lived within the sacramental traditions, I realized that my view of reading the Bible was impoverished by my privatistic perspective. But John Holland, in his gracious but artful way, began to open up for me, as did my friends from the sacramental traditions, a new understanding of the public dimension of that Word. It is powerful and sharper than any two-edged sword and is meant to be heard and read within the community of the faithful. It is also meant to cleave all of us, not just me, betwixt sin and redemption and to be a public experience. And so this tradition of Lectio Divina is an ancient practice that takes us beyond our own private reading of the Bible. It ushers us into the eternal congregation of the communion of saints where we "hear" from the author and finisher of our Faith. The authors and I herein pray that this book will be an introduction to divine reading, Lectio Divina, for each reader, and may we all be forever changed.

ROY M. CARLISLE

JANUARY

January 1

A Dream of Grace

"The Lord is righteous in all his ways and loving toward all he has made." —Psalm 145:17

"For it is by grace you have been saved, through faith — and this is not from yourselves, it is a gift of God." —Ephesians 2:8

In my dream it was winter, and it was dark. Melissa was only five or six. We were leaving the grocery store. I was pushing the cart across the icy parking lot. Melissa lingered to play with the automatic doors. I called to her. As she turned and started to run toward me, a car careened into the lot. Its headlights struck her face, and I saw in her eyes the terror of a white-tailed deer frozen on the highway. The driver of the mad car never braked. My voice rose, a wild, animal scream, for it was all that could reach her. She fell.

The car passed over her and disappeared into the wall of the store. She jumped from the pavement and ran into my arms. I woke.

I did not want to go back to sleep, so I got up and wrote down the dream. This morning I showed it to Lionel. "It's a dream about grace," he said. Seeing my puzzled expression, he went on. "You could do nothing to save her. It was beyond you. Yet she was spared — spared in an impossible way." —John Leax, *In Season and Out*

Lord, you have told us your strength is revealed in our weakness. If you are strong in this world, it must be so, for we are weak and needy. Fill us with your grace. Let us rise joyful when the cars of care knock us down. Let our weakness declare your salvation. Amen.

January 2

COMMUNION

"Words kill, words give life; they're either poison or fruit — you choose."
 — Proverbs 18:21, THE MESSAGE

When my daughter Karen was young, I often took her with me when I visited nursing homes. She was better than a Bible. The elderly in these homes brightened immediately when she entered the room, delighted in her smile, asked her questions. They would touch her skin, stroke her hair. On one such visit we were with Mrs. Herr, who was in an advanced state of dementia. She was talkative and directed all her talk to Karen. She told her a story, an anecdote out of her childhood that Karen's presence triggered. When she completed the story she immediately began at the beginning and did it again, word for word and then again and again and again.

After twenty minutes or so of this I became anxious lest Karen become uncomfortable and confused about what was going on. So I interrupted this flow of talk, anointed the woman with oil, laid hands on her, prayed, and left. In the car and driving home, I commended Karen for her patience and attentiveness. She had listened to this repeated story without showing any sign of restlessness or boredom. I said to her, "Karen, Mrs. Herr's mind is not working the way ours is."

And Karen said, "Oh, I knew that, Daddy. She was not trying to tell us anything; she was telling us who she is."

Nine years old, and she knew the difference, knew that Mrs. Herr was using words not for communication but for communion. It is a difference that our culture as a whole pays little attention to but pastors must pay attention to. Our primary task, the pastor's primary task, is not communication but communion.

— Eugene H. Peterson, *Under the Unpredictable Plant*

Communion with you, O God, and with each other is what I will seek today. Heighten my sensitivity as I go about the things I do, that I may experience the communion that waits for me and offer it to others. In Jesus' name. Amen.

January 3

MEDITATION: A PORTABLE SANCTUARY

"Here I am! I stand at the door and knock. If anyone hears my voice and opens the door, I will come in and eat with him, and he with me."
—Revelation 3:20

In meditation we are growing into what Thomas à Kempis calls "a familiar friendship with Jesus." We are sinking down into the light and life of Christ and becoming comfortable in that posture. The perpetual presence of the Lord (omnipresence, as we say) moves from a theological dogma into a radiant reality. "He walks with me and he talks with me" ceases to be pious jargon and instead becomes a straightforward description of daily life.

Please understand me: I am not speaking of some mushy, giddy, buddy-buddy relationship. All such sentimentality only betrays how little we know, how distant we are from the Lord high and lifted up who is revealed to us in Scripture. John tells us in his Apocalypse that when he saw the reigning Christ, he fell at his feet as though dead, and so should we (Rev. 1:17). No, I am speaking of a reality more akin to what the disciples felt in the upper room when they experienced both intense intimacy and awful reverence.

What happens in meditation is that we create the emotional and spiritual space which allows Christ to construct an inner sanctuary in the heart. The wonderful verse "I stand at the door and knock..." was originally penned for believers, not unbelievers (Rev. 3:20). We who have turned our lives over to Christ need to know how very much he longs to eat with us, to commune with us. He desires a perpetual Eucharistic feast in the inner sanctuary of the heart. Meditation opens the door and, although we are engaging in specific meditation exercises at specific times, the aim is to bring this living reality into all of life. It is a portable sanctuary that is brought into all we are and do.

—Richard J. Foster, *Celebration of Discipline*

Come! Spirit of Love!

Penetrate and transform us by the action of your purifying life. May your constant, brooding love bring forth in us more love and all the graces and works of love. Give us grace to remain still under its action, and may that humble stillness be our prayer. Amen.

—Evelyn Underhill, *Meditations and Prayers*

January 4

BEARING BURDENS

"This is how we know what love is: Jesus Christ laid down his life for us. And we ought to lay down our lives for our brothers. If anyone has material possessions and sees his brother in need but has no pity on him, how can the love of God be in him? Dear children, let us not love with words or tongue but with actions and in truth."

—1 John 3:16-18

Alan Paton, South African author of *Cry the Beloved Country,* holds up St. Francis of Assisi as a Christlike model of human response. One of the transforming moments of Francis Bernardone's life occurred when he was riding a horse as a young nobleman and came across a person with leprosy. Francis was bitter toward God at the time and felt a certain revulsion at the diseased man. But something within him overcame both those reactions. He dismounted from his horse, walked over, and embraced the beggar, kissing him full on the lips.

St. Francis could have cursed either God or the man with leprosy, says Paton. He did neither. Rather than spending his energy in accusing God for allowing the wound to creation, he chose instead to make his life an instrument of God's peace. That act transformed both the giver and receiver: "What had seemed bitter to me was changed into sweetness of body and soul," said St. Francis.

St. Francis's response was the very same response Alyosha gave his brother Ivan in *The Brothers Karamazov.* He could not resolve Ivan's or his own questions about the problem of pain. But he chose to put himself beside the sufferers and embrace them. And, pointedly, Dostoyevski portrayed Jesus giving that very same response to his enemy, the Grand Inquisitor.

If the church followed the pattern consistently, and responded to questions of suffering not with arguments but with love, perhaps those questions would not be asked with such troubled intensity. The united strength of Christ's body can be a powerful force on behalf of the lonely, suffering, and deprived. It can be like the tree in the gospel that grows so large that birds begin to nest in its branches.

In my visits in hospitals, I have been impressed by the huge difference between the measure of comfort that can be offered by believers ("We're praying for you") and unbelievers ("Best of luck — we'll keep our fingers crossed"). Today, if I had to answer the question "Where is God when it hurts?" in a single sentence, I would make that sentence another question: "Where is the church when it hurts?" We form the front line of God's response to the suffering world.

—Philip Yancey, *Where Is God When It Hurts?*

Dear Lord, my influence on others in pain comes from my willingness to offer love, to put myself beside the sufferers and "embrace" them — with thoughts, with physical acts of help, with prayers, with a listening ear. Help me to remember and to join with others in my church so that together we can become the front line of your response to suffering in the world. In Jesus' name. Amen.

January 5

A SEA OF MIDNIGHT TEARS

"Then Peter got down out of the boat, walked on the water and came toward Jesus. But when he saw the wind, he was afraid and, beginning to sink, cried out, 'Lord, save me!'" —Matthew 14:29b–30

In the people, and even the flowers and desert country next to the beautiful Gulf of Mexico, I saw a rugged loveliness, mingled with signs of fear, death, and failure. But I also found everywhere footprints of a saving God. But only when my own life met the "scorpion of the air" did I see that I am powerless — even with Texas-style courage — to save myself from the pain caused by sin and the need to be right and to be the savior of myself and those around me.

I saw it all clearly one moonlit night by the Gulf of Mexico, as I tried to walk across a "Sea of Midnight Tears."

> The moonbeam was a silver blade
> That cut the bonds of sleep too soon.
> At the beach, across the waves I saw
> A white-orange highway to the moon.
>
> I heard the Voice of Silence then,
> "Your pain has led you to the sea.
> Follow now My Son's clear light
> Across the waves of doubt to me."
>
> "You've cried a sea of midnight tears.
> You've almost drowned in work and fame.
> You've said a thousand faith-filled words
> Now leave them all, only say my name."
>
> I cried out, "But I've said your Name!"
> "No, listen closely, it was yours."
> I shook my fist through tears of shame,
> My rage and fear at least were pure.

I sank beneath the silver waves
And knew that all was lost to me.
The last words that I whispered were,
"Jesus, Lord — Master of the sea."

Then you came and set me free.

—J. Keith Miller, *Highway Home through Texas*

Lord, thank you, thank you that you are a saving God! So many times I've strayed from your Way, only to smash into walls of pain, fear, and frustration, or sometimes sink beneath the waves of emptiness, loneliness and lack of hope. Never give up on me, Lord. I need you in order to live. I want your Way to become more and more my own. Stay close by forever. In Jesus' name. Amen.

January 6

TO SEE THE STARS

"I, even my hands, have stretched out the heavens, and all their host have I commanded."
— Isaiah 45:12, KJV

The sky was enormous and terribly high. It's a funny thing: the colder it gets, the farther away the sky seems and the farther off the stars look. The sky was so thick with them it was almost as though it had been snowing stars, and down below us there was a white fog so it seemed as though we were looking out over a great lake. The Milky Way was a river of light, and John began pointing out the constellations, and I found the Big Dipper and the North Star and Cassiopeia's Chair and Scorpio and Sagittarius. Sagittarius is my favorite because it's my sign of the zodiac and I like the idea of shooting up to the stars.

Mother said, "I know you're both very upset about Uncle Hal and Maggy's father. We all are. I thought maybe if we came and looked at the stars it would help us to talk about it a little."

Just then a shooting star flashed across the sky, and John said, "There's a shooting star and I don't know what to wish. I want to wish it back to before yesterday and that none of this would have happened, but I know it wouldn't work."

I said. "Mother, I don't understand it," and I began to shiver.

Mother said, "Sometimes it's very hard to see the hand of God instead of the blind finger of Chance. That's why I wanted to come out where we could see the stars."
— Madeleine L'Engle, *Meet the Austins*

Lord, when we consider the work of your fingers, the moon and the stars which you have ordained, teach us our steps in the patterned dance of the universe. Amen.

January 7

FROM DUST TO DUST

"He is not the God of the dead, but of the living, for to him all are alive." —Luke 20:38

> Cold woman earth laughs loose and free.
> Her skin like fields taught me to sing.
> I wear her sweet dust like a ring,
> Desire her till eternity.
> How long before she will have me?
>
> I turn. I will seduce the sky
> The solemn mouth of endlessness
> To send some word strong as a kiss.
> In spirit with us all I cry
> May some world teach me how to die.
>
> When deserts smother fields of rye
> When waterfalls turn to stone
> Dust in my grave instead of bone,
> Still men will bless blank air and try
> To calculate the way to die.
>
> I stand beneath a calm green tree.
> Oh how the mouth of sky can sing
> What is and what is not, and bring
> From my dumb dust a saner plea;
> Before I die, God of what is,
> Be love to me. Teach me to be.

—Jeanne Murray Walker

Eternal Lord of the living, present in time and in flesh, teach me to apprehend, not the succession of passing moments that lead to death, but the present of your love, the eternal life that is mine through Jesus Christ, your Son. Amen.

January 8

GOD'S DAWN

"The night is far spent, the day is at hand."
—Romans 13:12a, KJV

Dawn creeps in stealthily from the east. Already an hour before the appearance of the sun, a mysterious glow rises from the horizon until the entire canopy of sky seems backlit. Grays dissolve into whites, and the sun itself, brighter than an orange in winter, peeks from a landscape drenched in gold.

There's a process to the day. We don't move from night to noon as if someone had flipped a switch. It's almost embarrassing to think about, isn't it? — that kind of radical change? Every day we'd walk into life with sleep lines creasing our faces. But the world is lit by a divine rheostat that gently and smoothly brightens the stage, each day, for our lives.

In some ways, our lives after conversion exist in a slowly rising dawn. The big day, the brightest day, comes only when the glory of Christ breaks over us.

That is as true today as it was in the day of the Apostle Paul, when conversions had to have been, in general, even more radical than they seem today. Speaking for himself and for the converts at Rome, he says, "Now it is [even though it's years after their conversions] high time to awake out of this sleep [their condition, even though they're converted].... The night is far spent, the day is at hand" (Rom. 13:11–12).

Like the dawn, however, these stages emerge slowly and not always visibly. Just as there is no switch for the day, no one pulls a chord and — just like that — becomes a mature Christian. Those who think they do are kidding themselves.

Even though the light we observe now in our renewed lives, our illuminated lives, doesn't reach the brightness we will know someday, that light still turns our narrow paths into freeways. It enriches human existence in all ways because it discloses to us the route we take to come to God. Everything looks more beautiful in the light of the Son.

Those who know God's light as richly as we can know it in this half-lit world, know absolutely nothing of standing still. By growing in their Christian walk, they enter more fully into the secrets of the infinite; when they awake in the morning, they do so in God's light, a light they carry with them every hour of the day, no matter where they work. Who are these people? — the salt of the salt, really. What's more, they are the salt of God's church. You know them, too.

These people are truly gifts to us. They're sanctified saints who preserve his church from desecration and dissolution. They're like planets.

They reflect the brilliance of divine light. They shine in the darkness of the world. Thank God. —James Calvin Schaap, *Near Unto God*

We have wakened in the dawn of your new life. Shine in us, Jesus. Brighten our day with your divine life. Amen.

January 9

THE PROMISE OF LIFE

"I have set my rainbow in the clouds.... I will remember my covenant between me and you and all living creatures of every kind."
—Genesis 9:13, 15

> Here in my winter breakfast room,
> the colors of rainbows are
> reduced to eight solid lozenges in a
> white metal tray. The child's brush
> muddies them to gray in a
> glass of water. Even the light breaks down
> as it pushes through the rain-streaked
> windows and polishes the wooden table
> imperfectly.
>
> Green leaves always turn
> brown. Summer died into the dark days
> a long while ago; it is hard even to
> remember what it was like, stalled
> as I am in this narrow slot of time
> and daylight.
>
> Until I look down again
> and see, puddling along the paper,
> under a painted orange sun
> primitive as the first spoked wheel,
> the ribbon of colors flowing out of
> my granddaughter's memory—a new
> rainbow, arc-ing wet over strokes of grass
> green enough to be true.

Such a simple, unremarkable moment. A dark, rainy day in late winter. My granddaughter Lauren, six, painting at a table near a window, quite unconscious of my scrutiny of her.

But the promise I received as I watched her laying the wet colors down on paper felt potent, as real to me as the covenant the Lord God made with Noah after the Great Flood.

He promised Noah that he would never again destroy by water all the living creatures on the earth. What I received in a child's painted rainbow was also a promise of life — that the days would lengthen, that the joy of spring and green would return, and that once again God would paint his iridescence wherever the sun shone on the rain's falling moisture. It is only when the two work together — sun with rain, joy with tears — that we see the flowing ribbon of a rainbow and the promise that comes with it.
—Luci Shaw, *Horizons*

Lord, you have made your covenant with all creation. In Christ you have established once more your order in the world. By grace I enter that order. As your sign in the sky reminds me — what joy is mine! Hallelujah! Amen.

January 10

HAVING IT ALL

"But everything exposed by the light becomes visible, for it is light that makes everything visible. This is why it is said: 'Wake up O sleeper, rise from the dead, and Christ will shine on you.' Be very careful, then, how you live — not as unwise but as wise, making the most of every opportunity, because the days are evil. Therefore do not be foolish, but understand what the Lord's will is."
—Ephesians 5:13-17

My fear of asking too little is greater, I find, than my fear of my own immorality. I don't want something to make into a tidy little life for me and mine; I want Life itself.

One must be willing to risk immorality as a spy, to sin, as Luther advised, boldly. With a spy there can be no divided loyalties; the single eye is everything. The very goodness of good activities can be seductive. One must, in the end, be content to let the dead bury the dead, to stop one's ears to the voice of the mother and brothers and sisters that stand outside and call, "Come out, come back. Give up this strange obsession with staring and stalking, this mean hoarding of your oil. Share with us." But there are no half measures. One must either sacrifice or hoard.

Yes, I have a family, a house, a cat. I sit close to my fire on January evenings as you do. But I know these cozy comforts, taken in themselves, are finally futile. They drain away into the darkness in only a few years. One irrational duplication in a gene's design as a cell divides, and it is a cancerous corpse that rocks before the fire.

Still, the fire, the house, the cat — these provide as good a place to spy as any. Domesticity makes a fine disguise. The housewife hiding the leaven in the loaf and finding the coin knows this.

Kafka vouches for the success of the stay-at-home spy: "You do not need to leave your room. Remain sitting at your table and listen. Do not even listen, simply wait. Do not even wait, be quite still and solitary. The world will offer itself quite freely to you to be unmasked, it has no choice, it will roll in ecstasy at your feet."

That is the spy speaking, the one who knows how to sit and wait in unlikely places, ready to pounce on reality, should it choose to reveal itself.

And it does so choose. Those who seek do find, as long as the seeking is their first and consuming passion. The door does open, gives way even as the knuckles strike it. "We may ignore, but we can nowhere evade, the presence of God," C. S. Lewis wrote. "The world is crowded with him. He walks everywhere incognito. And the incognito is not always hard to penetrate. The real labour is to attend. In fact, to come awake. Still more, to remain awake." —Virginia Stem Owens, *God Spy*

Develop in me a single eye, O Lord. Guide me toward your reality as I watch and wait throughout my days and nights. In Jesus' name. Amen.

January 11

Christian Joy

"And now, God, do it again —
 bring rains to our drought-stricken lives
So those who planted their crops in despair
 will shout hurrahs at the harvest,
So those who went off with heavy hearts
 will come home laughing, with armloads of blessing."
—Psalm 126:4-6, THE MESSAGE

It is clear in Psalm 126 that the one who wrote it and those who sang it were no strangers to the dark side of things. They carried the painful memory of exile in their bones and the scars of oppression on their backs. They knew the deserts of the heart and the nights of weeping. They knew what it meant to sow in tears.

One of the most interesting and remarkable things that Christians learn is that laughter does not exclude weeping. Christian joy is not an escape from sorrow. Pain and hardship still come, but they are unable to drive out the happiness of the redeemed.

A common but futile strategy for achieving joy is trying to eliminate things that hurt: get rid of pain by numbing the nerve ends, get rid of insecurity by eliminating risks, get rid of disappointments by depersonalizing your relationships. And then try to lighten the boredom of such a life by buying joy in the form of vacations and entertainment. There isn't a hint of that in Psalm 126.

—Eugene H. Peterson, *A Long Obedience in the Same Direction*

Dear Lord, help me to see where I may be trying to avoid pain, insecurity, or disappointments by numbing nerve ends, avoiding risks, distancing myself from a relationship. Bring me to the place of owning and experiencing my pain even as I experience the joy that I am yours and you are with me in the pain. In Jesus' name. Amen.

January 12

THE LIFT OF GOD'S GRACE

"They who wait for the Lord shall renew their strength, they shall mount up with wings like eagles." —Isaiah 40:31, RSV

Oil Spill

You are in the small gray light
that wakes from the east, the shore
that outlines my day. Empty
sky is your medium. You promise

nothing to me who beach
like a ruptured supertanker
glutting the shore with oil,
slick gull, dying of surfeit.

I wade out, coated
with unctuous night.
Stones cut my feet —
my tongue crusted with sand.

Immerse me again, wash clean
the broken feather of my will.

Dry me with your wind,
massage my sluggish heart.

Then drop me from the bluff
into sharpening light,
where for hours I may climb
the thermal updraft of your breathing.

—Robert Siegel, *In a Pig's Eye*

Hold me in the lift of your grace, O Lord. Let my voice call over sea and shore how you have cleansed me and made me whole. Let my flight testify to the breath of your love. Amen.

January 13

FEARS, REAL AND IMAGINED

"I cry aloud to the LORD, and he answers me from his holy hill. [Selah]"   —Psalm 3:4, RSV

Two moments of fear in the life of C. S. Lewis.

First, in 1926, when a young don at Oxford University, he planned to write a shocker play with a friend of his. First, they created the characters.

A Scientist with "a bright red beard, Mephistophelian in shape but reaching to the waist, very thick lips, and one leg shorter than the other."

A Corpse whose body lay in a coffin packed with ice, but whose brain and nerves were kept alive by injections.

A Hero and a Heroine who found "a poor fellow whose face was badly smashed in the war" huddling by the fire, complaining of the cold and how the Scientist was always chasing him about.

Of course, the Heroine would be the Scientist's next victim....

One night as Lewis slept, he dreamed that the Corpse had escaped and run amok, pursuing him about the streets of London and down into the Underground. He managed to reach the lift; the Liftman was terrified; and as the Corpse was about to strike, Lewis screamed, "There's going to be an accidennnnnt!" And then he awoke.

Clearly this was an imagined fear that seemed quite real to Lewis while he slept but, when he woke up, the scream was very real indeed.

Second, in 1929, after some vivid, even lurid, moments of introspection, Lewis came to the realization that Philosophy as the explanation of the universe fell rather short. At that moment he decided to stop philosophizing and start praying. But to whom? And then it happened. He heard a foot upon the staircase in New Buildings. The door to his rooms creaked open, and in walked a Mummy, heaving and throwing off its gravecloths to reveal a living presence. It was, Lewis could hardly wait to write to his old friend and collaborator, a sort of theological shocker. He even heard it say "I am," "I am who I am," "I'm the Lord God of creation."

Clearly, this was a real fear, God wrapped like a Mummy. Happily, Lewis's very real response was, not to the Mummy, but to God, acknowledging at long last that He existed.

Several morals present themselves. First, imagined fears sometimes have very real touches in them. Second, real fears are often festooned with bright, imaginative touches. Third, virtually all fears are not only grislies but also grizzlies quite willing to hug you to death, squeeze the living daylights out of you. Fourth, the God of all fears, real or imagined, comes whenever you call.

—William Griffin, *The High Calling of Our Daily Work*

Dear God, how good it is to be reminded that in the midst of our fears—both imagined and real—you promised to be with us. By calling out to you, we remind ourselves that you are near. Amen.

January 14

Darkness into Light

"If I say, 'Surely the darkness will hide me and the light become night around me,' even the darkness will not be dark to you; the night will shine like the day, for darkness is as light to you."   —Psalm 139:11-12

Because of the ice storm earlier this week the power is out all over town. I chanced on Chad Walsh's poem, "Why has thou forsaken me?" and heard the words from Psalm 22 echoing my frequent feelings:

> I have called to God and heard no answer,
> I have seen the thick curtain drop and sunlight die;...
> I have walked in darkness, he hung in it.
> In all my mines of night, he was there first;
> In whatever dead tunnel I am lost, he finds me.
> My God, my God, why has thou forsaken me?
> From his perfect darkness a voice says, "I have not."

How can darkness be perfect? When it is part of God's purpose. Perhaps he planned this darkness, this power outage, as a demonstration for me, just as he planned it for his Son, so that the darkness may be banished when the power comes on again. This way we see darkness for what it is — absence of light. It seemed a word of the Lord to me in the moment I read it. I can't see him — the darkness is too thick. All I want is a touch — hand, shoulder, robe — so that I know he is with me in this place until the lights come on and my eyes squint for the glory of it.

—Luci Shaw, *God in the Dark*

I can't always see you, Lord. Sometimes my darkness is too thick. In those moments let me feel your touch that I might follow fearlessly until your light blinds me once more with glory. Amen.

January 15

SACRIFICE

"And pray for us, too, that God may open a door for our message, so that we may proclaim the mystery of Christ, for which I am in chains. Pray that I may proclaim it clearly, as I should."

—Colossians 4:3-4

Mike preached from Colossians this morning. His theme was the necessity of sacrifice to validate one's witness. He kept returning to Paul's imprisonment, to the idea that it was the result and the proof of his faithfulness.

I have been thinking of sacrifice. I have been thinking of my writing, of the work I do here each morning typing these pages. How do I offer up this work as a sacrifice to God?

I begin with the nature of this work. Part of me does not want to do it; the core of journaling is discovery and revelation. In a journal a writer explores his personhood and his relationships. When he allows the journal to be read, he lets others into his life. He gives away knowledge of himself; he gives others power to invade his privacy. That bothers me greatly, for I am becoming an increasingly private person. My earlier willingness, as a writer, to reveal myself strikes me as somewhat self-absorbed and egotistical.

I often relate to my students E. B. White's observation that essayists must believe everything that happens to them is of interest to everyone else, that essayists are unrepentant egotists. I usually go on to justify that apparent egotism on the grounds that if what happens to a sparrow is of importance to God, what happens to humans must be of importance to humans. I argue that all experience is of consequence and that writing is giving testimony. I think that is true, but I fear it can only be true of a saint. For the rest of us it is ego.

The testimony is the ideal. It is what writing about the self reaches after. The necessary revelation, however, is corrupted by the egomania and the desire for safety, the desire to remain hidden.

What then does one do? Write on and hope for the best? Shut up? Frost has a poem called "How Hard It Is to Keep from Being King When It's In You and In the Situation." Perhaps if one is a writer, one can't shut up. No matter how the writing disturbs one, how the writing causes anxiety, irritability, fear, and doubt.

How do I offer this work up as a sacrifice? How can I offer up something I'd like to get rid of? Perhaps there is my answer, or part of my answer. I offer it up by taking it up, by not discarding it. I offer it up by affirming the goodness of the task — recognizing the complexity of motives at work, the testimony and the egomania — by putting aside my desire to sort it all out and be pure in heart or silent, by simply doing it and relying on grace to guide me wherever it will.

By laboring faithfully until someday I wake, in another world, to find myself a saint, one made perfect by the Christ who takes our work and makes it his.
— John Leax, *Standing Ground*

Lord, life seems to be full of things I'd rather not be doing, but that need to be done. In my work, in my daily living at home, in my relationships with my family and friends — I often find myself thinking I'd rather be elsewhere. I have trouble knowing if I'm giving up my time to someone or something as a testimony to your image of servanthood, or because I'm too much of a people pleaser, or to get brownie points I can collect in the future.

Help me to offer these times up to you as a sacrifice, without waiting until I can sort through my motives. And as I encounter each experience, may I increase my reliance on grace, simply doing what is before me, as I learn how to focus my questions to you, seeking your guidance. In Jesus' name. Amen.

January 16

LITTLE DEEDS

"Do nothing out of selfish ambition or vain conceit, but in humility consider others better than yourselves."   —Philippians 2:3

Thérèse of Lisieux, known only as "the Little Flower," devised a prayer-filled approach to life that has helped many. This Little Way, as she called it, is deceptively simple. It is, in short, to seek out the menial job, to welcome unjust criticisms, to befriend those who annoy us, to help those who are ungrateful. For her part, Thérèse was convinced that these "trifles" pleased Jesus more than the great deeds of recognized holiness. The beauty of the Little Way is how utterly available it is to everyone. From the child to the adult, from the sophisticated to the simple, from the most powerful to the least influential, all can undertake this ministry of small things. The opportunities to live in this way come to us constantly, while the great fidelities happen only now and again. Almost daily we can give smiling service to nagging co-workers, listen attentively to silly bores, express little kindnesses without making a fuss.

We may think these tiny, trivial activities are hardly worth mentioning. That, of course, is precisely their value. They are unrecognized conquests over selfishness. We will never receive a medal or even a "thank you" for these invisible victories in ordinary life — which is exactly what we want.

An incident from Thérèse's autobiography, *The Story of a Soul*, underscores the hiddenness of the Little Way. One uneducated and rather conceited sister had managed to irritate Thérèse in everything she did. Rather than avoid this person, however, she took the Little Way straight into the conflict: "I set myself to treat her as if I loved her best of all." Thérèse succeeded so well in her Little Way that following her death this same sister declared, "During her life, I made her really happy. Thérèse, I am sure, would be pleased."[1]

—Richard J. Foster, *Prayer, Finding the Heart's True Home*

To Do Some Work of Peace for Thee

O Lord,
open my eyes that I may see the needs of others;
open my ears that I may hear their cries;
open my heart so that they need not be without succor;
let me not be afraid to defend the weak because of the anger of the
      strong,
nor afraid to defend the poor because of the anger of the rich.

Show me where love and hope and faith are needed,
and use me to bring them to those places.

And so open my eyes and my ears
that I may this coming day be able to do some work of peace for
      thee. Amen. — Alan Paton, *The United Methodist Hymnal*

---

1. As quoted in Gloria Hutchinson, *Six Ways to Pray from Six Great Saints* (Cincinnati: St. Anthony Messenger Press, 1982), 87.

January 17

AN AMAZING SURPRISE

"I believe; help my unbelief!"
—Mark 9:24, RSV

But here... is the baffling paradox of a person seeking — yet running from God, as the moment of conversion is upon him or her.... John Knox helps clarify what is happening in the resolution of this conflict. He reminds us of Alfred North Whitehead's belief that religion runs through three stages if it evolves to its final satisfaction. It is the transition from *God the void* to *God the enemy*, and from *God the enemy* to *God the companion*.

What is meant by *God the companion*? Knox suggests that this stage, when realized (or to the extent it is realized), means a free and inward capitulation to the "enemy," an allowing of ourselves to be captured by the God who seeks us. This stage is the "final satisfaction" because we discover in the moment of surrender that the God who is on our trail is also the God we seek. In a strange manner, as we seem to be defeated, it dawns on us that we are in the only possible way, *victorious!* For we are free from having to run from God (who is everywhere), and we can turn and embrace him.

Our semiconscious fear of surrendering and being totally vulnerable is in that instant transformed into awe and relief. For we realize that God stood firm when we tried so frantically to push him away—not so he could destroy us or "control" us but in order to love us and help us find happiness. It is one of the most amazing surprises of the human pilgrimage.

As to what sort of response a person might make as he or she surrenders in the battle for the "God position" in his or her life, there are thousands of accounts. One classic statement is the prayer below, by Thomas à Kempis from the fifteenth century.

—Keith Miller, *The Becomers*

"O Lord, all things that are in heaven and earth are Thine. I desire to offer myself unto Thee, willingly and freely to be Thine forever.... In the simplicity of my heart I offer myself unto Thee this day." Amen.

January 18

A ROLE IN THE COSMOS

"Then Job replied to the Lord: 'I know that you can do all things; no plan of yours can be thwarted. [You asked,] 'Who is this that obscures my counsel without knowledge?' Surely I spoke of things I did not understand, things too wonderful for me to know. [You said,] 'Listen now, and I will speak; I will question you, and you shall answer me.' My ears have heard of you but now my eyes have seen you. Therefore I despise myself and repent in dust and ashes."   —Job 42:1-6

Very often, disappointment with God begins in Job-like circumstances. The death of a child, a tragic accident, or a loss of job may bring on the same questions Job asked. Why me? What does God have against me? Why does he seem so distant? As readers of Job's story, we can see behind the curtain to a contest being waged in the invisible world. But in our own trials, we will not have such insight. When tragedy strikes, we will live in shadow, unaware of what is transpiring in the unseen world. The drama that Job lived through will then replicate itself in our individual lives. Once again, God will let his reputation ride on the response of unpredictable human beings.

For Job, the battleground of faith involved lost possessions, lost family members, lost health. We may face a different struggle: a career failure, a floundering marriage, sexual orientation, a body shape that turns people off, not on. At such times the outer circumstances — the illness, the bank account, the run of bad luck — will seem the real struggle. We may beg God to change those circumstances. *If only I were beautiful or handsome, then everything would work out. If only I had more money — or at least a job — then I could easily believe God.*

But the more important battle, as shown in Job, takes place inside us. Will we trust God? Job teaches that at the moment when faith is hardest and *least* likely, then faith is most needed. His struggle presents a glimpse of what the Bible elsewhere spells out in detail: the remarkable truth that our choices matter, not just to us and our own destiny but, amazingly, to God himself and the universe he rules.

—Philip Yancey, *Disappointment with God*

Dear Lord, my choices do matter, more so than I can ever imagine! Help me to know how to choose — and when I am wrong, help me to correct my mistakes and return to the right path. In Jesus' name. Amen.

January 19

TO BE NEAR UNTO GOD

"But as for me, it is good to be near God."
—Psalm 73:28a

People can hold high admiration and deep respect for our nation, for nature, for beauty, for art, for the suffering of others, even for humanity itself. We can love what is honest and pure and good; we can adore our heritage, our theology, and our creeds.

We can even *have* a love for God, since all good that inspires love is from God and God himself is the highest good. But when the Psalmist says, "I love God," he implies something other than deep admiration and respect. What he is talking about is something intimate and personal, a relationship which makes the Good Shepherd, *our* shepherd; the Father, *our* source of life and happiness; the Covenant-God, the Divine Being with which *we* share an eternal and blessed agreement. That love brings us near.

What we're talking about here is a relationship so personal and intimate that it can't be described in words. If you don't understand, you don't *know* God at that level. But if you deeply desire to know him in that way, then you're already on the right track.

Today, in the public square, faith is frequently shunned. To some, belief in God is barbaric, some remnant silliness of the dark ages. Today, the world is not a haven for believers, if it ever was. There may have been a time when belief could more easily prosper in the marketplace, but today faith is scorned.

Such a world is an impediment to God's nearness, to say the least. But don't throw in the towel; we know very well God hasn't. In his eternal compassion, he will come nearer again and hold us up against the ridicule of a world that laughs him to shame.

The modern age is extremely dangerous to us — and even more so to our children. But he is here, as he always had been, awaiting our desire for the intimate fellowship with him that will sustain us no matter what happens in our world.

To know that, to seek him passionately, and to find him, face to face, in the muddle of our travail here on earth — all of that makes us testify with the Psalmist, "I love you, Lord."   —James Calvin Schaap, *Near Unto God*

Father, shepherd, you have loved us and sought us. That you have done so before we could love you is our hope, for you yourself are the source of our love. In the middle of our travail you lift us so we can say we love you. Thank you for such grace. Amen.

January 20

THE HEALING REMEDY

"Then Peter came to Jesus and asked, 'Lord, how many times shall I forgive my brother when he sins against me? Up to seven times?' Jesus answered, 'I tell you, not seven times, but seventy-seven times.'"
— Matthew 18:21-22

I had him by the scruff of his shirt front with my left hand, and was about to knock him out of the front door backwards! I could feel the resentment seething up from my chest into my face and arms, giving me an unreal strength.

Just then I heard my wife's voice. She was shaking my shoulder gently from the other side of the bed. "Keith, wake up, you're having a bad dream."

The fantasy of my beating up Charlie, my associate who'd shamed me at the office for the ump-teenth time, collapsed like a pop-up scene in a child's King Arthur book as I woke up and rolled over.

In that half sleeping/half waking state, I realized that resentments have plagued my life since I was a child. Usually they are about my perception that someone has slighted me, gossiped about me, been disloyal, or cheated me. But whatever the "crime," obsessing about resentments had caused many painful and helpless hours. I fluttered back into the pillow and closed my eyes.

I see a heavy walnut door swinging open in the basement video theater of my mind. A title rolls across the screen as I sit down: ACT I: "JUSTICE." The action is just beginning. We are in a great courtroom with a large walnut judge's bench. A huge white-haired figure in a long white robe is sitting behind the bench, looking remarkably like God. He is meting out justice from this "highest court in the land." My associate, Charlie, the one who humiliated me, is standing before the bench. The scene begins with the crashing of a thousand pound gavel and a roaring voice — deep and powerful enough to be heard across the Rose Bowl — "GUILTY!" I smile and nod my head.

Now a familiar dramatic scenario begins to unfold as the title ACT II: "REVENGE, THE COST THEY'LL PAY!" is rolling across the screen. And then, there I am, the prosecutor, the hero, delivering creative, brilliant, scathing, and cutting accusations about the heinous nature of the guilty party's crime, and calling for the most horrible sentence possible, as I subtly orchestrate the offender's fate — actually wanting to clobber him physically as "the enemy?"

I *know* that Act III is *supposed* to be "FORGIVENESS," but I also know that I usually just rewind Acts I and II and play them over and over, day after day, escalating the revenge and punishment scenes when I'm really into a big time resentment. But this time I hear the wise deep voice of the Judge telling me: "Mr. Prosecutor, when you keep resenting people, you are letting them live rent free in your head!"

I cry out, "But how can I quit? He's done it *before!* I've tried and tried, but there seems to be no 'Power Off' button in my mind."

The Judge replies as patiently as he can, "*Forgive* him! That's the healing remedy I've given you to stop the pain of resentment. Forgive him, and let the resentment go. *I'll* take care of it. You *can't.*"

So I tried to forgive my associate. Sure enough, I felt better — for about five minutes, and then I was back obsessing about the wrong he'd done to me.

"See," I whined to the Judge, "forgiveness just doesn't work for me!"

"*Forgive him again!* And get back to work at what is before you today, without congratulating yourself for forgiving him. Do this as many times as it takes, and one day it won't come back. Then you can move to Act III and the freedom I've provided for those under my jurisdiction through the miracle of forgiveness — which is the only way to get free when someone hurts you."

"No," I cried, "it's not fair!" But the giant gavel crashed on the judge's bench again.

"Next case," the deep echoing voice said, and a shrill bell rang.

I jumped awake with a start as my wife was leaning over me to answer the first call of the morning on the bedside phone.

"It's for you," she said sleepily. "It's Charlie, from the office."

—J. Keith Miller, *CrossPoint Magazine,* Fall 1996

Lord, thank you that there is a healing remedy for the pain of hurts from other people — even those who are repeaters — a remedy that doesn't depend on the other person, but on my willingness to let go of the desire for revenge, and to forgive. Help me to work through the pain of hurts from other people, and finally to be able to forgive and turn them, and my resentments, loose. In Jesus' name. Amen.

January 21

WORK IN THE PARTICULARS

"Be quick to give a meal to the hungry, a bed to the homeless — cheerfully. Be generous with the different things God gave you, passing them around so all get in on it." —1 Peter 4:9-10a, THE MESSAGE

When I work in the particulars, I develop a reverence for what is actually there instead of a contempt for what is not, inadequacies that seduce me into a covetousness for someplace else. A farm, Wendell Berry contends, is a kind of small-scale ecosystem, everything working with everything else in certain rhythms and proportions. The farmer's task is to understand the rhythms and the proportions and then to nurture their health, not bullyingly to invade the place and decide that it is going to function on his rhythms and according to the size of his ego. If all a farmer is after is profit, he will not be reverential of what is actually there but only greedy for what he can get out of it.

The parallel with my parish could not be more exact. I substitute my pastoral vocabulary for Berry's agricultural and find Berry urging me to be mindful of my congregation, in reverence before it. These are souls, divinely worked-on souls, whom the Spirit is shaping for eternal habitations. Long before I arrive on the scene, the Spirit is at work. I must fit into what is going on. I have no idea yet what is taking place here; I must study the contours, understand the weather, know what kind of crops grow in this climate, be in awe of the complex intricacies between past and present, between the people in the parish and those outside. —Eugene H. Peterson, *Under the Unpredictable Plant*

Dear Lord, help me to show up each day prepared to do the work you have given me to do, and to relate to others lovingly and in truth. Help me to let go of the outcomes of this work and these relationships... accepting instead that you are at work in all things, and I may not always know what outcomes you have in mind. Grant me the peace to trust that the Spirit is on the scene, long before I arrive, and after I am gone. In Jesus' name. Amen.

January 22

THE DISCIPLINE OF GOOD INTENTIONS

"For in this hope we were saved. But hope that is seen is no hope at all. Who hopes for what he already has? But if we hope for what we do not have, we wait for it patiently." —Romans 8:24-25

> Though snow crusts the fields
> my mind moves to the small failures
> of autumn's labor.
>
> I bear them forward into summer,
> by imagination enter the discipline
> of good intentions,
> and by thought begin
> the reclamation of the earth.
> —John Leax, *The Task of Adam*

To confess our sins is good, Lord Jesus. To give them up and set our minds on you is better. You are our hope and our redeemer. We give you first our thankfulness and then we give, as we are enabled by your grace, our lives. Amen.

January 23

FEET

"How beautiful on the mountains are the feet...."
—Isaiah 52:7a, NRSV

I get perversely silly at formal church affairs. For instance, on the Sunday morning I was ordained as an elder, I became suddenly self-conscious about my feet. There I was, kneeling alone on the steps at the front of that huge sanctuary, wearing my best Sunday outfit, hair and fingernails groomed, heart clean and prepared, too (I hoped), when it occurred to me that everyone in the congregation could see the bottoms of my shoes. I was wearing my best pumps, but they were old nevertheless, and I hadn't checked the soles in a long time for worn heels, for gum, whatever. It was certainly a part of myself I hadn't planned to display to the public.

Then I pictured my feet inside the shoes, the peasant feet I'd inherited, broad toes, low arches, hardly Grecian, meant for walking in pastures to call the cows. And I thought about foot washing, a ritual abandoned now in most congregations. The church has managed to get communion "all cleaned up," sterilized really, but you can't make foot-washing neat, and maybe that's why it's seldom done.

In civilized Presbyterian style ("all things decently and in order") my feet were covered, but they were still there under the scruffy shoes when a dozen people came forward to lay hands on my head. It occurred to me that they might lay hands on my feet, too, but nobody did.

In the Swedish-American culture in which my husband grew up, to be "good with your hands" held priority, to be skilled at the practical things of life. When I first met his family, I remember someone asking, "Are you good with your hands?" No one asked me if I was good with my feet. How would I have answered if they had? Yet it's the feet the prophet calls beautiful — knobby, calloused, corned, ingrown, aching, and probably flat, but beautiful when they are "on the mountains," bringing good tidings and peace.

Of all the metaphorical uses of our bodies in Scripture (heart, head, throat, bowels, hands, feet) I like feet best, I think, because they are closest to the ground. So with the authority endowed upon me with the laying on of hands, I bless my own feet and consider them formally and properly ordained. —Shirley Nelson, *Notes and Files*

Lord of the mountain: We don't ask for swift or graceful or even beautiful feet. Just keep us moving, as carriers of the good news. Amen.

January 24

RELUCTANT PROPHET

"The sacrifices of God are a broken spirit; a broken and contrite heart, O God, you will not despise." —Psalm 51:17

> Both were dwellers
> in deep places
> (one in the dark
> bowels of ships
> and great fish
> and wounded pride.
> The other
> in the silvery belly
> of the seas).
>
> Both heard God saying
> "Go!"
> but the whale
> did as he was told.

Jonah's circumstances were unique; he was sent as a prophet to a warlike enemy people, a Hebrew running from God and angry at God, a man who was thrown overboard into the sea as unlucky, a drowning man who was swallowed by a whale but survived, "damp but undigested." We all have a fellow feeling with Jonah. Like most of us he was stubbornly set on his own way, and he made Jehovah work hard to change his mind.

For Jonah the most difficult thing in the world was to obey. He based his willful disobedience on his human logic. "Why should I have to preach to the Ninevites?" he asked. "They don't deserve a chance to repent. They're cruel, corrupt, heartless. They *deserve* God's punishment." And when he was finally cornered in Nineveh and the wicked people he was forced to preach to were actually repenting in sackcloth and ashes, Jonah was furious. They should be punished, not forgiven. He felt so bad about it all he wanted to die.

This lesson of obedience to a higher wisdom than our own, an obedience that some creatures in the universe seem to give naturally (whales, for instance), goes against our grain. Today "self-determination" and "freedom" and "individuality" sound like good words, and they make "obedience" sound restrictive and overly meek.

But obedience is a discipline that brings its own insights and rewards. Could it be that the Lord's demands on Jonah (and on us today) were as much for his own growth and benefit as for the sake of the wicked Ninevites?
—Luci Shaw, *Horizons*

Lord Jesus, I would be more like the whale than Jonah, but I admit I am willful. Though I know I am not wise enough to rule myself, I desire my own way. By your grace break my heart, and I will give you my obedience in return. Amen.

January 25

GIVING IT UP

"For to me, to live is Christ and to die is gain."
—Philippians 1:21

Life without sacrifice, Annie Dillard wrote, is an abomination. Never to give oneself up, always to hoard and protect. Without heat constantly being given up and taken in, this world would grind to a halt of absolute zero temperature. There would be no more being, which after all depends on the continual exchange of energy to maintain its existence. Elementary particles must suffer a continual state of dissolution and regrouping. Trees, in order to live, must suck up the soil and exhale the air. Our jellied corpses melt into meadow rue. All dying does somebody good. The meanest miser must unclench his fist and unfold it, one day, in a flower, even if that is the only graceful gesture he ever makes.

The heart of the universe is sacrifice, not the stone-cold nirvana of oblivion. To live in Christ we must die to ourselves, be careless of our own substance.
—Virginia Stem Owens, *God Spy*

Dear Lord, help me to give more and protect less. I trust you to bring into my life the things I need to nurture within myself so that I have whatever it is you want me to give. Help me to direct my giving to the proper places, not just spewing it out until I am drained and useless, but focusing it through the lens of your love and guidance. In Jesus' name. Amen.

January 26

TOGETHER WE CAN DO IT

"I can do all things through him who strengthens me."
— Philippians 4:13, NRSV

This Scripture verse is a heartening message, and it describes how I feel on days when I am well and strong, when my body is beginning to respond to exercise. But then, like a sudden cloudburst out of nowhere, discouragement and boredom can appear to banish my enthusiasm. Suddenly I'm no longer the least bit interested in even getting out of bed — much less doing any more sit-ups, jogging any more miles, or looking at one more bowl of whole-wheat cereal.

At times like these I remember the way I felt a few days before — springy, cheerful, and in tune with God and the world — and I wonder, can I really "do all things through him who strengthens me."? What was Paul talking about? And I begin to suspect that Paul probably wrote that on a day when he, too, felt springy and cheerful and didn't have any blisters from his sandals or tired muscles from walking all day.

One such day, when I wasn't feeling at all energetic, I read in *The Imitation of Christ*, "One thing withholds many from growing in virtue and from an amendment of life, and that is a horror and a false worldly fear that they may not be able to stand the pain and labor needed to win virtue."

"Boy, that's me," I thought. I don't even want to *mention* to anybody that I'm trying to get in shape, because then, if the pain is too much and I decide to quit, they'll know I blew it.

I read on: "But they will profit most in virtue who force themselves vigorously to overcome those things that are most grievous and irksome to them. A woman [my editorial change] profits most and wins most grace in those things in which she has most overcome herself, and in which she has most subjected her body to her soul." I read again Paul's claim: "I can do everything through him who gives me strength." I decided to believe that if Paul could do it, so could I. And I began to pray silently at difficult times during the day for the strength to do the things I knew I had to do to get in shape.

On days when I feel I can do all things with or without God, I forget easily that I need to rely on him. But there are more days when I know I'd never make it if I didn't have Jesus as the player-coach on my team!

— Andrea Wells Miller, *BodyCare*

Dear Lord, you are my strength, and when I'm in touch with you I can do more than I can without you. Even the last three sit-ups. Even exercising when I'd rather be doing something else. Help me to remember that when I'm feeling inadequate and lazy. Forgive me when I forget you're there. And thank you for loving me so much that you'll patiently watch me go through all my struggles and failures, knowing that, when I finally stop and ask you to help me, together we can do what seemed impossible for me to do alone.

Be with me today and in the days ahead as I try to learn to remember to call on you for strength. In Jesus' name. Amen.

January 27

CHOOSE LIFE

"I have set before you life and death, blessing and cursing: therefore choose life, that both thou and thy seed may live."
—Deuteronomy 30:19, KJV

"The last time Urs and I were at your house, Rosy and Johnny were blowing bubbles, lovely little iridescent orbs floating in the breeze. And when one thinks of the macrocosm, size makes no never mind, as Nettie would say." She laughed gently. "Is a galaxy bigger than a quark? I lean more and more on the total interdependence of all creation. If we should be so foolish as to blow this planet to bits, it would have repercussions not only in our own solar system but in distant galaxies. Or even distant universes. And if anyone dies—a tree, a planet, a human being—all of creation is shaken."

How different that was from Zachary. Frightening, but in a completely different way, because it gave everything meaning.

"Never think what you do doesn't matter," Max said. "No one is too insignificant to make a difference. Whenever you get the chance, choose life. But I don't need to tell you that. You choose life with every gesture you make. That's the first thing in you that appealed to me. You are naked with life."

And wasn't that what drew me to Max, that abundant sense of life?—pointing out to me the fierce underside of a moth clinging to the screen; fireflies like a fallen galaxy on the dunes in front of our house; the incredible, pulsing life of the stars blooming in the night sky, seeming to cling to the Spanish moss on the old oaks.

—Madeleine L'Engle, *A House Like a Lotus*

Lord, when we glimpse what Life really is, how could we not give up our lives in order to choose the life you offer us? Amen.

January 30

ONE AFTER THIS MANNER AND ANOTHER AFTER THAT

"Every man hath his proper gift of God, one after this manner, and another after that." —1 Corinthians 7:7, KJV

Dog: a domesticated, quadruped carnivore, adorned with fur, a tail (sometimes), and given to bark (some worse than others); often proudly loyal and even slavish (from a cat's point of view anyway).

Even though any mention of the word "dog" brings an immediate picture to everyone's imagination, every image is different. One's "dog" tent has to be pretty wide to admit both a German shepherd and a dachshund. Cockers are known for their floppy ears, Dobermans for their ferocity, English sheep dogs for their uncanny ability as shepherds. But they're all dogs.

Everywhere in creation we see the same kind of diversity. You want copies, go to a Xerox. You want differences, look at life. No two roses are the same; no two fingerprints, no two elms, no two wood ducks, or no two earthworms. And no two believers. Unanimity is a quality diligently sought on an assembly line, but unavailable in life.

And yet Christians — and good Christians — fall victim to a desire for the unnatural condition of sameness. Somewhere at base, pride may be the cause; but more likely the desire to turn out Christians as stiffly patterned as Christmas cookies emerges from motives which are, in intent, good and sweet.

We are — each of us — an intricately designed piece of work, an almost impossible conglomeration of diverse, individual forces: the powers of our ancestry, the sensitivity of our nerves, the vigor of our imagination, the depth of our understanding. And more. We are formed by the way our hearts are strung, by our disposition, our inclinations and sympathies, the range of our consciousness, our susceptibility to emotions and sensations, our education, our environment, our calling. All of these put a stamp on us and our spirituality.

What all of this forms is a uniqueness created by the Holy Spirit, not just a garment we wear through life, but what we are. Each of us has his or her own beauty, and only when our walk with God is uniquely ours will we be free and spirited. —James Calvin Schaap, *Near Unto God*

We thank you, Father, that you have not made us all alike. Give us eyes to see your beauty, wisdom, and infinite love in the diversity of your body the church. Amen.

January 31

FAR AND NEAR

**When we look at your heavens...
at the stars which
you have established,
what are we humans
that you are mindful of us...
that you care for us?...
Yet you crown us
with glory and honor.**

—Psalm 8:3-5, author's paraphrase

It was one of my favorite places in our old house — the little landing halfway up the stairs. There through the evening window I could see the whole wide sky uninterrupted by streetlights or lights from other houses.

One severely cold winter all the windows in the house were decorated with flakes and scrolls of frost like a baroque patterned foil, all silver and white. That night I stood on the landing and looked out through the glass, between the stars of frost, to where, millions of light years away, the stars twinkled through space. The infinitely far stars seemed as close to my eyes as the tiny touches of frost on the glass. And when I breathed on them, lightly and warmly, they melted and melded, swimming together, the very far joined to the very near.

Years later, after photography had become my passion, I loved to record on film this aspect of the cold. The images were clearest on early mornings, with the rising sun highlighting the window frost. The marvel was that once again the far and the near, the immense and the infinitesimal, the powerful and the fragile were collaborating to create a moment of beauty and revelation for me. The sun was in service to these small frost feathers — lighting them into radiance. Is it fanciful for me to think of the sun on the frost as a metaphor of God's face shining on me, small and insignificant as I am? —Luci Shaw, *Horizons*

In your service, Lord, the sun fires the world with radiance. As small as I am, give me light to show that radiance as well. Let me declare with my life your glory. Amen.

FEBRUARY

February 1

THE FREEDOM IN SUBMISSION

"'Has not my hand made all these things, and so they came into being?' declares the Lord. 'This is the one I esteem: he who is humble and contrite in spirit, and trembles at my word.'" —Isaiah 66:2

Every Discipline has its corresponding freedom. What freedom corresponds to submission? It is the ability to lay down the terrible burden of always needing to get our own way. The obsession to demand that things go the way we want them to go is one of the greatest bondages in human society today. People will spend weeks, months, even years in a perpetual stew because some little thing did not go as they wished. They will fuss and fume. They will get mad about it. They will act as if their very life hangs on the issue. They may even get an ulcer over it.

In the Discipline of submission we are released to drop the matter, to forget it. Frankly, most things in life are not nearly as important as we think they are. Our lives will not come to an end if this or that does not happen....

In submission we are at last free to value other people. Their dreams and plans become important to us. We have entered into a new, wonderful, glorious freedom — the freedom to give up our own rights for the good of others. —Richard J. Foster, *Celebration of Discipline*

A Prayer of Relinquishment

Today, O Lord, I yield myself to you.
  May your will be my delight today.
  May your way have perfect sway in me.
  May your love be the pattern of my living.

I surrender to you
  my hopes,
    my dreams,
      my ambitions.
Do with them what you will, when you will, as you will.

I place into your loving care
  my family,
    my friends,
      my future.
Care for them with a care that I can never give.
I release into your hands
  my need to control,
    my craving for status,
      my fear of obscurity.
Eradicate the evil, purify the good,
and establish your kingdom on earth.

For Jesus' sake, Amen.

—Richard J. Foster, in *Prayers from the Heart*

February 2

SHARING OUR BURDENS

"Bear ye one another's burdens, and so fulfill the law of Christ."
—Galatians 6:2, KJV

"Justin and Katherine. Katherine and Justin. I thank God for you every day. Why did it take Michou's death to bring us back together as we were before?"

"It's not as we were before, Wolfi. I'm not as I was before. And you're not, either."

"No. We have both moved a long way. I do not think you know how much you have taught me." This last was murmured in so low a voice she was not sure she had heard.

She told him, then, about a concert she had given in Munich a few weeks before. She had gone back to the cathedral. To the ancient statue of the Virgin and Child. How could a wooden face have so many changes of expression?

Now the young woman looked old, and full of grief. She held the baby as she might have held the man when he was taken down from the cross, and the baby's face was ancient; the painted eyes held all the wisdom of the world. Katherine had bowed her head against all that wisdom, and when she looked at the mother again, the carved face was bright with love. Grief, and the acceptance of grief, yes. But love was the strongest expression, and the love seemed to be saying: You can bear this. You can bear it and go on living.

"And I am bearing it, Wolfi. At first I didn't think I could, but I am, because I know that if I didn't bear it, Justin couldn't."

"You do know that? That you have to bear it with him, for him?"

—Madeleine L'Engle, *A Severed Wasp*

> O Divine Master,
> Grant that I might not so much seek
>   to be consoled as to console;
>   to be understood as to understand;
>   to be loved as to love.
> —St. Francis of Assisi

February 3

A TONGUE TO TRUTH

> "For this is what the Lord says —
> he who created the heavens, he is God;
> he who fashioned and made the earth, he founded it;
> he did not create it to be empty, but formed it to be inhabited —
> he says: 'I am the Lord, and there is no other.'" —Isaiah 45:18

Incarnation is not an abstraction, not some distant theological principle. It is reality itself. *Res;* things. Accessible to everyone. It starts with fragrant infants' flesh, blood, breath, and tears, and radiates from that single point to include the whole world. Straw, mites, dung steaming in the chill night air, eyes, stars, smells, songs.

It is the spy's purpose to raise this actuality to consciousness, to give a tongue to this truth, not because it will not be truth unless he tells it, but because there is no light in a truth untold, and no joy. In apprehending the flying photons, the electrical charges the world is made of, the spy becomes the film emulsion that traces the signs of their passing. And more than that. In the spy's mind, the passings become pattern. He is an anemometer that scores the will of the wind that creates the world. And only when it whistles through such caverns of comprehension is the movement of the spirit recognized as will. For the spy to fail in this mission is to fall himself into a broth of unapprehended being; to fail is to subject creation to futility. —Virginia Stem Owens, *God Spy*

Dear Lord, help me to experience light and joy as I "give a tongue" to the truth of your promise! Help my comprehension come alive to capture the reality of your incarnation for myself, and then be able to bring it alive for others! In Jesus' name. Amen.

February 4

OUR CARETAKER

"Rest all your cares on him...
he does care for you."
—1 Peter 5:7, author's paraphrase

We are the beneficiaries of God's two ways of revealing himself: his special revelation, through Scripture and Jesus Christ, shows us how God looks and acts; his general revelation is the whole universe, the manuscript in which the Creator has written his character and signed his name.

So I take comfort not just from the words on a page but also from a different message — the images I see written on the sky, the configurations of a flock of birds, the gift of a glossy chestnut. In dew, rocks, rain, flowers, finches I see divine "syllables of light and color" that say, "I care for you." The deer and the great blue heron, daily visitors to my woodland home, remind me of how wild things find their way through the wilderness, as I do, guided by God.

Most of all, I want to be lit like a burning bush, to blaze and shine. I see myself in the leaf fires of autumn and am lifted in the dancing flame.

We say "I care about you" to someone for whom we have deep personal affection. We "care for" someone for whom we are lovingly responsible. In both these senses God has promised to be our Caretaker.

—Luci Shaw, *Horizons*

For being a Caretaker who shows himself I thank you, Lord. In your revelation in the world about me, and in your revelation in Jesus Christ, I recognize and acknowledge you. Accept my love and my praise. Let me burn for you and you only. Amen.

February 5

MY SOLITARY ONE

"Deliver my soul from the sword, my solitary one from the power of the dog."
—Psalm 22:20, Dutch KJV

Some people avoid crowds at all costs, while others flee solitude like the plague. Some people desire, even ache, to get on every committee they can; others prefer root canals.

Despite our differences, however, each of us has a solitary self, a soul, that which David calls twice in the Psalms, "my solitary one." Our souls, our solitary selves, are our most precious commodities. Think about it — anything else we own can be replaced. Even our bodies can be destroyed, lowered into the grave. All that remains is the soul.

It is, of course, individual and private. It contains places not even those closest to us ever know. That kind of privacy often creates two kinds of problems. Sometimes we withdraw too deeply in sadness, grief, or hurt to a hideout where even suicide lurks at the gates of our possibilities. We get "the blues," and worse.

But then again, sometimes we run so gingerly through life that the very essence of the soul withers in the frantic zaniness of our public madness.

Perhaps we should think of it this way: the soul is like a tabernacle. In each, there is a general court, where close friendships and even intimacy enter. But beyond the most precious gates lies the holy of holies, and no one really enters there.

Except the Lord. He is the only remedy for imperiled souls.

Only God can save us from our loneliness and also give us the society so necessary to the health of our most secluded lives. Those who know God there, in their own inner sanctums, know him most fully and wonderfully. They are nearest to God.   —James Calvin Schaap, *Near Unto God*

We zig and zag, O Lord, from the zaniness of activity to the darkness of withdrawal. You are our one true point of stillness. Hold us in the society of your love. Keep us close that we might know you fully and wonderfully. Amen.

February 6

A NEW WAY TO SAY IT

"Are your ears awake? Listen. Listen to the Wind Words, the Spirit blowing through the churches."   —Revelation 3:22, THE MESSAGE

I do not read the Revelation to get additional information about the life of faith in Christ. I have read it all before in law and prophet, in gospel and epistle. Everything in the Revelation can be found in the previous sixty-five books of the Bible. The Revelation adds nothing of substance to what we already know. The truth of the gospel is already complete, revealed in Jesus Christ. There is nothing new to say on the subject.

But there is a new way to say it. I read the Revelation not to get more information but to revive my imagination.

—Eugene H. Peterson, *Reversed Thunder*

Dear Lord, help me to release my imagination as I develop ways to say the truth of the gospel. In Jesus' name. Amen.

February 7

HEALTHIER, WEALTHIER, AND WISER
DO ONLY GOOD THINGS HAPPEN TO GOOD PEOPLE?

"When your herds and flocks grow large and your silver and gold increase and all you have is multiplied, then your heart will become proud and you will forget the Lord your God, who brought you out of Egypt, out of the land of slavery." —Deuteronomy 8:13-14

Do Christians have car accidents? Do they get cancer? Are they ever fired from their jobs? The answer to all three questions is, of course, yes. But that answer causes big problems for some new Christians. Doesn't the Bible promise that God will look out for and protect his followers? How can such bad things occur?

People puzzled by such questions often refer to Old Testament books where God clearly promised success and protection to the Israelites. In Deuteronomy, Moses spelled out God's promises in complete detail. Israelite wives would have many babies. All the crops — grain, grapes olive trees — would produce bountifully. Cattle and sheep would multiply. And Moses even included this extraordinary promise: "The Lord will keep you free from every disease" (7:15).

A Message for Us Today. The promises of Deuteronomy were given to a particular people, the Israelites, in a special covenant relationship — a covenant that God prophesied would be broken. The formula was simple: "Do good, get rewarded; do evil, get punished." But Christians of today cannot simply turn to those flagrant promises of wealth and prosperity and apply them directly. Rather, we must look at this book in light of the new covenant introduced by Jesus Christ and spelled out in the New Testament.

When Jesus came, he promised certain rewards for Christians, but he also predicted poverty, rejection, and even persecution. Rewards on this earth cannot be reduced to such a simple "Do good, get rewarded; do evil, get punished" formula. Jesus' disciples proved faithful to him, and yet most of them lived through poverty and persecution and died martyrs' deaths. For them, full rewards had to wait until heaven.

Deuteronomy may offer a clue to why God does not exempt his followers from every bad thing in life. Ironically, prosperity and health may make it harder to depend on God. Moses' fears came true: the Israelites proved least faithful to God after they moved into the prosperity of the promised land. In the desert, at least, they had been forced to lean on God just for daily survival. But after a very short time in Canaan, they forgot about him. There is a grave danger in finally getting what you want. —Philip Yancey, *The Student Bible*

Lord, like the Israelites in Deuteronomy I tend to think about you more often when I am in trouble and less often when things are going well. Help me to seek your will and to rely on you all the time. In Jesus' name. Amen.

February 8

SIGNS OF CHRISTIAN GROWTH

"But Jesus called the children to him and said, 'Let the little children come to me, and do not hinder them, for the kingdom of God belongs to such as these.'" —Luke 18:16

My ideas about what Christian growth is have changed a lot over the years. Growth for the Christian, whatever else it is (I decided) has to be toward a kind of pervasive integrity, not a *quantitative* model (e.g.: *How many* books have you read? or *How many* people have you fed or evangelized, or *How much* do you pray, give, counsel, etc.). And I began to see that the saints were not people with the greatest education or even who had the largest results. But they did have a couple of traits in common that were almost invisible: What they *said* correlated almost 100 percent with what they *were* and what they *did*. And Jesus was exactly what he said and did. I saw that when a person "comes together" in a surrender to Christ and begins to walk through the pain of life with eyes open—when this happens, and that person's words and his inner self finally match, touch all around the rim of his or her life, then an amazing and invisible power may be released through that life that can touch a generation.

It's as if Christian growth were not so much "up" and "out" toward bigness as it is a permeation toward a congruence, a healing unity of all the separated and conflicting parts of our lives—so that each of us might become "Natural," the persons we were made to be. We might then be able to live simply again, like children in some ways, in the clarity and integrity of our persons.

—J. Keith Miller, *Witness,* Summer 1985

Lord, I desire to grow in the ways that bring me closer to you. Show me the honest, childlike person you made me to be, and make me aware of places where my words and actions are not the same. Open my eyes to experience all of life—pain and joy alike—and, after bringing what appropriate love and support I can to those around me, help me to surrender to you the resolution of each circumstance and problem I encounter. In Jesus' name. Amen.

February 9

THE PLUNGE

"The people living in darkness have seen a great light; on those living in the land of the shadow of death a light has dawned."

—Matthew 4:16

I knew I was ready now to take The Plunge. The escape from the harpoon, the storm, the encounter with men, and the hours of solitude had made me ready. For three days I ate nothing. I swam along slowly, far from other creatures, ignoring the occasional gossipy bird.

Fasting changed things. For one, after the initial hunger passed, I felt lighter and stronger. I found it easier to concentrate, whether on a color of the ocean current, a thought, or a song. I felt both more inside myself and more keen at the edges. I at once felt detached from things and more *with* them. The world filled with an alert, sinewy peace.

I slept lightly those nights and the dream of the Whale of Light returned several times. The third night I hardly slept at all, singing my song over and over. That morning at sunrise I would take The Plunge.

When the first ray touched the whitecaps pink, I drew deep breaths, flooding my lungs and heart with air. After a last look at the sun, I heaved myself up and over and, with one strong twitch of my flukes, dove. Down I plunged through the green, the blue, into the black deep. Darker and darker it grew, colder and colder. Unafraid, I continued downward, past the luminary fish swimming in constellations through the black space of sea, down till they faded above me to the merest pinpoints of light, down into total darkness. Still I sank, feeling the terrible pressure crush me on all sides, feeling much like a stone. Still I knew no fear and I sang my song within me.

After a long time something rose under me and held me up like my mother. It was a second or two before I realized I'd touched bottom. I lay there for a long while, barely aware of time, of the ocean, of anything. I'd grown used to the pressure by now. The blood crept through my heart, lungs, and brain. The only noises were my heart beating — slowly, very slowly — and the swish of blood through my veins.

There I lay till I no longer noticed my heartbeat. I noticed nothing, suspended in darkness. All thought had gone, even the sense of myself. The deep quiet became an alert and living substance that I was spread out in.

The rest is difficult to tell. But I shall try, even though I fail.

I felt I was where I should be, where I had always wanted to be. The past was not there, nor the future. There was only the present, infinitely full. Rather, the past was there as a small picture in my mind, to look at and enjoy, and also the future — something to look at and delight in, but not really there. All reality was in the present. The sense of want, of wanting to be back in the past or wanting to be ahead in the future, was gone. The sense of *want* was gone, because the want was filled in this darkness. I felt totally free, as if I were expanding through the darkness.

Suddenly, right at the center — of my heart, perhaps — there shone a tiny seed-pearl of light. It was a light that shone on my inner eye, so bright I couldn't focus on it. It grew and grew until it shone like a sun and swallowed up the darkness. And even though bright, it was soft; its radiance ceased to hurt my inner eye and I looked about with delight. I was swimming in a sea of light.

I remembered the tales of the Ocean of Light and felt — not afraid — but ashamed and a little silly for being there. Only then did I notice the singing. A low hum surrounded me. Whether it came through that light or was that light, I cannot tell. All I know is that I could now focus upon the light and see it moving even while it remained still. Then it became one long, low indescribable sound. I started to weep — really weep. I could feel the oil flow from my eyes as the sound drew forth tears.

And then, in the midst of the light, an even greater Light appeared, a flaming Light too great to look upon, in the shape of the whale of my dream. The whale drew closer and I knew I would be burned, but I didn't care, for I felt I would gladly die if only I could approach that Light. The Light sang to me, a voice musical and soft, and the words took shape in my head.

I saw my mother and father swimming together, with the Light moving between them. Then I saw a tiny light in my mother and I knew it was me and I heard the Whale of Light sing louder — a note in a peculiar tone I'd never heard before, but recognized as *myself.* My heart leapt and I started to sing with him.

I saw myself grow in my mother's belly and be born, and I saw how her song became part of mine. I saw Lewtë flash across the shallows as her song wove itself with mine, and then the deep bass of my father joined us and made a chorus. As we swam to the polar seas Caloon's funeral made a note, and the romp with the sea lions made light grace notes, and so with every experience up to the present: each became part of the music. My brush with the whalers made a harsh note that nevertheless blent in, and the waterspout and typhoon a ponderous and majestic phrase. The note when I rescued the whalers sounded soft and sweet and was the most beautiful of all.

The Whale of Light stopped singing and turned to face me. Somehow I could look upon that Brightness without burning. His face had the most beautiful smile on it and even something of laughter, as if he found humor in all this. He showed me the future — not what would happen, but what I was meant to be. It was all tied in with what Hralekana had said, but mostly it was like that musical note sung at my conception. He showed me things I cannot express, things impossible to put into words.

All at once he turned and swam away in sport, beckoning me to follow. I chased after him, almost catching him, but never quite; he would dart away laughing, and I would chase after again. He would leap and I would leap, and at each leap I grew larger and stronger — though he always grew larger and stronger too.

At last we rested, and I looked full into his face and felt such love as I had never known, not even for my own mother and father. And I asked, "Are you the Spouter of Oceans?" He smiled and the smile grew infinitely wide and bright, and the brightness moved into me and wrapped me around, and I saw *that* before which all words drop away.

At length the light faded and I floated in a dark peace lit by a faint glow. How long I rested in darkness I do not know, but it was a long time. Finally my lungs told me they needed air, and I rose slowly — almost floated up — past the dim galaxies of fish. I surfaced in the middle of the night. The moon was half-nibbled away and I lay there breathing softly. Never had air tasted so sweet and never had waves appeared more beautiful as from each of them flashed sparks from the Sea of Light.

—Robert Siegel, *Whalesong*

True Light of the World, shine in our darkness. Show us by your light what we are meant to be and the way that we should go. Amen.

February 10

MAPLE WEATHER

"John wore clothing made of camel's hair, with a leather belt around his waist, and he ate locusts and wild honey. And this was his message: 'After me will come one more powerful than I, the thongs of his sandals I am not worthy to stoop down and untie. I baptize you with water, but he will baptize you with the Holy Spirit.'"   —Mark 1:6-8

Four clear nights —
the woodsmoke rising blue
against the quarter-moon black,
the house cracking in the below
zero plunge into dark —
say *Winter holds.*

The Earth, however, dumb and slow,
turns, leans into the light
and day lengthens.

The ground, caught in the altercation
of freeze and thaw, heaves,
and in the maples the run
of sweetness augurs the water
baptism, the scouring melt,
and the planted seed.

— John Leax, *The Task of Adam*

The earth itself awaits the descending fire of your baptism, O Galilean. Do not keep it from us. We lean to receive your light. Speak in our lives like the rush of spring. Amen.

February 11

DISAGREEMENT VERSUS DISSENT

"A man had two sons; and he went to the first and said, 'Son, go and work in the vineyard today.' And he answered, 'I will not'; but afterward he repented and went. And he went to the second and said the same; and he answered, 'I go, sir,' but did not go. Which of the two did the will of his father?" — Matthew 21:28-31, RSV

"And he came to the disciples and found them sleeping; and he said to Peter, "So, could you not watch with me one hour?" — Matthew 26:40

At first blush both "disagreement" and "dissent" seem like such good concepts when it comes to conflict resolution. They appear to be opposites, perhaps contraries, perhaps even contradictories. In reality, they seem more like first cousins once removed. Something like the Hatfields and McCoys. But upon closer examination more like "disagreement versus dissent."

Disagreement has been defined as the "agreement to disagree," with the possible hope of trying again to set things straight in the near future. Dissent has been defined as the "assent to dissent" with no possible hope of setting things straight ever again. There has to be a better way to understand agreements and disagreements, assents and dissents. Perhaps something like the binary computer language made up of zeros and ones, offs and ons.

To illustrate, I would refer to *The Vicar of Dibley,* a ragged, ribald television series from England. The vicar is a middle-aged three-hundred-pound woman of great hilarity. Dibley is Church of England, of course, but what takes place in that parish is, funnily enough, generally applicable to most churches in most denominations. Which is perhaps another way of saying that the parish board is the Board from Hell.

One of the half-dozen loquacious scruffians is Jim Trott, an unshaven, gravelly-voiced old man in fairly decent clothes who prefaces his agreement/assent by five disagreements/dissents; and vice versa. Hence, when asked if he's going to vote for a new stained-glass window, he says,"No, no, no, no, no, yes!"

When his wife, Doris, once appeared at the doorway of their thatch-roofed cottage, he asked her if the kettle was on. She replied "Yes, yes, yes, yes, yes, no!"

Are the Trotts' responses so far-fetched?

I turn to the New Testament for some examples.

(Alas, the sixteenth-century lads who did the Bible into English — the King James Version on the one side of the Channel, the Douai-Rheims on the other — didn't distinguish themselves when it came to expressing agreement and disagreement colloquially. The following illustrations are done in modern paraphrasal.)

"No, no, no, no, no, yes!" was surely the response of the first apostles and disciples as Jesus called them.

"Yes, yes, yes, yes, yes, no!" was surely the response of those who promised Jesus they'd stay awake and pray those last few hours before the arrest.

In summary, the binary computer language made up of zeros and ones, offs and ons, noes and yeses, would seem to open new horizons in the "conflict resolution" theories of the future. —William Griffin

Dear God, for the times I drift off — sleepwalking through my life — in spite of my resolve to stay close to you, forgive me! Amen.

February 12

HELP US TO PRAY

"That their hearts might be comforted, being knit together in love…"
—Colossians 2:2, KJV

"I'm going to help Father get ready for bed," Daddy said.
Suzy demanded, "So, are you going to ask him to pray for Jeb?"
"Why not?" Daddy responded mildly.
"You mean, it may not do any good but it probably won't do any harm?"
Daddy's voice was still mild. "I think it may well do good."
Suzy snorted and turned away from Daddy, so that she was facing Mother.
Mother put her hand against Suzy's cheek. "I believe in prayer. You know that."
"But you don't even know Jeb. You've never even met him!"
"What's got into you?" John demanded sharply.
Suzy still sounded angry. "Prayer didn't keep Jeb from being hit by a motorcycle. It didn't stop Grandfather from having leukemia."
"Prayer was never meant to be magic," Mother said.
"Then why bother with it?" Suzy scowled.
"Because it's an act of love," Mother said.
—Madeleine L'Engle, *A Ring of Endless Light*

Heavenly Father, when we are angry about terrible things happening to people we care about, help us to remember that you care, too, and are with us and them. Help us to pray. Amen

February 13

THE BEAUTY OF CREATION

"There is a time for everything, and a season for every activity under heaven: …I have seen the burden God has laid on men. He has made everything beautiful in its time. He has also set eternity in the hearts of men; yet they cannot fathom what God has done from beginning to end."
—Ecclesiastes 3:1, 10-11

One morning in late winter I stopped the car on impulse, left it parked on the road's gravel shoulder, and dove impulsively with camera into the prickly, thickly-bristling elderberry undergrowth just southeast of Van Kampen's brook.

An unseasonably warm rain the night before had been stopped in its tracks by a sudden cold wave so that everything flowing, running free, was swiftly solidified as by the wand of the White Witch of Narnia.

Through all the sloping woods bordering the road the small creeks and streams formed by the torrent of rain had been drowning the layered, copper-brown leaves. With the cold — temperatures plummeting from a mild sixty-five degrees to ten below — the swirls and eddies of water froze so fast that their lovely, abstract lines and curves are now perfectly preserved. My camera caught the leaves embedded in crystal or lifted on crests of paralyzed rainwater. When the air seeps under ice, its shape shows white, so that every bubble and ripple is outlined and highlighted. The thin skin of baroque ice, from which the water has now drained away, created a sculpture striking as Orrefors lead crystal.

The air is so still and sunny, with the ping of frost still in it, but I know how impermanent ice can be, like joy, like health, like life. Even if it warms up tomorrow, though, the images of ice will stay frozen on my film and I can repeat this moment of wonder, this epiphany, whenever I wish, as I look at my slides.

Have matted two prints for friends: the burst milkweed pod with seeds and silk silhouetted in light, and the two fallen elderberry leaves caught in the ice the night the temperature dropped. It has been one of my perceptions this year that the beauty of creation suffuses even decay and death — the *fallen* leaf, the fragile, *shattered* shell of ice, the *frozen* stream, the *burst* pod. 　　　　　—Luci Shaw, *God in the Dark*

Your ways are beyond our ways, O Lord. You have made everything beautiful — even the fallen leaf and the frozen stream. Death and decay play a part in the making of your world. But you have not made me for this world only. You have set in my heart the desire for you and made me restless for eternity so that I walk, here, incomplete, waiting for the day when you call all to yourself and make it new. Come quickly, Lord Jesus. Amen.

February 14

Heart

"Keep this desire in the hearts of your people forever, and keep their hearts loyal to you." 　　　　　　　　　　　—1 Chronicles 29:18b

Valentine's Day is just behind us, the day when that fat little fellow Cupid sneaks around with his quiver full of arrows. You know how it works:

One hit and you're out of commission for weeks or more. Can't study, can't think, can't eat.

Rollo May, in his wonderful book *Love and Will,* sheds some light on the history of Cupid. He started out as Eros in Greek mythology, symbolizing a creative life force. This was recognized by the Greeks as sexual drive — human passion — but closely tied to creativity and discovery. In other words, imagination. In the course of his long biography, Eros gradually lost this powerful role and became, as the Roman god Cupid, the funny fellow we all know with his arrows of infatuation. He no longer represented the full force of love, with all its risks and creative power.

The reduction is easy to understand. The earlier Eros represented something hard for the human spirit to manage — constructive and destructive at exactly the same moment. As Cupid, he is much less threatening. We receive the arrows of Cupid more or less passively. Uh-oh, in love again. But Eros demands active participation. The force he represents calls for our whole hearts and minds.

Most of the references to the imagination in the Bible are negative. The word shares a root with "image" and implies idolatry. Paul told the Corinthians to "cast down imaginations." It's true that imagination is the source of both light and darkness, balance and madness, cruelty and compassion, heroic justice and megalomania. It opens the door on family secrets, laughs at popes and Protestant pomposity. It tells terrible lies one minute and life-giving truths the next.

Yet the one instance in which the word "imagination" is used positively in Scripture nails it down exactly. David, in turning his kingship over to his son Solomon, asks God to keep this precious moment forever in the "imagination *of the thoughts of the heart*" of his people. Without imagination, we have no memory or projection of our emotions, and therefore no life beyond the mundane.

The healthy imagination, says Rollo May, is fueled by "active love" — disciplined, nurtured, never idolized, but never suppressed. We must accept the whole package with its dangerous potential: new thoughts, new emotions, brave ideas, ambiguity, darkness and light.

This is hard. It is lifetime work. It requires prayer and caution and guidance and maturity — and it brings to our lives and our faith enormous and unquenchable joy.

—Shirley Nelson, chapel address, Nyack College

Be Thou my vision, O Lord of my heart. Amen.

February 15

ANGER HAS A PROPER PLACE

"Speaking the truth in love, we will in all things grow up into him who is the Head, that is, Christ.... 'In your anger do not sin': Do not let the sun go down while you are still angry.'" —Ephesians 4:15, 26a

When my wife and I began to share feelings that might threaten each other, it was a frightening experience for me. I had spent a lifetime "stuffing" threatening feelings, often for days. I have always been terribly afraid that if someone really knew my inner reality, they would not be able to accept me, particularly some of the hostility, resentment, fear, and controlling habits that have always lurked around the edges of my mind. I have denied much of this because I was "too good a person" to have such "negative" reality (really too afraid of rejection to express it). But I learned... that expressing a real thought, fear, or anger is very different from acting these feelings out in an abusive way.

For example, for years I was afraid to express the fact that I was angry with my wife for fear that it would trigger rage in her, or that I would be rejected and punished for expressing my anger. I was also afraid that if I truly let my anger out, it would be too big for me to handle. I might hit someone or hurt them with it. As it turned out both of these were delusions fostered in my own family of origin.

After we'd been married a while, one day I began simply to state my anger in response to something she had said that triggered anger inside me. I said to her, "When you say that, I feel angry." Another time I said at breakfast, "I am angry this morning. I don't know exactly why, but I have feelings of anger and I just want to share them with you. I don't think they are about you, but I don't want to hurt you like I will if I stuff them."

I found that just saying those things out loud in a nonabusive way drained off some of their energy and also informed my wife that this anger, which was apparent to her, was something I was not focusing on her. Even in cases where the anger was focused on her, I was aware that there was a component of it that had to do with my own fear rather than about her being a "bad person."

This openness in owning and expressing feelings the day they happen has led to a greater security in our intimate life and a greater sense of being accepted and loved, for which I have always longed. When I chew on my feelings as a cow chews its cud, the feelings swell, and are harder and harder to choke down. When I express my true reality in a nonjudgmental, nonpunishing, nonmanipulative way, and I am accepted — even if my wife does not like the feelings expressed — then it means that the *real* I, the precious, wounded, but maturing Person inside, is accepted. This sense of being accepted affects everything in a positive way. The walks we take together, our vacations, the way we handle money, our intimate love life.   —J. Keith Miller, *Compelled to Control*

Expressing anger, O Lord, is for me a potentially dangerous undertaking. Since neither holding anger in, nor "taking it out on someone else" solves the problem, I thank you that you taught us in your word to get the feelings out and if possible to deal with them before the sun goes down. Teach me to be open about my feelings without clobbering someone else — emotionally or physically! In Jesus' name. Amen.

February 16

GOD CREATED MAN AFTER HIS OWN IMAGE

"Let us make man in our image, in our likeness."
—Genesis 1:26a

Our practice of faith, every speck of righteousness we have, every vestige of the faithfulness we carry into our lives — all of it stems from one indisputable fact of our existence: we are made in the image of God.

We can pray fervently, avoid murder, adultery, and idol-worship, and do good all the days of our lives; but nothing we do or achieve will make us any more devout or Godly. Only when our very souls come into fellowship with God can we joyfully and even effortlessly abide under the cover of his wings.

Think of it this way: every outward manifestation of our practice of religion changes throughout our lives: what we sing, how we sing, what we wear to church, how we pray, even the breadth and width of our smiles. What doesn't change is what goes on inside us the moment we rise in the morning to a consciousness of God's reality. What doesn't alter is our fellowship with him, and that fellowship occurs in a relationship even more intimate than that which we have with any human being. It happens when our souls dwell in God's tabernacle — and when his Spirit dwells in ours.

When God said, "Let us make man in our own image," what he designed to carry out was to fashion beings fully capable of close fellowship with him. If true religion is defined most precisely by an intimate fellowship with God, then when God created us in his image, he was creating religion.

Birds are wonderfully blessed with beaks, elephants with trunks, trees with bark, and cats with nocturnal vision—in all these ways God filled nature with glory; but on nothing else in his world did he invest his image. Only human beings can fully *know* his love by intimate fellowship with him.

Everything we do out of faith, everything we know of God, begins in the fact that we are his kin. —James Calvin Schaap, *Near Unto God*

Creator Lord, you blessed us with your image and called us to fellowship with you. Forgive us for the times we have hurt you with our refusal of that fellowship, for the times we have hidden because of our nakedness. Reclothe us in your righteousness. We would dwell with you forever. Amen.

February 17

You Won't Get What You Pray For

"But when you pray, go into your room, close the door and pray to your Father, who is unseen. Then your Father, who sees what is done in secret, will reward you." —Matthew 6:6

I had always viewed prayers as focused on and determined by me, the person praying. But Jesus' prayers showed that the focus ought to be on the Father, the one prayed to. Jesus used prayer as a time to commune with the Father, to refresh himself in God's will, to ask for strength. He also used it to thank God for the world and to mention his friends who had needs. It was a conversation, not a shopping list.

Charlie Shedd calls prayer "an inner dialogue with your best friend." I had instead viewed it as a magic wand I could wave to make God do what I wanted. I am not the one in charge of prayer, however; God is.

Many people share the misconception I once had. For example, Mark Twain, who was bothered by unanswered prayer, expressed the dilemma in *Huckleberry Finn*. Huck got a lesson from Miss Watson in prayer.

> She told me to pray every day, and whatever I asked for I would get it. But it warn't so. I tried it. Once I got a fishline but no hooks. It warn't any good to me without hooks. I tried for the hooks three or four times, but somehow I couldn't make it work. By and by one day I asked Miss Watson to try for me, but she said I was a fool. She never told me why. I couldn't make it out no way.

> I set down one time back in the woods and had a long think about it. I says to myself, "If a body can get anything they pray for, why don't Deacon Winn get back money he lost on pork? Why don't the widow get back her silver snuffbox that was stolen? Why can't Miss Watson fat up? No! says I to myself, there ain't nothing in it."

Obviously, Huck wanted a genie in a bottle who would perform his wishes on command, not a God who would be Lord of his life. Faith, to him, was a mental flex to get what he wanted. But faith should be in God, trusting his love and willingness to respond wisely.
—Philip Yancey, *What They Never Told Me When I Became a Christian*

Lord, my prayers are an inner dialogue with you, as with my very best friend! Thank you that you are Lord of my life. In Jesus' name. Amen.

February 18

BLOWN AWAY

"The wind blows wherever it pleases. You hear its sound, but you cannot tell where it comes from or where it is going. So it is with everyone born of the Spirit." —John 3:8

The wind, the wind, the unremitting wind. For a week it has assaulted us without ceasing. Waking and sleeping, indoors and out, its noise is a continual roar, bellow, blast, shriek. From down below on the canyon floor, we hear it high on the tops of the ridges, rumbling like a rocketing freight train. Making the stovepipe shudder, whipping the reaching limbs of the trees, sailing snow in enormous clouds across the lake. In some places people wait for such a gale to blow itself out. But not in Wyoming. This is the origin and heartland of winds. They are manufactured here.

A power company set up an experimental wind turbine just outside Medicine Bow. Its propellers were immediately wrecked and mangled by the wind it was supposed to harness.

The porch roof of one of the cabins higher up blew off two nights ago. It sags several feet on one corner now, the support post dangling like a broken bone. Roofing paper litters the snow all around.

The great roaring wind of Pentecost must have been engendered in Wyoming. Fierce and implacable, blowing at eighty miles an hour, these winds bend everything before them — beast, plant, man. The stones themselves wear away under their breath. This wind blows where it wills. Ruthless in its own hidden purposes, oblivious to the entreaties of the lowly, earth-gripping creatures.

Jesus made a play on words with wind and spirit, trying to teach us its wildness. The wind blows where it wills. But, as with all things spiritual, we have tried to tame it. If anyone really wants a taste of the Spirit, let him come to Wyoming, climb Gannet Peak, and there, struggling to stand upright in the blast of suffocating snow that can suck the breath right out of his lungs, there let him dare to mutter his platitudes about the Spirit. When the Lord answered Job, it was out of the whirlwind, a typhoon, a hurricane. And after his baptism in the Jordan, the Spirit *drove* Christ into the wilderness, drove him the way the wind drives the leaves, the waves, the snow before it.

Those who try to tame this wind had better beware. Try to harness its power and you may end up like the Medicine Bow wind turbine. Better to let it drive you, head over heels, into the wilderness.

—Virginia Stem Owens, *Wind River Winter*

Dear Lord, your Spirit is awesome in its power and strength. Help me to trust myself to it, and to let it drive me where I need to go next. In Jesus' name. Amen.

February 19

Look at Her Now

"God said to Moses, 'I AM WHO I AM. This is what you are to say to the Israelites: "I AM has sent me to you."' God also said to Moses, 'Say to the Israelites, "The Lord, the God of Abraham, the God of Isaac and the God of Jacob — has sent me to you." This is my name forever, the name by which I am to be remembered from generation to generation.'" —Exodus 3:14-15

    What kind of chime, anyhow, sounds
    over God's eternal choirs? What bell
    sings over those sonorous saints
    whom all the world could not quell?

    I remember my grandmother well —
    a gentlewoman with thin ankles
    who took me and took me and took me aside
    and spoke in a singing knell
    about trees which weep with real voices,

> about kings and queens alive for no reason
> at all — except me. She fell
> wholeheartedly out of favor
> with mother and father and entire worlds,
> and still (dangerously) I overheard her tell
> many a winter afternoon
> that deeper in man than all snow is a name
> to which he will answer yes. Her bell
> voice became my deep name.
> Look at me now. And at her:
>
> Over God's choirs she somewhere plays
> in a voice which all the world could not faze.
>
> —Jeanne Murray Walker

God of Abraham, Isaac, and Jacob, you have made yourself known in the history of your people, in the words of your Scripture, and in my heart by the movement of your Spirit. Your grace is endless. My only word to you is yes. Amen.

February 20

LIFE IN DEATH MYSTERIES

"So will it be with the resurrection of the dead. The body that is sown is perishable; it is raised imperishable." —1 Corinthians 15:42

Over the years I've grown fond of compost. I crumbled some "finished stuff" in my hand the other day and wondered that the wastes of my life can be so profitably conserved. But so much is in perspective. Last night I came across a poem in Whitman that contrasts and balances my response. He wrote:

> Now I am terrified at the Earth, it is that calm and patient,
> It grows such sweet things out of such corruptions
> It turns harmless and stainless on its axis, with such endless
>   successions of diseas'd corpses.

Seeing through Whitman's eyes, expanding my vision through his, I realize that there is something terrifyingly "other," something alien to the human in the fecundity of nature, in the ability of the earth to absorb offal and make itself. It is terrifying to realize that humus is not inert. It is, according to John H. Storer, a "hive of living things.... The bacteria alone may range from comparatively few up to three or four billion in a single gram of dry soil."

I suppose in looking at compost I am looking at a sign of the resurrection, of life proceeding out of death. But I have a hard time accepting the analogy, for it is badly flawed. In nature the life that rises out of the dead is never new life for the dead; it is always merely another life feeding on the one that died. The resurrection begins a life unimaginable within the confines of nature. —John Leax, *In Season and Out*

Here, O Lord, we are bound in the sacrament of exchange. Our lives are sacrifices we make for each other and for your creation. Receiving and giving, we rejoice in our place in this order. But we long for the fulfillment of what this birthing, dying, and birthing so imperfectly reflects, the new life of Christ's resurrection, our place in your perfect order where all our sacrifice will be everlasting praise. Amen.

February 21

THE PRAYER OF REST

"Come to me, all you that are weary and are carrying heavy burdens, and I will give you rest. Take my yoke upon you, and learn from me; for I am gentle and humble in heart, and you will find rest for your souls." —Matthew 11:28-29, NRSV

Through the Prayer of Rest God places his children in the eye of the storm. When all around us is chaos and confusion, deep within we know stability and serenity. In the midst of intense personal struggle we are still and relaxed. While a thousand frustrations seek to distract us, we remain focused and attentive. This is the fruit of the Prayer of Rest.

There is perhaps no more appealing invitation in all the Bible than Jesus' gracious words, "Come to me, all you that are weary and are carrying heavy burdens, and I will give you rest" (Matt. 11:28). Nothing is more needed today than this rest of body, mind, and spirit. We live so much of our lives in "an intolerable scramble of panting feverishness," as Thomas Kelly calls it in *A Testament of Devotion*. All of the grasping and grabbing, all of the controlling, all of the manipulative dynamics of life exhaust us.

If only we could slip over into that life free from strain and anxiety and hurry! If only we could know that steady peace of God where all strain is gone and Christ is already victor over the world! If only.... But listen, my friend, I am here to tell you that this way of living can be ours.

We *can* know this reality of rest, and trust, and serenity, and firmness of life orientation. We *can* know as lived experience the words of Jean Sophia Pigott:

> Jesus, I am resting, resting
> In the joy of what Thou art;
> I am finding out the greatness
> Of Thy loving heart.[1]

Today, this very moment, Jesus is inviting you, Jesus is inviting me, into his rest: "Take my yoke upon you, and learn from me; for I am gentle and humble in heart, and you will find rest for your souls" (Matt. 11:29).

—Richard J. Foster, *Prayer: Finding the Heart's True Home*

Blessed Savior, I am not good at resting in the hollow of your hand. Nothing in my experience has taught me this resting. I have been taught how to take charge. I have been taught how to be in control. But how to rest? No, I have no models, no paradigms for resting.

That is not exactly right. Jesus, when you walked among the Jerusalem crowds and in the Judean hills, you pioneered this way of living. You were always alert and alive. You lived utterly responsive to the will of the Father. Manifold demands were placed upon you, and still you worked in unhurried peace and power.

Help me to walk in your steps. Teach me to see only what you see, to say only what you say, to do only what you do. Help me, Lord, to work resting and to pray resting.

I ask this in your good and strong name. Amen.

—Richard J. Foster, *Prayer: Finding the Heart's True Home*

February 22

WE FIND OUR VOICE IN THE DIALOGUE

> "What can I give back to God
> for the blessings he's poured out on me?
> I'll lift high the cup of salvation—a toast to God!
> I'll pray in the name of God;
> I'll complete what I promised God I'd do,
> and I'll do it together with his people."
>
> —Psalm 116:12-14, THE MESSAGE

---

1. *Hymns for the Family of God* (Nashville: Paragon Associates, 1976), Hymn 86.

Prayer is everywhere and always answering speech. It is never initiating speech, and to suppose that is presumptuous. *Miqra,* the Hebrew word for Bible, properly means "calling out" — the calling out of God to us. "God must become a person," but in order for us to speak in answer to him he must make us into persons.

We become ourselves as we answer, sometimes angrily disputing with him about how he rules the world, sometimes humbling ourselves before him in grateful trust. Prayer is language used to respond to the most that has been said to us, with the potential for saying all that is in us. Prayer is the development of speech into maturity, the language that is adequate to answering the one who has spoken comprehensively to us. Prayer is not a narrow use of language for specialty occasions, but language catholic, embracing the totality of everything and everyone everywhere. This conversation is both bold and devout — the utterly inferior responding to the utterly superior. In this exchange we become persons.

The entire life of faith is dialogue. By means of the Psalms we find our voice in the dialogue. In prayer we do not merely speak our feelings, we speak our answers. We can answer, we are permitted to answer. If we truly answer God there is nothing that we may not say to him.

—Eugene H. Peterson, *Answering God*

Dear Lord, our conversations are precious to me. Help me to hear you better and to remember that we are in a dialogue, and my prayer is my answer to what you have put before me in my life and relationships. Here is my answer now about my life today...[add personal comments]. In Jesus' name. Amen.

February 23

GOD LOVES US ALL

"Jesus...said to her, 'O woman, great is your faith!'...And her daughter was healed from that very hour." —Matthew 15:28, NKJV

This is one of the most multileveled of all the Jesus-stories. According to many theologians, it was the moment when Jesus, the son of Man, realized the enormity of his vocation. He was to fulfill the law and the prophets, but he was to fulfill them not only for the Jews, but for the whole of creation. God made all people, every single one of us. We may not exclude the woman from Canaan or the bag lady down the street or the person who is slightly crazy and yet insists on being in the front row in church. God made us all. You. Me. God loves all. You. Me.

We tend to think God loves the good people better than the wicked. Luke reminds us that God loves the wicked and the greedy just as much as those who come to church, pay their tithes, and try to live good and moral lives. This reminds us that only God can bring out the best in us, as Jesus brought out the faith of the woman from Canaan.

But God calls us not to be rewarded but to spread the Good News of God's love come to us in Jesus. God calls us to speak to all those we might otherwise shun.

It is not easy. We tend to be afraid, and then out of our fear, we tend to condemn anybody who is different. But Jesus was different, wholly different! How can we not be different too?

—Madeleine L'Engle, *With the Angels in Lent*
(written by and for the People of All Angels Church, New York, 1996)

Dear God, help us to know that your love shines on both the just and the unjust, and that it is so brilliant that ultimately the unjust will turn to you for forgiveness. Forgive us, Jesus. Help us to love as you turned to love and heal the Canaanite woman and her child. Amen.

February 24

FROM VERSE TO VERSE WITH HANNAH

> "My heart exults in Yahweh
> my horn is exalted in my God
> my mouth derides my foes
> for I rejoice in your power of saving."
> —1 Samuel 2:1, JB

Since I work in an office, dealing with the constant influx of mail and faxes and phone calls and projects and deadlines and meetings and pressure—there are times I just have to get away. Even if I set up a schedule for prayer and frequent liturgies, the schedule falls apart, or if it doesn't, it becomes another pressure point. In order to spend time with God I have to get beyond the schedule.

I have a vivid memory of spending a day alone in prayer: the first retreat experience I designed for myself. I was working at a high-pressure job, one which demanded long hours and frequent travel, with a high level of hostility in the workplace. It was a frenzied atmosphere. In that assignment I felt far away from the spirit of silence and prayerful discipline.

The office allowed three personal days a year; I arranged to spend one of them in prayer at a retreat house in the country about an hour's drive from my home, not a planned retreat, but my own day, improvised by me. I began with that day's reading from 1 Samuel, chapter 1, about how Hannah prayed in the temple. "I will be Hannah today," I thought, "beseeching the Lord just as much. I will take on her way of praying, I will appropriate her style of prayer."

As I drove out onto the expressway, I felt a sense of high excitement and release. It was all very freeing, giving myself a whole day with the Lord. And I kept on praying with Hannah, in the chapel, in the silent hallways, walking the grounds. By now I had moved into Hannah's Song (1 Sam. 2:1).

Going from verse to verse with Hannah, praising God for his power and favor, I thought this canticle held the whole story of God's love for his people. Not only that: God's love-story was being retold to me through my praying of the canticle again. I felt connected with the pray-ers of other times and places, all the holy people who had prayed this canticle before me, even connecting with those who would come after me and find solace in Hannah's song. And in this way, it seemed that by going away to pray I had found the whole world.

But no, it wasn't over. Next came Samuel in the temple, learning awkwardly, by fits and starts, that God was actually speaking to him. So I went from being Hannah to being Samuel. "Eli then understood that it was Yahweh who was calling the boy. And he said to Samuel, 'Go and lie down, and if someone calls say, "Speak, Yahweh, your servant is listening."' So Samuel went and lay down in his place" (1 Sam. 3:9).

All these things flowed into me very powerfully. They became my word from Yahweh for the day. I was both Hannah and her child. And through me I felt the prophetic message streaming: "He is Yahweh: let him do what he thinks good" (1 Sam. 3:18). I also took comfort in the next thought: "Samuel grew up and Yahweh was with him and let no word of his fall to the ground" (1 Sam. 3:19). Later I learned that this story of Hannah in the temple is regarded by some as the origin of contemplative prayer.

The best space for a real spiritual life is not on some exalted plane. It's back at square one. Over and over, we have to make clean breaks and fresh starts and sudden flights from escalating pressure and routine.

—Emilie Griffin

Lord, teach me to find you in and through the schedule; and if the schedule is a barrier to you, teach me to throw the schedule away and flee into your presence. Help me to find you, Lord, when I need you most. Show me the where of my spiritual life, and the what of it, and the why of it. Let me be like Hannah and Samuel, alert to the sound of your voice and the whisper of your demands, the joy of your presence, and the awe of your companionship. Amen.

February 25

A Sun

> "The Lord God is a sun and shield."
> —Psalm 84:11a

You may have heard loving parents say of their kids, "Our children are the sunshine of our lives." True it is, of course, and probably even more so to those who have tried for a long time to have children.

But the happiness brought into life by a child pales in comparison with the far greater joy ushered into our lives by God Almighty. When the Psalmist says, in effect, "The sun of my life is my God," his testimony of God's love is total and eternal.

The sun is an apt and glorious metaphor for God, because when we are near to him, his very presence casts a sheen over all of life and makes visible that which otherwise would seem formless in the gloom.

The only idolatry really understandable from a human point of view is confusing the sun for God, or making an idol of the sun. No image, no spirit, no pagan temple can illuminate with such fervency, can warm us so fully and bring us vision, as the sun. It's no wonder that people throughout the ages have looked up in the sky and simply assumed that the sun *was* God, and they worshiped the sun.

But the words of the Psalmist steer us clear of that idolatry: "God is *a* sun" (not *the* sun) is a way of describing God as being to *my* life as the sun is to the Universe, the center around which the Psalmist's life revolves.

This simple phrase "God is a sun..." reflects other profound images of God as the sun of our lives. Without the sun, darkness flattens our shadows into obscurity. But when the dawn rises, we measure distances, perceive forms and tints. In the same way, without God we stagger in the darkness and stumble through life as if careening off tombstones. But God's holy magic wand lays light all around us, breaks through the darkness with heavenly clarity.

Sometimes the sun burns. Sometimes our own heart's hardness willfully rejects the touch of his hand. When we try to come near unto God at those moments when our spirits are still afflicted by secret sins, his warmth will ignite into conflagration. Then there is a range fire.

But God, our sun, never reneges on his blessings of light and warmth, even when we harden our hearts. He promises glorious quickening to those who know him deeply as the sun of their lives.

—James Calvin Schaap, *Near Unto God*

Lord, thank you for the light that illumines our lives even on days of cloud cover. Thank you for providing a secure, true center around which we can revolve, and for the warmth of your love that can break through our resistance like a range fire! Amen.

February 26

GOD IS MY FOREST RANGER

"I will instruct you and teach you in the way you should go; I will counsel you and watch over you." —Psalm 32:8

As a seasoned tent-camper I rendered Psalm 23 in my own idiom:

> God is my Forest Ranger who equips me for the wilderness.
> Each night he finds me a level campsite
> and helps me set up my tent.
> He searches out clear streams to cool my blistered feet
> and goes ahead of me to make sure
> I find the right path and don't get lost.
> Even though I hike down Death Valley
> I won't be anxious if he's with me.
> He provides me with a sturdy hiking stick,
> packs a picnic lunch for me,
> and keeps the bears at bay.
> He supplies me with a sun hat for my bare head,
> sun block for my face, insect repellent against bug bites,
> and Gatorade for my thirst.
> His personal presence and care is always there for me,
> and when we reach home together
> I want to be with him always
>
> —Luci Shaw, Psalm 23, author's paraphrase
> Journaling Workshop Exercises: How to Paraphrase a Scripture

Lord of the mountains and valleys, I delight in your faithfulness. In your presence enable me to release anxieties. In all circumstances may I learn to rejoice in your presence, and at the end of every day may I find my rest in you. Amen.

February 27

YOU'RE BLESSED

When Jesus saw his ministry drawing huge crowds, he climbed a hillside. Those who were apprenticed to him, the committed, climbed with him. Arriving at a quiet place, he sat down and taught his climbing companions. This is what he said:

"You're blessed when you're at the end of your rope. With less of you there is more of God and his rule.

"You're blessed when you feel you've lost what is most dear to you. Only then can you be embraced by the One most dear to you.

"You're blessed when you're content with just who you are—no more, no less. That's the moment you find yourselves proud owners of everything that can't be bought.

"You're blessed when you've worked up a good appetite for God. He's food and drink in the best meal you'll ever eat.

"You're blessed when you care. At the moment of being 'care-full,' you find yourselves cared for.

"You're blessed when you get your inside world—your mind and heart—put right. Then you can see God in the outside world.

"You're blessed when you can show people how to cooperate instead of compete or fight. That's when you discover who you really are, and your place in God's family.

"You're blessed when your commitment to God provokes persecution. The persecution drives you even deeper into God's kingdom.

"Not only that—count yourselves blessed every time people put you down or throw you out or speak lies about you to discredit me. What it means is that the truth is too close for comfort and they are uncomfortable. You can be glad when that happens—give a cheer, even!—for though they don't like it, *I do!* And all heaven applauds. And know that you are in good company. My prophets and witnesses have always gotten into this kind of trouble."

—Matthew 5:1–11, Eugene H. Peterson, THE MESSAGE,

Dear Lord, your guidelines are never clearer than in this lesson. Help me to become more content with who I am, to remember that less of me means more of you, and to cooperate more. Help me to look boldly at the meaning behind the rejection of people to know whether I am in error, or my truth has hit too close to home. Help me, above all, to remember that I am in good company, and that I am blessed! In Jesus' name. Amen.

February 28

A FILM OF ICE HINTS AT RESTORATION
(ASH WEDNESDAY)

"And the God of all grace, who called you to his eternal glory in Christ, after you have suffered a little while, will himself restore you and make you strong, firm and steadfast." —1 Peter 5:10

Today it is bitter cold on Remnant Acres. The temperature is not so low, but a hard wind sweeps across the field from the northwest and swirls the snow into drifts. Because I have been away, my cabin has been unattended for a week. When I came in, carrying my little propane heater, the thin film of ice that forms in the low spot of my writing table was larger than usual. I could not begin to write until I thawed it and wiped it up with a towel I keep for that purpose.

The regular appearance of that sheet of ice (which on warm days is a puddle of water) disturbs me, for I cannot find its source. To all appearances my cabin is tight. I've caulked at least twice every crack I can find. Still the water, insistent and insidious, finds its way in and waits in the center of my table to disrupt my work. What is maddening is that the trail that should allow me to follow the water to the leak has always evaporated.

Today, as I waited for the ice to melt, I saw the water as an analogy for the way sin finds the hidden cracks in my life, flows to the center of my work, and disrupts my relationships with people and with the creation. That is a good analogy to consider on Ash Wednesday, for an awareness of sin and a determination to be cleansed are the order of this day, but since the passing of my adolescence, I have never been able to focus long on my evil nature, nor on any particular acts of either omission or commission. I live rather in the awareness of my redemption, of the work of restoration Christ is doing in me and in creation.

Almost as soon as I drew the analogy of sin infiltrating like water, my imagination leaped ahead to another: Christ, the living water, infiltrating, coming on his own even when we are unaware, uninviting, to bring life to the land. These woods I love are filled with springs. In a few weeks the thaw will come, and everywhere I walk I will walk in water.

—John Leax, *Standing Ground*

Lord, I am coming to see that living my life as you would lead me to live it — would be having the best life I could have. At times I am disturbed by the appearance of disruptive elements in my thinking, feelings, and actions, and can't find answers. Come into my life especially then. Infiltrate it with your living water, so that I may be restored. Lead me into faith, and help me to trust and keep moving forward. In Jesus' name. Amen.

February 29

SUFFICIENT GRACE

"My grace is sufficient for you, for my power is made perfect in weakness."
—2 Corinthians 12:9

Every time I begin an exercise program after not working out for months at a time, I go through the same series of feelings: Boy, it doesn't take long for my body to get out of shape. Why do I let this happen?

During what is usually a two-week period of readjusting to hard exercise, I feel embarrassed and discouraged that I've let myself slide. I often make silly jokes about being flabby and hope other people around me won't think I'm awful because I haven't kept up with exercising. Exercising just seems like such a drag sometimes!

But in Philip Keller's book *Lessons from a Sheep Dog*, there is a passage that really hit me. He writes,

> The greatest delusion any man or woman can ever come under is the idea that it is a "drag" to do God's will. Just the opposite is true! Yet our old natures, our strong, selfish self-interests, our sensual society, our arch-foe Satan — all endeavor to deceive us into believing that it is a bore and bondage to serve the Master, to carry out His commandments in glad-hearted cooperation.

I realized that he was right! I do consider it a bore to exercise every day and bondage to "restrict" myself from certain foods. Maybe it's my attitude that needs changing.

When I read in 2 Corinthians that God's power "is made perfect in weakness," I realized that my best hope is to admit that I am weak and selfish, and that my old habits are strong. Paul seems to me to be saying that the power of God can work in a person like me, that when I am willing to confess my weakness, God's kind of power has room to come into my life and be perfected. I could see that without my weaknesses I would never have to call on God for anything. These repeated failures to keep myself in shape were what kept driving me to look deeper for answers about myself — answers that I find come from God.

Good ol' Thomas à Kempis said it for me again. In *The Imitation of Christ* he wrote,

> When a good person is troubled or tempted or is disquieted by evil thoughts, then he or she understands and knows that God is most necessary, and that he or she may do nothing that is good without God.

As I continue to try to break my old habits and to wrestle with feelings like "It isn't fair that I have to exercise every day," I am trying to learn to tell Jesus about them. I am trusting a little more each time that he can work through me to bring me to a condition of health that will make me most able to carry out his will. —Andrea Wells Miller, *BodyCare*

Dear Lord, thank you for your grace to me — that unconditional love that forgives me for my weaknesses and inspires me to keep on trying to be all I can be for you. Your grace is sufficient for me. And as I learn to trust you with my physical well-being as well as my spiritual health, I find more and more that I need your strength. I ask you to fill me with your grace today and to help me understand clearly what your intentions for my life are. In Jesus' name. Amen.

MARCH

March 1

THE MEGAPHONE

"Their idea of pleasure is to carouse in broad daylight. They are blots and blemishes, reveling in their pleasures while they feast with you."
—2 Peter 2:13b

C. S. Lewis introduced the phrase "pain, the megaphone of God." "God whispers to us in our pleasures, speaks in our conscience, but shouts in our pains," he said; "it is his megaphone to rouse a deaf world." The word "megaphone" is apropos, because by its nature pain shouts. When I stub my toe or twist an ankle, pain loudly announces to my brain that something is wrong. Similarly, the existence of suffering on this earth is, I believe, a scream to all of us that something is wrong. It halts us in our tracks and forces us to consider other values.

The animal fable *Watership Down* tells of a colony of wild rabbits uprooted from their homes by a construction project. As they wander, they come across a new breed of rabbits huge and beautiful, with sleek, shiny hair and perfect claws and teeth. How do you live so well? the wild rabbits ask. Don't you forage for food? The tame rabbits explain that food is provided for them, in the form of carrots and apples and corn and kale. Life is grand and wonderful.

After a few days, however, the wild rabbits notice that one of the fattest and sleekest of the tame rabbits has disappeared. Oh, that happens occasionally, the tame rabbits explain. But we don't let it interfere with our lives. There's too much good to enjoy. Eventually, the wild rabbits find that the land is studded with traps, and death "hangs like a mist" over their heads. The tame rabbits, in exchange for their plush, comfortable lives, had willingly closed their eyes to one fact: the imminent danger of death.

Watership Down is a fable with a moral point. Like the fat, sleek rabbits, we could — some people do — believe that the sole purpose of life is to be comfortable. Gorge yourself, build a nice home, enjoy good food, have sex, live the good life. That's all there is. But the presence of suffering vastly complicates that lifestyle — unless we choose to wear blinders, like the tame rabbits.

It's hard to believe the world is here just so I can party, when a third of its people go to bed starving each night. It's hard to believe the purpose of life is to feel good, when I see teenagers smashed on the freeway. If I try to escape toward hedonism, suffering and death lurk nearby, haunting me, reminding me of how hollow life would be if this world were all I'd ever know.

Sometimes murmuring, sometimes shouting, suffering is a "rumor of transcendence" that the entire human condition is out of whack. Something is wrong with a life of war and violence and human tragedy. He who wants to be satisfied with this world, who wants to believe the only purpose of life is enjoyment, must go around with cotton in his ears, for the megaphone of pain is a loud one.

—Philip Yancey, *Where Is God When It Hurts?*

Dear Lord, at times I get "cotton in my ears" and block out the megaphone of pain and suffering around me as I become too focused on pursuing "the good life." At such times, increase my sensitivity to others. Help me to remember that the proper object of my love is you and people, not money and things. And guide me ever in your will concerning the proper use of what you have given me. In Jesus' name. Amen.

March 2

A Sign or a Sham?

"Do you not know?
Have you not heard?
The Lord is the everlasting God,
 the Creator of the ends of the earth.
He will not grow tired or weary,
 and his understanding no one can fathom."
—Isaiah 40:28

All the world is one great sacramental loaf. We are not — nor will we ever be, God save us — solitary intelligences spinning in the dark void of space. He crowds upon us from Sheol to the sea; he jostles our thoughts along the pathways in our brains. He hides in the bushes, jumping out in flames to startle us into seeing. He sequesters himself in stables and swaddling so as to take us unawares. He veils himself in flesh, the same flesh that drips into fingers at the end of my arms and sprouts into hair on my head.

Either the world is holy or it's not. Either the Creator's work is a sign of himself or it's a sham. Where else can one draw the line between sacred and profane except around all the cosmos?
—Virginia Stem Owens, *God Spy*

As I move throughout my world today, Lord, let my awareness of your presence in it grow. The world outside me, full of traffic, weather, people, and nature, and the world inside me, full of thoughts, emotions, and physical conditions — both are full or your reality, if only I can detect it. In Jesus' name. Amen.

March 3

THE MIND OF CHRIST

"We have not received the spirit of the world but the Spirit who is from God, that we may understand what God has freely given us."
—1 Corinthians 2:12

The sun is shining so seductively here today that I spread a sleeping bag on the narrow balcony and, in spite of the wintry forty-five degrees, I put on my swimsuit and luxuriated like a cat in a sheltered spot. My skin welcomes the naked heat of the sun. For two contented hours I have lain here, knitting, reading, dozing, meditating on a poem by George MacDonald.

> O Son of man, to right my lot
> Naught but thy presence can avail;
> Yet on the road thy wheels are not,
> Nor on the sea, thy sail.

> My fancied ways, why should'st thou heed?
> Thou com'st down thine own secret stair —
> Com'st down to answer all my need,
> Yea, every bygone prayer.

Again, as so often before, I feel the secret thoughts rising in me, trusting them to be God-thoughts making themselves known. Which started me reflecting on the Spirit, and how he teaches us all things and guides us into truth, as Jesus promised. I checked 1 Corinthians 2:10–16 in my New International Version of the Bible — about how God reveals things to us. My spirit knows my thoughts; God's Spirit knows God's thoughts.

Because I am God's daughter, a bridge, a path, a secret stair has been built from his heart to mine so that by the Spirit God's thoughts can step into my mind. "This is what we speak, not in words taught us by human wisdom, but in words taught by the Spirit.... The spiritual person makes judgments about all things" because she has "the mind of Christ." Even these journal words are part of the process — this mysterious inner interweaving of observation and reflection and verbalization.

—Luci Shaw, *God in the Dark*

Holy Spirit, dwell in me. Give me the mind of Christ that I might discern the way I should go, that I might do the things I should do, and that I might be the person I am called to be. Amen.

March 4

GOD DOWN HERE

"I have called thee by thy name; thou art mine. When thou passest through the waters, I will be with thee." —Isaiah 43:1-2, KJV

Back when it was still possible to believe that this planet was the center of everything, that the sun and the moon and the stars were hung in the sky entirely for our benefit, it was quite possible to think of God as our Maker, Out There. God took nothing, and created a planet with water and land and fish and land animals, and proclaimed it good, looking at it all from a heavenly distance. We have too often thought of God as being *outside* the universe, creating us, and looking at what happens to us, concerned, but Out There. But as I contemplate the vastness of the night sky on a clear, cold night, God Out There does not work. Out There is *too* far out; God becomes too remote; I cannot hide under the shelter of el's protecting wings.

Scripturally, God is always in and part of creation, walking and talking with Adam and Eve, taking Abraham out to see the stars, wrestling with Jacob.

And, in the most glorious possible demonstration of God *in* and *part of* creation, God came to us in Jesus of Nazareth, fully participating in our human birth and life and death and offering us the glory of Easter.

If we shed our idea of God as being someone Out There, separate from all that has been made, and begin instead to think of God as within all creation, every galaxy, every quantum, every human being, then we cannot hold ourselves "out there" either: We cannot set ourselves apart from anything that happens. Anywhere.

—Madeleine L'Engle, *A Stone for a Pillow*

Lord God, may we look for you where you may be found: everywhere! Amen.

March 5

ACTION OR FEELING?

"My Father, if it is possible, may this cup be taken from me."
—Matthew 26:39

I was sitting on my front porch one day when my children were small, thinking about the love Christ showed us when he went to the cross, and what it might look like if I were acting with the same kind of love. In my mind, I saw my daughter pedaling her tricycle down the driveway straight into the path of a huge truck. With no time to think, I vaulted over the iron railing, ran into the street and shoved her out of the way, just in time to hear and feel the awful crunch as the truck ran over my back!

Though it was only a daydream, I was covered with perspiration. *That was really an act of love!* I thought. But then the scene started replaying itself. Except now the tricycle rider was the mean little boy from down the street, the one who teased and threw rocks at my daughter. And he was heading right into the path of the truck. This time, I did not want to risk my life for that kid. But I couldn't stop myself and I vaulted over the iron railing, pushed the kid to safety and was killed myself.

Which of these two actions was the greater act of Christian love? I wondered. Any father might risk his life for his own child. But to do that for someone unworthy — or an enemy, even — that was more like Jesus' actions. In his humanness Jesus did not want to go through with the loving act of dying on the cross. Three times, Matthew tells us, he prayed in great distress to be spared from the ordeal. At the end of his praying, he said in effect, I still don't want to go ("Let this cup pass from me"), but if you won't change your mind, I'll do it out of obedience to your will ("My Father, if this cannot pass unless I drink it, thy will be done," Matt. 26:42, RSV).

If that is true, then to love as Jesus did, I don't have to have warm, loving feelings. My job is to do loving acts for others, out of obedience to him, no matter how I feel. —J. Keith Miller, *Daily Guideposts,* 1996

Lord, help me not to sit around waiting to feel loving before I agree to be your loving representative. Help me always to act in loving ways. Amen.

March 6

SEWING

"Instead [your beauty] should be that of your inner self, the unfading beauty of a gentle and quiet spirit, which is of great worth in God's sight."
—1 Peter 3:4

I remember, that morning, how
I stayed home from school to sew a dress,
how instead I watched snow
bandaging the city. Pour it out, Muse,
how I tended the window, how I was
patience itself, how still
I sat, how I became
the chair. And that's when
you flocked down, drowsy angel,
clever seamstress. Say anything,
say how those mothy flakes
charmed you, how you tucked
the snow around the buildings,
how you swathed them,
how you worked with the material,
how you were nowhere visible
but in the spaces.

    Sing how, that afternoon,
when I laid out the flimsy pattern
dancing around the fabric on my knees
the rug's whiskers buffing my knees
till they were numb and rosy,
how I worked with the material,
squinting at the arrow on the bias,
dovetailing the plackets,
making Tab 1A kiss Tab 1B.
As I pointed the sharp snout of scissors
and whispered *Dear Lord, make me*
good at geometry, don't let me
ruin this,

        as I started to cut,
I could feel myself move
beyond the pattern, move
toward beauty, move toward
the empty spaces.

—Jeanne Murray Walker, in *Gaining Time*

Dear Lord, I want to sense you in the empty spaces of my life as well as in the center of my heartbeat. Calm my frantic days, let me become still, a chair, a rug, a garden bench, until I can find you anywhere — to thank you, praise you, love you. Amen.

March 7

Enduring Mercy

"Then the trees of the forest will sing, they will sing for joy before the Lord, for he comes to judge the earth. Give thanks to the Lord, for he is good; his love endures forever." —1 Chronicles 16: 33-34

The afternoon we bought our trees it rained, so we had to wait a couple of days to plant them. When I started to dig, I expected to find heavy, wet soil, but spring had been so dry that only the top inch or two, those inches held together by grass roots, contained moisture. I set each tree, filled the hole halfway with soil, and then ran it full of water.

While I waited for the water to soak in, I pruned. That was hard, for I tend to put my faith in the seen, not the unseen, and the budding tops looked strong. But I followed directions. Since the roots had been reduced by one-third to one-half in transplanting, I nipped the branches off the same, bringing the size of the tree into conformity with its source of nourishment.

Brutal as it seemed then, I can see in the lush green of their present flourishing that it was good. —John Leax, *In Season and Out*

Great husbandman of earth's orchard, you have planted us for your Father's pleasure. Tend us kindly. Prune the wild limbs from us. Be enduring mercy to us, and nurture our roots in the soil of your love. Transform our heartwood so that we shall stand supple, responsive to the wind of the Spirit blowing through our branches. Amen.

March 8

MOVING IN THE DARK

"The sheep hear his voice, and he calls his own sheep by name."
—John 10:3, RSV

Sheep at Nightfall

They are foam collecting
   on the shore of the field.
Backs yellow with dust
   they lean against the gate,
now one, now another, lifting a voice
   vibrating and torn as the Irish.

They are richly dressed, each wigged
   like a British justice. Yet
they move together like slaves
   bent under Pharaoh,
to be folded into the dark
   eating every green thing
and complaining at the dust of their daily bread.

If March shows the icy
   back of his robe,
they will go no further.
   Eyes thick with rheum
they feel death's finger shake the ground:
   Thousands in one night
rot where they fall like patches of late snow.

Still the old ram carries his head
   like the treasure of Persia,
uttering a melodious question,
   knowing he will be answered
when the sun comes striding
   from the oratorio of the hills
touching his fleece with gold.
—Robert Siegel, *In a Pig's Eye*

Lord, sometimes I feel like a sheep at night, moving in the dark with a herd of other sheep, all of us without answers to many questions. Strengthen my trust to be like that of the old ram, who knows he will be answered and will again experience your presence. And lead me to safety in the doing of your will. Amen.

March 9

THAT THEY MAY KNOW YOU

"Now this is eternal life: that they may know you, the only true God."
—John 17:3a

If Christ had a rich prayer life, Scripture doesn't offer us the record. We can only imagine how active he must have been in prayer — as a boy in his father's house in Nazareth, as an adolescent taking on the wizened elders in the temple, and as a man, a sufferer and a redeemer, on the road to Golgotha. There must have been thousands of prayers. Just imagine what a great book that would make — all by itself: *The Prayers of Jesus Christ.*

We don't have that book. Very few of Christ's own prayers are recorded in Scripture, and that fact alone makes what we have particularly precious. Consider this short prayer, for instance: "Now this is eternal life: that they may know you, the only true God" (John 17:3). In this few words lies the entire picture of our happiness, overheard in the intimate conversation between the Father/God and the son he sent to dwell among us.

It's one of the very few prayers Christ's disciples actually wrote down for our benefit, and it's less an outright request for something than it is an act of receiving. Christ is repeating back to the father the very cornerstone of our happiness — this is the whole package: that your people might know you as the one true God. That's what life is all about. That's eternity.

Listen. There is no question that this world offers great blessings. Music thrills us. Our work offers rewards. What greater comfort can we feel than to be loved by family and friends? But all of that, at death, is left behind. What is most obviously eternal about our lives is the individual soul, this germ of divinity within each of us.

And that soul, just like our bodies, must be fed — not by vitamins and minerals and the four basic food groups. The soul requires sustenance after its own eternal nature. If the soul is to grow and blossom through our lives, it requires a different kind of nurturing — it requires *knowing God.* —James Calvin Schaap, *Near Unto God*

Our happiness, O Lord, is knowing you. You are our joy, for we have received your love and live, even now, the eternal life infused with your Spirit. Amen.

March 10

A WOMAN OF FAITH
(BASED ON JOHN 8:1-12)

> "Jesus bent down and wrote with his finger on the ground. And as they continued to ask him, he stood up and said to them, 'Let him who is without sin among you be the first to throw a stone at her.'"
> —John 8:6b-7, RSV

"You boys don't give up, do you?"

"No, sir, we don't," said the Scribes and Pharisees as they dragged in a woman and made her stand facing Jesus.

"Teacher, she's just been caught in the act."

"The act of what?"

"Adultery. Caught her in *flagrante delicto*."

"Am I supposed to have an opinion?"

"Well, you do about everything else!"

"I suppose I do."

"The law of Moses says women like her have to be stoned. So what do you say?"

Jesus thought for a moment, then bent down, and with his fingers wrote something confidential on the ground. Even as he was doing this, they peppered him with questions.

"Yes, that's what the law says," said Jesus standing up, "and, yes, do stone her."

That was the answer they wanted to hear. No more of his wishy-washy, lovey-dovey interpretations of the law.

"One thing, though," he said to them as they were getting in a few last squeezes before dragging the woman off to the stoning place. "To stone her to death, you have to be without sin yourselves, stainless creatures right from the start, not a blot on your record."

"Since when?"

"Since now!"

Then he bent down and continued his calculations in the dust.

Well, when they heard this, the Scribes and Pharisees weren't happy at all. The older ones weren't quite the lions, and the younger ones weren't quite the tigers they thought they were.

And then there were two. Jesus and the rather ragged yet handsome woman. He stood up and looked her in the eye, and she returned his look eyeball for eyeball.

"Thank you, Lord," she said.

"Well, where are they, the hotshots who wanted to stone you?"

"Gone with the wind, I guess."

"Who's left to condemn you?"

"No one, Lord, unless of course you want to. I do deserve it, you know."

"Yes, you do and, yes, I could but, no, I won't."

"Thank you, Lord.

"So, you enjoy your work, do you?"

"Not really."

"So why do you do it?"

"It's a job."

"I thought so."

"And I'm good at it."

"I think our paths will cross again one day."

"I'd like that, Lord."

"Just one thing, though."

"Anything, Lord."

"Please do me a favor."

"Yes, Lord."

"Don't do it again."

"No, Lord."

"But you probably will."

"And if I do?"

"Then you'll become just like them, and wouldn't that be a sad end for a woman of faith like you!"

"Thank you, Lord."

—William Griffin

Dear God, thank you that you do not condemn me even though I deserve it and even though you could. Amen.

March 11

STEP ON IT

"For there is one God and one mediator between God and men, the man Jesus Christ, who gave himself as a ransom for all men — the testimony given in its proper time." —1 Timothy 2:5-6

> All these broken bridges —
> we have always tried to build them
> to each other and to heaven.
> Why is it such a sad surprise
> when last year's iron-strong,
> out-thrust organization, this month's

shining project, today's
far-flung silver network
of good resolutions
all answer the future's questions with
rust, and the sharp, ugly jutting
of the unfinished?
We have miscalculated very time.
Our blueprints are smudged.
We never order enough steel.
Our foundations are shallow as mud.
Our cables fray.
Our superstructure is stuck together
clumsily, with rivets of the wrong size.

We are our own botched bridges.
We were schooled in Babel
and our ambitious soaring sinks
in the sea. How could we hope to carry
your heavy glory? We cannot even bear
the weight of our own failure.

But you did the unthinkable.
You built one bridge to us
solid enough, long enough, strong enough
to stand all tides for all time, linking
the unlinkable.

There is always a gap between present reality and future potential.
   A gift unwrapped has never been truly received. An uncashed check cannot be spent. A bridge that spans a raging river is useless to us unless we begin to advance across it.
   The divide between earth and heaven, between us and God, is one that only Jesus Christ could reconnect. He is our link to life and eternity — a bridge to be stepped onto so that it bears our whole weight as we cross the space from one side to the other.   — Luci Shaw, *Horizons*

I have tried, O Lord, to be the engineer of my salvation. I have sunk piers, but they have tilted and fallen in the mud. I have strung cables, but they have twisted and tangled in the winds of my capriciousness. Forgive me my foolish ambition, my refusal to set aside my will and walk the bridge, Christ Jesus, who waits for me. Today I yield. He is my way. I shall follow him to you. Amen.

March 12

GOD, PLEASE BOTHER!

> "Trust in the Lord with all your heart, and lean not on your own understanding; in all your ways acknowledge him, and he will make your paths straight. Do not be wise in your own eyes; fear the Lord and shun evil. This will bring health to your body and nourishment to your bones."
> —Proverbs 3:5-8

I've mentioned how many times I've tried to rely on my own understanding and strength and how I have to keep running back to God over and over with my frustration and failure. But I'd never known anybody to write about why this might happen until I read *The Southampton Diet* by Dr. Stuart Berger.

Dr. Berger warns about an emotional danger that comes with dieting. He said that after we've been on a diet for a week or so and we've lost some weight, we'll probably start feeling pretty cocky. We'll feel like we're really in control of getting good results and success. These feelings can lead us to start thinking things like, "I'm doing so well, I can afford to eat this one extra little piece of cheese," or "I think I'll add another slice of bread to my diet today. Surely it won't hurt." That's when it all starts to fall apart. And you know what? That's exactly what's happened to me many times, and it's usually the point at which I stop losing weight, even though I "think" I'm still dieting.

As a matter of fact, it seems that the closer I get to my goal, the more likely it is to happen. I start to think the momentum I've begun by losing weight will carry me on to my new weight goal without my having to stick to the diet. It's like pushing a grocery cart around the store, then assuming the momentum it built up from being pushed all over the grocery store will carry it through the checkout line! Most of the grocery carts I've ever seen have to be pushed constantly or they stop dead on their flat little wheels. And that's the way my weight-loss momentum seems to work.

Richard Foster, in *Celebration of Discipline,* also talks about this cocky feeling. Foster points out that "the moment we feel we can succeed and attain victory over our sin by the strength of our own will alone is the moment we are worshiping the will."

Henri Arnold, in *Freedom from Sinful Thoughts: Christ Alone Breaks the Curse,* also looks at this problem of attitude. He said, "As long as we think we can save ourselves by our own will power, we will only make the evil in us stronger than ever."

So, after reading these things in the Bible and in these three books, and after thinking things over, I'm recommitting myself today as I write this to try to drop my cocky attitude and get back to work. I'm going to trust in the Lord more than I ever have and try to stop thinking I can handle this myself.

I keep thinking I can find a shortcut around what it takes to shape up my body. But now I know that one of the problems I have is in my head. And I believe the cure for the problem in my head is to let God change my attitude about who is God around here.

—Andrea Wells Miller, *BodyCare*

Dear Lord, I want the refreshment to my flesh and healing to my bones that is promised in these Scripture verses. Help me to trust in you and to stop pretending that "I can handle it now, so you don't have to bother, God." Please bother! I need you.

Thank you that you can make my paths straight — straight past the refrigerator and out of the kitchen. In Jesus' name. Amen.

March 13

TUNING IN TO GOD'S FREQUENCY

"I will not leave you as orphans; I will come to you. Before long the world will not see me anymore, but you will see me. Because I live, you also will live." —John 14:18-19

We may be just beginning to learn about the transmission of information between persons and between God and people. If God is personal in nature and we are to pray, "Our Father..." as Christ suggested (Matt. 6:9), then we should expect some sort of response in meaningful terms. It may be that our ability to tune in to God's frequency is blocked by our own self-centered absorption. Perhaps our sin is like "filling our receiving screens with snow." Yet occasionally people get very clear "pictures" of God's answer to a prayer in terms of a meaningful word or image. And whether the contact was actually with God or not, sometimes the depth of the experience carries with it the power to change the life of the person praying, and through him or her, the lives of many others.

Several years ago a good friend told me about a startling encounter he had just been through. My friend is an intelligent professional man and in some ways a little cynical about things he hears. I certainly do not know if the experience had a transcendent reference, but my friend had been deeply moved by the account he related.

A Christian, an automobile salesman, decided he was going to make hospital calls two days each week as a part of his response to Christ's admonition to visit the sick. During a routine business telephone call to a man named Bennie Abernathy, with whom he had talked earlier about buying a new car, the salesman, Bert Johnson, spoke with his potential customer's wife. She said, "Mr. Johnson, I don't think my husband will be needing a new car. He is in the hospital and has incurable cancer. He will probably never get out."

Bert thought, "I'll go by to see him, just to say 'Hello.'" When he got to the man's room in the hospital, he had a very superficial conversation. Bennie was nice enough, but Bert didn't know him very well and had no idea how he felt about death. Finally, just before leaving, Bert decided to get in at least a word about the real situation. He turned to the sick man, "Well, I hope the Lord gives you peace about all this," nodding toward his body.

When the man heard Bert, his face lighted with a wonderful smile. "Let me tell you something," he said. "All my life I have never really known what I felt about God. I have heard that a person must 'commit his life to Christ' or 'be born again' — but I didn't really know how. Yesterday I was lying here, very depressed, because I did not know what to do to tie my life into God. In desperation I decided to pray. I simply asked God how I could come close to him." The man's face was very sincere and intense as he remembered his experience. Now he looked into Bert's eyes with great clarity. "And do you know what happened as I prayed? I saw Jesus — here in this room, as real as you are. He was standing over there (he nodded toward the corner), and there were people coming to him. As they got to where he was, each one would reach inside his own robe and lift out his heart... and hand it to Jesus. First there were grown men, all kinds, and then there were the children...." Bennie paused as he saw it all again in his mind against the wall in the corner of the room. Bert did not know how long they sat like that, but finally the man looked up calmly and said, "And I gave him my heart, too. He took it, put his other hand on my shoulder and smiled as he said, 'Peace.' And then he was gone."

Bert could only nod his head slightly as if in agreement. "That's... wonderful," he said softly.

The man in the bed went on thoughtfully, "You know, Mr. Johnson, I realize this whole thing sounds absurd, but it's true. It's the truest thing that ever happened to me. And I am going to tell every person who comes in that door before I die."

And he did.
—J. Keith Miller, *Habitation of Dragons*

All I can do is indicate indirectly certain events in man's life, which can scarcely be described, in which some people experience spirit as meeting; and in the end, when indirect indication is not enough, there is nothing for me but to appeal, my reader, to the witness of your own mysteries — buried, perhaps, but still attainable.
—Martin Buber, *I and Thou*

A miracle is "not contrary to nature," but contrary to what we know as nature.
—Augustine, *The City of God*

In the dispute concerning the true God and the truth of religion, there has never happened any miracle on the side of error, and not of truth.
—Blaise Pascal, *Pensées*

Lord, sometimes in my cynicism I feel as if prayer is autosuggestion and that we are playing games with ourselves when we talk of communicating with you. And then I see the miracles of modern science and realize that we are already experiencing things which point beyond our intellectual horizons to a time when people may be able to communicate mind to mind across thousands of miles. With regard to you, we seem to see through a dim lens now; but I believe with Paul that someday we may communicate face-to-face. I believe, and I appreciate your help with my unbelief. Amen.
—J. Keith Miller, *Habitation of Dragons*

March 14

The Reality of Our Lives

"Like an open book, you watched me grow from conception to birth; all the stages of my life were spread out before you, the days of my life all prepared before I'd even lived one day."
—Psalm 139:16, THE MESSAGE

Before Jeremiah knew God, God knew Jeremiah: "Before I formed you in the womb I knew you." This turns everything we ever thought about God around. We think that God is an object about which we have questions. We are curious about God. We make inquiries about God. We read books about God. We get into late night bull sessions about God. We drop into church from time to time to see what is going on with God. We indulge in an occasional sunset or symphony to cultivate a feeling of reverence for God.

But that is not the reality of our lives with God. Long before we ever got around to asking questions about God, God has been questioning us. Long before we got interested in the subject of God, God subjected us to the most intensive and searching knowledge. Before it ever crossed our minds that God might be important, God singled us out as important. Before we were formed in the womb, God knew us. We are known before we know.
—Eugene H. Peterson, *Run with the Horses*

Dear Lord, I am learning to hear your questions to me about my response to you and your love. Guide me as I look inward at the person you made me to be, and look outward at the world into which you have set me. Help me to answer you in accordance with your plans for my life. In Jesus' name. Amen.

March 15

LOVE IS WHAT YOU DO

"And walk in love, as Christ also hath loved us, and hath given himself for us an offering and a sacrifice to God for a sweetsmelling savour."
—Ephesians 5:2, KJV

"... Meg, there's no more time. They'll be back any moment now."

Panic churned in her. "Progo, if I don't Name right, if I fail, what will you do?"

"I told you. I have to choose."

"That's not telling me. I want to know which way you're going to choose."

Proginoskes's feathers shivered as though a cold wind had blown through them. "Meg, there isn't much time. They're on their way back. You have to Name one of them."

"Give me a hint."

"This isn't a game. Mr. Jenkins was right."

She shot him an anguished glance, and he lowered several sets of eyelashes in apology. "Progo, even for Charles Wallace, how can I do the impossible? How can I love Mr. Jenkins?"

Proginoskes did not respond. There was no flame, no smoke; only a withdrawing of eyes behind wings.

"Progo! Help me! How can I feel love for Mr. Jenkins?"

Immediately he opened a large number of eyes very wide. "What a strange idea. Love isn't *feeling*. If it were, I wouldn't be able to love. Cherubim don't have feelings."

"But—"

"Idiot," Proginoskes said, anxiously rather than crossly. "Love isn't how you feel. It's what you do...."   —Madeleine L'Engle, *A Wind in the Door*

Living God, raise us by your Eternal Spirit to love not in word, neither in tongue, but in deed and in truth. Amen.

March 16

BODY BLESSING

"Bless the Lord, O my soul: and all that is within me, bless his holy name."
—Psalm 103:1, KJV

The Hesychasts, high on Mount Athos, bowed their heads upon their breasts, took a deep breath, and plunged in. What they plunged into was prayer. It began with a tack with which to fix the attention. It became breath itself, an inlet for the universe to invade one's body until the entire cosmos, drawn in, heaved out, was transformed into prayer. The body's posture was important. The breathing was to be carefully controlled so as to keep time with the words. Eventually the prayer, breathed in, united with their very blood and heartbeat; breathed out, it blessed the world. And some monks claimed after a while to have indeed seen the Light of the Transfiguration, uncreated energy beheld by bodily eyes.

For it is bodies that are baptized, bodies that eat and absorb the Body of Christ, bodies that will be raised, glorified and incorruptible. It is tongues that confess and knees that bow. Perhaps we are so willing to reduce ourselves to abstractions of thought, principles of personality, because God, too, could then be an abstraction or a principle, and not a person.

How dare we say we feed Christ in the hungry, harbor him in the stranger, succor him in the sick, if we believe the Incarnation is over and done with? God save us from perverting metaphors to moralizing. Is "Christ in us" only sentiment? Is time stronger than eternity, and has it kicked God himself back upstairs into his properly ethereal realm? Do we gloat over our own transience and our decaying corpses, thinking that can hold him at bay?

He is here, rushing in our blood, melting in our mouths, oscillating in our synapses. In him all things hold together. He pierces us with photons, skewering us like Tinker Toys to all creation. When we lift up our hearts we must also lift up, on that slender pinnacle of purpose, the whole world. We carry mountains on our tongue. Bless the Lord, O my soul, we say, and all that is within me. And within us is the Sahara, the salty seas, the muddy Mississippi. The flora and fauna of the equator swarm our throats. Asphalt and ashes. The cedar tree. The pond. All the world that we have discovered, one way or another. That is what is within us and what must be made to bless the Lord.

—Virginia Stem Owens, *God Spy*

Lord, you inhabit my mind and soul, and every inch of my body. These hands touch others with love and do work dependably and this head bows in prayer. My physical being is dedicated to carrying out your will. I praise you with my body as well as my mind, heart, and soul! In Jesus' name. Amen.

March 17

KNOWING THE TRUTH

"Do not be conformed to this world but be transformed by the renewal of your mind, that you may prove what is the will of God, what is good and acceptable and perfect." —Romans 12:2, RSV

The apostle Paul tells us that we are transformed through the renewal of the mind. The mind is renewed by applying it to those things that will transform it. "Finally, brethren, whatever is true, whatever is honorable, whatever is just, whatever is pure, whatever is lovely, whatever is gracious, if there is any excellence, if there is anything worthy of praise *think* about these things" (Phil. 4:8, RSV; emphasis added). The Discipline of study is the primary vehicle to bring us to *"think* about these things." Therefore, we should rejoice that we are not left to our own devices but have been given this means of God's grace for the changing of our inner spirit.

Many Christians remain in bondage to fears and anxieties simply because they do not avail themselves of the Discipline of study. They may be faithful in church attendance and earnest in fulfilling their religious duties, and still they are not changed. I am not here speaking only of those who are going through mere religious forms, but of those who are genuinely seeking to worship and obey Jesus Christ as Lord and Master. They may sing with gusto, pray in the Spirit, live as obediently as they know, even receive divine visions and revelations, and yet the tenor of their lives remains unchanged. Why? Because they have never taken up one of the central ways God uses to change us: study. Jesus made it unmistakably clear that the knowledge of the truth will set us free. "You will know the truth, and the truth will make you free" (John 8:32, RSV). Good feelings will not free us. Ecstatic experiences will not free us. Getting "high on Jesus" will not free us. Without a knowledge of the truth, we will not be free. —Richard J. Foster, *Celebration of Discipline*

Dear Lord Jesus, in my better moments I want nothing more than to be like you. But there are other moments.... Help me to see how good conformity to your way really is. In my seeking for you may I be found by you. I love you, Lord. Amen. —Richard J. Foster, *Celebration of Discipline*

March 18

ROYALTY

"'Not by might nor by power, but by my Spirit,' says the Lord Almighty."
—Zechariah 4:6b

> He was a plain man
> and learned no Latin
>
> Having left all gold behind
> he dealt out peace
> to all us wild ones
> and the weather
>
> He ate fish, bread,
> country wine and God's will
>
> Dust sandaled his feet
>
> He wore purple only once
> and that was an irony.

Jesus contradicted all their presuppositions.

They were looking for a warrior king, with political and military power, a leader who would free them from the iron rule of Rome. Jesus was indeed born into the kingly line of Judah, but rather than leading the people into battle he told them to love their enemies and forgive the wrongs done to them. He told them: "Blessed are the meek, the merciful, the peacemakers," and he gave them himself as their prime example. He had no army; his following was a ragged bunch of fishermen and a few women, and his kingdom a secret one. Instead of publicizing his power, he worked underground. "Don't tell," he'd say to a healed leper.

They wanted a figurehead, dominant, educated, handsome, autocratic, magnetic, one who could give them again a sense of national pride. Jesus was strong but humble, wise but simple. Though he was decisive his decisions ran counter to popular opinion. He gave his listeners *radical* instructions — "Give away your shirt...." " "When you're hit, turn your other cheek for another blow...." " "Be happy when you are persecuted...." " "Don't worry so much about eating and drinking and what you wear...."

They wanted a man of action, a messianic figure who would effect major changes in their world. Jesus talked of small but potent things — salt, a mustard seed, yeast, a coin, a pearl, a cup of cold water. He spoke of quiet realities — light, and water, and narrow roads, and shepherds. He taught his followers to be seed-scatterers, dough-kneaders, light-bearers.

They wanted a monarch in a grand palace, eating and dressing extravagantly, holding court surrounded by nobles, with stables full of horses and chariots. But Jesus wandered by foot from place to place, without a home to call his own. The only time he was called a king and wore a robe to match was at his own trial. It was done in mockery; everyone thought the whole thing a farce.

They didn't see what was going on because they were searching for something superficial and transient. Jesus, who really was royal, invaded the heart and revolutionized what went on *inside* people — a change that would be forever, outlasting all earthly kings and kingdoms.

—Luci Shaw, *Horizons*

Jesus, you unsettle me. I want a celebrity to lead the country, a general for president, a great figure out of some movie to step in and right the world. You, God with us, will have none of that. You become flesh and walk about in the body of the poor. You go homeless and call me when I am looking for anyone but you. I pray for you to come in power, and you ask me for a quarter. Giving it costs me my life. Here, take it. Change me. Make me powerless that your grace might live through me. Amen.

March 19

THE PEBBLES ARE TRICKY RIGHT ALONG HERE (A REFLECTION ON TRUST)

"For he shall give his angels charge over you, to keep you in all your ways. In their hands they shall bear you up, lest you dash your foot against a stone." —Psalm 91:11–12, NKJV

For some time now I have thought of myself as a spiritual writer. I am confident enough to say so when someone wants to know. "Emilie, what do you do?" I say, "I'm a writer." And the person says, "Oh, what do you write about?" And I generally say, "spirituality," or "Christian living."

I remember framing "spiritual writer" as my personal goal some years back. Sitting in my editor's office at Doubleday, and saying, "Oh, I want to be like..." trailing off. And hearing him say... "like Henri Nouwen?"

But I was afraid. Afraid of being laughed at. There I was, writing a book on conversion, and working in a big ad agency at the same time. I was sure my book on conversion would be greeted with critical scorn and whoops of condescending laughter.

After awhile I saw the issue clearly. To write a book about trusting God, I had to trust God.

Why was I writing a book on conversion, anyhow? Well, because I had found the Lord in a ragged, fits-and-starts process, assaulted by doubt and confusion. A strange quest in which I needed the support of other believers, some who were my personal friends, others my friends in books. Like many others, I had read my way into Christian belief. I had followed every thread, veering from books by very charming atheists to those by very beguiling Christians.

I had been buffeted around by yearnings, promptings, not knowing what to call them, lacking a full vocabulary of grace. But when I found out others had followed this same bumpy path, wanting to believe, losing heart, being afraid, I felt floods of recognition. In the vivid stories of other conversions, I saw myself, running away from God, but wanting the consolation of God's love.

So, imagine my embarrassment when my book was greeted with respectful praise. Why hadn't I trusted God more?

If you actually become a spiritual writer, things may get harder.

Father Henri Nouwen, from the platform, used to voice fears about thinking he was some kind of spiritual genius, just because he had written seventeen or eighteen books. He worried that his bit of fame might go to his head. He thought he might forget that he was there to serve, not for the spotlight.

Recently, while editing the writings of British spiritual writer Evelyn Underhill, I found out something about her worst doubts and temptations. She was afraid that her great experiences in prayer were self-induced, delusionary. Which connected well with my earliest worry, that Christianity was too beautiful to be true.

Being a spiritual writer is a rare subcategory for writers. Few would claim this offbeat designation.

But, judging by the amount of help I've received from reading spiritual writers, they're needed. As much as in biblical times.

Sure, the creative imagination plays tricks on us: peculiar shadows, rough stones, even serpents in the path. In Latin, the word *scrupulus*, little stone, is what gives us the word for "scrupulous" or "scrupulosity." A spiritual ailment for which the major remedy is trust.

Rufus Jones, a Quaker writer of some years back, spoke about spirituality as something like sailing in fog. Spiritual writers steer in the darkness, too. —Emilie Griffin, *The High Calling of Our Daily Work*

Wonderful God, give me what I need to trust in you. I am constantly being tripped up by my own grandiose ambitions to serve you, by my foolish scrupulous attitudes, by my fearfulness. Give me simplicity; give me confidence. Let me take one step at a time, and not be afraid of falling. Amen.

March 20

LOVE YOUR ENEMIES

"You are not a God who takes pleasure in evil; with you the wicked cannot dwell. The arrogant cannot stand in your presence; you hate all who do wrong. You destroy those who tell lies; bloodthirsty and deceitful men the Lord abhors." —Psalm 5:4-6

Since the other day, I've been thinking about enemies. Having once introduced them to my thoughts, I can't seem to get rid of them. Yesterday I got a letter from my friend the distinguished poet John Bennett. In it he wrote, "... and perhaps you can't write satire because you have not yet become angry enough. Hate the sin and love the sinner? I can't do that: a grave weakness in my Christian being-ness, I suppose.... Yep. Perhaps all that makes my satire strong (I think it is) but it also makes me contemptible/unreadable/unacceptable to a society in which what I condemn prevails — blandly, arrogantly, stupidly — and in death."

I read in Psalm 5 yesterday morning, "For thou art not a God that hath pleasure in wickedness: neither shall evil dwell with thee. The foolish shall not stand in thy sight: thou hatest all workers of iniquity. Thou shalt destroy them that speak lies.... Destroy thou them, O God; let them fall by their own counsels." The psalmist sounds like us. He seems to make no distinctions between sinner and sin either.

There is a sense, perhaps, in which, in practice, we are our actions, in which we are our sins incarnated. (I intuit that sentence. I'm not sure I understand it.) Apart from me, my sins would not exist. By myself I am sin to the world. Redeemed, I am somehow made Christ to the world. Paul, I think, spoke of Christ becoming sin for our sakes. Here, perhaps, is where the twist comes, is where we must learn to encounter our hates and make them somehow redemptive. As Linda and I read evening prayer last night, these words from the intercession stood out to me: "Reward all who have done us good, and pardon all those who have done or wish us evil, and give them repentance and better minds. Be merciful to all who are in trouble; and do thou, the God of pity, administer to them according to their several necessities; for his sake who went about doing good, thy Son our Savior Jesus Christ."

Three things struck me. First the prayer to give those who would do me evil better minds. Evil is not just in the heart. It is intellectual and chosen. It can be rejected. Second, those who do evil are in trouble and have needs. The trouble is not so much that they are under the judgment of God. He is merciful and desires them to be whole. The trouble is they reap the consequences of their own actions — they become their sins. And third, our concern in this is Jesus Christ our Savior, who because of all this has become sin. We must become whole for his sake. There is some sense in which he who is whole and complete in himself in his place in the Trinity, needs also our wholeness, our redemption, and the re-establishment of the order of creation before we chose sin.

Perhaps holy hatred is, like love, relational. Perhaps it is a necessary beginning for valid witness. Perhaps the tolerant are the lukewarm to be spewed out into nothingness, into the nothingness of their own acceptance of evil. Another paragraph in John's letter comes clear. He added a word of caution.

One cannot hate without regret, or one cannot hate without restraint, or one cannot hate without discrimination, or one cannot hate with enjoyment — else what is hated becomes the hater, the moral trap is sprung, the "good" man becomes subject (deeply subject and oddly subject) to the evil he would oppose. So there is my caveat: don't sentimentally forgive evil, don't (or rarely) turn the other cheek, don't gloss over the fact of the world's murder by industry, by greed, by stupidity, by mindless evil turning natural good to corruption and death. But always be aware, always be very much aware, that the hatred, if it is to be good hatred and morally usable, is really another aspect, side, dimension of love.

—John Leax, *Standing Ground*

Lord, as I begin to grow in my life with you, I am often confronted with how short I fall of loving those who harm me or wish me ill. It seems that acting as if I am tolerant, and burying my anger and pain, only prolongs my agony and blocks me from experiencing love — from you and from people around me.

May I learn to remember that people will reap what they sow — and so will I. Help me to fully embrace my feelings of anger and pain, emotions you created for good and useful purposes. Guide and guard me as I work through the process of acknowledging the injury I have experienced and expressing my emotions appropriately, so that I may heal, let go, forgive, and eventually even come to love, as you do, the one who delivered the injury.

I put such people in your hands to keep as they encounter the consequences of their own behavior. Help me to leave these consequences in your hands and to focus on you and your love for me and everyone. In Jesus' name. Amen.

March 21

JELLY BEANS

"One who is slack in his work is brother to one who destroys."
—Proverbs 18:9, NIV

The seeds of sloth sowed themselves early in my heart. I was seven. Friend's birthday party. Jelly-bean hunt. A prize for the one who finds the most. I amassed a sizable pile in five minutes, decided I was well ahead, got bored, stretched out on a sofa and began to eat my cache. "I don't think eating them is the idea," said one of the mothers. I shrugged her off and lost the prize by something like three beans.

Without being too hard on that seven-year-old soul (she is forgiven), I wish she had seen that the error of her ways was not so much in laziness or greed or even cockiness, but *ennui*. It was pulling herself out of the fun, sitting on her bum while others played the game, a kind of arrogant distancing, maybe what M. Scott Peck would call "Giving away power." Perhaps that sounds a little like a speech by an athletic coach, but it's not inappropriate. In my meager athletic experience, I remember being ordered to play the game in my head from the sidelines (where I spent most of the time) as zealously as I would out on the gym floor.

The deadliness of this Seventh Deadly Sin, it seems to me, is in the self-protection it implies — isolation from engagement and confrontation, repressing talent, excusing ourselves from involvement by any false reason — elitism or ersatz humility. And with the trickiness inherent in all "serious sin," sloth can disguise itself as much in play as it can in work — when we fail to find joy in life, sitting out with passive faces what Thomas Merton has called God's "Cosmic dance."

—Shirley Nelson, *Notes and Files*

Lord of the dance, teach us the steps. Amen.

March 22

Seek Your Servant

"I have strayed like a lost sheep. Seek your servant, for I have not forgotten your commands." —Psalm 119:176

Wandering searchlights thrown over a darkened neighborhood by a circling helicopter bring a chill to the bone. Yet the lights themselves are an apt metaphor for the eye of God. Wherever he looks, the light of his face makes hiding foolhardy.

But the Psalmist is not talking like a criminal here. What's behind his utterance in this line of Scripture is a whole different scenario. The image he uses is no helicopter spotlight; it's the familiar presence of a shepherd. The intent is wholly different. Here we have the heart's prayer of someone who is not interested in hiding, but wants instead, deeply, to be found. The words of the Psalmist are the bleating of a heart that knows God but has lost its way.

They are not the words of the unconverted. Only believers fear the nothingness that exists outside the presence of the Almighty. Only believers who've fallen away are capable of the intensity of the Psalmist's bleating in this passage.

And it happens. Often. Like this. Faith becomes old hat to us or maybe too difficult. A species of doubt grows within the mind — not doubt of God actually, but doubt that what he's given us is enough to satisfy our hunger for joy and happiness. That kind of uncertainty makes the heart restless and comfortless, and the influences of all kinds of things below come to cloud the possibilities God brings to us from above. Our worlds are turned upside down.

God is gone. Darkness reigns in the soul. Loneliness possesses the heart.

That's when our serious bleating begins: "seek your servant."

Just exactly how God engineers our return in itself a mystery, but he accomplishes it through the very ordinariness of our lives. Maybe we read an idea on a page. Maybe pain and suffering brings us back, hard or perilous times flatten our wills. Perhaps God brings someone of sincere and deep inspiration into our lives. Perhaps he uses something definable only as vision.

All avenues lead to the same end: nearness. He seeks us and finds us, and once we discover that, our hearts stop their desperate bleating and begin to sing.   —James Calvin Schaap, *Near Unto God*

Except you find me, Lord, I am lost. Seek me where I have strayed and return me to the safety of your fold. Then my cries will turn to song, and I will lift my voice to praise your name. Amen.

March 23

SHARING IN SUFFERING

"For just as the sufferings of Christ flow over into our lives, so also through Christ our comfort overflows. If we are distressed, it is for your comfort and salvation; if we are comforted, it is for your comfort, which produces in you patient endurance of the same sufferings we suffer. And our hope for you is firm, because we know that just as you share in our sufferings, so also you share in our comfort."
—2 Corinthians 1:5-7

The Bible tells us that we are "the body of Christ." This description of the community of faith is not some romantic metaphor but is a genuine reality. Jesus Christ through the Spirit continues to live within his church, and our sufferings are his sufferings. John Calvin writes in his *Commentaries on the Epistles to the Philippians, Colossians, and Thessalonians:* "As, therefore, Christ has suffered *once* in his own person, so he suffers *daily* in his members." And these sufferings are redemptive; they are actually used of God to change and transform and draw people into the way of Christ.

As our sufferings are his, so his sufferings are ours. Every now and then we are given the privilege of sharing in the sufferings of Christ over some special need in his Body. According to an account recorded by Paul Yonggi Cho in *Prayer: Key to Revival,* a minister in Africa once woke up in the middle of the night in tears. A strange name came to him over and over, a name he did not know. He sensed it was a call to pray, but for whom, for what? He did not know. Still he prayed in the Spirit over this name that he did not know, suffering intense pain as he did so. After several hours the burden lifted, and he knew his intercessory work was complete. The next day the newspapers carried the sad story of a Christian village whose inhabitants had been massacred during the night. The village had the same name the minister had been weeping over. In some way that we do not now understand, this minister was allowed to share in the sufferings of the village people and so share in the sufferings of Christ. Our prayer privilege may never be this striking, but it will be just as important.

—Richard J. Foster, *Prayer: Finding the Heart's True Home*

O Holy Spirit of God, so many hurt today. Help me to stand with them in their suffering. I do not really know how to do this. My temptation is to offer some quick prayer and send them off rather than endure with them the desolation of suffering. Show me the pathway into their pain.

In the name and for the sake of Jesus. Amen.

—Richard J. Foster, *Prayer: Finding the Heart's True Home*

March 24

ACCESS TO THE CREATOR

"I wait for the Lord, my soul waits, and in his word I put my hope. My soul waits for the Lord more than watchmen wait for the morning, more than watchmen wait for the morning." —Psalm 130:5-6

From the *World Book* my parents bought when I was in elementary school, I learned that our word "Lent" comes from the old English word "lenten," which means "spring." It hardly seems up to bearing the burden of meaning it has come to have. It seems so pagan.

Sitting here this morning with nothing much on my mind such paganness seems okay. These woods are far from "church." Far from the muttered words that tame the wildness of God. Here I sit on the edge between the domestic and the wild. Along the fence line I've piled brush. Birds inhabit it and pass berry seeds. Brambles grow up. More birds come to them. Rabbits hide in the cover. In the summer, deer bed down in it to escape the midday heat.

I walk along the edge of the brambles choosing to stay near, but choosing not to invade or destroy them for they are my access to lives not mine. And those lives are an access to the life of the Creator.

He is here revealing himself as surely as he reveals himself in words. But as I cannot seize the lives of the creatures, I cannot seize the life of the Creator. I must wait and let it occur about me and in me. Wordlessly. Silently.

And it is good.

I am filled. Sunlight spills across the floor.

—John Leax, *Standing Ground*

Lord, how often I want to rush the process, but I am realizing that access to you comes best when I am still and watchful. In this way I can more often perceive your presence and your guidance as it occurs about me and in me. Cultivate in me a desire to spend the necessary time—wordlessly, silently—listening and watching for you. In Jesus' name. Amen.

March 25

EYES OF THE HEART

"For with thee is the fountain of life: in thy light shall we see light."
—Psalm 36:9, KJV

"Why is it so dark in here," Meg asked. She tried to look around, but all she could see was shadows. Nevertheless there was a sense of openness, a feel of a gentle breeze moving lightly about, that kept the darkness from being oppressive.

Perplexity came to her from the beast. "What is this dark? What is this light? We do not understand. Your father and the boy, Calvin, have asked this, too. They say that it is night now on our planet, and that they cannot see. They have told us that our atmosphere is what they call opaque, so that the stars are not visible, and then they were surprised that we know stars, that we know their music and the movements of their dance far better than beings like you who spend hours studying them through what you call telescopes. We do not understand what this means, *to see.*"

"Well, it's what things look like," Meg said helplessly.

"We do not know what things *look* like, as you say," the beast said. "We know what things *are* like. It must be a very limiting thing, this seeing."
—Madeleine L'Engle, *A Wrinkle in Time*

Domine, fac ut videamus: Lord, make us to see. Make us to see in your light. Make us to see with the eyes of the heart. Amen.

March 26

THE SHAPE OF MY LIFE

"I pray that out of his glorious riches he may strengthen you with power through his Spirit in your inner being, so that Christ may dwell in your hearts through faith. And I pray that you, being rooted and established in love, may have power, together with all the saints, to grasp how wide and long and high and deep is the love of Christ, and to know this love that surpasses all knowledge — that you may be filled to the measure of all the fullness of God."   —Ephesians 3:16-19

When my youngest daughter, Kristin, was a small child, I would take her with me wherever I went, as mothers of young children are likely to do. One day, driving to the grocery store in early spring, we passed a field in which a pool of melted snow water glinted under the sun.

Kris was an observant little girl. A light breeze began to ruffle the water's surface and seeing the sun's reflected image broken into shining fragments she cried out, "Look, Mommy, the sun's not round any more!"

At the next stoplight I scribbled the following lines on the back of my grocery list:

Spring Pond

Look how the sun
lies on the low water!

Spread ripple-shaped he
has lost roundness:

Light joined to the pond
in fluid fusion

And I, earthy,
wed now to the high sun

Give God a new shape
to shine in.

—Luci Shaw, *Horizons*

Let the shape of my life be the fullness of God, living in me through Christ Jesus. Amen.

March 27

You Have to Try It

"One day Jesus was praying in a certain place. When he finished, one of his disciples said to him, 'Lord, teach us to pray, just as John taught his disciples.'"
—Luke 11:1

When I finally did begin to learn to pray, I found some very positive changes taking place in my attitudes and feelings. But I was so cynical at first that I didn't want *anybody* to know I was praying. And the more I undermined my prayer time by telling myself that it wouldn't help — which is in effect saying that "not even God can help me when I am this miserable" — the less good I felt from the experience. But the more I believed that "this will really help me get over some bad feelings (maybe not this hour or this day, but eventually)," the better I would seem to feel about myself, my situation, and what I was doing. My energy level perked up a little by little until I was sometimes whizzing through a day, surprised by how much I was getting done!

This may sound too simple, but I started approaching prayer this way by saying to myself, "I'm going to find out for myself if this will really help or not." Some people say that prayer is just a psychological manipulation and that it's not really God working in me. After thinking about that for a while, I realized that prayer is like a laboratory hypothesis — you have to try it to know if it's true. And my constant doubting seemed to be only a part of the undermining process by which I had closed myself off from God's love for years. I finally said one morning, "I don't care if it is a psychological manipulation. God created our minds, and maybe he has to manipulate me somehow to get me out of the rut I have created for myself. I'm just glad when it helps!" And it did.

—Andrea Wells Miller, *The Single Experience*

Lord, I still don't pray about everything I could pray about, but I'm getting better. Draw me to you and calm my doubting, so that I can hear you better. In Jesus' name. Amen.

March 28

WHERE THE SUFFERER IS, GOD IS

"Surely he has borne our griefs and carried our sorrows."
—Isaiah 53:4, NRSV

"But God put his love on the line for us by offering his Son in sacrificial death while we were of no use whatever to him."
—Romans 5:8, THE MESSAGE

The biblical revelation neither explains nor eliminates suffering. It shows, rather, God entering into the life of suffering humanity, accepting and sharing the suffering. Scripture is not a lecture from God, pointing the finger at unfortunate sufferers and saying, "I told you so: here and here and here is where you went wrong; now you are paying for it." Nor is it a program from God providing, step by step, for the gradual elimination of suffering in a series of five-year plans (or, on a grander scale, dispensations). There is no progress from more to less suffering from Egyptian bondage to wilderness wandering, to kingless anarchy, to Assyrian siege, to Babylonian captivity, to Roman crucifixion, to Neronian/Domitian holocaust. The suffering is there, and where the sufferer is, God is. —Eugene H. Peterson, *Five Smooth Stones for Pastoral Work*

Dear Lord, in times of suffering help me to be open to experiencing your presence in it through the presence of others, sharing it with me. And help me to be your representative in the lives of others who are suffering, not with answers or actions to eliminate their suffering, but rather simply by my presence. In Jesus' name. Amen.

March 29

GIVING THE GIFT OF LOVE

"Whoever receives one such child in my name receives me; and whoever receives me, receives not me but him who sent me."
—Mark 9:37, RSV

When people focus their interest deeply into my life, they are receiving the private childlike part of me somehow, and something happens between us — we move into the warmer arena of the "personal." The situation changes, and I am suddenly alive with them. At such moments *agape* love rides down the beam of our attention into people's hearts. And I think that this basic attention to ordinary individuals in the present moment may be the greatest kind of love we can give them. For in a strange way we give them our lives in that instant, when we are giving them our whole attention. If that is true, perhaps the most real way to value people as human beings is to really be *with* them and take them seriously as they are. A single such contact may change the whole direction of a life — a single experience of helping someone realize that he or she is really of some value.

    Several years ago a young woman came several hundreds of miles to a conference I was also attending at Laity Lodge. Elton Trueblood was the guest speaker. In a small group we were talking about the people who had had the greatest influence in our lives. The last person to speak was a very attractive young woman in her twenties. She told us that when she was a pre-adolescent child, Elton Trueblood was speaking in the city in which she lived. He was staying in her parents' home. She told us that during the day or two he was there he talked to her, asking her questions and listening to what *she* had to say, just as he did to her parents. She said that, although he never knew it, that brief experience as a young girl of being treated as an authentic, intelligent Christian had made her want deeply to be one and had changed the direction of her life.
—Keith Miller, *A Second Touch*

Lord, thank you that you walked around listening to people and being interested in what is important to them, that your idea of loving was to be salt, bringing out the flavor of other people's lives. Help me to quit trying to impress people or change them long enough to listen to the heart-beat of their childlike hopes and dreams. Amen.

March 30

THE BETTER PART

"As Jesus and his disciples were on their way, he came to a village where a woman named Martha opened her home to him. She had a sister called Mary, who sat at the Lord's feet listening to what he said. But Martha was distracted by all the preparations that had to be made. She came to him and asked, 'Lord, don't you care that my sister has left me to do the work by myself? Tell her to help me!'

"'Martha, Martha,' the Lord answered, 'you are worried and upset about many things, but only one thing is needed. Mary has chosen what is better, and it will not be taken away from her.'"

—Luke 10:38-42

Unlike her sister Martha, an active, practical person, Mary of Bethany is quiet and introspective. Not the sort we would ordinarily call sensual. But there is more to Mary than first meets the eye. Though ordinarily she stays in the background, she is drawn irresistibly toward the man Jesus with an intensity found in no other person in the gospels.

In Luke's story about the two sisters, Mary never speaks, not even to defend herself from her sister's implicit charge of laziness. Her only act is in choosing. Otherwise she was passive. She sits at Jesus' feet and listens to his words. When her sister bustles in to point her accusing finger, Mary remains silent, allowing Jesus to speak for her.

The "good part," Jesus calls Mary's choice, "which shall not be taken away from her." And we still have a hard time accepting that judgment. In order to protect that choice of Mary's, the Roman Catholic Church institutionalized the quiet stillness called contemplation by setting up communities of prayer. In the Protestant tradition, Mary's choice has an even harder time gaining acceptance, much less respect. Cultivation of the inner life, which requires sitting and listening, looks like loafing to those whose work ethic often becomes a works theology.

—Virginia Stem Owens, *Daughters of Eve*

Lord, thank you that I have the right to choose, as Mary did, what is right for me, regardless of what others may say or think. Help me to know what my options are and to make the choices you would have me to. Forgive me for times when I comply with unacceptable conditions. I recognize that I make that choice, even though it may seem as if I had no choice. Help me to live my life conscious of the choices I make and to begin to make the choices you would have me to make. In Jesus' name. Amen.

March 31

THE JUDAS IN US

"Now Judas, who betrayed him, knew the place, because Jesus had often met there with his disciples." —John 18:2

A garden traditionally has been an enclosure, a place for humans, a place made safe from the terrors of the wild. Though I have no sure way of knowing, I think that safety must have been on my father's mind when, at night before tucking me into bed, he'd hold me and sing, "I come to the garden alone, while the dew is still on the roses...." Those times make up one of my earliest memories. I was three or four. My father had just returned from Germany and a war he would never in his life tell me about.

The writer of Genesis describes the Lord planting a garden eastward in Eden and placing the man he had formed there. The image is a tender one, a protective father providing a safe place for his child. And there is more. The garden is not just a safe place; it is a fruitful place, a place filled with good things for the man and eventually his wife to enjoy.

We all know what happened. In that garden a serpent spoke, and as surely as the world came into being at the voice of the Lord, sin and alienation came into being as a consequence of his silvered words. No garden would ever again be safe. No matter how high we build a garden wall or how tight we string a fence, we cannot come to the garden alone. The Judas in us knows the place. —John Leax

For what you planned for us, Father, we give you thanks. We acknowledge that we have listened to the silvered words of the lying serpent and have lost our place in Paradise. We come to you broken, dependent on your grace to stand us once more, upright, in your presence. Amen.

APRIL

April 1

THERE IS NO PRIVATE PRAYER

"While it was still night, way before dawn, he got up and went out to a secluded spot and prayed. Simon and those with him went looking for him. They found him and said, 'Everybody's looking for you.' Jesus said, 'Let's go to the rest of the villages so I can preach there also. This is why I've come.'" —Mark 1:35-38, THE MESSAGE

The single most widespread American misunderstanding of prayer is that it is private. Strictly and biblically speaking, there is no private prayer. "Private" in its root meaning refers to theft. It is stealing. When we privatize prayer we embezzle the common currency that belongs to all. When we engage in prayer without any desire for or awareness of the comprehensive, inclusive life of the kingdom that is "at hand" in both space and time, we impoverish the social reality that God is bringing to completion.

Solitude in prayer is not privacy. The differences between privacy and solitude are profound. Privacy is our attempt to insulate the self from interference; solitude leaves the company of others for a time in order to listen to them more deeply, be aware of them, serve them. Privacy is getting away from others so that I don't have to be bothered with them; solitude is getting away from the crowd so that I can be instructed by the still, small voice of God, who is enthroned on the praises of the multitudes. Private prayers are selfish and thin; prayer in solitude enrolls in a multivoiced, century-layered community: with angels and archangels in all the company of heaven we sing, "Holy, Holy, Holy, Lord God Almighty." —Eugene H. Peterson, *Earth and Altar/Where Your Treasure Is*

Dear Lord, in solitude I join a multivoiced, century-layered community in prayer. Put into my mind and heart the faces of those whom you would put into my life today. Give me the awareness to listen and serve them as you would have me to. Heighten my awareness of your still, small voice. I love you and praise you. In Jesus' name. Amen.

April 2

HOW TO FAIL SUCCESSFULLY

"Then Jesus told them, 'This very night you will all fall away on account of me, for it is written: "I will strike the shepherd, and the sheep of the flock will be scattered." But after I have risen, I will go ahead of you into Galilee.'" —Matthew 26:31–32

In the New Testament we are shown pictures of two people — Judas and Peter — who were failures at critical points in their lives. One merely failed. The other learned the singular lesson of how to fail successfully.

The relationship of Master and follower has never been an easy one. To be a Christ-follower means to give up one's independence, to choose rather to listen and obey and learn, to repattern one's thinking, to put the Leader first in such a radical way that by comparison the claims of family, friends, reputation, and possessions grow shadowy and insubstantial.

A disciple cannot use a special relationship to the Leader to win political favors or make money on the side. Somehow, Judas never saw this. Or if he did, he could never divest himself of his not-so-secret love of silver and the power it brings. Perhaps when Jesus said, with quiet emphasis, "You cannot serve God and Mammon," it was Judas whom he looked in the eye. For all his easy piety about giving to the poor Judas had a miserly spirit devoid of real love. In betraying Christ with that false kiss in the midnight Garden for thirty silver coins, he ended up betraying himself.

Peter, on the other hand, lived hard and loved hard. He was pigheaded, impulsive, short-fused, talkative, and often dead wrong. But he was wholehearted. That saved him in the end, after his miserable mistake of fearing to acknowledge his relationship to the fettered Criminal in the center of the courtyard and of not wanting to look like a fool in front of the high priest's servants. He learned, the hard way, that not being willing to look like a fool may be the most foolish attitude of all.

But his strong love for Jesus produced in him equally strong shame when he recognized his failure for what it was — not just betrayal but *denial* of his Master. He saw the truth about himself, and rather than deny his denial, he cried. Peter's kind of crying is the secret to failing successfully. It comes when the truth penetrates our hearts. It signals light breaking — a new day, a fresh chance to find the healing of forgiveness, of saying yes to a voice that asks with gentle persistence, "Do you love me?"

    Judas, Peter

        because we are all
        betrayers, taking
        silver and eating

body and blood and asking
(guilty) is it I and hearing
him say yes
it would be simple for us all
to rush out
and hang ourselves

but if we find grace
to cry and wait
after the voice of morning
has crowed in our ears
clearly enough
to break our hearts
he will be there
to ask us each again
do you love me?
—Psalm 51:17,
author's paraphrase

—Luci Shaw, *Horizons*

Merciful Savior, I am both Judas and Peter. I would serve you, but I am quick to seek my own advantage, quick to use your name to achieve my own ends, and I am slow to risk my self-esteem for your sake. I have both kissed you in the garden and denied you by the fire. Forgive me. Reinhabit me with your resurrection power. I love you. Give me the strength of your love. Amen.

April 3

OF VERY LIGHT

"'You are a king, then!' said Pilate. Jesus answered, 'You are right in saying I am a king. In fact, for this reason I was born, and for this I came into the world, to testify to the truth. Everyone on the side of truth listens to me.'" —John 18:37

It is not information we seek as humans, but illumination, that sudden irradiation of our understanding that has no real relationship to the accretion of data. We have known since 1897 about the photoelectric effect of light on matter, a shower of electric charges liberated from a material bombarded with radiant energy. But illumination, sudden and sometimes shattering insight, has been a part of our experience ever since we began recording it.

Only light can have a true nature. Perhaps that is, after all, the important point. Although generations of schoolchildren have no doubt been frustrated by the definition of dark as the absence of light (and that of cold as the absence of heat), that is the nearest one can come to the truth about the dark and cold. Light is a "thing" in a way dark is not. There are neither waves nor corpuscles of darkness. St. Augustine's explanation of evil provokes a parallel here. Just as darkness is not a thing in itself but an absence, a void, so evil is not the created counterpart to good. Only goodness, like light, has being. The diminishing of that being is what we call in one case evil and in the other case darkness. As long as some form of being continues, both goodness and light continue. Small wonder that humanity has always connected light with goodness, truth, understanding. The bottom of Dante's hell is not fire, which gives both heat and light, but ice, a frozen lake. And his heaven is merely a movement from lesser light to greater until one reaches the source:

> That light doth so transform a man's whole bent
> That never to another sight or thought
> Would he surrender, with his own consent;
> For everything the will has ever sought
> Is gathered there, and there is every quest
> Made perfect....

But mankind as a species is still bent on solving problems rather than singing praises. The vital connection between matter and what we were made for has been broken. And that is why, as C. S. Lewis observed, "A true philosophy may sometimes validate an experience of nature; an experience of nature cannot validate a philosophy.... Nature never taught me that there exists a God of glory and of infinite majesty. I had to learn that in other ways. But nature gave the word "glory" a meaning for me. I still do not know where else I could have found one."

Making the connection between glory and God. That is what light does. There first has to be that second creation, that other flash of lightning that reveals to our marred vision what should be as natural as rain, as obvious as the air we breathe. "For this reason I was born, and for this I came into the world, to testify to the truth." This is the illumination we long for — the Light of the world himself. And the truth that he illumines is our own true destiny: that we ourselves are children of light, intended for glory. —Virginia Stem Owens, *A Taste of Creation*

O Lord, you reign in glory and bring light into the world to wipe out darkness. Enter into the dark corners of my soul and illumine them, fill them with your truth, so that I may know better how to do your will! In Jesus' name. Amen.

April 4

Extravagance

"Then he said, 'Jesus, remember me when you come into your kingdom.' Jesus answered him, 'I tell you the truth, today you will be with me in paradise.'"
—Luke 23:42-43

A few mornings ago when I was filling up at Bill Yanda's Quaker State, Bill got to talking about the end of the world. He pointed out the station door to the park across the road and shook his head. "Look at that beautiful world," he said, "To think that it's fallen! You just can't imagine it made new!" Another customer pulled in, ending our conversation. But as I drove off, I was surprised at how intensely I felt what Bill was saying, for I've never been much interested in talk of heaven. I've never felt it was necessary.

After thinking about it the last few days, I'm convinced that heaven's unnecessariness is what makes it important. It's important because it has no relevance to this life. (It does not follow that this life has no relevance to it.) Heaven is simply a glorious, gratuitous extra, totally unnecessary, but totally in character with the extravagant goodness and boundless creativeness of the Maker and Redeemer of this world.
—John Leax, *In Season and Out*

Jesus, we are petty thieves of experience. The beauty of this fallen world exceeds our capacity to enjoy. How should we imagine the wild riches of your kingdom? Yet you have spoken: we will be with you, for you have called us to be in you and where you are is Paradise. Amen.

April 5

Proof of God's Love

"Not only so, but we also rejoice in our sufferings, because we know that suffering produces perseverance; perseverance, character; and character, hope. And hope does not disappoint us, because God has poured out his love into our hearts by the Holy Spirit, whom he has given us."
—Romans 5:3-5

In my study of the Bible, I was struck by a radical shift in its authors' attitudes about suffering, a shift that traces directly back to the Cross. When New Testament writers speak of hard times, they express none of the indignation that characterized Job, the prophets, and many of the psalmists. They offer no real explanation for suffering, but keep pointing to two events — the death and resurrection of Jesus — as if they form some kind of pictographic answer.

The apostles' faith, as they freely confessed, rested entirely on what happened on Easter Sunday, when God transformed the greatest tragedy in all history, the execution of his Son, into a day we now celebrate as Good Friday. Those disciples, who gazed at the cross from the shadows, soon learned what they had failed to learn in three years with their leader: When God seems absent, he may be closest of all. When God seems dead, he may be coming back to life.

The three-day pattern — tragedy, darkness, triumph — became for New Testament writers a template that can be applied to all our times of testing. We can look back on Jesus, the proof of God's love, even though we may never get an answer to our "Why?" questions. Good Friday demonstrates that God has not abandoned us to our pain. The evils and sufferings that afflict our lives are so real and so significant to God that he willed to share them and endure them himself. He too is "acquainted with grief." On that day, Jesus himself experienced the silence of God — it was Psalm 22, not Psalm 23, that he quoted from the cross.

And Easter Sunday shows that, in the end, suffering will not triumph. Therefore, "Consider it pure joy...whenever you face trials of many kinds," writes James; and "In this you greatly rejoice, though now for a little while you may have had to suffer grief in all kinds of trials," writes Peter; and "we also rejoice in our sufferings," writes Paul. The apostles go on to explain what good can result from such "redeemed suffering": maturity, wisdom, genuine faith, perseverance, character, and many rewards to come. —Philip Yancey, *Disappointment with God*

Dear Lord, that you, too are "acquainted with grief" means so much to me. The three-day pattern — tragedy, darkness, triumph, happens over and over. Help me to learn to rejoice in anticipation of the end of the darkness and the onset of the triumph, and to cling to you during the tragedy and darkness. In Jesus' name. Amen.

April 6

WE HAVE TO DO THE FORGIVING

"In the midst of the street of it, and on either side of the river, was there the tree of life, which bare twelve manner of fruits, and yielded her fruit every month: and the leaves of the tree were for the healing of the nations." —Revelation 22:2, KJV

There was silence on the drive until Chantal said, "Emma, you have to forgive Adair."

Emma looked at her in surprise. "I have, oh, I have. There was never a question in my heart about forgiving Adair."

"Do you think Adair was ever able to forgive himself?"

Emma looked out the window. The leaves were turning. Chrysanthemums were blooming in front of many of the houses. The roadsides were full of goldenrod. "Perhaps," she suggested tentatively, "we have to do the forgiving? If Adair can't, well, we can."

"Can we?"

"We have to."

"Does that mean forgiving Billy?"

Emma did not answer.

Chantal spoke in a small, chill voice. "If we have to do the forgiving for Adair, then we have to forgive Billy, too."

Emma closed her eyes. There was a terrible empty space where Etienne and Adair should have been. "What is forgiveness?"

Chantal's long fingers gripped the steering wheel. "It's not forgetting. That's repression, not forgiveness."

Emma looked over at her sister.

"Remembering," Chantal said, "but not hurting anymore."

—Madeleine L'Engle, *Certain Women*

Lord, on the cross you opened the way for us to forgive even as you forgave; on the cross you gave up all claim to exact a penalty against those who wronged you. By that same power may we give up any desire to punish. For it is in forgiving that we are healed. Amen.

April 7

Easter Morning

"Jesus acted as if he were going farther. But they urged him strongly, 'Stay with us, for it is nearly evening; the day is almost over.' So he went in to stay with them. When he was at the table with them, he took bread, gave thanks, and broke it and began to give it to them. Then their eyes were opened and they recognized him."

—Luke 24:28b–31a

In the cornfield
where winter thin
deer have browsed,

a single tractor
growls slowly
back and forth.

Behind it the
earth, like an
old grave, opens.
—John Leax,
Country Labors

How, Risen Lord, do we fail to know you, when you have filled your creation with signs of your life among us? Open us to receive the seed of your word. Let us be good soil, a place where you will be pleased to dwell. Amen.

April 8

Craftsmanship

"Through him all things were made; without him nothing was made that has been made. In him was life, and that life was the light of men."
—John 1:3–4

Carpenter's son, carpenter's son,
is the wood fine
and smoothly sanded, or rough-grained,
lying along your back? Was it well planed?
did they use
a plumbline
When they set you up? Is the angle true?
Why did they choose
that dark, expensive stain
to gloss the timbers
next to your feet and fingers? You
should know — who,
Joseph-trained, judged all trees
for special service.
Carpenter's son, carpenter's son,
were the nails new and cleanly driven
when the dark hammers sang?
Is the earth warped from where you hang;
high enough for a
world view?
Carpenter's son, carpenter's son,
was it a job well done?

Think of it — Jesus, Creator of the universe, grew up to be a small-town carpenter, moving from the macrocosm to the microcosm. But he continued to be a *maker* who shaped and crafted raw materials into usefulness and beauty, trained by his human father, Joseph, a skilled carpenter.

We can be sure that in Jesus' careful hands the yokes he carved and sanded were comfortable around the necks of farm animals, that the doors and doorframes he planed and hung were solid and square, as were his tables and boxes and shelves. And his scythe handles didn't blister the farmers' hands with rough spots; his carpentry jobs were always well done.

When he was hung, at last, on a wooden cross made by some other carpenter, perhaps he judged its workmanship. As to the nailing of his hands and feet to that wood — we must ask of God, was it "a job well done"?

It was all too well done. The cross didn't crack under his weight, and the nails didn't pull out. But the craftsmanship of the job made all the difference in the world to us. His dying, on a carpentered cross, now means our living forever.

—Luci Shaw, *Horizons*

Carpenter's son, Creator Lord, fill me with your conscience, make me sensitive to the work of my hands and the work of my mind that all I do might be done well to your honor and glory. Amen.

April 9

DIRECTIONS FOR SPRING

"And if Christ has not been raised, your faith is futile; you are still in your sins. Then those also who have fallen asleep in Christ are lost. If only for this life we have hope in Christ, we are to be pitied more than all men." —1 Corinthians 15:17-19

Watch the daffodils. though they are not up yet,
already they are unstable, their high yellow
waving by the deep riverbed like a gang of suns.

Beware of how you plant them. Place the side marked
MADE IN HOLLAND down. Burn the box. Dig holes
at night and do not admit hope to your neighbors.

In winter, do not read Wordsworth, whose fields
permit riots of heat in the most implacable freeze,

whose breeze never stops shuffling pages of stamens.

Do not think of them in the dark, in basements,
while scanning the *New York Times* on the rise of crime,
or while making necessary arrangements with people.

Daffodils will take advantage. If one of them gets her green foot
into your last permanent room, nothing can follow but
bliss, crouching on every threshold, blocking all exits.

Should the strong arms of daffodils succeed in their terrible
    shove,
you will lose your last method of knowing sorrow:
you will recognize only love.
                        —Jeanne Murray Walker, in *Fugitive Angels*

What joy, O Christ, we learn in being lost. Giving up our claim to sorrow, looking to the terrible shifting of the rock that closed your tomb, we find ourselves alive. The spring of your resurrection breaks about us and we dwell in love. Amen.

April 10

C. S. LEWIS'S SPIRITUAL LEGACY

"Finally, all of you, have unity of spirit, sympathy, love of the brethren,
a tender heart and a humble mind."   —1 Peter 3:8, RSV

C. S. Lewis's spiritual legacy, if it's anything, is to believe oneself, and to encourage others to believe, the basic doctrines of Christianity and to put into action the basic practices of Christianity as they are taught by one's denomination. All Christians are included; none excluded. It doesn't require hopping, skipping, and jumping to another denomination. Oddly, the merer the Mere Christian's [MC's] Christianity becomes, the closer the MC moves to the center of his or her own denomination and the warmer the MC feels toward members of all the other denominations. Presumably, that's where Jesus may be found discoursing on one thing or another.

That one denomination should crow its supposed superiority over others in this regard is lamentable. It would be sheer knavery to prefer one nave to another. They're all one to Screwtape,[1] the knave of naves,

---

1. A character from C. S. Lewis's *The Screwtape Letters*.

and they're all trouble to him. That's not to say that denominationalism is unimportant; indeed, it's even necessary. But Lewis would never encourage a Christian to denounce one denomination for another. He'd say that ecumenism, however broadly or badly one defines it, is an historical movement, and hence will require inventions as revolutionary as the wheel and the passage of many eons before it's accomplished. Mere Christianity, on the other hand, can begin on a Monday morning....
—William Griffin, *C. S. Lewis: Spirituality for Mere Christians*

Dear Lord, keep me focused on you and the basic truths you taught. Help me to grow a tender heart and a humble mind. Amen.

April 11

BODY AND BLOOD

"Jesus took a loaf of bread, and after blessing it he broke it, gave it to them, and said, 'Take; this is my body.' Then he took a cup, and after giving thanks he gave it to them, and all of them drank from it. He said to them, 'This is my blood...'" —Mark 14:22-24, NRSV

Around the world, at every stage of history, humans have needed two essentials for survival—*food* and *drink*.

At the end of his earthly ministry Jesus ate a meal with his friends. Because he wanted them to go on remembering him, he gave them two pictures of himself— *bread* and *wine* — basic food and drink that can be found in any culture. He linked the bread and wine to his own body and blood in a unique way. Holding out the cup of wine and the loaf of bread, he said, "This is my body. This is my blood."

Ask yourself, How is bread like Jesus' human body (solid like flesh, ground from grain and baked to picture his suffering for us, textured, cellular)? And how is wine like Jesus' human blood (fluid, red, made from crushed grapes)?

Jesus also said, "Do this...until I come again." He wanted them, and us, to enact this metaphor of his enfleshment, his being born human— flesh and blood like you and me so that he can relate to us and we to him.

Paul tells us that we are now Christ's body. That means that we can be the *fingers* of Jesus, touching others in love and healing; his *feet* going where he would have gone; his *voice*, saying his words to people who need to hear from God; his *eyes,* looking with compassion and discernment into the eyes of others; his Shepherd *arms,* carrying home lost lambs. We are even the wounded *side* of Jesus, feeling some of his brokenness, and that of the world.

As we take the communion bread and wine into our mouths, these elements can picture not only Jesus but what he wants us to be — his body and blood broken and poured out for the needs of the world.

—Luci Shaw, *Horizons*

I would be your fingers, Lord. And your feet. And your voice. And your eyes. And your arms. I would even be your side. Be in me. Give me grace to touch, to go, to speak, to see, to hold, and to feel the brokenness of the world you love. Amen.

April 12

Creation Redeemed

"The fear and dread of you will fall upon all the beasts of the earth and all the birds of the air, upon every creature that moves along the ground, and upon all the fish of the sea; they are given into your hands." —Genesis 9:2

Children, and many adults, are fascinated by tales of talking animals. Some writers have suggested that this fascination has its root in a collective human memory, a haunting recollection of a prelapsarian paradise where communication between species was a reality. Whether there is such a thing as a collective memory or not, the creation account of Genesis suggests that once the relationship between humanity and the other creatures of God's extravagant love was more congenial than it is now. Adam knew the creatures intimately enough to name them. And even after the expulsion of humanity from the garden, when Noah, exercising his stewardship, called the animals to the ark, they came.

Now, however, even the frog in the my garden pond flees my presence. And well he should, for a human is an unreliable friend. Some adore frog legs. Many live in houses built on filled wetlands. Most participate in the economy that produces acid rain. But nothing is finished. The tending of the garden where I walk and the frog swims will someday be taken from my hands by a gardener greater than I, and then....

Who knows what word we might exchange with our fellow creatures, what song we might lift in praise together.

—John Leax

Christ, on your cross you announced, "It is finished." The work of your heart is done. Yet it is not done. In history sin survives. We long for your return, for the day when you will come triumphant and the whole of your creation will raise a single voice of praise. Amen.

April 13

LONELINESS OR PRESENCE?

"But all those who knew him, including the women who had followed him from Galilee, stood at a distance, watching these things."
— Luke 23:49

As I have read through the Gospels' accounts of Jesus' death, I have come to identify most with Matthew. What follows are the thoughts I might have had the day after Jesus' crucifixion if I'd been walking in Matthew's sandals.

Saturday was probably the worst day of my life. I'd never known grief like this. All of us just kept out of sight. There wasn't anything we could do for Jesus, or for ourselves, or for anybody.

I'd watched his crucifixion from a distance, heartsick. *This was not the Messiah!* I thought. Nothing that looked as pitiful as he did could possibly be from God. He didn't call down the angels to help him, as he said he could. He failed completely in what he'd come to do. And he failed me. I felt sorry for him, but more, I was sorry for myself. I felt more alone than I ever had in my life.

In the past three years, as we ate and laughed and sang and prayed together, Jesus filled the empty loneliness in our lives. Never again would that emptiness be filled.

Then I began to cry. Because I didn't care what Jesus was. I didn't care if he was a fraud. He was the only man in my whole life who ever really knew me, who saw the misery, the selfishness and guilt behind the mask I wear. He let me know that God loved me — that he loved me. And now my life was going to be totally lost without him.

In that moment I knew that I loved him. And I wished with everything in me that I'd died for him. I just sat there and ached inside.

—J. Keith Miller, *Daily Guideposts*, 1996

O God, help me to put my trust in you, while there is still light for me. Thank you that you use your story and even the failure of others to trust in Jesus, to awaken our desire to trust you now. Help us to accept you, even before we understand how you come to us in Jesus. Amen.

April 14

THE LAST TEMPTATION
(GOOD FRIDAY/EASTER)

> "At the sixth hour darkness came over the whole land until the ninth hour. And at the ninth hour Jesus cried out in a loud voice, 'Eloi, Eloi, lama sabachthani?' — which means, 'My God, my God, why have you forsaken me?'"
> —Mark 15:33-34

Long before, at the very beginning of his ministry, Jesus had resisted Satan's temptation toward an easier path of safety and physical comfort. Now, as the moment of truth drew near, that temptation must have seemed more alluring than ever.

Everybody, it seemed, was demanding a miracle. At the Sanhedrin trial, the priests who slapped Jesus challenged him, "Prophesy! Who hit you?" Pilate and Herod, who had heard rumors about Jesus' powers, begged for a show. The grieving women, who had followed Jesus all the way from Galilee, yearned for a miracle of rescue. The disciples, cowering in fear, ached for one.

On the cross, a criminal at Jesus' left taunted him, "Aren't you the Christ? Then save yourself and us." The crowd milling about the site took up the cry: "Let him come down from the cross, and we will believe in him.... Let God rescue him now if he wants him."

But there was no rescue, no miracle. There was only silence. The Father had turned his back, or so it seemed, letting history take its course, letting everything evil in the world triumph over everything good. How could Jesus save others when, quite simply, he could not save himself?

Why did Jesus have to die? Theologians who ponder such things have debated various theories of "the Atonement" for centuries, with little agreement. Somehow it required love, sacrificial love, to win what could not be won by force.

Mark's account presents the facts, not the theology, but one detail he includes may provide a clue. Jesus had just uttered the awful cry, "My God, my God, why have you forsaken me?" He, God's Son, identified so closely with the human race — taking on their sin! — that God the Father had to turn away. The gulf was that great. But, Mark adds, just as Jesus breathed his last, "The curtain of the temple was torn in two from top to bottom."

That massive curtain served to seal off the Most Holy Place, where God's Presence dwelled. No one except the high priest was allowed inside, and he could enter only once a year, on a designated day. As the author of Hebrews would later note (Hebrews 10), the tearing of that curtain showed beyond doubt exactly what was accomplished by Jesus' death on the cross. No more sacrifices would ever be required.

Jesus won for all of us — ordinary people, not just priests — immediate access to God's presence. By taking on the burden of human sin, and bearing its punishment, Jesus removed forever the barrier between God and us. —Philip Yancey, *A Guided Tour of the Bible*

Dear Lord, having immediate access to your presence is a gift beyond belief! Help me to remember your presence more often, especially at those times when I have most wanted a "miracle" in my life — and felt you did not provide one. In Jesus' name. Amen.

April 15

TRANSFUSION

"For the life of a creature is in the blood, and I have given it to you to make atonement for yourselves on the altar; it is the blood that makes atonement for one's life." —Leviticus 17:11

Until five years ago in the emergency room of our local hospital, I had never seen blood for what it is. Earlier that day I'd gone bicycling with Kristin, my teenage daughter. As I coasted along down a hill on a fresh autumn evening, not paying close attention to what I was doing, my front wheel had accidentally touched her rear wheel. It sent me off balance, spilling me over the handlebars onto the rough country road, scraping the skin off my forehead, nose, chin, hands, and knees. I must have looked appalling, with blood flowing freely and my scraped skin bruised and swelling fast. As soon as Kris saw that I was reviving, she sped off on her bike for help.

Twenty minutes later, rescued by my husband in our station wagon and trundled off to our local hospital, I was finally paying attention to my surroundings. And I realized with astonished empathy that every other patient in the unit was also bleeding.

Blood, a startling color, not the kind of evidence you can ignore, is designed to be almost invisible, doing its essential work, unheralded and unseen within the body, hidden, protected within the water-tight envelope of human tissue and skin. Nearly always the red of blood is a signal that something is wrong, that there's a breach in the system.

The incident stayed with me, sinking in, moving deeper from body to mind to heart, reminding me of another event when blood had flowed, a blood that from the foundations of the world was destined by God to be spilled, to be clearly evident to a watching world, to signal both death and life.

Trauma Unit

It was never meant
to burst from the body
so fiercely, to pour unchanneled
from the five wounds
and the unbandaged brow,
drowning the dark wood,
staining the stones
and the gravel below,
clotting in the air
dark with God's absence.

It was created for
a closed system — the unbroken
rhythms of human blood
binding the body of God,
circulating hot, brilliant,
saline, without interruption
between heart, lungs,
and all cells.

But because he was once
emptied, I am each day refilled;
my spirit-arteries
pulse with the vital red
of love; poured out,

it is his life that now pumps through
my own heart's core. He bled and died
and I have been transfused.

—Luci Shaw, *Horizons*

O Wounded Healer, because you have suffered and bled, I am healed. In me the blood courses, every beat of my heart sounds the redemption you have worked for me. I cried to you and you touched me. You said, "Life." Life more abundant than I in my broken body could imagine. Amen.

April 16

To Trust Again

"Behold, God is my salvation; I will trust, and not be afraid: for the Lord Jehovah is my strength and my song; he also is become my salvation."   —Isaiah 12:2, KJV

Canon Tallis pushed his empty coffee cup across the counter. "How many people can you trust here in New York?"

Dr. Austin looked about him at the unknown people seated at the counter, at the little tables crowded along the wall. "I believe that people become trustworthy only by being trusted."

The priest gave a startled smile at hearing his own words come back at him from this gentle doctor so completely different from himself.

Dr. Austin continued, "I know that I'm infinitely more trustworthy because of my wife's faith in me. I know that there are all kinds of things I'll never do or say because she trusts me, and so do my children. But how sure am I of myself, really? Haven't you ever spoken when you should have kept your mouth shut, or not spoken when you should have stood up to be counted?"

The Canon looked somberly into the dark dregs remaining in his cup. "I am constantly being reminded by my own behavior that I am a fallen human being in a fallen world."

The Doctor smiled. "You sound like my father-in-law, who is not far from being a saint—"

"I am," the Canon put in.

"He would add that when we fall, as we always do, we pick ourselves up and start again. And when our trust is betrayed the only response that is not destructive is to trust again. Not stupidly, you understand, but fully aware of the facts, we still have to trust."

         —Madeleine L'Engle, *The Young Unicorns*

Lord, we trust you for those we trust, for those who trust us, and for those we have difficulty trusting. Amen.

April 17

Is He the One?

"When John heard in prison what Christ was doing, he sent his disciples to ask him, 'Are you the one who was to come, or should we expect someone else?'"   —Matthew 11:2-3

John's message from prison, sent through his disciples to Jesus, has always struck me as the most poignant question in all the Scriptures: "Are you the one who was to come, or should we expect someone else?" A whole lifetime is contained in those words. Years of abnegation, sacrifice, zealous aberrations lived out on sheer nerve. And he only wants to know, from the horse's mouth, if it has all been to some point, of some worth, or if it has been as vain as water poured out on the desert sand.

Jesus, replying to the one who will go before him in death as he has preceded him in life, again uses the same Scripture passage he had read that day in the Nazareth synagogue. By now Isaiah's prophecy of healing and hope had been fulfilled. And Jesus attaches to it an almost pleading admonition to his cousin: *Blessed is he who takes no offense at me.*

Perhaps it is only in such extreme circumstances as John's, imprisoned and on the point of death, that anyone is vouchsafed even this answer. Jesus, who at times went out of his way to offend people, was anxious that this one not be offended. He was at pains that this Epiphany, sent secondhand, should be inoffensive and efficacious. While John's messengers are still within earshot, he delivers his eulogy to John, calling him Elijah. —Virginia Stem Owens, *Wind River Winter*

O Lord, thank you for your straightforward answer to John's question, a question that is asked by many, even today. Help me in times of doubt to remember that even John the Baptist just had to ask, even after having baptized you and seen the dove descending. In Jesus' name. Amen.

April 18

BESIDE THE STILL WATERS

"He leadeth me beside the still waters."
—Psalm 23:2b, KJV

Some people lack time or opportunity to study the complexities of God's reality and truth. Some simply, and sadly, lack the brain power. Others work so hard at their day-to-day lives that they have little time or energy for thinking about these things.

No matter. We know very well that no human soul ever earned salvation by the number of hours he parked his nose in a book. If knowledge of God is itself a foretaste of eternal life, then some knowledge of him must be available to all, no matter where believers stand or sit or serve, in the factory, the kitchen, the think tank.

Will is something we all have. It acts in us every day. Without it, we're mere vegetables. Very little simply "happens" in our lives. Like a river within us, our will is always flowing outward, carrying us into life.

Because everyone has will, it is in everyone's power to take a closer walk with God — provided, of course, that our wills align themselves with his. We need to be led to the quiet waters, but we need to will our going there.

When we know his presence, cruelty disappears from the office, the shop, the classroom. The first lady, the farm hand, the professor — all submit quietly and spend their hearts in love. Knowing God takes no study time, nor is it dependent on occupying a certain station in life. Everyone can do it.

All our activity here is an expression of our will, and the more closely we align ourselves to the love that is the Father's the closer we will come to the *eternal life* that begins in our being led to the quiet waters that are near unto God.
—James Calvin Schaap, *Near Unto God*

Father, your love is patient, and you choose to lead us. But we are impatient, desiring our own ways, seeking our own ends. By your Holy Spirit enliven our wills to love you and teach us to choose your ways. Amen.

April 19

POETS

"Be gracious in your speech. The goal is to bring out the best in others in a conversation, not put them down, not cut them out."
—Colossians 4:6, THE MESSAGE

Poets are caretakers of language, the shepherds of words, keeping them from harm, exploitation, misuse. Words not only mean something; they are something, each with a sound and rhythm all its own.

Poets are not primarily trying to tell us, or get us to do something. By attending to words with playful discipline (or disciplined playfulness), they draw us into deeper respect both for words and the reality they set before us.

I also am in the word business. I preach, I teach, I counsel using words. People often pay particular attention on the chance that God may be using my words to speak to them. I have a responsibility to use words accurately and well. But it isn't easy. I live in a world where words are used carelessly by some, cunningly by others.
—Eugene H. Peterson, *Subversive Spirituality*

Lord, teach me to respect the everyday words I hear today, the expressions of children, loved ones, friends, co-workers, and strangers. Help me to discern their use of words, whether careless, cunning, or sincere. Guide me to think before I speak or write, so that I may use my words accurately and well. In Jesus' name. Amen.

April 20

EACH BREATH SINUOUS WITH PRAISE

"Shout for joy to the Lord, all the earth.
Worship the Lord with gladness;
come before him with joyful songs."
—Psalm 100:1-2

Rinsed with Gold, Endless, Walking the Fields

Let this day's air praise the Lord—
Rinsed with gold, endless walking the fields,
Blue and bearing the clouds like censers,
Holding the sun like a single note
Running through all things, a *basso profundo*
Rousing the birds to an endless chorus.

Let the river throw itself down before him,
The rapids laugh and flash with his praise,
Let the lake tremble about its edges
And gather itself in one clear thought
To mirror the heavens and the reckless gulls
That swoop and rise on its glittering shores.

Let the lawn burn continually before him
A green flame, and the tree's shadow
Sweep over it like the baton of a conductor,
Let winds hug the housecorners and woodsmoke
Sweeten the world with her invisible dress,
Let the cricket wind his heartspring
And draw the night by like a child's toy.

Let the tree stand and thoughtfully consider
His presence as its leaves dip and row
The long sea of winds, as sun and moon
Unfurl and decline like contending flags.

Let blackbirds quick as knives praise the Lord,
Let the sparrow line the moon for her nest
And pick the early sun for her cherry,
Let her slide on the outgoing breath of evening,
Telling of raven and dove,
The quick flutters, homings to the green houses.

Let the worm climb a winding stair,
Let the mole offer no sad explanation
As he paddles aside the dark from his nose,
Let the dog tug on the leash of his bark,
The startled cat electrically hiss,
And the snake sign her name in the dust

In joy. For it is he who underlies
The rock from its liquid foundation,
The sharp contraries of the giddy atom,
The unimaginable curve of space,
Time pulling like a patient string,
And gravity, fiercest of natural loves.

At his laughter, splendor riddles the night,
Galaxies swarm from a secret hive,
Mountains lift their heads from the sea,
Continents split and crawl for aeons
To huddle again, and planets melt
In the last tantrum of a dying star.

At his least signal spring shifts
Its green patina over half the earth,
Deserts whisper themselves over cities,
Polar caps widen and wither like flowers.

In his stillness rock shifts, root probes,
The spider tenses her geometrical ego,
The larva dreams in the heart of the peachwood,
The child's pencil makes a shaky line,
The dog sighs and settles deeper,
And a smile takes hold like the feet of a bird.

Sit straight, let the air ride down your backbone,
Let your lungs unfold like a field of roses,
Your eyes hang the sun and moon between them,
Your hands weigh the sky in even balance,
Your tongue, swiftest of members, release a word
Spoken at conception to the sanctum of genes,
And each breath rise sinuous with praise.

Let your feet move to the rhythm of your pulse
(Your joints like pearls and rubies he has hidden),
And your hands float high on the tide of your feelings.
Now, shout from the stomach, hoarse with music,
Give gladness and joy back to the Lord,
Who, sly as a milkweed, takes root in your heart.
—Robert Siegel, *In a Pig's Eye*

Hear, Lord. I raise my voice. I sing. My whole body shouts your praise. Hallelujah! Amen.

April 21

Eyes Right

"Let each esteem other better than themselves."
—Philippians 2:3, KJV

There it is again. I never read it now without remembering what it offered on one morning long ago. Age twenty-one and not very mature, spurned in love, trapped in pity for myself, arguing inwardly for months — this was not the answer I wanted, this particular "verse for the day." If it had read "Go hang thyself," it might have seemed more to the point. It looked impossible, in fact. My heart would not be in it, I protested. I'd be a phony. That's all right. Do it anyway. Call it a simple matter of obedience.

So I entered the exercise, a moment by moment game: Focus on anyone but yourself; act on it. By the end of the day I was hooked. By the end of the week my feet found themselves standing in a "large place," and the crisis was over.

Looking back, I'm amazed at how precisely the remedy matched the need. The dilemma itself seems childish to me now, yet I know the inner chaos was real and potentially serious. It never occurred to me to go for professional help. It was not really available. I knew nothing of the theory of dealing with "symptoms." Yet I knew that was happening. It was not a case of being rescued from the "cause." No change in my circumstances was promised. I was simply to divert my eyes from myself, a process not possible by negative will-power, but viable as obedience to what I could recognize as safe and healthy scriptural injunction — what I ought to be doing anyway, in any case.

It's usually unclear when intervention in our lives can be called divine, and that's probably best. I knew only that my first experience of healing was not something done to the patient, but through the patient, a participating agent. That in itself seems divine indeed.

—Shirley Nelson, *Notes and Files*

> "Drop Thy still dews of quietness
> Till all our strivings cease.... " Amen.

April 22

CONSECRATING OURSELVES

"Each of you should give what you have decided in your heart to give, not reluctantly or under compulsion, for God loves a cheerful giver."
—2 Corinthians 9:7

If our spiritual vitality seems low, if Bible study produces only dusty words, if prayer seems hollow and empty, then perhaps a prescription of lavish and joyful giving is just what we need. Giving brings authenticity and vitality to our devotional experience.

Money is an effective way of showing our love to God because it is so much a part of us. Economist Edward W. Bauman put it this way in *Where Your Treasure Is:* "Money as a form of power is so intimately related to the possessor that one cannot consistently give money without giving self." In a sense, money is coined personality, so tied to who we are that when we give it we are giving ourselves. We sing, "Take my life and let it be, consecrated, Lord, to Thee." But we must flesh out that consecration in specific ways, which is why the next line of the hymn says, "Take my silver and my gold, not a mite would I withhold." We consecrate ourselves by consecrating our money.

—Richard Foster, *The Challenge of the Disciplined Life*

> Take my life and let it be
> Consecrated, Lord, to Thee;
> Take my hands and let them move
> At the impulse of Thy love,
> At the impulse of Thy love.
>
> Take my lips and let them be
> Filled with messages for Thee;
> Take my silver and my gold,
> Not a mite would I withhold,
> Not a mite would I withhold. Amen.
>
> —Frances R. Havergal

April 23

REALITY OR SUCCESS

"Jesus entered the temple area and drove out all who were buying and selling there. He overturned the tables of the money changers and the benches of those selling doves." —Matthew 21:12

Some years ago, my Christian ministry was going better than I could have ever imagined. I was faithful in church attendance, I tithed, I read the Scriptures, I prayed daily. I had helped to start many Christian fellowship and study groups and had written several successful books about living for Christ.

So when I read about Jesus' overturning the tables and seats of those who were exchanging money for the purchase of the sacrificial animals used in temple worship, I cheered him on — never realizing that the cleansing of the temple had anything to do with me.

But one day, Jesus walked into the inner temple of my life and turned over my delusion that I was a good, unselfish, Christian husband and father. Suddenly, the things that had seemed so stable in my life began going out the window, including my marriage and my sense of myself as one of the white knights of the faith. Eventually, I was divorced, wound up in a recovery program and was rejected by many of those who had read my books.

Because I had focused so intently on myself and my ministry, I had fouled up my relationships and was far from the closeness with God that earlier had changed my life and given it purpose. And I hadn't even seen the change taking place, because I *felt* sincere.

I am grateful that Jesus came into my inner life and overturned the tables of my complacency and success. My failures forced me to take an honest look at my life, and with his help — and forgiveness — I began once more to focus on loving God and my family.

—J. Keith Miller, *Daily Guideposts*, 1996

Lord, I'm glad you didn't pass by and leave me in my religious unreality. May I always be ready for your cleansing touch. Amen.

April 24

PURE SILVER WORDS

Quick, God, I need your helping hand!
The last decent person just went down,
All the friends I depended on gone.

> Everyone talks in lie language;
> Lies slide off their oily lips.
> They doubletalk with forked tongues.
>
> Slice their lips off their faces! Pull
> The braggart tongues from their mouths!
> I'm tired of hearing, "We can talk anyone into anything!
> Our lips manage the world."
>
> Into the hovels of the poor,
> Into the dark streets where the homeless groan, God speaks:
> "I've had enough; I'm on my way
> To heal the ache in the heart of the wretched."
>
> God's words are pure words,
> Pure silver words refined seven times
> In the fires of his word-kiln,
> Pure on earth as well as in heaven.
> God, keep us safe from their lies,
> From the wicked who stalk us with lies,
> From the wicked who collect honors
> For their wonderful lies.
> —Psalm 12, THE MESSAGE

Dear Lord, keep me safe from the lies all around me — the pull of today's culture that is not aligned with your principles. Inspire me to immerse myself in your words, pure silver words refined seven times, so that I may discern truth, beauty, peace, and love... and walk in your ways. In Jesus' name. Amen.

April 25

WAS, IS, AND WILL BE

> "And he is before all things, and by him all things consist."
> —Colossians 1:17, KJV

When they got to the standing stones there was someone lying on the altar. With a low cry, Anaral hurried forward, then drew back. "It is Bishop talking with the Presence."

While Polly watched, the bishop slowly pushed himself into a sitting position and smiled at her and Anaral. Then he returned his stare to some far distance. *"But, Lord, I make my prayer to you in an acceptable time,"* he whispered. The words of the psalmist. How did he know that the time was acceptable? How do we know? An acceptable time, now, for God's now is equally three thousand years in the future and three thousand years in the past."

"We are sorry," Anaral apologized. "We did not mean to disturb your prayers."

The bishop held out his hands, palms up. "I have tried to listen, to understand."

"Who are you trying to listen to?" Polly asked.

"Christ," the bishop said simply.

"But, Bishop, this is a thousand years before—"

The bishop smiled gently. "There's an ancient Christmas hymn I particularly love. Do you know it? *Of the Father's love begotten—*"

"*E'er the worlds began to be.*" Polly said the second line.

"*He is alpha and omega, He the source, the ending—*" the bishop continued. "The second person of the trinity always was, always is, always will be, and I can listen to Christ now, three thousand years ago, as well as in my own time, though in my own time I have the added blessing of knowing that Christ, the alpha and omega, the source, visited this little planet. We are that much loved. But nowhere, at any time or in any place, are we deprived of the source. Oh, dear, I'm preaching again."

"That's okay," Polly said. "It helps."

—Madeleine L'Engle, *An Acceptable Time*

> *Christ be with me,*
> *Christ within me,*
> *Christ behind me,*
> *Christ before me,*
> *Christ beside me*
> *Christ to win me,*
> *Christ to comfort*
> *and restore me.*
> —adapted from
> St. Patrick's Breastplate

April 26

LIVING OUT OF THE CENTER

"Those who listen to the word but do not do what it says are like people who look at their faces in a mirror and, after looking at themselves, go away and immediately forget what they look like. But those who look intently into the perfect law that gives freedom, and continue to do this, not forgetting what they have heard, but doing it — they will be blessed in what they do." —James 1:23-25 NIrV

I hope you understand what I mean when I speak of living out of the Center. I am of course referring to God, but I do not mean God in an abstract theoretical sense, nor even God in the sense of One to be feared and revered. Nor do I mean God only in the sense of One to be loved and obeyed. For years I loved him and sought to obey him, but he remained on the periphery of my life. God and Christ were extremely important to me but certainly not the Center. After all, I had many tasks and aspirations that did not relate to God in the least. What, for heaven's sake, did swimming and gardening have to do with God? I was deeply committed, but I was not integrated or unified. I thought that serving God was another duty to be added onto an already busy schedule.

But slowly I came to see that God desired to be not on the outskirts, but at the heart of my experience. Gardening was no longer an experience outside of my relationship with God — I discovered God in the gardening. Swimming was no longer just good exercise — it became an opportunity for communion with God. God in Christ had become the Center. —Richard J. Foster, *Freedom of Simplicity*

> *Dear Lord and Father of mankind,*
> *Forgive our foolish ways!*
> *Reclothe us in our rightful mind;*
> *In purer lives Thy service find,*
> *In deeper reverence, praise.*
> *Drop Thy still dews of quietness*
> *'Til all our strivings cease;*
> *Take from our souls the strain and stress,*
> *And let our ordered lives confess*
> *The beauty of Thy peace.*
> —John Greenleaf Whittier

April 27

WITH ALL THY SOUL

"And thou shalt love the Lord thy God...with all thy soul."
—Deuteronomy 6:5a, KJV

How exactly does God excite thirst for him within us? Does it happen through the intellect? By way of the understanding or will? Is coming to

God a matter of feelings? Is it borne out of the imagination? Is it simply something mystical?

The answer is, all of the above. How God calls us to him is different in every human case. Some come by learning, some by feeling. Imaginative souls find him in their own visions. Analytic types come by the arrangement of complex ideas. It's always been that way, and always will be. There is no unanimity among humankind — and that fact alone argues for a great deal of freedom of expression in our worship and searching.

Our problem in taking that truth to heart stems from our continual violation of the first and greatest commandment — to love God with all your heart, all your soul, and all your mind. Let's face it, heinous public sin — adultery, murder, theft — prompts its own regret. We know we've done wrong. Shame tells us as much. But who among us really feels him or herself in violation of the command to love him with everything? Very, very few.

What's more, all too often our individual paths to God work against our understanding of our limitations. We come to God thoughtfully, and we think everyone should. We come to him in intense feelings, and we believe everyone else should find the same path. We raise our hands in praise, and we don't trust those who don't. Those who come to Christ in social action believe all of us should work tirelessly to bring shelter to the homeless, alms to the poor, empowerment to the marginalized. But only a block away, a different believer, someone who finds God through emotional gratification, wants everyone else to feel the same shimmering gratification in the soul.

We are a neighborhood of individuals whose varied perceptions and gifts — good in design and beneficial in expression — create a complex beauty. But too often we begin to idolize the path of our individual pilgrimage and thereby disregard the avenues others have walked as they have approached the face of God.

When Jesus said, "With all they heart, with all thy soul, and with all thy mind," he meant that God wants every last component part of our being. Even the most pious among us need to remember that no single part of what we are should be restrained from the full blessings of his love and grace. — James Calvin Schaap, *Near Unto God*

We are a people of many talents and dispositions. We come to you, Lord, by many paths. Teach us to understand that our individual ways are not the measure of your ways. Help us to see in the diversity of our responses the infiniteness of your love and grace. Amen.

April 28

MY BODY, MY SELF

"I appeal to you therefore, brothers and sisters, by the mercies of God, to present your bodies as a living sacrifice, holy and acceptable to God, which is your spiritual worship." —Romans 12:1, NRSV

When I first read this Scripture verse in the light of Keith's and my new commitment to go on the adventure of discovering how to get in shape, I imagined a scene, an encounter between Jesus Christ and me. It seems kind of corny, in a way, but it helped me start thinking about how God might view my physical condition.

The scene opens in a large hall, such as I imagine the old Roman courts of law might have been. Christ is sitting at one end, and I can see him far away as I enter the building. There are two rows of columns, one on my left and the other on my right, and I am supposed to walk across this room between the two rows of columns until I reach the place where Christ is seated, waiting for me.

He looks friendly enough, so I take a deep breath and start walking. As I go, I become conscious of my body. I'm aware that my untoned muscles are jiggling as I walk, my tummy sticks out too much, and my thighs brush each other with each step I take. I try to stand up straighter, hoping I can diminish some of these uncomfortable feelings.

Before I even get to the end of the room, I push the image from my mind. "Wait a minute!" I think. I'm not ready to do this. The full meaning of "presenting my body as a living sacrifice" isn't clear yet, but it's beginning to be. If I "sacrifice" my body to Christ, what does he want with it?

I am told that the Hebrews believed that the body and soul were wrapped up together somehow. This would mean that to offer my body to God would be to give my whole self to him, to dedicate myself to doing whatever he wants me to do with my life.

God has created the human body with certain capacities. But these capacities can be lessened by lack of care — by nonactions as well as actions. Nonactions include not thinking of good health as a vital part of a spiritual life, not exercising, and not knowing how foods and their nutrients work together to bring health. Actions include doing harmful things to the body — putting fat-loaded foods into the digestive system, putting cigarette smoke and alcohol into our circulatory systems, staying up too late, and taking on too many responsibilities for one person to reasonably handle.

As I followed this line of thinking, the concept of "BodyCare" came to mean learning about the capacities of my body for health, energy, and vitality, and trying to do the things I need to do to fulfill those capacities, just as I try to develop my soul through spiritual activities like prayer, Bible study and participation in the church's life and worship. While I live on this earth, I have the opportunity to achieve and maintain a level of fitness which will allow me the energy, strength, and endurance to do a lot more for God than I could if I'm not in shape.

Now a quick look around any room full of people tells me that God didn't give all people the kind of body that fits our current standard of "beautiful." We must deal with various physical dimensions like height, nose length, facial shape, skeletal structure, and fat distribution. In fact, I've read that there are almost no people who really like they way they look—even models and movie stars who "set the standard" for what is considered fashionably beautiful.

But that "beautiful" standard is not what I'm talking about. Each of us has a maximum potential. Each of us can move toward that potential—improving our muscle tone, the distribution of our body fat, and the condition of our hair, complexion, nails, and overall skin tone. And we can add much to our lives by enjoying the maximum energy levels possible. To me, that is the goal of BodyCare—not just losing weight or looking good or being stronger (although these things are important to me), but becoming as fit as I can be to do God's will.

With these things in mind I return to my visualized encounter with Christ. But things are different this time. Now I am sitting at the table with him. My body is the same body I'd felt embarrassed about before. Only now I can feel that Christ loves me any way I come to him, regardless of whether I'm up to my best potential. Now that I'm aware of how far away from my potential I am, I want to talk to him about it.

I tell him, "Lord, I want to dedicate myself to you, to being the woman you meant for me to be. I am beginning to see the ways I am missing out on the full potential you gave me by not being in shape. Will you help me as I learn about how to exercise and nourish my body properly so that it can be the best possible sacrifice to you?"

And in my vision Christ smiles and says, "Of course I'll help."

—Andrea Wells Miller, *BodyCare*

Dear Lord, I am becoming so aware of how much potential I have in my physical body for energy, for health, for strength. I want very much to present my body as a living sacrifice to you, and I want to begin now to improve my knowledge of how to do this. Help me as I read and study to begin to see concrete ways in which I can put exercise and good nutrition into my life, not as a temporary thing just to help me look prettier, but as a permanent, lasting way of living.

As Paul says in the passage above, "by the mercies of God" I am to present my body "as a living sacrifice." Grant me your mercies, your love, your patience, and your forgiveness as I begin, falter, and begin again to care for my body. In Jesus' name. Amen.

April 29

I LOVE

"I love the Lord."
—Psalm 116:1a

Lots of us know by personal experience the way love can send us reeling. It seems so overwhelming, so unreasonable in its power, that we go blind to everything else.

Heart-throbbing love is almost mystical in the way it takes us out of everyday reality and becomes obsession. It abandons reason so fully that it reaches its ends in only two ways: full reciprocity or death.

Want to define love's ecstasy? Look at Christ's own description: "Love the Lord your God with all your heart, all your soul, all your mind, and all your strength." That's total. We are, ourselves, consumed by our attraction to him.

The commandment works two ways actually. In knowing God's love, we're more able to know how to love each other. The Bible is a kind of how-to manual when it comes to love. Our relationships are made exalted and holy when we understand the character of love given as grace to us. What's more, this pattern helps us understand why it is that, when we break the contract ourselves, despair stands at the door. What results is the worst of evil from the best of blessings.

Psalm 16 begins with this song: "I love the Lord." Yet, in the original, the idea is more gripping because the utterance is simply, "I love." We'd say it this way, "I am in love!" People who trumpet that to others are almost gone in their devotion.

Tons of people don't dislike God — most even like him, even if they don't know him. What's not to like, after all? — he is good and kind and offers us blessing. But those who admire God, who respect him, still don't *know him*. We're talking about a relationship here, a knowledge, that leaves abstract formulas in its dust.

Holy passion is ours now in being near unto God. But it's not total yet, for one day the wall of separation will crumble, and God in us — and we in him — shall attain the perfection of the holiest love ever.

—James Calvin Schaap, *Near Unto God*

Lord, in loving us you have taught us to love you. Incarnate, you gave yourself. Your image, we give ourselves to you, and in that giving we commit ourselves to loving all you love. Amen.

April 30

THE PEARL OF EXISTENCE

"Again, the kingdom of heaven is like a merchant in search of fine pearls; on finding one pearl of great value, he went and sold all that he had and bought it."
—Matthew 13:45-46, NRSV

It used to be commonplace to talk about our "crosses," the trials and burdens of everyday living we couldn't walk away from or forget. The phrase was, "We all have little crosses to bear." But becoming open to the cross is somewhat different from that. This is the tension that seems to split existence in two. At moments we sense it. We recognize the harsher truth that underlies everything. It is an invitation, yet one we're not so eager to accept.

When we surrender, we too are marked with the painful tension that scars all reality. The world is maimed, distorted, out of whack. The time, as Hamlet says, is out of joint, not just for one generation but all generations. But Hamlet misses the mark when he supposes he was born to put it right. There is only one who can put it right and he has already done so, bearing the tension, the division of existence in his body, so to speak. Not just at Easter, but always, the mystery is played out in history as one, once-for-all event: the Son pouring out his blood for the Father and for us, sending the Spirit to bind and heal us once and for all.

I think we grasp this reconciliation for ourselves only when we are willing to undergo the cross, not just romantically but practically in the way we live. Are we shouting too much? Drinking too much? Giving way to the peer-demands and pressures around us? Just ahead is the path we should we walking, the footprints painfully clear. Are we walking with him, yielding to what he asks? Or are we forgetting, denying, not living for him but living for number one? How am I living the Cross? If I can't feel the edge of it in my consciousness, then the fullness of reality is lacking. I need to lean into the whirlwind of his presence, accept the storm he stirs up in me. I have to relent and die with him to be sure of knowing how to be alive. I have to open my heart, my consciousness, to see him, crucified, changing the meaning, transforming the event. There, just beyond the cross, in the sky getting darker hour by hour, I can see the outline of the universe, God designing everything, and us, for himself, to be swept up into his flaming heart.

Is the way narrow? How are we supposed to enter in? We do it by consenting, leaning into the particular, feeling the nails in our hands.

Do not weep for me, daughters of Jerusalem. He knows the outcome.

Master, how can I thank you for this gift? This depth of vision that lets me live your story, knowing it as my own? Do I value enough the pearl of your existence?

In the surrender of one man the broken pieces of existence are made whole again.
—Emilie Griffin, *Homeward Voyage*

Master, teach me to connect my story with yours in ways that are not hyperdramatic, not grandiose, but simple and straightforward. Give me the gift of interpretation, so that I may value the pearl of your existence in history and in my own life. Let me not trifle with other kinds of ornaments, but go in search of you, the precious pearl. Amen.

MAY

May 1

THE LOST GARDEN

> "Taste and see that the Lord is good."
> —Psalm 34:8

Imagine Adam and Eve in the garden. Imagine them walking about in innocent wonder, adoring each other, tasting every wild fruit and finding it good to satisfy their hunger. Imagine them conversing with God.

Then imagine them, stuffed full with the knowledge of good and evil cast out of the garden, cautiously touching the thorny stalks of briers, picking berries and carefully touching them to their tongues to discover sometimes sweetness sometimes bitterness.

Imagine how tasting sweetness they must have felt first elation and then the enormity of their loss. Imagine how tasting bitterness they must have mourned their disobedience and longed to return to the joyousness of their first state.

Last imagine them learning to cultivate those fruits their tongues found good and their bodies nourishing. Imagine them, in their loss, becoming what only God before had been: providers for themselves and each other.

Imagine them and weep.

—John Leax

We live, O Lord, in a world turned over by sin. Teach us to mourn for what has been lost. Unite us with the creation that groans for the coming day of redemption, and give us grace to taste and see your unimaginable goodness. Amen.

May 2

THE RELUCTANT VISIT

"In Christ Jesus you who once were far off have been brought near in the blood of Christ. For he is our peace, who has made us both one, and has broken down the dividing wall of hostility."
—Ephesians 2:13-14, RSV

Several years ago I attended a weekend conference at which a very close friend of mine, a businessman, was one of the conference leaders. We had talked about Christian love a lot that weekend. At one of the final sessions, this friend, whom I shall call Dick, told the people at the conference the following story: When he was a small boy, his father, a restless man who drank quite a bit, had left his mother and had married a much younger woman. Although his mother had remarried and Dick had a stepfather whom he came to love and respect, he had always deeply resented his birth father for leaving the family. Over the years they had met only a few times — and their meetings had often left additional scars, as Dick's dad would promise to bring him presents and then forget, adding disappointment to the rejection he had known.

Then, as an adult, my friend had met a man who really believed in God. Through this man's presentation of the Christian message, Dick tried to give God a life he felt was shaky and insecure on the inside, though outwardly very successful. And Dick had become an outstanding Christian layman. Then, almost ten years later, he had been asked to speak at this weekend Christian conference.

As he was preparing to come to the conference, Dick got word that his real father was dying with cancer of the throat in a city near the conference center. He did not want to see his dad at all. He simply had nothing to say to him. The cancer had advanced until his father could not talk or hear and was going blind. His friend told Dick that his father was already virtually a dead man. His only communication with the world outside his mind was through the process of writing and reading on one of those little toy magic slates, which he could barely see.

One of Dick's Christian friends had gone to see the father and told him on the magic slate that his son had grown into a fine man. He asked the older man if he knew that Dick had become a Christian. The father, who was not a Christian, shook his head. He then wrote on the slate that more than just about anything he would love to see his son. He said that although he had never been much of a father, he had been very proud of his boy. He was sorry that he had hurt his mother and him.

The friend left the hospital and wrote to Dick. Although Dick did not want to see his dad, since he was coming that way anyway, he decided to go by the hospital before the conference to see him. When Dick got there he went into the room alone and faced his father. They just looked at each other for several minutes; then Dick began to write on the slate. He told his dad that he loved him and about how his own life had changed since they had last been together because he had tried to give his future to God. His dad did not really understand, but was glad and wanted to hear more about what had happened. As the minutes moved on in silence, one man wrote and then, after changing the slate, the other. Dick gently told his dying father about the Lord who had saved him from so much of the misery that his father had known. Afterwards they just sat and looked at each other.

Finally Dick got up to leave. Then, with all his experience of the rejections of a lifetime telling him not to do it, he turned back and picked up the slate. "Dad," he wrote, "would you like to give your life to Christ too?" His dad stared at the slate for a long time in silence, frowning. Then he took the stylus and wrote, "Yes, I would. But I don't know how. Will you show me, Dick?" And with tears welling up in his eyes, Dick led his own father to a new beginning as he gave as much of himself as he could to as much of God as he could accept. Then they prayed together for the first and only time in their lives — on a magic slate.

—Keith Miller, *A Second Touch*

God, how can it be that doing the very thing we fear for you and one of your lonely, frightened ones can swing open the largest bolted steel doors in the deepest dungeons and free a human soul. Thank you for the mystery of your redeeming power. Amen.

May 3

THE MOUNTAIN OF VISION

"The Lord will lay bare his holy arm in the sight of all nations, and all the ends of the earth will see the salvation of our God."

—Isaiah 52:10

For half of every year, I live where the land is flat — prairie country stretching to the horizon, quilted in a patchwork of fields of corn, wheat, oats. But I miss the mountains, and as I travel west to the coast, its ranges — the Rockies, the Bighorns, the Cascades — seem to lift their summits like holy altars.

Mountains stand for strength; in their enormity and stability they remind us of God, who made them, who is bigger than we are and bigger than they are, who makes us look up, who has *promised* us his powerful arm to hang on to. In times when my heart sinks and I feel wholly inadequate, I imagine myself leaning into the flanks and shoulders of a towering mountain, feeling its solidity, which draws my heart even higher — to my mighty Father-Creator.

Because of their height, mountains are places of vision. From their peaks we can see clearly in any direction without interruption. We can survey the land below us like a map — the shining threads of rivers, the shapes of lakes, the deep clefts of valleys, with towns punctuating the landscape. And somehow at that height we feel there is less distance between us and God.

In the Bible mountains are often scenes of pivotal action. Think of the signs Jehovah gave on mountains: He unfurled a rainbow, a promise of life, over Ararat, where the ark unloaded its precious cargo after the Flood. On Sinai he ignited a bush as a sign to Moses of his unquenchable presence. Many years later, on the same mountain, Moses received from the hands of the Almighty the two tablets of stone engraved with God's standard for human conduct. And on Mount Carmel God unleashed a power unmatched by the pagan baals as he kindled Elijah's water-soaked sacrifice into flame.

On Mount Moriah Isaac was bound on an altar by his father, Abraham, in obedience to God, but was saved from slaughter when a ram was divinely provided as a substitute sacrifice. It was on the same mountain — Moriah — that the Lord "broke forth" on Uzzah for his brashness in touching the sacred ark of the covenant.

And there he blessed Obed-Edom for secluding the ark in his threshing floor, the very spot where Solomon eventually built the temple as God's house on earth.

And finally, Jesus' ultimate sacrifice, the focal event of all time, which gave meaning to all the others, was enacted there. —Luci Shaw, *Horizons*

Father-Creator, you have made bare your mighty arm for me to hang on to. You have shown me your works in all the earth, and you have shown me yourself in your Christ, the one who will return as he departed. Keep me looking forward in the light of your promise, that I may be found faithful on that day. Amen.

May 4

DESERT UNICORN

"Canst thou bind the unicorn with his band in the furrow? or will he harrow the valleys after thee?" —Job 39:10, KJV

In counterpoint to their heavy footsteps came the sound of a delicate prancing, like silver hooves against crystal. The child looked out across the desert to the horizon, where a unicorn stood silhouetted against the path of the moon. With a toss of his head the unicorn danced lightly across the shining diamonds of sand. As he neared the circle of firelight he bowed his horned head and his flanks quivered with tension as though he were preparing to charge, but he continued lowering his horn until it touched the sand before the child in a gesture of loving reverence. Then he walked past the child to the young mother, lay down quietly beside her, and put his head in her lap. For a moment she stroked his wild mane. When she raised her hand he rose, bowed his horn once more to the child, and galloped across the desert into the path of the moon. —Madeleine L'Engle, *Dance in the Desert*

Lord of the Universe: Thank you for the unicorn that runs free on the sand. Thank you for the lion, the desert mice, the wild asses, the eagles, the adder, the ostriches, the pelican, the owl, and the dragons that dance together in a circle. Thank you for a safe crossing on the journey through the desert. Amen

May 5

KEEPING SENSE

"How sweet are your words to my taste, sweeter than honey to my mouth!" —Psalm 119:103

Two basic dangers plague the human race. We are both physical and spiritual beings, yet we find it almost impossible to balance those two supposedly contradictory aspects of our nature. Some of us, preferring the pure ideal to messy reality, are tempted to live in a realm of ethereal abstraction where bodies are only a nuisance and encumbrance. Others, impatient with what they can't see or touch, insist that the senses are the only reality and their gratification life's sole reward.

Dealing with the senses is particularly perplexing for contemporary women. For one thing, our culture assumes we are made of nothing but nerve endings constantly screaming to be stimulated. Ads for clothes, jewelry, perfume, and makeup pay the freight in women's magazines. Articles in those publications routinely feature food, sex, and something called "beauty" as their primary stock-in-trade. Unfortunately, the women's movement has done surprisingly little to change these assumptions.

Sensory perception is essential to being human. We ignore that at our peril. Even more, our senses are the good gift of God. He put the first man and woman in a garden where he planted "trees that were pleasing to the eye and good for food" (Gen 2:9). specifically to gratify their senses. The name of the place is most accurately translated "Garden of Delight." Realizing that these creatures required more than spiritual communion, he provided them flesh-hand-blood comfort through each other's body.

Yet it is also through the senses that Eve is tempted. The fruit of the forbidden tree that she eats to make her wise first attracts her because it was "pleasing to the eye" (Gen. 3:6). And ever afterwards, women have found it difficult to achieve that lost balance between wisdom and feeling. They have been caught in the web of desire, often reduced to objects of appetite themselves. When love becomes lust, the garden becomes a jungle. —Virginia Stem Owens, *Daughters of Eve*

Dear Lord, help me to hone that delicate balance between wisdom and feeling. Improve my awareness of my sensory perceptions, a gift from you. In Jesus' name. Amen.

May 6

LISTENING WITH THE HEART

"Whether you turn to the right or to the left, your ears will hear a voice behind you, saying, 'This is the way; walk in it.'" —Isaiah 30:21

In Meditative Prayer God is always addressing our will. Christ confronts us and asks us to choose. Having heard his voice, we are to obey his word. It is this ethical call to repentance, to change, to obedience that most clearly distinguishes Christian meditation from its Eastern and secular counterparts. In Meditative Prayer there is no loss of identity, no merging with the cosmic consciousness, no fanciful astral travel. Rather, we are called to life-transforming obedience because we have encountered the living God of Abraham, Isaac, and Jacob. Christ is truly present among us to heal us, to forgive us, to change us, to empower us.

There is a technical word for what I have been describing, and it might be helpful for you to know it — *lectio divina* (divine reading). This is a kind of reading in which the mind descends into the heart, and both are drawn into the love and goodness of God. Henri Nouwen once pointed to a lovely picture hanging in his apartment and said to me, "That is *lectio divina*." It depicted a woman with an open Bible in her lap, but her eyes were lifted upward. Do you get the idea? We are doing more than reading words; we are seeking "the Word exposed in the words," to use the phrase of Karl Barth. We are listening with the heart to the Holy within. This prayerful reading, as we might call it, edifies us and strengthens us. —Richard J. Foster, *Prayer: Finding the Heart's True Home*

The Sacrament of the Word

Today, O Lord, I'm listening to the proclamation of the Word. Help me to listen as much with the heart and the will as I do with the head. Amen.
—Richard J. Foster, in *Prayers from the Heart*

May 7

RAINSTORM

"...he makes his sun rise on the evil and on the good, and sends rain on the just and on the unjust." —Matthew 5:45b, RSV

Television tells us at least two things about rain.

The Weather Channel tells us when rain is coming, how it's going to ruin our day, wreak havoc with our schedule, cause misery in our car pool.

The Movie Channel tells us just the opposite. Or at least one line in one lyric amid the many songs and dances in *Top Hat* (1935) tells us.

"Isn't this a lovely day to get caught in the rain?"

Fred Astaire and Ginger Rogers do indeed get caught, momentarily imprisoned as it were in a gazebo or summer house during a sudden downpour. Boy meets girl. Thunder and lightning. He's agonized, she's antagonized. He sings and dances. She follows suit, matching his every note and step. And so it is when Gods runs, unexpectedly, into us. After all, He's the one who rains on the just and the unjust, the fertile and the fallow. —William Griffin, *The High Calling of Our Daily Work*

Dear God, yes, do rain on my parade and, yes, do open my eyes to your presence and, yes, do reveal to me that the downpour was just your crazy idea of arranging a casual meeting that wouldn't otherwise have taken place. And yes, every time it rains, do let's make it another excuse to meet again. So what's a little wet, a little singing, a little dancing, a little praying in the rain? Who can ask for anything more? Amen.

May 8

NIGHT VISION

"Where there is no vision, the people perish: but he that keepeth the law, happy is he." —Proverbs 29:18, KJV

> Often the geese fly
> at night. I watch them,
> dark against dark sky,
> beat northward.
>
> Tonight, when I heard
> their wild calling, one
> darkness filled my eyes;
> I saw nothing I could see.
>
> Joyous in the music
> of their flight, I cried
> to all I saw. *Thanks be!*
> *for Vision Vision Vision.*
>
> —John Leax, *The Task of Adam*

You have given us eyes to see, O Lord, and hearts inclined to do your will. For the grace that moved us to turn to you, we give you thanks. You are our vision, the light by which we see. Amen.

May 9

NOT AS I WILL

"Thy will be done." —Matthew 26:42b, KJV

Although Ann's pregnancy had not been without problems, she carried her first child confidently, so sure she was of God's hand on this new life within her. The delivery was difficult but not harrowing with her husband Daniel beside her. She felt pain, sure, but a blessedness and a calm that seemed a gift of grace once the doctor gave her Emily, pink and healthy with life.

A year later, Emily and Daniel were both killed at an intersection not more than a mile from their new home, a place Ann can't pass anymore. She will deliberately drive five miles out of her way and choose to be late to work rather than see the overpass where a distracted driver forced them to... but what does it matter how? Everything she ever loved died at that spot. She can visit the cemetery, but she can't pass that intersection and won't.

For months, Ann couldn't pray. She had always believed in a God of love, and quite simply there was no way to square what he had done in taking everything she loved with that image. How could a loving God wreak that much horror on the soul of someone who loved him? — that's what she thought.

In life, some of us, by God's own hand, avoid such despair; but many don't. Most believers feel abandoned at one time or another. A life that was beautiful goes up in a conflagration, the image of a loving God along with it.

In the garden of Gethsemane, when Christ said, "May your will be done," he was asking to be avoided. Sometimes when we say to the Lord, "May your will be done," we are gaining in our knowledge of God but that gain costs us dearly.

Ann's attitude toward life and her understanding of God were nearly destroyed. Before the accident, everything was wonderful. An overwhelming sense of happiness kept her soul aloft in joy and praise, so great was the love of the Father. The Lord had seemingly made her the center of his life, bestowing blessing after blessing. Sadly, this notion of God was false.

Ann learns the God she has loved and worshiped is much, much bigger than her own sweet perceptions. What she learns is the lesson of Christ at Gethsemane: she learns the immense reality of God.

Then a whole new education begins. At that point, the troubled heart, understanding its weakness, comes on its knees before the Almighty. The will to drink the cup, as Jesus did on Golgotha, to drink it with a broken heart, and to thus cooperate in God's work and attune one's will to his, is the will to find eternal life.

Our entering into God's great will for his creation, whether it be through joy or sorrow, is our honor and the self-exultation of our soul. He becomes our peace. —James Calvin Schaap, *Near Unto God*

How easy it is for us to say, "May your will be done," when all is well. How easily we forget your ways and purposes are not always the same as our wishes and dreams. Lord Jesus, be in us so that all we wish is your will. Be our peace, and we will walk where you lead. Amen.

May 10

Answers to Riddles

"O Lord, thou hast searched me and known me! Thou knowest when I sit down and when I rise up; thou discernest my thoughts from afar. Thou searchest out my path and my lying down, and art acquainted with all my ways.... For thou didst form my inward parts, thou didst knit me together in my mother's womb. I praise thee, for thou art fearful and wonderful. Wonderful are thy works! Thou knowest me right well; my frame was not hidden from thee, when I was being made in secret, intricately wrought in the depths of the earth."
—Psalm 139:1-3, 13-15, RSV

The first time I remember hearing this Psalm, I was at a women's prayer group meeting in Georgia with twenty-nine others. A woman read the entire Psalm as a morning devotion, and before she had finished I realized I had tears streaming down my face.

I was crying from relief — a mixture of embarrassment and joy which came from the realization that I could admit to myself and to God that I couldn't do everything I needed to do to improve my health. I didn't have to keep on pretending that it was easy for me.

I had been studying nutrition and exercise and trying to fit all I was learning into my life — with much difficulty. I was at a "fed up with it all" stage and was almost ready to throw it out the window. But I still pretended to be "gung-ho" and enthusiastic. The truth was, I wasn't interested in sweating and hurting and cutting chocolate chip cookies out of my life. I just wanted to be healthy *without* all that!

Also, I had begun to get the feeling that God would love me better as soon as I lost my ten pounds and ran three miles (every day... Without skipping any) and had *fun* doing it! It hit me like a bucket of cold water that I was trying to earn some kind of approval from God by getting trim. But that morning I realized in a way I could really see that God loves me just because he is God and I am his child. God's grace, as I understand it, means that he loves me. Period. Not because of *anything* I am (trim and fit) or anything I do (run a marathon or even a mile).

The words, "Thou knowest me right well: my frame was not hidden from thee, when I was being made in secret," mean so much to me. God knows about my weak knees, my sluggish metabolism, my pot tummy, my attraction to unhealthy foods. In fact, the reason he knows all this is that he made me. "Thou didst form my inward parts, thou didst knit me together in my mother's womb." If he made this puzzle that is my body, then he knows the answers to the riddles of why I'm not trim and fit.

How many times I've said to myself, "But Lord, if you only knew how easy it is for me to gain weight!" Or, "If you only knew how busy I am. I'll never find time to exercise every day!" "Lord, you know how my knee hurts when I run very far." When I heard these Scripture verses, I thought, "Yes, God knows all those things. And he is involved in my process to become fit" The Scripture had come to me at a turning point in my struggle, and it means a lot to me today.

—Andrea Wells Miller, *BodyCare*

Dear Lord, instead of complaining about all my physical problems, I want to praise you like this psalmist did—because you made me and know me. You even know what I'm thinking, and what I am doing.

Help me to learn to ask you for the patience and faith to keep on my plan even when my body doesn't seem to respond to my efforts to shape it up. Forgive me for quitting so often, and thank you for understanding and taking me back when I return. You are acquainted with all my ways so you know the answer to the riddles of why my body isn't as healthy as you know it could be. Teach me, Lord, and help me to listen, to recognize your voice, and to learn. In Jesus' name. Amen.

May 11

GOD GETS EVEN

"He is the image of the invisible God, the firstborn over all creation. ...For God was pleased to have all his fullness dwell in him."

—Colossians 1:15, 19

When we see an elm tree growing in a square of green grass in front of a house, we can point to it and say, "There's an elm." And we can go on to describe it scientifically, in terms of its botanical species and structure; practically—in terms of the shade it casts or the suitability of its wood for building; poetically—how it looks to us, what emotions it evokes, what it reminds us of, what it seems to mean.

To the tangible, visible, audible objects in the world around us (a bell, a book, a field mouse, a politician, a long-distance runner) we can assign names and values and physical descriptions. They are part of the "known world," which we take for granted because we are so familiar with it.

But how can we know a God who is intangible, invisible, inaudible? To describe him in human terms seems like shrinking him down to our own size, our level of understanding—the One who is infinite, all-powerful, all-knowing. When the only other self-conscious, intelligent, immortal beings we know are people, our tendency is to describe God like a bigger, stronger, better-informed *person*. We have an anthropomorphic view of God.

The only way for us to know what God is really like is *if he describes himself* to us. And at Bethlehem God did that; he shrank *himself* down to the dimensions of a human baby who grew up to become a small-town carpenter; he "got even" with us, as it were, by coming into history at our own level, showing us what God looks like and what his love and sacrifice signify.

Jesus was the Word, God's descriptive message, that still speaks the truth about him. In Christ, God sent the human race an unmistakable "signal from himself." And we must be daring enough to take his Word for it! —Luci Shaw, *Horizons*

Jesus, you restricted yourself by coming to us in a human body, showing us how much God loves us, identifying with our human feelings of joy or sorrow, exuberance or fatigue, satisfaction or frustration. I thank you today for coming down to us, and especially to me, and raising us up with you. Amen.

May 12

Peeps: 1948

"O Jerusalem, Jerusalem, you who kill the prophets, and stone those sent to you, how often I have longed to gather your children together, as a hen gathers her chicks under her wings, but you were not willing."
—Matthew 23:37

>Inside the dark of early spring,
>I trailed across the lane
>and clambered up the ramp
>behind Pap. As the door
>swung open, yellow light
>spilled, like cracked corn,
>onto the yard. I stepped
>through its welcome sweep
>and followed Pap
>into the chicken house it warmed.
>
>Broody hens shifted and clucked
>in their beds of straw,
>and clamoring in the life
>of an old lamp,

> the new fuzzed chicks
> tossed their shrill *peep peep*
> into the rising joy
> of the Easter world.
> — John Leax, *Country Labors*

We toss our cries unto you, O Prophet of Jerusalem. Gather us in the warmth beneath your wings and keep us safe from the predators that would devour us apart from your unceasing love. Amen.

May 13

CHRIST'S PERSPECTIVE

> "When they measure themselves by one another and compare themselves with one another, they are without understanding."
> — 2 Corinthians 10:12, NAB

When I talked with other Christians...I discovered that "consistency" is considered to be one of the most important and desired characteristics of living the Christian life. I felt ill. Because the more I was living in what I thought was Christ's perspective on this adventure of faith, in one sense the more *inconsistent* my behavior seemed to be — according to some evangelical teaching about how to live and witness. Being very insecure, I would go back and try to conform.

I was pretty discouraged and confused. But then I saw a surprising thing in reading the New Testament. Whereas I had always blindly assumed that Christ was very consistent in his life, I saw suddenly that he was *not*. In fact, Jesus was very *inconsistent* in his life! And it was his inconsistency, according to the religious habits of his day, which kept him in hot water and eventually led to his death. For example, on one hand he said that he had not come to change even the smallest punctuation mark of the Jewish law (Matt. 5:17–20), and then he proceeded to break their sacred rules one after the other — even on the Sabbath — to love the people from his Father's perspective in obedience to him (Mark 2:15–17, 18–22, 23–28; 3:1–5). He told his followers not to use physical violence to conquer the world; in fact, he told them that they should turn the other cheek (Matt. 5:39). But in a later situation we see a furious Jesus driving employees out of the Temple and throwing over their stalls (Matt. 21:12). Or on another occasion we see him telling a group of scribes and Pharisees that they were so rotten inside that from his perspective they had internal B.O. (Matt. 23:27–28). Then a few days or weeks later, he died for them. These are just a few of the acts of a

Man who was notoriously *inconsistent*. Why did he behave that way? As I thought about this, I knew I was on the track of something very important if I was ever going to see life in Christ's perspective.

So I began to examine my old ideas about consistency. And I realized that, in my insecurity, I had unconsciously assumed that *consistency* in Christian living meant *uniformity* — that we were all supposed to act *alike* and to respond the *same* way all the time.

Where had this idea come from that Jesus lived a consistent life and, therefore, we ought to also? Then I knew. Jesus was not consistent with regard to a set of rules. (I am not talking about the Ten Commandments, which Jesus did obey, of course. But with regard to human relationships, he and Paul both tried to summarize all these laws into a *perspective of love* to avoid the kind of legalism of which I am speaking; Matt. 22:37–40, Rom. 13:9–10.) He lived out his days in consistent obedience to a Living Creative Composer, who was composing a masterpiece of lives and giving Jesus his part in it to play — a line, an hour at a time — as he listened and watched in his life. To be obedient to the perspective of his Father in new situations, Jesus transcended the old rules. He tried to bring God's vulnerable but healing love to *each* situation in a way that brought *wholeness to the people involved*, however inconsistent his behavior might seem to the secular mind or even to the Jewish keepers of the truth and defenders of the faith.

But Jesus' consistency was to a perspective of loving obedience. This has always made him and his way very threatening, especially to religious people, because we cannot control this kind of life in others. And if we try to live it, we must take the risk of being considered unrighteous by our religious peers. Being misunderstood about our faith and accused of self-centered motives or "lack of discipline," etc., is hard for a sensitive Christian to take. Some religious leaders have always thought people who talk about this kind of creative freedom from consistency are talking about a kind of irresponsible license, a kind of freedom from discipline and responsibility. But of course this is *not* true. As a matter of fact, I am finding that trying to discover and live creatively in Christ's perspective is far more demanding in terms of prayer and study of the Scriptures and risking than it was to follow the standard little personal habits and rules outlined by our part of the Christian community. This is not speaking against personal or corporate disciplines. *Quite the contrary.* In my own life I find that time alone each day in prayer, reading of the Bible and devotional classics, and public worship are a continuing necessity. It is the practice of these disciplines which, in fact, acts as a valuable check against a rootless subjectivism.

—J. Keith Miller, *A Second Touch*

Dear Lord, draw me to you through the consistent discipline of daily prayer, Bible reading, and worship so that I may learn more about living creatively in your perspective in new situations — situations that perhaps you did not encounter during your life in Palestine. Somehow, by immersing myself in your word through study, prayer, and meditation, I can begin to absorb that informative perspective and become more and more consistent with it. In Jesus' name. Amen.

May 14

Windows to God

"But we all, with open face beholding as in a glass the glory of the Lord, are changed into that same image from glory to glory, even as by the Spirit of the Lord." —2 Corinthians 3:18, KJV

What do I mean by icon?

If it's impossible for me to describe the wild wonderfulness of Antarctica, it is equally impossible for me to describe what I, personally, mean by an icon. I am not thinking of the classic definition of the icons so familiar in the Orthodox church, icons of Christ, the Theotokos, saints, painted on wood and often partially covered with silver. My personal definition is much wider, and the simplest way I can put it into words is to affirm that an icon, for me, is an open window to God. An icon is something I can look through and get a wider glimpse of God and God's demands on us, el's mortal children, than I would otherwise. It is not flippant for me to say that a penguin is an icon for me, because the penguin invited me to look through its odd little self and on to a God who demands of us that we be vulnerable as we open ourselves to intimacy, an intimacy which leads not only to love of creatures, but to love of God.

I have some icons that are more traditional. On the night stand in my cabin I placed a small travel copy of the famous icon of Abraham's three angelic guests, three beautiful, winged angels, who are also, understood iconically, Father, Son, and Holy Spirit. It is what we think of as a classic icon, saying something that cannot be said in words, that cannot even be said in the painting. It transcends our experience and points us to something larger and greater and more wonderful. Yes, it is an open window to God. —Madeleine L'Engle, *Penguins and Golden Calves*

God our Creator, open wide our windows for a clearer view of you, that our image may reflect what we see. Amen.

May 15

HELP

"I call to you, God, because I'm sure of an answer.
So — answer! bend your ear! listen sharp!
Paint grace-graffiti on the fences;
    take in your frightened children who
Are running from the neighborhood bullies
    straight to you."   —Psalm 17:6-7, THE MESSAGE

To the objection "I prayed and cried out for help, but no help came," the answer is "But it did. The help was there; it was right at hand. You were looking for something quite different, perhaps, but God brought the help that would change your life into health, into wholeness for eternity. And not only would it change your life, but nations, society, culture."

Instead of asking why the help has not come, the person at prayer learns to look carefully at what is actually going on in his or her life, in this history, its leaders, its movements, its peoples, and ask, "Could this be the help that he is providing? I never thought of *this* in terms of help, but maybe it is."

Prayer gives us another, far more accurate way or reading reality than the newspapers. "Think of it!" exclaims Bernanos's country priest, "The Word was made Flesh and not one of the journalists of those days even knew it was happening" (*The Diary of a Country Priest*).

—Eugene H. Peterson, *Earth and Altar/Where Your Treasure Is*

Dear Lord, help me to relax in the knowledge that your help is here. My inability to recognize it creates discontent, unease, irritability. Show me how your help is at work in my life in what actually is going on in my world right now. Open my mind to see you at work. And thank you for the help. In Jesus' name. Amen.

May 16

A TRINITY OF VOICES

"Now it is God who makes both us and you stand firm in Christ. He anointed us, set his seal of ownership on us, and put his Spirit in our hearts as a deposit, guaranteeing what is to come."
—2 Corinthians 1:21-22

Think of God's plan as a series of Voices. The first Voice, thunderingly loud, had certain advantages. When the Voice spoke from the trembling mountain at Sinai, or when fire licked up the altar on Mount Carmel, no one could deny it. Yet, amazingly, even those who heard the Voice and feared it — the Israelites at Sinai and at Carmel, for example — soon learned to ignore it. Its very volume got in the way. Few of them sought out that Voice; fewer still persevered when the Voice fell silent.

The Voice modulated with Jesus, the *Word* made flesh. For a few decades the Voice of God took on the timbre and volume and rural accent of a country Jew in Palestine. It was a normal human voice, and though it spoke with authority, it did not cause people to flee. Jesus' voice was soft enough to debate against, soft enough to kill.

After Jesus departed, the Voice took on new forms. On the day of Pentecost, tongues — *tongues* — of fire fell on the faithful, and the church, God's body, began to take shape. That last Voice is as close as breath, as gentle as a whisper. It is the most vulnerable Voice of all, and the easiest to ignore. The Bible says the Spirit can be "quenched" or "grieved" — try quenching Moses' burning bush or the molten rocks of Sinai! Yet the Spirit is also the most intimate Voice. In our moments of weakness, when we do not know what to pray, the Spirit within intercedes for us with groans that words cannot express. Those groans are the early pangs of birth, the labor pains of the new creation.

The Spirit will not remove all disappointment with God. The very titles given to the Spirit — Intercessor, Helper, Counselor, Comforter — imply there will be problems. But the Spirit is also "a deposit, guaranteeing what is to come," Paul said, drawing on an earthy metaphor from the financial world. The Spirit reminds us that such disappointments are temporary, a prelude to an eternal life with God. God deemed it necessary to restore the spiritual link *before* re-creating heaven and earth.

In two places the New Testament compares being Spirit-filled with the state of drunkenness. Both states change the way you view life's trials, but there is a profound difference between them. Many people turn to drink to drown out the sadness of unemployment, illness, and personal tragedy. Inevitably, however, a drunk must awake from the fantasy world of inebriation and return to an unchanged reality. But the Spirit whispers of a new reality, a fantasy that is actually true, one into which we will awake for eternity.

—Philip Yancey, *Disappointment with God*

Dear Lord, your Spirit comforts, helps, and counsels me during the hard times in my life. I feel your presence as Spirit in joyful, peaceful times as well. That Presence does indeed change the way I view life's trials. Thank you, Lord, for that Presence. In Jesus' name. Amen.

May 17

IN MIND, AND OUT

"...and you will do well to pay attention to it, as to a light shining in a dark place, until the day dawns and the morning star rises in your hearts." —2 Peter 1:19

I know a man who had a tumor and, along with it, a sizable chunk of the right hemisphere of his cerebral cortex excised from his brain. He survived the surgery with no complications, woke up, functioned well, even talked to the doctors and nurses. There was only one problem: he was convinced he was dreaming. Nothing could persuade him that he was actually awake and aware. Descartes would have been proud of him. Perhaps he would have gone on in this dream world forever if it hadn't been for television. He finally decided that his own mind could not possibly produce the meager and unsatisfying scenarios he found on the screen. If he had been dreaming, he would have made a better job of it.

But it is only brain most of us want, not consciousness. And in itself, the organ seems marvelous enough. Its endless compartments hold codes for the way to get to work, the way home again, what we like to eat, the names and faces of friends. Even when consciousness is suspended, the brain continues to function, although it may miss a few red lights on the way to the office. An epileptic suffering a *petit mal* seizure will continue to breathe, walk, open the door, sit down, though no memory remains of those actions. And most of us live our lives in a constant state of *petit mal* seizures. The difference is that epileptics have their brains blown about by unsought electrical storms whereas we decide to detach consciousness through a failure of nerve.

—Virginia Stem Owens, *God Spy*

Dear Lord, awaken my consciousness to a sense of your presence in my life. Quicken my senses to the world around me and how I am to do and be according to your will. Strengthen my nerve, so that I may live more and more fully awake and aware of truth, love, peace, and grace. In Jesus' name. Amen.

May 18

OH, YOU KID!

"This is what the Sovereign Lord says to these bones: I will make breath enter you, and you will come to life." —Ezekiel 37:5

"Look at my hands and my feet. It is I myself! Touch me and see."
—Luke 24:39

"The body's coming later," the cop shouted,
handing her the arm and driving off,
while she stared at the hump of forearm,
steadied the cold fingers slithering like rubber.
She was the night nurse, my mother,
younger then than my daughter
as I write this, finally,
after fifty years, telling
how the lights burned low
to save juice for boys in Okinawa,
how the hemorrhage stained her white uniform.
I tell her that her nurse's oath
must have billowed like MISS AMERICA
across her chest. *Oh no!* she laughs,
she was pinned to that arm
like St. Peter in the Baptist window,
no faith, barely knowing how she got there.
She tells how she scrubbed,
but even undiluted bleach
wouldn't forgive that stain.
She had to throw her uniform away,
go without breakfast for a month to buy another.
It's coming back to her, now that she's eighty,
how nothing she did was ever wasted.
She's shifting into high gear.
She wants us to know how she stuffed the arm
into the freezer, and when the body came,
she helped sew the thing back on, Raggedy Andy style.
Years later, the man stopped in to thank her.
"Oh, you kid!" he shouted, and shook her hand,
to show off his good arm.

She presses his handshake into my palm.
I pass it to my laughing daughter.
It is the vagrant lost-arm signal,
the secret message, proof
of how far down the road toward dead

a thing can be and still
get turned around in the other direction.
—Jeanne Murray Walker, *Gaining Time*

Lord, that you conquered death gives me so much hope! I've felt so low at times it's as if I were deadened, anesthetized, numb—to the people around me, to the tastes, smells, and sights in my world, and to you. I've wanted to reach out and touch you somehow, to really know that you are there. Yet I know that you can restore me to life again because you have before. I've experienced it first hand. It is truly amazing to me how low I can get and still be rejuvenated by your healing presence. Thank you. Amen.

May 19

Beauty in the Ordinary

"So God created man in his own image, in the image of God he created him; male and female he created them." —Genesis 1:27

Quiltmaker

I make them warm to keep my family from freezing.
I make them beautiful
to keep my heart from breaking.
—Prairie woman, 1870

To keep a husband and five children warm, she quilts them covers thick as drifts against the door. Through every fleshy square white threads-needle their almost invisible tracks; her hours count each small suture that holds in place the raw-cut, uncolored edges of her life.

She pieces each one beautiful and summer bright to thaw her frozen soul. Under her fingers the scraps grow to green birds and purple, improbable leaves; deeper than calico, her mid-winter mind bursts into flowers. She watches them unfold between the double stars, the wedding rings.

When the world was created, it would have been enough to have it work, wouldn't it? A functioning universe would have seemed sufficient. To include beauty seems gratuitous, a gift of pure grace. The creation of beauty links us with our Creator. God, the first Quilter of prairies, the prime Painter (sunsets, night skies, forget-me-nots, thunderheads), the archetypal metal Sculptor (mountain ranges), the Composer who heard the whales' strange, sonorous songs in his head long before there were whales to sing them, the Playwright who plotted the sweeping drama of life, the Poet whose Word said it all—

God made us humans in his image; we participate in creative intelligence, giftedness, originality.

Most of all we have the faculty of imagination deep within us, waiting like a seed to be watered and fertilized. Imagination gives us pictures by which to see things the way they can be or the way they are underneath. The prairie woman, hemmed in with her small children by months of cold and snow, used her imagination redemptively. Around the traditional quilt patterns—double stars, wedding rings—her imagination pieced in the exuberant flowers and leaves that redeemed the long winter, that thawed her soul. She created beauty and richness from the ordinary stuff of life.
—Luci Shaws, *Horizons*

Creator God, First Quilter, Prime Painter, Archetypal Sculptor, Composer of All Songs, Life's Playwright, Word-breathing Poet, how many names will you be known by? I say them over and over. Praise you Father, Son, and Holy Spirit! Amen.

May 20

Giving Frees Us

"He also saw a poor widow put in two very small copper coins. 'I tell you the truth,' he said, 'this poor widow has put in more than all the others. All these people gave their gifts out of their wealth; but she out of her poverty put in all she had to live on.'"
—Luke 21:2-4

When we give money we are releasing a little more of our egocentric selves and a little more of our false security. John Wesley declared that "if you have any desire to escape the damnation of hell, give all you can; otherwise I can have no more hope of your salvation than that of Judas Iscariot."

Giving frees us from the tyranny of money. But we do not just give money; we give the things money has purchased. In Acts the early Christian community gave houses and land to provide funds for those in need (Acts 4:32–37). Have you ever considered selling a car or a stamp collection to help finance someone's education? Money has also given us the time and leisure to acquire skills. What about giving those skills away? Doctors, dentists, lawyers, computer experts, and many others can give their skills for the good of the community.

Giving frees us to care. It produces an air of expectancy as we anticipate what God will lead us to give. It makes life with God an adventure of discovery. We are being used to help make a difference in the world, and that is worth living for and giving for.
—Richard J. Foster, *The Challenge of a Disciplined Life*

Lord! Give me courage and love to open the door and constrain you to enter, whatever the disguise you come in, even before I fully recognize my quest!
Come in! Enter my small life!
Lay your sacred hands on all the common things and small interests of that life and bless and change them. Transfigure my small resources, make them sacred. And in them give me your very Self. Amen.
—Evelyn Underhill, *Meditations and Prayers*

May 21

WHERE ANGELS FEAR TO TREAD

"When he came near the place where the road goes down the Mount of Olives, the whole crowd of disciples began joyfully to praise God in loud voices for all the miracles they had seen.... Some of the Pharisees in the crowd said to Jesus, 'Teacher, rebuke your disciples!' 'I tell you,' he replied, 'if they keep quiet, the stones will cry out.'"
—Luke 19:37, 39-40

Simple Simon

Now he wags his head, now beats the floor,
out of time with all the dignity,
pomp, and music in this service of our Lord,
this tread and pause of elders steady as trees.
Constrained inside his head all leaps and pushes
to a blur of light, to a hugger-mugger joy,
as if a wind would take each hand and rush
him birdlike to the altar with a cry.

We see his ungainly shadow, not
what his soul by its sharp hunger proves—
that we are fickle with our faculties
and by our spastic wills evade our love—
unlike this simple child whose spirit easily
outstrips where angels groan and dare not.
—Robert Siegel, *In a Pig's Eye*

We are slow, O Lord, halting in our praise. Make us as like this child whose spirit knows no hesitation. Make us quick as the stones to name your name. Amen.

May 22

A LITTLE LOWER THAN THE ANGELS

"What is man that you are mindful of him, the son of man, that you care for him? You made him a little lower than the heavenly beings, and crowned him with glory and honor. Thou made him ruler over the works of your hands." —Psalm 8:4-6a

All day Saturday as we worked in the woods, I watched the tractor wear and compact the path. Our tractor is light, and we are careful, but by afternoon the earth was marked by our presence. It will heal in a few seasons, for the path we made is crooked, twisting around saplings and trees that will grow into timber. As they grow, they will drop their leaves and build the soil beneath them, gradually erasing all traces of our labor.

Climbing on and off the tractor, I began to recognize that my angle of vision and my ability to relate to the nonhuman altered as I changed my position. On the tractor I saw trees and concentrated on steering around them. I was a power, apart from the woods. Walking, I saw woodpeckers and red efts; I moved more as a creature that belonged. But riding or walking, I was aware of my separateness from the rest of nature.

Some writers on ecology and some poets would have me comprehend this separateness as alienation. It seems to me that a better term would be "distinctiveness." I am not a pantheist. I do not want to be taken up in the sameness of the All. I want red efts to be red efts. I want to enjoy the individuality of each part of creation, experiencing it as something other than myself. Admitting this distinctiveness does not diminish my ability to be related to the nonhuman. Rather it defines the terms of the relationship. It admits consciousness into my living and allows me to stand apart from the world without denying I remain a creature of the world. — John Leax, *In Season and Out*

Creator Father, with David we stand amazed that you have made us, a part of your creation, to serve as stewards in this world. May we begin in humility, remembering that our will is subject to yours; may we proceed in faith, recognizing that all we do is unto you; and may we end in love, serving with honor your Christ in whom all things exist. Amen.

May 23

THE TRUTH IN THE DETAILS

"When... the spirit of truth comes, he will guide you into all truth."
—John 16:13

My walk this morning brought me back along the beach east to west. A high wind was blowing, throwing heavy waves at the beach and eating away at the slope of sand and shells. It has taken the beach out from under our wooden walkway and steps, undercutting them by several feet.

I love the way the sea-grapes grow, each leaf a joining of two flattened circles to a central rib. The new buds push out first as a glossy lime green, then, unfolding, enlarging, burnish into copper and finally a fiery red — losing the sheen with time, but gaining color — a parable of youth and age?

I am *alive,* and the magnificence of this created universe surrounds me. What I must learn to discern in its impersonal forces and phenomena is the Spirit, not only brooding upon the face of the waters, but coming closer — residing in me, linking me to my Creator and through him to other created beings.   —Luci Shaw, *God in the Dark*

Creator Father, for the covenant you have made with your creation I give you thanks. Bless me with insight that I might see in my relationship to your creatures a sign of your relationship to me. Let me live generously in this world, both loving you and loving what you love. Amen.

May 24

THE MANNA SHORTAGE

"You did not see him, yet you love him; and still without seeing him, you are already filled with a joy so glorious it cannot be described, because you believe; and you are sure of the end to which your faith looks forward.... It was this salvation that the prophets were looking and searching so hard for; their prophecies were about the grace which was to come to you."   —1 Peter 1:8-10, JB

It's only after the fact that a desolate experience can be seen as a gift. In the middle of it our vision is dim. We can't see past the present moment. The main response that comes to mind is a howl. This alienation isn't a spiritual exercise that can be scheduled when it's convenient. It rarely seems to coincide with our plans. God's unpredictability is a constant. Now, the question is: How can I get out of this? How can I be glad the spiritual life is never boring?

Maybe the Israelites' story has its own answer coded in. The manna that was sent was barely enough for each day's need, no grace left over for the day to come. (He did send an extra supply to tide them over the Sabbath.)

Each day's anxiety has to be lived in trust. That's theory, not practice. Are the shortages meant for my growth? I can't see it. (My gravest temptation is to stage-manage everything, write the script, and demand that God play his assigned role.) Instead, I need to hold on minute by minute. The more we hold on, give in, the more the actual moment hollows us out. By a gift of imagination, we endure; we grope; we tough it through. "We do not know where you are going, Lord. So how shall we know the way?" (1 John 2:11)

Living the cross is giving ourselves when we have nothing to give: breaking, for a moment, the whine of the TV, the drone of conversation behind the hospital curtain. This is an unidentified location somewhere between Horeb and Sinai. We live in hope that tomorrow's manna will fall, as promised.

I know it is time to drop all my disguises, the ways I hide from God. "Down in the dust I lie prostrate: revive me as your word has guaranteed. I have chosen the way of fidelity, I have set my heart on your rulings. I cling to your decrees" (Ps. 119:25, 30, 31). A new role has been assigned to me; one that gives me a chance to be vulnerable, open, naked, needy, loving, trusting, hour by hour, day by day. Whatever time of year it comes, this is my Lent, an undressing, a stripping off of assumed and false identities. In another sense it is also its own drama or play: our acting-out of Jesus' ordeal in the wilderness. Putting on Christ, as Paul says, is dressing up to be like our Lord.

I am called to walk through times of confusion and doubt playing a new part, keeping my eyes fixed on the Jesus who walks just ahead. Time to ask again, Who is this man? What is he calling me to? And why do we care about him so? —Emilie Griffin, *Homeward Voyage*

Dear Christ, I run a little short of manna; also I'm lacking in vision now and then. But I want to experience the joy that your first followers knew, so that they were transported and happy even during times of hardship. I want to love you, without visions, without revelations, but with a vivid knowledge of your presence in my life. Help me. Pour your grace and joy into me, so that I may be a consolation and inspiration to others, and so that I can stay on an even keel. Thank you, my blessed Lord. Amen.

May 25

THE ENEMY

"...And hath redeemed us from our enemies: for his mercy endureth for ever." —Psalm 136:24, KJV

After [Simon's] mother's death the local minister, Dr. Curds, had come to call, and had immediately alienated Simon by talking of this premature death as the will of God.

Aunt Leonis looked down her long, aristocratic nose at the middle-aged man in his dark suit. "I wonder how it is, Dr. Curds, that you are so certain that you understand the will of God?"

Dr. Curds looked at her with patient gentleness. "You must not fight the Lord, my dear Miss Phair. Trust in his will, and he will send you the Comforter."

"Thank you. I believe he has already done so. I also believe that my niece's illness and death were not God's will. I doubt very much if he looks with approval on such suffering. It seems to me more likely that it has something to do with man's arrogance and error. However, being mortal and finite, I do not presume to understand God's will, so I am not certain."

Dr. Curds murmured something about it being part of God's plan.

Aunt Leonis replied, "It may be part of God's plan that a young woman should suffer and die, or it may be the work of the enemy."

"The enemy?"

"Don't you believe in the devil, Dr. Curds? I do."

Dr. Curds murmured again, "The Church in these more enlightened times...the devil seems a little old-fashioned."

Aunt Leonis raised her left eyebrow. "I haven't noticed many signs of enlightenment. And I am undoubtedly old-fashioned. But I do believe that God can come into the evil of this world, and redeem it, and make it an indispensable part of the pattern which includes every star and every speck of hydrogen dust in the universe—and even you, Dr. Curds."

Despite his grief, Simon nearly laughed.

—Madeleine L'Engle, *Dragons in the Waters*

Lord, thank you for turning what was meant for harm into the missing piece that fits the whole pattern. Amen.

May 26

CARING OR TALKING?

"I tell you the truth, whatever you did not do for one of the least of these, you did not do for me." —Matthew 25:45

Bill and I were sitting alone at the breakfast table the morning after his wife's funeral. She had died of lung cancer, leaving two small children. I've known Bill most of his life, and over those thirty-odd years I've given him lots of advice, spiritual and otherwise, from my vantage point of age and experience. Often, though, I had sensed his anger at me. Now he began to speak a little hesitantly about his pain, and then went on to tell me what he planned to do about his financial obligations, and about setting up an educational fund for his small children.

As in the past, all kinds of advice flooded my mind. But this time, something told me to be still and let him talk out his feelings and plans. After almost an hour, he looked up and there were tears in his eyes. "You really heard me!" he said in surprise. "Thank you! I know that you *do* care because you're not just talking to me about religion and what I *should* do. You're listening to me and caring about what's happening to me."

It had taken me thirty years to learn what Jesus was teaching his disciples during his last week. Being on God's side isn't a matter of behaving religiously, or knowing the Bible and being able to give a lot of spiritual advice. To be part of God's kingdom, Jesus said, involves giving people what they need: food for the hungry; cold water for a thirsty traveler; clothes for the naked. *And,* I heard him say to me, *a loving ear, rather than advice, for someone in emotional pain. Because, whatever you did not do to love one of the least of these, my brothers and sisters, you did not do for me.* —J. Keith Miller, *Daily Guideposts,* 1996

Lord, help me not to miss meeting you where you want to meet us — in the lives of the hungry, the poor, and all your lonely brothers and sisters imprisoned in pain. Amen.

May 27

WITH ALL THY STRENGTH

"And thou shalt love the Lord thy God...with all your strength." —Deuteronomy 6:5b

Love is the very essence of the gospels, isn't it? In fact, if you compare all the world's religions, what's common to all of them and universal in its reality is love itself. It makes me nervous to have to read through the Old Testament, with its macabre rituals, its barbaric warfare, and its avenging God. And Paul? — some of his invectives are simply insulting. They wouldn't be there if the Good Book had had an enlightened editor. Love is the whole truth. It's the one word worth building your life around. And Christ is love's most endearing example. Love is all you need, as the Beatles said.

Sound familiar? It's easy to idealize love, and today we have a penchant for doing exactly that. Love *is* the first and great command — that's not a lie. But love is not simply an ideal — it's a practical reality that Christ makes most definite when he says we must love him with *all our strength.*

What he is not talking about is gathering one's strength and giving one's all for some feeling, some grand idea, some vision. What Christ asks us to do is give of ourselves in the touchable existence of the real world. He wants our muscles and tendons. For what? To love him.

The last thing we should do is buy into some kind of false spirituality. He's not asking us to invest our strength in religious things, in visions and ecstasy, in feelings and warm fuzzies. That's not it at all. There are no special "spiritual" categories into which he wants our strength deposited. A doctor can love God with all his strength just as fully as a preacher. A carpenter can give God all his might just as gloriously as a missionary.

A sculptor gives thanks in her work, just like a preacher. A lawyer glorifies God in the courtroom just as substantially as a Christian teacher in a classroom. No callings are omitted. A dairy farmer who holds church office serves God as fully in the milking parlor as the council room. Motherhood is a calling fully as God-glorifying as mission work. Nothing stands outside his reign and authority. He wants our strength in his world. Every inch of this world belongs to him.

— James Calvin Schaap, *Near Unto God*

Father, the world is yours. You have placed us in it and called us to the work of loving you. What more joyous task could you have set before us. Strengthen us that we might love more, that we might in our weakness be made strong to give you glory. Amen.

May 28

Turning to Jelly

"Create in me a pure heart, O God,
and renew a steadfast spirit within me.
Do not cast me from your presence
or take your Holy Spirit from me."
— Psalm 51:10-11

Christians are big on butterflies. What they don't realize is that the caterpillar undergoes complete dissolution within those chitin walls, turns to mush, undifferentiated slime, before its cells are rearranged into the new, flying creature it becomes.

The purpose of hibernation is entirely different from the purpose of death. Hibernation is a hedge against death. It is conservative. It saves the old life. No doubt the creatures who hibernate, hoarding their starches in their complex fat cells, are worth saving as they are.

But we are not, you and I. Our current mode of existence is imperfect, incomplete. You must feel it too, that straining against sloth, against the reptilian brainstem, that backward fall into inadequacy. I do not put this to you as a matter of morality. It is not a matter of being good; it is a matter of being perfect. Morality is at best only a stopgap; a snow fence; a sea wall. If we were perfectly fulfilling our destiny, morality would have no meaning, would be beside the point. For a helium atom, there is no such thing as morality.

But there are holes in us, great moth-eaten holes, and through them we are leaking away into oblivion. We are all less than we are capable of imagining — less wise, less true, less simple, less beautiful. And each of these imperfections is a fissure through which seep our strength and our hope. Don't try stopping those cracks with your moral practices — not your chastity, your temperance, your pacifism, your generosity. No matter how chaste, temperate, gentle, or generous you are, it will never be enough. Not enough to stop the holes where chaos sucks at your very substance. It's not just money you can't take with you to the grave; you can't take your virtues either. If all you have in mind is hibernation, then by all means tuck away the odd good deed to dig up again for a lean winter day. But hibernation does not end in metamorphosis. The same creature will crawl out of its hole at the end of the winter, only weaker and hungry. Butterflies do not eat at all inside the chrysalis. They simply turn to jelly. To be re-created demands at least that much.

— Virginia Stem Owens, *Wind River Winter*

Dear Lord, am I hibernating or cocoon-ing, awaiting metamorphosis? Help me not to settle for mere hibernation, but to wrap myself in the cocoon of your word, your promises. Help me to relax in trust within this cocoon, turn my will to jelly, so that you can re-create me anew! In Jesus' name. Amen.

May 29

ASKING ON THEIR BEHALF

"I pray for them.
I'm not praying for the God-rejecting world
But for those you gave me,
For they are yours by right."
—John 17:9, THE MESSAGE

Jesus' ministry with us is not finished when he speaks God's word and demonstrates God's presence. He continues to guide and shape our lives by his prayers of intercession on our behalf.

How do Jesus' prayers affect you? —Eugene H. Peterson, *Praying with Jesus*

What a difference it makes as I pray, Father, to know that Jesus is praying for me; that my prayers to you are surrounded by his prayers for me. That makes me want to pray more than ever in the name of Jesus. Amen.

May 30

TEMPLE OF THE SPIRIT

"Do you not know that your body is a temple of the Holy Spirit, who is in you, whom you have received from God? You are not your own; you were bought at a price. Therefore honor God with your body."
—1 Corinthians 6:19-20

Many thoughts and feelings tumble around in me as I think about this passage. Without studying any scholarly commentaries, I first thought that Paul was referring to keeping free from immoral sexual activities. And I still think he is. But I think he is also referring to other sins which make our bodies less than they were created to be, such as being overweight or physically out of shape.

I don't want to concentrate on trying to decide whether overeating or not exercising are sins. From one perspective, I think they are, if they separate us from God by becoming the focus of our lives, or if they lead to poor health which disables us with sickness so that we aren't able to do his will. Another way to think of excess fat and weak muscles is to regard them as "encumbrances" which prevent us from being our best for God.

Whichever it is, I think it's clear that my physical body is all I have with which to serve God while I am in this life. Out of love for him and gratitude for all he has done for me I want to do everything I know to keep healthy and free from illness.

When I compare my body to a building which was built for a rare and special guest (the Holy Spirit), I get an interesting picture of what I might look like from God's perspective when I let myself get out of shape.

"Out of shape" could mean I am overweight, bogged down with cholesterol and layers of fat on the internal organs or within muscle tissue, lungs wheezing along at minimum capacity, kidneys overworked with trying to flush out waste materials. Or it could mean that I catch every cold that comes along, get knocked off my feet regularly by the flu, and am chronically too tired to do anything but the minimum each day.

Either way, it's as if I am a building whose floors are never mopped or dusted, whose furniture is buried under mounds of garbage, whose plumbing is clogged with things not meant to be flushed down the drains! It's as if the air conditioner filters are never cleaned so that fresh air can circulate, as if mildew and mold are allowed to accumulate inside, making the atmosphere unhealthy.

If I am weak, sick, or cause my own premature death by not keeping my internal systems clean and efficient, then it seems to me that I am not "glorifying God in my body" as Paul suggests we should. By exercising and eating properly, I can "clean house" within my body and help keep it operating smoothly and efficiently. —Andrea Wells Miller, *BodyCare*

Dear Lord, I know that my body is a temple of your Holy Spirit within me, and I want to glorify you. I am so grateful to you for paying the price you paid for me. Help me to be willing to pay a price to honor you. As I learn to trust you with control of this part of my life, help me to begin to see what changes I can make to become more healthy. In Jesus' name. Amen.

May 31

PERFECTION

"Be perfect, therefore, as your heavenly father is perfect."
—Matthew 5:48

Nothing like an ultimate standard. The word "perfect" has gotten us into trouble for a long time in the Christian church. It has not only led us into excruciating self-examination and condemnation, but has given us an excuse for getting rid of anything in our midst that threatens the illusion of purity: the heretics, the witches, the worldly, those who walk funny or speak with a sibilance.

I lean toward another reading of perfect, meaning not freedom from error, but maturity. "Be adult as your heavenly father is adult." Not just "grown up" (as in "Oh, grow up!") but complete. Actually, I'm cheating a little. In this verse, the word for perfect is *teleios,* meaning "finished." In the context Jesus gives us, it refers to the capacity to think radically, to love enemies and bless those who curse us — being expansive enough (big, like Daddy) to occupy spaces we never dreamed we could fill.

Some of those larger spaces can seem rangy and full of risk.

1. to re-enter the human race. No more "we/they," using redemption as an excuse for separation or exclusion.

2. to openly acknowledge our own history, which includes the appalling history of the church. All the skeletons out of the closet.

3. to no longer have anything to prove, accepting at last the unprovability of faith, which makes it a pearl of even greater price

And that's first grade. Where do we go from there? I'm still in elementary school, but I'm acquainted with the syllabus. The courses, which are arduous, go something like this: Ambiguity, Compassion, Humor, Irony, and Imagination. There are no twelve-step programs to these.

—Shirley Nelson, address, Wheaton College, Colloquium

Abba... Amen.

JUNE

June 1

WHAT'S IN A NAME?

"Hallowed be thy name."
— Matthew 6:9b, KJV

Most of us become irritated with little name tags, but try to imagine an important meeting where no one knows anyone's names, where everyone is simply, "Sir" or "Madam" or "You at the end of the table." Doing business would be awful.

Even though today there are millions of Scotts or Theresas or Lees, names still personalize us. If you want to distance yourself from people you know, just forget their names. You want to make God impersonal, call him "the force."

When we call upon "Our Father in Heaven," we're defining a relationship in those very words. We're personalizing him — and the nature of the relationship which exists between us. That relationship is not vague or foggy or whimsical. What exists between us is defined by the name we use when we call upon God.

But it's not simple. Christ's addressing God as "our Father who art in Heaven" defines our relationship. God is as close as a loving parent, and yet as far as heaven away. With his name, we begin to consciously understand the Lord our God, we begin to know him consciously, as something very much "other than" ourselves, a being to be hallowed.

However — and this will come as no surprise — frequent repetition dulls our perception of what we're saying. When the name of God is repeated as if by rote, its meaning becomes empty. Habit dulls spiritual consciousness.

But when there's a crisis, something big happens. For the first time in years, we pray with a whole new knowledge of what "our Father in heaven" really means. The reality of God is impressed upon us, and even as we speak we think through what we're saying.

Here's the bottom line: if we enter our discourse with the Father with any less consciousness, any less attention to what we're doing than when we turn on our computers to begin our day's activity, we're not hallowing the name of God.

The complex that is "our Father in Heaven" is God. His name is not Scott or Theresa. His name is hallowed — and should be in both our prayers and our lives.
—James Calvin Schaap, *Near Unto God*

Our Father, as children we were taught to pray. We knelt, closed our eyes, and folded our hands. We came before you aware of who you were. The familiarity of godtalk has turned our senses dull. Make us children again. Amen.

June 2

Keeping in Touch

"But we will give ourselves continually to prayer."
—Acts 6:4, KJV

To work on a book is for me very much like the same thing as to pray. Both involve discipline. If the artist works only when he feels like it, he's not apt to build up much of a body of work. Inspiration far more often comes during the work than before it, because the largest part of the job of the artist is to listen to the work, and to go where it tells him to go. Ultimately, when you are writing, you stop thinking and write what you hear.

To pray is to listen also, to move through my own chattering to God, to that place where I can be silent and listen to what God has to say. But, if I pray only when I feel like it, God may not choose to speak. The greatest moments of prayer come in the midst of fumbling and faltering prayer, rather than the odd moment when one decides to try to turn to God.

We used to call my mother (usually collect) once a week; then, in her last years, several times a week, just to keep in touch. We, in our turn, like our children to keep in touch with us. If they never called, then they might be so far from our own busy lives that they might not even know if the phone number was changed.

A faltering analogy. But it is good for the children to keep in touch. It is good for all of us children to keep in touch with our Father.
—Madeleine L'Engle, *Walking on Water*

Heavenly Father, help us to keep in touch with you, that we may know your touch in our everyday lives. Amen.

June 3

FINDING FREEDOM

"We will all be changed, in a flash
in the blink of an eye."

"Caught up together in the clouds
to meet the Lord in the air."

"Where the spirit of the Lord is
there is freedom."
—1 Corinthians 15:51-52; 1 Thessalonians 4:17;
2 Corinthians 3:17; author's paraphrase

One of our natural human restrictions is that we are land bound, tied to *terra firma*. Human inventions such as submarines and space craft show our strenuous efforts to extend our boundaries. But they are at best artificial. We are still bipeds; we haven't grown fins or wings.

On holiday in the Bahamian island of Eleuthera (whose very name means freedom in Greek), I sampled what it might *feel* like to be free. It was snorkeling that gave me the dreamlike experience of floating on the surface, equipped only with face mask, breathing tube, and flippers. I experienced the release from gravity, the buoyancy of the clear, aquamarine salt water, the entry into another world lit with filtered light, feeling like one of the fish that swarmed unafraid in schools around me as I glided effortlessly above the corals and kelps and anemones on the ocean floor.

I realized that fish swim with the same kind of fluidity as birds fly. And I wanted to take that further step — to break through the skin of the sea and lift up, up into the sun's eye, to soar on the updrafts, to view from the height the flour-white sands hemming the land, the palms and casuarinas like green fringes around the rug of island, the water the color of a gemstone.

Such physical freedom, of fish, of birds, of snorkelers or hang gliders, reminds us of the deeper, more eternal freedoms that entice us toward heaven. What is your heart-dream of heaven? One of the things I long for is release not only from the body but from the earthy bondages of fear and guilt and fatigue and failure that chain both body and mind. I want metamorphosis. Like a pupa developing into a larva and then a flying insect, I yearn to grow toward heaven where my body shell will drop away like the empty skin of a dragonfly.   —Luci Shaw, *Horizons*

Father of Freedom, one of the things I long for is release not only from the body but from the earthy bondages of fear and guilt and fatigue and failure that chain both body and mind. I want metamorphosis. Like a pupa devel-

oping into a larva and then a flying insect, I yearn to grow toward heaven where my body shell will drop away like the empty skin of a dragonfly. Amen.

June 4

UNDERSTANDING JESUS

"Such large crowds gathered around him that he got into a boat and sat in it, while all the people stood on the shore. Then he told them many things in parables.... 'He who has ears, let him hear.'"
—Matthew 13:2-3, 9

Jesus never lectured; he told stories. And the stories he told were narratives readily understandable in the agrarian culture in which he lived. Yet his audiences frequently went away puzzled. They could not make the connections between his stories and their lives. Even his disciples asked for explanations. This should cause the modern reader of Scripture, who lives in a largely urban world, to read with caution. One dwelling in the abstraction of the supermarket where all evidence that one's meat ever lived is obscured by specialty cuts and plastic wrap should expect difficulty comprehending the complexity of relationships contained in a story about a sower or a mustard seed. Too often modern readers proceed arrogantly assuming the passage of time has given them access to wisdom. It is not so.

Wendell Berry has written, "Living in our speech, though no longer in our consciousness, is an ancient system of analogies that clarifies a series of mutually defining and sustaining unities: of farmer and field, of husband and wife, of the world and God. The language of both our literature and of our everyday speech is full of allusions to this expansive metaphor of farming and marriage and worship." A recovery of this system of analogies, an ability to live within them, whether one lives in the city or the country, is necessary to an understanding of the teachings of Jesus. —John Leax

Lord Jesus, we have heard the words of your stories. Strip us of our arrogant surety. Grant us humility to understand your mystery. Allow us to be as little children hearing for the first time a story of great wonder. Let us squeal with delight at your word. Amen.

June 5

CRUSHED HOPES

> "'They will be mine,' says the Lord Almighty, 'in the day when I make up my treasured possession. I will spare them, just as in compassion a man spares his son who serves him. And you will again see the distinction between the righteous and the wicked, between those who serve God and those who do not.'" —Malachi 3:17–18

Malachi is the last Old Testament voice, and his book serves as a good prelude to the next four hundred years of biblical silence. From the Israelites' point of view, those four centuries could be termed "the era of lowered expectations." They had returned to the land, but that land remained a backwater province under the domination of Persia (then Greece, then Rome — imperial armies took turns tramping through Israel). The grand future of triumph and world peace described by the prophets seemed a distant pipe dream. Even the restored temple caused stabs of nostalgic pain: It hardly rivaled Solomon's majestic building, and no one had seen God's glory descend on this new temple as it had in Solomon's day.

A general malaise set in among the Jews, a low-grade disappointment with God that showed in their complaints and also in their actions. They were not "big" sinners like the people before the Exile, who had practiced child sacrifice and brought idols into the temple. People in Malachi's time went through the motions of their religion, but they had lost contact with the God whom the religion was all about.

Malachi is written in the form of a dialogue, with the "children" of Israel bringing their grievances to God, the Father. They were questioning God's love and his fairness. One gripe bothered them more than any: "It is futile to serve God. What did we gain by carrying out his requirements?" Following God had not brought the anticipated reward.

In reply, Malachi calls his people to rise above their selfishness and to trust the God of the covenant; he has not abandoned his treasured possession. "Test me," says God, "and see if I will not throw open the floodgates of heaven and pour out so much blessing that you will not have room enough for it."

At least some of Malachi's message took hold. During the next four hundred years, reform movements like the Pharisees became increasingly devoted to keeping the Law. Unfortunately, many of them would cling fiercely to that Law even when Jesus, the "messenger of the covenant" prophesied by Malachi, brought a new message of forgiveness and grace.

—Philip Yancey, *A Guided Tour of the Bible*

Forgive me, O Lord, when I focus on whether you have done enough for me, when I wonder what I gain by serving you. Help me to rise above my own selfishness, as Malachi entreated the Israelites, and to trust you more. In Jesus' name. Amen.

June 6

WITNESS

> "If God hadn't been for us
> —all together now, Israel, sing out!—
> If God hadn't been for us
> when everyone went against us,
> We would have been swallowed alive
> by their violent anger."
>
> —Psalm 124:1-3, THE MESSAGE

The proper work for the Christian is witness, not apology, and Psalm 124 is an excellent model. It does not argue God's help; it does not explain God's help; it is a testimony of God's help in the form of a song. The song is so vigorous, so confident, so bursting with what can only be called reality, that it fundamentally changes our approach and our questions.

No longer does it seem of the highest priority to ask, "Why did this happen to me? Why do I feel left in the lurch?" Instead we ask, "How does it happen that there are people who sing with such confidence, 'God is our help'?" The psalm is data that must be accounted for and the data are so solid, so vital, have so much more substance and are so much more interesting than the other things we hear through the day that it must be dealt with before we can go back to the whimpering complaints.

The witness is vivid and contagious. One person announces the theme, and everyone joins in. God's help is not a private experience; it is a corporate reality—not an exception that occurs among isolated strangers, but the norm among the people of God.

—Eugene H. Peterson, *A Long Obedience in the Same Direction*

Refocus my questions, O Lord, toward the confidence of those who sang Psalm 124. Help me to trust that your hand is at work in the pain of my situation, and to allow my own confidence that you are there to blossom and grow in my soul. In Jesus' name. Amen.

June 7

BODY PRAYER

"But if from there you seek the Lord your God, you will find him if you look for him with all your heart and with all your soul."
—Deuteronomy 4:29

A striking feature of worship in the Bible is that people gathered in what we could only call a "holy expectancy." They believed they would actually hear the *Kol Yahweh,* the voice of God. When Moses went into the Tabernacle, he knew he was entering the presence of God. The same was true of the early church. It was not surprising to them that the building in which they met shook with the power of God. It had happened before (Acts 2:2, 4:31). When some dropped dead and others were raised from the dead by the word of the Lord, the people knew that God was in their midst (Acts 5:1–11, 9:36–43, 20:7–10). As those early believers gathered they were keenly aware that the veil had been ripped in two, and, like Moses and Aaron, they were entering the Holy of Holies. No intermediaries were needed. They were coming into the awful, glorious, gracious presence of the living God. They gathered with anticipation, knowing that Christ was present among them and would teach them and touch them with his living power.

How do we cultivate this holy expectancy? It begins in us as we enter the Shekinah of the heart. While living out the demands of our day, we are filled with inward worship and adoration. We work and play and eat and sleep, yet we are listening, ever listening, to our Teacher. The writings of Frank Laubach are filled with this sense of living under the shadow of the Almighty. "Of all today's miracles," he writes in *Learning the Vocabulary of God,* "the greatest is this: to know that I find Thee best when I work listening.... Thank Thee, too, that the habit of constant conversation grows easier each day. I really do believe *all* thought can be conversations with Thee."

—Richard J. Foster, *Celebration of Discipline*

I pray today with my head, Lord, lifting it heavenward in adoration.
I pray today with my eyes, Lord, looking for the things that are not seen.
I pray today with my hands, Lord, raising them in jubilant praise.
I pray today with my knees, Lord, bowing in submission and contrition.
I pray today with my feet, Lord, working with all my might.
May you be pleased with my prayer.
Amen.

—Richard J. Foster, in *Prayers from the Heart*

June 8

A Message from God

"I can do everything through him who gives me strength."
—Philippians 4:13

But he said to me, "My grace is sufficient for you, for my power is made perfect in weakness." —2 Corinthians 12:9a

Most of the problems in intimate relationships seem to stem from the fear of pain and failure. People often see pain only as "the enemy" and in their impatience and fear flee from it in any way possible — even over the bodies of their loved ones. But many of us have learned... that pain can be the doorway to intimacy and to personal wisdom and a deeper kind of strength that comes from somewhere beyond us and our situation.

I was told that a mature person will not run from necessary emotional pain, but will stand in it and ask what its message is. Many of us feel that whatever its source, pain virtually always has a message from God about something we need to learn or attend to in our lives. A person with this belief will have a very different attitude toward the pain in an intimate relationship than one who is trying to escape pain at any cost. A wise person uses pain as a farmer uses organic fertilizer, to support increased growth. And this takes time. —J. Keith Miller, *Compelled to Control*

Dear Lord, help me to face whatever pain I encounter in my relationships. Give me grace and courage to admit I am wrong and don't have the strength and "answers" I pretend to. And Lord, give me the ability to offer forgiveness to others gracefully. And as I admit my powerlessness to "fix" everything for them, help me to release those close to me from my critical fix-them focus, to concentrate on changing my own life, and to open myself to your kind of patience, and to the possibility of depending on your strength to do everything I need to do. In Jesus' name. Amen.

June 9

Mary of Bethany

"When the Jews who had been with Mary in the house, comforting her, noticed how quickly she got up and went out, they followed her, supposing she was going to the tomb to mourn there." —John 11:31

The impractical, impulsive side of Mary of Bethany's nature shows when her brother Lazarus dies and the mourning party from Jerusalem arrives at the sisters' home. Martha, hearing that Jesus is approaching, slips out of the house to warn him that potential enemies are there. But Mary thoughtlessly rushes out of the house to meet him, not stopping to consider the consequences for her Lord.

Some who witness the miracle hurry back to the religious officials in Jerusalem and report that this man is a worse threat than they had heretofore imagined. The marvel in Bethany sets in motion the plans to arrest Jesus.

However, not all of the Jerusalem Jews who witness the raising of Lazarus react negatively. This unmistakable sign of Jesus' divine power, in fact, convinces some of them that he is the Messiah. *Mary's impetuous rush to see Jesus was the catalyst that eventually brought them to belief.*
—Virginia Stem Owens, *Daughters of Eve*

Lord, let my impulsive, impractical side about my relationship with you be a catalyst that may convince someone else to believe in you. Help me let whatever joy and excitement you bring into my life show! In Jesus' name. Amen.

June 10

Gingerbread

"Do your best to present yourself to God as one approved, a workman who does not need to be ashamed and who correctly handles the word of truth."
—2 Timothy 2:15

On one of my visits back to Shiloh hilltop in the early sixties, I brought along my five-year-old daughter. Standing in the front hall of Shiloh Proper, gazing up the staircase that led its five flights to Jerusalem Turret, she amazed me by exclaiming, "I like this place! Why don't we live here?" She knew nothing of the significance of the building, or that those were the stairs her grandmother had once washed down on winter mornings. Maybe she was enchanted by the smell of gingerbread, for the hall was full of it. It floated up from the kitchen below, but for me it came charging straight out of the past, with all the appeal and challenge Shiloh represented, and along with that its danger.

More than anything else as I have studied the movement I have seen a body of people struggling with the same old things that all of us have trouble keeping straight. I am amazed by the heap of confusions that can pile up in one small corner of history—the blurred lines between liberty and responsibility, between authority and tyranny, between goodness and self-righteousness, between righteousness and being right, between faith and piety, obedience and mindlessness, passion and sentiment, heroism and bravado, self-sacrifice and self-destruction. In the cracks of the differences our most threatening perils hide.

Shiloh longed for human qualities that seem less and less common in the world — courage, endurance, personal discipline, ardor, and fire. It trained itself in the hardship of lonely heroism. Their leader taught them that it is hard to be a Christian and do it right, and so it is. But the lure of the gingerbread is this — the appeal of what purports to be a justified hardship. —Shirley Nelson, *Fair, Clear and Terrible*

Oh, God my Shepherd: Sometimes it seems that the harder I try to be Christlike, the more mistakes I make. Give me a sound mind, clear vision, and a spirit of discernment on this adventurous climb. Amen.

June 11

Who Dwelleth on High and Beholdeth the Things of the Earth

"Who is like unto the Lord our God, who dwelleth on high, who humbleth himself to behold the things that are in heaven, and in the earth!"
—Psalm 113:5-6, KJV

The Lord's Prayer begins with these words: "Our Father who art in heaven." In the very first words we bring to God in this model prayer, we establish a distance. We don't say, "Our Father who dwells here in me," even though that is also true. We bring him our humility by looking above where he reigns.

That God, Creator and King of our world, actually comes to live in our individual hearts *is* the good news of the gospel. That a Being of such loftiness would slum with us is the miraculous testimony of his love. But he wants to be reverenced, nonetheless. And as politically incorrect as this phrase is in contemporary society, with respect to God Almighty, *we need to know our place.*

And what is our place? We are the receivers of his grace. He comes to us. He entered the garden after Adam and Eve fell. In Christ, he laid himself down in a manger for us. At Pentecost, he sent his Spirit. We don't grab grace. He gives it. Our place is to receive it. It comes from him, from above. For he is and always will be *above* us. Understand that and we *know our place.*

In fact, only when we understand that are we capable of bringing him our love can we become not only recipients, but actors in the process. "Unto thee O Lord, do I lift up my soul," says the Psalmist (25:1). We bring our lives before him, only after we know his grace has come into our lives. Knowing God is knowing he *first* loved us.

Efforts to bring God down to our level — whether they occur in the language we use to him or of him, the songs we sing, or the images and the trinkets we create seemingly to remind us of his grace — bring us only his contempt.

We come near him only by grace, by his gift, by his coming to us. There's no room for our pushiness or arrogance or manipulation in that confession. What he wants is our humility.

—James Calvin Schaap, *Near Unto God*

We are graduates of assertiveness training, Lord. We call on you and expect results. Having swallowed possibility thinking, we are swollen with our own importance. But there is none other like you. You dwell on high. We cannot manipulate you for our ends. Forgive us for trying. Amen.

June 12

LIKE LITTLE CHILDREN

"And he said: 'I tell you the truth, unless you change and become like little children, you will never enter into the kingdom of heaven.'"
—Matthew 18:3

If roads went nowhere
and rain fell dry,
if birds crawled low
and worms flew high,
if faces were flat
and the midday sky
looked always dark
and the sun shone square,
if beauty were costly
and God unfair,
if densest earth
were as thin as air,
if clocks went backwards
and grass grew blue
and lions were happiest
in the zoo

and five were the sum
of two and two
would you be me?
Might I be you?

How would we think
if all sprouts grew down
and the sea churned pink
and the clouds turned brown
and God's face was fixed
in an awful frown?
I'm thankful, I'm thankful
(are you too?)
that grass is green
and sky is blue
and the sun is round
and fact is true
and we can count on
gravity,
and God is good
and beauty free,
and, for the sake of
our sanity,
that you are you
and I am me.

I wrote this child's poem to enflesh in whimsical verse something philosopher Duns Scotus called *haeccitas,* or "this-ness," our intuition that every individual person or thing has its own unique essence and importance. To make this distinctiveness more striking I tried to imagine things in opposite terms from our usual perceptions of them, making my descriptions so outrageous we'd laugh (we all know that grass doesn't "grow blue" and that lions aren't "happiest in the zoo") and in our laughter we might gain something.

C. S. Lewis embodied some pretty hefty theology in his captivating tales *The Chronicles of Narnia,* but families read them for the pure enjoyment. Jesus wanted us to become as free and happy as small children. Again and again he told truth in stories that may have seemed like mere entertainment (in our modern English translations we miss much of Jesus' ironic humor). Wisdom doesn't have to be dour and stodgy; we profit from the enjoyment of play as much as from hard work.

—Luci Shaw, *Horizons*

I delight, O Lord, in the world that you have made. I think you for its order, its beauty, and its sheer delightfulness. I thank you for the reversal you require — that we become like children. We pray that we might go open-eyed, able to see at every moment the good things that you have made. Amen.

June 13

BELIEVING IN THE UNBELIEVABLE

"A new commandment give I unto you, that ye love one another, as I have loved you, that ye also love one another." —John 13:34, KJV

To love one another as Jesus loved us. As Christ loves us. Can we do it? Can we love one another as Christ loves us? We have to. It isn't going to be any easier than trying to understand the Ascension, or the coming of the Spirit in tongues of flame at Pentecost.

God expects us to believe in the — not so much the unbelievable as in the unprovable, that which leads us into the glorious love of God.

Believing in the unbelievable is not believing in human constructs, like *Star Wars,* but believing in God's love, which surrounds us in all we do and at all times unless we reject it, or limit it. Even then, I suspect, it is still all around us, but we have blinded ourselves to it. The Holy Spirit has come to help us to understand — the Comforter Jesus promised to send to us.

So must we. We must want to be changed by Jesus' marvelous act of loving, Christ willing to be Jesus, to live for us, to show us how to be human, to die for us, to rise from the grave for us, to ascend into heaven for us, to send us the Holy Spirit — and all for love. How splendid! It is so splendid that it cannot be understood by our finite minds alone; it cannot be understood literally. Literalism is death to Christianity, despite the protests of the fundalits, and we are left with Jesus' feet vanishing up into the air. The story is far, far greater than that. It is the truth we live by. It is glory! —Madeleine L'Engle, *Penguins and Golden Calves*

Change us radically, O Lord, that we may offer our altered love on your altar of love. Amen.

June 14

C. S. LEWIS ON PRAYER

"Likewise the Spirit helps us in our weakness; for we do not know how to pray as we ought, but the Spirit himself intercedes for us with sighs too deep for words." —Romans 8:26, RSV

The Mere Christian (MC) can pray anywhere, anytime, in any position. That seems so obvious, but it bears repeating many times. And if a person follows the advice, then one will find himself or herself praying in the most surprising places.

Some prayers, ready-made prayers, have words, and the petitions in these prayers may be festooned with spiritual ornaments of one's own making; the way one festoons a Christmas tree; the way a daydream festoons an actual event; a drawing festoons a letter; a suit, a man; a rug, a floor; a tablecloth, a dinner table.

Other prayers have no words. They consist in affections of the soul; that is to say, they are acts of love, not words; the lover communing with the beloved. In a manner of speaking, they're festoons of the soul; adornments without the material things adorned. And it's but a hop, skip, and jump from adornment such as this to adoration.

Does prayer work? That's the powerful question all prayerful practitioners must ask themselves virtually every time they pray. When Jesus prayed for others, lepers leaped, paralytics pranced, the possessed smiled and made new friends, the newly dead arose from their cold sleep and asked for a nice warm meal. But when he prayed for himself, nothing happened. Does prayer work?

As in the natural life, so in the spiritual life, a little rain must fall. Things aren't better when one feels good about them; and they're not necessarily worse when one feels bad about them. And it's certainly all right if one has no feelings one way or the other.

The classical terminology of prayer denominates these ups and downs as consolation and desolation. And the spiritual masters have consistently said — and our spiritual experience has consistently proven to be true — that the one follows the other as night follows the day, and day follows the night.

But what about the volcanoes and tornados? Can irruptions and conniptions be considered a good for the geological part of creation and, at the same time and under the same aspect, as a devastating evil for that part of humankind who got caught camping out in the wrong place? Lewis hasn't a prayerful answer to that, nor indeed have the masters and mistresses of prayer before him.

Last of all, Lewis turns our minds to distraction in prayer, and distinguishes four kinds. There's no prayer without it if the one praying is of humankind. It's a natural flaw in a supernatural act, a brownish vein in the whitest cup, which shows that it's been used by humans and has suffered in the process. When all is said and done, temptation was, and is, a deadly game.

One good thing about festoonery in prayer is that it's a mechanism, albeit a clumsy one, for turning the inevitable distractions in a highly active intellect and imagination like Lewis's into the very fabric of prayer itself.

Time was, in the history of prayer, when distractions were considered imperfections. Stories abound in ascetical literature about holy people being bedeviled by distractions during time of meditation. Such distractions inevitably had something to do with the problems they faced in everyday life. These men and women retaliated by ignoring such solutions as were presented during the meditation time. A noble strategy perhaps, but how many tactics in the turbulent history of the church have come a cropper because solutions were presented, willy-nilly, during prayer!

In fact, Lewis's notion of festoonery just might make sense to contemporary western society when it comes to pray. The distractions are the prayer, and the pray-er can offer these distractions to the Lord.

—William Griffin, *C. S. Lewis: Spirituality for Mere Christians*

Holy Spirit, as I stumble and mumble through my prayers, festooning them with all my innermost longings, not knowing how to pray as I ought, it is wonderful to know that you intercede for me with those deep sighs beyond words. Thank you! Amen.

June 15

LET NOT MAN PUT ASUNDER

"In the original creation, God made male and female to be together. Because of this, a man leaves father and mother, and in marriage he becomes one flesh with a woman — no longer two individuals, but forming a new unity. Because God created this organic union of the two sexes, no one should desecrate his art by cutting them apart."

—Mark 10:6-9, THE MESSAGE

Committed by command and habit to fidelity
I'm snug in the double bed and board of marriage:
   spontaneity's built-in
   to the covenantal dance
   everyday routines arranged
   by the floor plan of the manse.

This unlikely fissiparous alliance
embraces and releases daily surprises.
   The ego strength we'd carefully hoarded
   in certain safe-deposit boxes
   we've now dispersed, unlamented,
   in dozens of delicate paradoxes.

A thousand domestic intimacies are straw
for making bricks resistant to erosion:

with such uncomely stuff we've built
our lives on ordinary sod
and grow, finally, old. My love is
not a goddess nor I a god.

"Asunder" is the one unpronounceable word in the world
of the wed, one flesh the mortal miracle.
What started out quite tentatively
with clumsy scrawls in a billet doux
has now become the intricacy
of bold marriage's pas de deux.

—Eugene H. Peterson, *Christianity Today*, October 1977

Lord, teach us in the world of the wed how to strengthen our commitment to each other with erosion-resistant bricks made from the "straws" of the thousands of domestic intimacies we experience. Guide us all to pray for the Sacrament of Marriage, that each marriage may be guided, strengthened, healed, and blessed by your love and grace. Amen.

June 16

MAKING A LIFE THAT COUNTS

"Take therefore no thought for the morrow: for the morrow shall take thought for the things of itself. Sufficient unto the day is the evil thereof." —Matthew 6:34, KJV

While hoeing his garden St. Francis was approached by a villager who had his own idea about how a saint should spend his time. The villager demanded of Francis, "What would you be doing if you knew the Lord would return this afternoon?" Francis replied, "I would be hoeing my garden." This I think is the meaning of "Take therefore no thought for the morrow: for the morrow shall take thought for the things of itself." Care is implied, not carelessness. If the present is lived in Christ, the Creator of this world, we will do nothing to limit the possibilities of the future.

This is not simplistic; this is the meaning of the verb to be; this is the work of God.

At twenty, filled with religious jargon and the assurance of salvation, I knew all the answers. I could quote Scripture in response to any question. I believed in Christ, born of the Virgin, crucified, buried, resurrected, and coming again. I still do. But as the years pass, I realize these things I affirm are far more mysterious and complex than I ever imagined them being. The hope of the Second Coming and a future in Heaven is just that, a hope, something unseen. What I have is the present here on earth. This present is the life I've been given to live. It's my concern and my only concern. My work is to be a husband and father, to make a few poems as well as I can make them, and most of all, by husbanding, fathering, and craft, to make a life where Christ can meet himself.

I like this life. I make my way through it learning its meaning as I go.
— John Leax, *Grace Is Where I Live*

Lord, thank you for this life, for what I am learning though you about its meaning. Guide me in my relationships with family and friends and in my work to make my life one where you can meet yourself. Guide me in reconciling the things that trouble me, by taking action if it is my responsibility, and by withdrawing from and relinquishing what belongs to someone else. In Jesus' name. Amen.

June 17

CUMBER

"The Lord is my shepherd; I shall not want. He maketh me to lie down in green pastures." —Psalm 23:1-2, KJV

A Psalm of Midlife

Christian simplicity... liberates us from what William Penn called "cumber." —Richard Foster

Cumber is my Lord: it's more than I want.
It maketh me to carry in from the station wagon: it maketh me to carry out to the curb.
It distresseth my soul: it leadeth me in the paths of acquisitiveness for Wall Street's sake.
Yea, though I walk through the valley of forgetfulness, I know no peace: my clock and my calendar, they remind me.
It prepareth a caloric table before me in the presence of mine colleague: it hath put a mortgage on my head, my budget runneth over.
Surely lender and tax-collector shall follow me all the days of my life, and I shall make monthly payments forever.
— Robert Siegel

Deliver me, O Lord, from my wants. Free me from the encumbrances of my false needs, and teach me to trust in your goodness and love. Amen.

June 18

NOT BY BREAD ALONE

"It is written: 'Man does not live on bread alone, but on every word that comes from the mouth of God.'" —Matthew 4:4

One weekend I attended a conference at which my husband, Keith, spoke. He was talking about how we might begin to recognize things in our lives that are more important to us than trying to live the way God wants us to. He asked, "What thoughts fill your mind when it's free, when it doesn't have to be busy thinking about something you're doing?"

At first, I couldn't think of anything, but then it hit me. I spend most of my free mental time thinking about food! This was true during all my previous attempts to lose weight, and even when I wasn't particularly trying to lose. I thought about what I could eat, what I wasn't going to eat, what I wished I could eat, what I didn't like to eat, what I had just eaten, what I was going to eat next.

After I focused on this startling discovery, my next thought was, "What does that mean?"

Keith suggested to us that these things may be perfectly good things in themselves — like vocation, health, food, our mates, or our children. But they might also be what we worship instead of God because after all, worship can be defined as freely giving our primary attention to something when we could choose to concentrate on anything. He also said that this can be compared to worshiping "idols."

I didn't like what I had discovered, but I felt he was right. For much of my life, I have thought a lot more about food than I have thought about God.

If we want to begin to change and to move closer to God, the next step, according to Keith, is to be honest with God by telling him, "God, I don't want you most in my life after all. What I want most is this thing I think about all the time. I'd *like* to want you most, but I can't seem to do it right now. So I ask you to come into my life and help me put that thing aside, and to want you most of all."

Boy, for some reason saying that prayer was hard for me! I didn't *want* to stop thinking about food. It was fun, it was a habit, and it didn't seem like such a bad thing to think about. And I thought I *needed* to think about it.... To keep tabs on it so I could lose weight.

But then I realized something else. Even though I believed I had to think about food all the time so I could keep my weight down, I still didn't seem able to keep it down. Hmmmmm. Maybe I *did* need to change my attitude.

So in the next few days I decided to give it a sincere try. I prayed, "Lord, I've just seen how much I worship food, and not you. I'm afraid to ask you this, but, just the same, would you come into my life and help me stop thinking about it all the time and to learn to think more about you?" After I prayed, I wondered what would happen next.

At first, the only difference I felt was that I was now *very aware* of how much I thought about food. I'd be sitting in the car at a traffic light and catch myself — "Oops, there I am again, imagining eating a big cheesy pizza!" just because I saw the pizza place across the street. I couldn't *believe* how many times I caught myself doing things like that!

But as the weeks went by I began to relax about food. I found I could go through a whole morning and be surprised that it was lunchtime and I hadn't even given a thought about what to eat.

There have been times during my study of nutrition when I have spent a lot of time planning menus, thinking about making healthy changes in the way I cook, and reading labels in the grocery store. But this doesn't feel like the old daydreams of forbidden foods that I used to have all the time.

I thought about the verse in Matthew: "Man does not live on bread alone..." And I realized that, for me, the best way to begin to take the emphasis of my thoughts off of food is to concentrate on something I need more — a relationship with Jesus Christ and a knowledge of his will for my life.
— Andrea Wells Miller, *BodyCare*

Dear Lord, you know how much I like to think about food. Even though food is meant to be fuel for my body, I have managed to turn it into a full-time entertainment enterprise for my own benefit. Help me to stop misusing food in this way and to turn to you. Thank you that there are times when I realize I haven't had these recurring thoughts. Let me begin to learn how to love other people, to study your Word, and to take care of my health in a way that is wholesome and good. In Jesus' name. Amen.

June 19

MOLECULES AND MINDFULNESS

"I have been crucified with Christ and I no longer live, but Christ lives in me. The life I live in the body, I live by faith in the Son of God, who loved me and gave himself for me." —Galatians 2:20

My dog died the other morning on the floor beside the bed. As the last of his mortal breath rattled his throat and his eyes glazed over like tough gelatin, I knew that what he had been wasn't there any more. A corpse lay beside the bed, something that once had been a dog but now was only short-hand, an abbreviation, a sign with "dog" printed on it, growing stiff as a cipher. My dog was — is — more than I know, more than all the coded engrams for him my brain has collected over ten years' time. There were, for example, all those hours — days, even — when I was not particularly conscious of him, when I did not, could not pay attention. He caught my wandering awareness from time to time with a deep, disgusted sigh and a desultory flop of his tail. Did my attention call him into being, or at least into *more* being? Is that why he so often demanded it? Was he non-existent when I wasn't looking? These are precisely the questions physicists ask themselves today about bits of matter smaller than a medium-sized mammalian. And the answer has something to do with C. S. Lewis's contention that our dogs will be "raised" in us as we are raised in Christ.

Certainly my dog had being as molecular movement, just as I do. But as another writer has pointed out, "molecular movement is not sound; molecular movement is not light. The vibrational effects — or whatever we wish to call them — are interpreted by *us* as sound and light. Could we see the waves or vibrations, *per se,* we would not see redness or blueness, loudness or music. Yet when cells in our brains begin to be shaken up in certain ways light and sound enter our minds."

It is at this point that phenomena are conceived. Or, as Ruskin put it, "Let there be light, is as much, when you understand it, the ordering of intelligence as the ordering of vision."

So the answer is yes. As a phenomenal dog he did depend on my attention. Or on the attention of the cat that was always pestering his ears and tail. Or perhaps, in some dim way, he depended on himself. Dogs are surely not as self-conscious as we, but they know enough to stage a little drama of their own to distract us from time to time.

Still, it is ourselves — alert, aware, attentive — who are the universe knowing itself, perceiving the patterns, imagining ourselves bacterial chromosomes or organic compounds, building the steely structures of Bach, finding the suburbs rasping the shape of beauty in our eye. And we are the ones who perceive the evaporation of consciousness in death and yet decide, in some place undiscoverable by spatial coordinates, to believe beyond the brain in the implication of consciousness.

St. Paul, in that uncanny way saints as well as scientists have of staging possibilities before us, promised an interpenetration of consciousness, a participation in divine life. We live in Christ; he lives in us. The consciousness that upholds us in being, that attends us into being, that conceptualizes all the "levels, domains, and aspects" of the universe simultaneously, will expand, open its arms, and ask us to dance.

—Virginia Stem Owens, *God Spy*

Help me, O Lord, to say "YES!" as you ask me to dance and lead me more fully to participate in divine life, with you as my partner. Awaken my senses to deeper awareness of your consciousness within me in the everyday events of my life. In Jesus' name. Amen.

June 20

A GOD WITH SKIN

"And surely I am with you always, to the very end of the age."
—Matthew 28:20

It's the ache of being alone. All of us feel it sooner or later. For the unmarried it's now, every day, every night. For couples, it's an inevitable and unwelcome prospect; unless separation comes through instantaneous death for both at once, they must anticipate that splitting of the "one flesh" in which one partner exits, moving away from the other in space and time. The seam of marriage is unraveled by death or, even more unhappily, divorce.

After the numbing paralysis of bereavement I tried all the ploys recommended to widows — "develop new interests," "keep busy," "reach out to others in need," "give yourself time," "pamper yourself," "just rest in the Lord." But the emptiness, the aloneness refused easy answers; it had to be lived through.

But it was during that time that I felt, more than in any other crisis time in my life, the need to know experientially that my God is personal. It wasn't hard for me to recognize the power of God in creation, to see the evidences of his handiwork in nature — the seasons, the earth textures, the colors of flowers and plumage and sunsets, the three-dimensional flow of earth-life before me, like a living mural. But I wanted a God "with skin."

And then I held in my arms my first grandson. And the squirm and squall of the baby reminded me that I did, indeed, have a God "with skin." In Mary's womb God had formed himself into a baby much like little Jack, who sucked and slept and grew muscles and got tired and loved his friends.

I am a friend of Jesus. I *have* a God with skin and a lover who stays with me night and day; my faith in him and his closeness may move the mountain of loneliness.
—Luci Shaw, *Horizons*

Jesus, lover of my soul, your constant presence has moved the mountain of my loneliness. Where once the crags of isolation cast their cold shadows, your light abounds and a pleasant meadow blossoms at your word. For this I give you thanks and adoration. Amen.

June 21

THY VISITATION HATH PRESERVED

"Thou hast granted me life and favor, and thy visitation hath preserved my spirit."
—Job 10:12, KJV

Although first impressions can sometimes be surprisingly accurate, they are never completely accurate. Perhaps a white shirt and tie say as much about who we are as do pierced body parts, but what's behind the physical image—that which we see immediately—is likely a great deal more than can be read in a tattoo, a diamond broach, or a black turtleneck.

We are *more* than our bodies. "She gave up the ghost" is an old way of avoiding the word "death," but it's implication isn't inaccurate. When we die, something of us, our spirit, leaves our body behind like snake skin. All of us have this *spirit,* this breath of life. If we say someone "has spirit," we usually mean they've got get-up-and-go.

The two words "spirit" and "soul" are used very similarly, even in the Bible. When the Psalmist cries out, "O Lord, thou hast delivered my soul from death" (116:8), he's referring, pure and simple, to his life. However, at times the word "soul" is used to mean one's spiritual existence. "My soul thirsteth for God, the living God" has little to do with a dry throat and everything to do with a parched spirituality.

Scripture doesn't distinguish between our life and our spirit. In God's word our physical and spiritual existences are one. God formed humanity from the dust of the earth, but humanity came alive only when he breathed his breath into a set of lungs he'd already fashioned. *Soul* or *spirit* doesn't have much existence without a self, a person.

This soul or spirit isn't disposable. We can make it dirty ourselves, but we can't take it off like a dirty sweatshirt. Our souls live on long after we've shucked our physical selves.

Whatever it is, however it looks, and wherever it abides in our bodies, we know this—God keeps an eye on it, on all of our souls. This is Job's confession: "Thou hast granted me life and favor, and thy visitation hath preserved my spirit." God *visits* our spirits, not simply as if he were observing tea time. That's not exactly the meaning here. He's *always* there, watching, guiding, directing. He's in charge. He's supervising.

One can, without too much problem, seriously grieve the Holy Spirit in rejecting God's supervision of our souls and spirits; or one can choose to work with him. There is that much freedom. But whatever we choose, he's there, watching and waiting. —James Calvin Schaap, *Near Unto God*

Thank you, Lord, for making me a free creature. By your grace I choose to love you. Be in me. Supervise my every thought and deed. Amen.

June 22

RESPONSE, NOT CAUSE

"Then the Lord spoke to Job out of the storm: 'Brace yourself like a man; I will question you, and you shall answer me. Would you discredit my justice? Would you condemn me to justify yourself? Do you have an arm like God's and can your voice thunder like his?'"

—Job 40:6–9

Although God's speech resolved Job's questions, it may not resolve ours. (Looking back, we may have trouble understanding why Job felt so satisfied with a seemingly evasive answer, but, then, we didn't hear God speak out of a whirlwind either.) In the end, it was God's presence that filled the void. But what lessons apply to the rest of us, those of us who did not have the privilege of hearing God's speech in person?

In my view the book of Job reinforces the pattern followed by Jesus in Luke 13 and John 9. Suffering involves two main issues: (1) *cause*— Why am I suffering? Who did it? — and (2) *response*. By instinct, most of us want to figure out the cause of our pain before we decide how to respond. But God does not allow Job that option. He deflects attention from the issue of cause to the issue of Job's response.

It's as if God has walled off two areas of responsibility. He fully accepts responsibility for running the universe, with all its attendant problems. To someone like Job, who focuses on those problems, God has one word of advice: "Stop your whining. You have no idea what you're talking about." Or, as Frederick Buechner puts it, "God doesn't explain. He explodes. He asks Job who he thinks he is anyway. He says that to try to explain the kind of things Job wants explained would be like trying to explain Einstein to a little-neck clam.... God doesn't reveal his grand design. He reveals himself."

As for Job, he had only one thing to worry about: his response. God never explained the origin of Job's suffering, but rather moved the focus to the future. Once the tragedy has happened — *now what* will you do? Casting about for blame would get him nowhere; he needed to exercise responsibility in his response, the one area he, and not God, had control over.

This biblical pattern is so consistent that I must conclude the important issue facing Christians who suffer is not "Is God responsible?" but "How should I react now that this terrible thing has happened?"

—Philip Yancey, *Where Is God When It Hurts?*

Whenever life's tragedies happen, O Lord, help me remember to ask the forward-looking question, "What will I do now?" Keep me mindful of what is your responsibility and what is mine: You handle the universe, I handle my response. In Jesus' name. Amen.

June 23

THE SPIRITUAL DIRECTOR

> "For this reason, since the day we heard about you, we have not stopped praying for you and asking God to fill you with the knowledge of his will through all spiritual wisdom and understanding."
>
> —Colossians 1:9

In the Middle Ages not even the greatest saints attempted the depths of the inward journey without the help of a spiritual director. Today the concept is hardly understood, let alone practiced, except in the Roman Catholic monastic system. That is a tragedy, for the idea of the spiritual director is highly applicable to the contemporary scene. It is a beautiful expression of divine guidance through the help of our brothers and sisters.

What is the purpose of a spiritual director? The seventeenth-century Benedictine mystic Dom Augustine Baker writes, "In a word, he is only God's usher and must lead souls in God's way, not his own." His direction is simply and clearly to lead us to our real Director. He is the means of God to open the path to the inward teaching of the Holy Spirit.

All this talk of "soul" and "spirit" might lead us to think that spiritual direction deals only with a small corner or compartment of our lives. That is, we would go to a spiritual director to care for our spirit the way we might to go an ophthalmologist to care for our eyes. Such an approach is false. Spiritual direction is concerned with the whole person and the interrelationship of all of life. In *Spiritual Direction and Meditation* Thomas Merton tells of a Russian spiritual director who was criticized for spending so much time earnestly advising an old peasant woman about the care of her turkeys. "Not at all," he replied, "her *whole life* is in those turkeys." Spiritual direction takes up the concrete daily experiences of our lives and gives them sacramental significance. We learn "the sacrament of the present moment" as Jean-Pierre de Caussade put it. "So, whether you eat or drink, or whatever you do, do all to the glory of God" (1 Cor. 10:31).   —Richard J. Foster, *Celebration of Discipline*

A Prayer for Spiritual Leaders

I intercede, O Lord, for our spiritual leaders.
Grow in them the fruit of gentleness
that they might understand our frailty.
Grow in them the fruit of peace
that they might be free of manipulation.
Grow in them the fruit of love
that they might always serve out of a divine wellspring.
All these things I ask in the name of Jesus Christ. Amen.

—Richard J. Foster, in *Prayers from the Heart*

June 24

LIGHT, EVERYTHING IS LIGHT

"So the Lord God caused the man to fall into a deep sleep; and while he was sleeping, he took one of the man's ribs and closed up the place with flesh. Then the Lord God made a woman from the rib he had taken out of the man, and he brought her to the man. The man said,

> "This now is bone of my bones
> and flesh of my flesh;
> she shall be called "woman"
> for she was taken out of man.'"
> —Genesis 2:21-23

> From bells to bells I progress into day.
> The first bell falls upon the pale sidewalks
> of sleep: jangle of newsboy's bike. I finish up
> my dream (a midget eating the sun with a fork),
> descend into my body where I find my tongue
> cracked and stiff again. I wait. It moves. It swabs.
> My arm comes to itself. I throw an absent-
> minded leg across your thigh. Our thighs
> together light the bell of the alarm,
> which flares. Hello, body, flesh of my flesh.
> The rosy morning starts, a palpitating
> ring on growing ring. How could my body,
> dumb as iron, articulate such light
> unless the clapper were the very sun?
> —Jeanne Murray Walker

Lord, you have filled our days with awakenings. We wake to your sun, to each other, and to you. With each awakening new life fills us. Such extravagance is your nature. Such abundance is your gift. In receiving these gifts we give ourselves back to you. Amen.

June 25

GOD AND LOVE

"My beloved friends, let us continue to love each other since love comes from God. Everyone who loves is born of God and experiences a relationship with God. The person who refuses to love doesn't know the first thing about God, because God is love — so you can't know him if you don't love." —1 John 4:7-8, THE MESSAGE

The two most difficult things to get straight in life are love and God. More often than not, the mess people make of their lives can be traced to failure or stupidity or meanness in one or both of these areas.

The basic and biblical Christian conviction is that the two subjects are intricately related. If we want to deal with God the right way, we have to learn to love the right way. If we want to love the right way, we have to deal with God the right way. God and love can't be separated.

—Eugene H. Peterson, THE MESSAGE

Dear Lord, help me to both deal with you and learn to love — the right way. Forgive me for my willful avoidance of these lessons. Thank you for your patience with my clumsy attempts to get it right. In Jesus' name. Amen.

June 26

FINDING THE SAWDUST

"Do not judge, or you too will be judged.... Why do you look at the speck of sawdust in your brother's eye and pay no attention to the plank in your own eye?" —Matthew 7:1, 3

I've always had the delusion that if I can blame someone else for what has gone wrong or been done imperfectly, I will not be shamed. Even if I can shift *part of the blame* on to my wife so that we were *both* responsible for something, the sense of failing does not seem to be quite as bad.

Blame almost always triggers anger and defensive control behaviors in our mates, which is a method of self-defense against internal shame attacks on their inner Person for being wrong. Blame never helps.

Some people use blame as a way to justify an attack on their partner. If I am angry at my loved one, just to walk up and hurt her with a nasty comment is too dastardly for a good-guy perfectionist like me who needs to be right. But if I, as Mr. Righteous, can blame my loved one for a wrong I perceive she has done, then it is amazing how justified I can feel in "getting her back."

Pointing out a loved one's faults or mistakes without specific blaming is another abusive shaming control device that is fairly common — even if you are correct about the fault or mistake. The fact that you "caught them" often triggers the shame they felt as children when their parents (who at least had a teaching responsibility as parents) pointed out their faults and mistakes. This control habit puts you in a parental role and usually turns off the desire for intimacy in the other partner. Who wants to share their reality with someone who's going to point out what's wrong with it (and with you) in the process?

Blaming and pointing out the faults of people around us are parts of a very unpleasant intimacy-killer — judgment. When I put myself in the center of my life and the lives of those around me, I think I know better than they do how our lives should be lived. That puts me in the position of God and judge above them — and in my case those close to me have all resented this deeply.

It was very difficult for me to see that it is *not my business* to judge my loved ones about their behavior. They are adults under God. Just because I am spouse, parent (of adult children) or friend, does not mean that I have been automatically appointed to correct them and shame them into their full potential.

When we try to judge people and control them to get them to change in accordance with our judgment, intimacy sneaks out the back door. Our delusion, as controllers, is that we can get them straightened out and they will be grateful to us for doing it. In only a very few cases has this been true in my experience. I'm not talking about a formal intervention here or helping people who have come and asked for your advice. I'm talking about the picking, badgering, shaming sort of correcting that seems to go on when we are in our most intimate relationships without anyone else around. — J. Keith Miller, *Compelled to Control*

Let me tend to the plank (even if it seems at first like a "splinter of sawdust") in my own eye, O Lord. Help me correct myself according to your guidelines for living in Christ. Remove from me the desire to blame, point out faults, or judge others. And when I do blame or judge someone, help me be quick to realize it, and take it back promptly. In Jesus' name. Amen.

June 27

REACHING FOR HOLINESS
(FATHER'S DAY)

"Make every effort to live in peace with all men and to be holy; without holiness no one will see the Lord." —Hebrews 12:14

In my father I had an example of wholeness, of what a man by conscious effort might become. I didn't know it then, and I am only coming to understand it now, but his life was a pursuit of holiness worked out in terms of devotion, faithfulness, and craft. My understanding has been so slow in coming because as a college student I was distracted and confused by the religious jargon which intending to honor, effectively debases the idea of holiness. Nevertheless I feel it is imperative to try.

I remember when my father and my mother picked out and bought four treeless acres twenty miles outside of Pittsburgh. Then working long evenings and weekends, they began the slow discipline of building and making a place worthy of the word "home."

Two years ago my father died. Last Thanksgiving I drove from my home in the wide, comfortable valley of the Genesee River down through the mountains and narrow valleys of Pennsylvania to those acres. It was probably the last time I will ever drive those particular roads, for I was going to help my mother move from that place of their making to a new place which would be one of her making. I approved completely of her move. Yet it was hard to think of that house and those acres without one of us.

Early Friday morning I walked outside and stood on the back porch. I went down the bank, past the pond and across the lawn toward the forsythia hedge and the gate to the pasture. The lawn where we had played ball was thick with trees; small maples, evergreens, walnuts, and others I do not know. Just before I reached the hedge, I stopped. At my feet was the feeder where my father had kept cracked corn for the pheasants. I remembered looking out the windows on winter mornings and seeing ringnecks and hens clustered like barnyard fowl around the corn. I remembered the pleasure my father took in drawing them to the yard. Raising my eyes, I looked through the hedge and over the gate to where he had kept a salt block to attract deer. It was gone.

I turned and walked back to the house. The lesson my father had been teaching me by his life was complete.

The place he had made, as I viewed it that morning, was not the end of his life. His end was to achieve something far more difficult to measure and price than an "estate." His end was to realize the moment of building and to live a full and abundant life in the only time life is alive, the present. As a result, he was free of the burden of the future, free of the burden of finishing that diminishes the working. And free of those burdens, he was free to concentrate on the act of working. He was free to reach for holiness. I say reach for holiness because ultimately holiness is never achieved. It is setting one's mind in the direction of God. It is setting aside what one is to become what God wills. This setting aside does not imply discontinuity. The new, that is the present, is based on the past. One can only become what one already is. "In my beginning is my end," said T. S. Eliot. — John Leax, *Grace Is Where I Live*

Lord, today I will focus on the act of doing the things I am in the midst of now. I let go of the "burden of finishing that diminishes the working" and turn my attention to what is around me at this moment. I feel the surface on which I sit as I read this, I hear the sounds around me and smell the aromas in the air. I set my mind toward you, and set my own agenda aside in order to make room for yours. In Jesus' name. Amen.

June 28

BACKING DOWN

"Forbearing one another, and forgiving one another, if any man have a quarrel against any: even as Christ forgave you, so also do ye."
—Colossians 3:13, KJV

"I'm sorry, Father Noah, but I still don't see why you won't help him."

"I told you." Noah's voice was gruff. "I work long hours in the vineyard. There is not time for coddling the old man."

"Is speaking to your father coddling, or whatever you call it? Sandy and I get mad at our father. He pays more attention to our sister and our little brother than he does to us, because they're the geniuses and we're only—but even when we're mad at him, he's still our father."

"So?"

"When we get home, we're going to have a lot of explaining to do to our father. He will probably be very angry with us."

"Why?"

"Well, we sort of got in the middle of something he was working on."

"I don't know what you're talking about," Noah said.

"Neither do I, exactly," Dennys admitted. "The thing is, we're going to have to talk to our father when we get home. It would be a stupid thing if we tried to avoid him."

"So why are you telling me this?"

"Well—I really do think you should talk with your father."

"Umph."

"I don't mean to be rude or anything, but it sounds to me as though all this argument about wells and stuff has gone on for so long it doesn't make sense anymore. And he's an old man, and you're much younger, and you should be strong enough to back down."

"Backing down is being strong?"

"It takes a lot of courage to say, 'I'm sorry.' That's what Sandy and I are going to have to say to our father when we get home."

"Then why say it?" Noah growled.

"Because things won't be right between us till we do."

—Madeleine L'Engle, *Many Waters*

God our Father, help us to let go of our "rights" and set things right by making amends. Amen.

June 29

BEACH COMBING

"Praise the Lord, for the Lord is good; sing praise to his name, for that is pleasant. For the Lord has chosen Jacob to be his own, Israel to be his treasured possession." —Psalm 135:3-4

I am amazed at how effortlessly I slip into a beachcomber role. As I pad along the shore, eyes scanning the millions of shells in their textured banks, or scattered, embedded in the film of the pulled-back waves, my mind keeps saying to me, *This is pure happiness. This is the state of purest happiness.*

Bright bits of color catch me in the eye — rosy, rubbery seaweed, a pearly jingle shell, a ribbed calico cockle patterned in bright tangerine, a live sea-star, a glistening angel-wing — undeserved gifts of Grace winking up at me with the sheen of sun and sea on them, waiting to be fondled with the eye or carried away with me a thousand miles to where they can remind me of these perfect moments. As I bend and lift each one and love it with my touch and glance, I wonder if this was how God bent and lifted me, how he chose me and treasures me, how he wants me with him. I must seem singular and precious to him if he came so far to find me. —Luci Shaw, *God in the Dark*

Lord, in the vastness of your world, I am a small thing. How you see me I do not know. But I have felt you lift me and hold me up as if I were a bright shell. You have treasured me and loved me. And in that love I have found myself made whole and lovely. Amen.

June 30

GIFTS FROM THE SEA

"The whole congregation of the Israelites complained against Moses and Aaron in the wilderness. The Israelites said to them, 'If only we had died by the hand of the LORD in the land of Egypt, when we sat by the fleshpots and ate our fill of bread; for you have brought us out into the wilderness to kill this whole assembly with hunger.'" —Exodus 16:2-3, NRSV

I write this from mid-ocean, not knowing my way. My directions are unclear. My supplies are running short. Darkness is darkness. I know what it means to be at sea.

I can't help thinking that an experience of darkness can never be fully staged. We can't really orchestrate an experience of emptiness; it's not a matter of chosen hardships or fasting. Wilderness is always impromptu, a gift that comes out of nowhere, without rehearsal or warning. When a real desert experience sets in, there's no time to prepare. We're up against it. Trapped in a place without comfort, without support.

Things that fed us before don't seem to nourish us now. Who are we? Where are we going? Why don't the plans and dreams we had yesterday add up? Isn't there a structure, a design we can cling to? The map doesn't match the circumstances. We're going in circles, exhausted, lost. Now's the time to grumble, to tell Moses and Aaron they've betrayed us. This experience isn't play-acting. The lines we memorized don't work for these situations. "Why did we not die at Yahweh's hand in the land of Egypt? As it is, you have brought us to this wilderness to starve the whole company to death!" (Exod. 16:3). As so often, when dealing with God, he seems to have changed the rules. We're inclined to tell him he's not playing fair. "Why did you bring us out of Egypt? Was it so that I should die of thirst, my children, too, and my cattle?" (Exod. 17:3–4).

In the blush of my first enthusiasm for the spiritual life I once wanted to take on penances and deliberately chosen fasts. Then my spiritual director counseled me wisely: "Better the penance that you don't choose." Now that I have come into such a place, a place not of my own choosing, it is painful even to remember the false heroics of my earlier plan.

In the past, I volunteered to help those who had to stay put. As a lay minister in my New York congregation I became a regular Sunday visitor to nursing homes. In a sense, I think I was trying to compensate for the ways I couldn't be attentive to my own family, living far away. Whatever my intention, I saw a lot of anguish, people trapped in loneliness with less than adequate care.

Yes, it was a generous act; yes, it was worth doing. But some of that overenthusiastic ministry seems to me now less than holy, an effort to take center stage in a publicly Christian way.

How much better to stay put and stand toe-to-toe with my own challenges. Now I am fenced in as they were; now it's not so easy to voice my Christian enthusiasm. Now I can't romanticize the experience of tending the sick. Now I see that I am not "caring for the elderly" but becoming one of the elderly for whom others must care. My impulse is to make a break for freedom, for irresponsibility, to cut loose from being the good, obedient child.

How can we grow beyond our fears? Only perhaps by yielding to experience, and keeping a sharp eye for God's guiding presence: angelic sentinels and guardians can protect us from ourselves, our own deepest fears and anxieties, our continuing fear of change.

—Emilie Griffin, *Homeward Voyage*

Dear Lord, why is it, when you've sent your messengers and leaders to lead me into a new place, I'm always hanging back and dwelling in my fearfulness? I find myself constantly in mid-ocean, midway between departures and destinations, not fully trusting the map or the directions given. Lord, teach me to trust and follow faithfully, to put one foot in front of another. Let me outgrow my fearfulness. Give me courage, just for today. Amen

JULY

July 1

KYRIE ELEISON

"The Lord is good to all: and his tender mercies are over all his works." —Psalm 145:9, KJV

Righteousness leads directly into *blessed are the merciful, for they shall obtain mercy.*

But mercy goes further than that forgiveness taught us in the Lord's Prayer. The human being is given the ability to forgive, but that capacity of mercy which not only forgives but also removes the sin is more than human.

The English language, despite what we have done to it with all our jargons, is still extraordinarily rich and powerful in quality, though not in quantity, of words. Both the Greeks and the Hebrews used many words where we have been satisfied with one. As there are many words for our one *love,* so with *mercy.* The Hebrew *chesed* is seen over and over again in the Psalms, and Coverdale frequently translates it as *loving kindness,* that continued forbearance shown by God even when his chosen people are slow to keep his commandments and swift to turn to foreign gods.

Another Hebrew word for mercy is *rachamim,* which has to do with tender compassion, the care of the shepherd for the stray lamb, the pity shown to the weak and helpless. And there is *chaninah,* a joyful, generous mercy, loving and kind.

So mercy, as all the other Beatitudes, is a Christlike word, and I must look for understanding of it in the small and daily events of my own living, because if I do not recognize it in little things I will not see it in the great. —Madeleine L'Engle, *The Irrational Season*

> Kyrie eleison. *Lord, have mercy,*
> Christe eleison. *Christ, have mercy,*
> Kyrie eleison. *Lord have mercy.*
> Amen.

July 2

SALVATION

> "As high as heaven is over the earth,
>   so strong is his love to those who fear him.
> And as far as sunrise is from sunset,
>   he has separated us from our sins."
> —Psalm 103:11-12, THE MESSAGE

What God has done for us far exceeds anything we have done for or against him. The summary word for this excessive, undeserved, unexpected act of God is "salvation." Prayer explores the country of salvation, tramping the contours, smelling the flowers, touching the outcroppings. There is more to do than recognize the sheer fact of salvation and witness to it; there are unnumbered details of grace, of mercy, of blessing to be appreciated and savored. Prayer is the means by which we do this. —Eugene H. Peterson, *Psalms: Prayers of the Heart*

O Lord, I come to you full of appreciation for the many incidents of grace, mercy, and blessing you have put into my life. I can't begin to comprehend what you have done for me through my salvation, but I enter this prayer time with you full of awareness that it is too big to comprehend. Here are some of the details I am savoring today. . . . In Jesus' name. Amen.

July 3

AND TO WHOMSOEVER THE SON WILL REVEAL HIM

> "Neither knoweth any man the Father, save the Son, and he to whomsoever the Son will reveal Him." —Matthew 11:27, KJV

In the beauty of the lily and the machinations of the human mind, one can see something of the reality of God. But then how do we read this verse? "Neither knoweth any man the Father, save the Son, and he to whomsoever the Son will reveal him?" An apparent contradiction?

Knowledge of God is all around us and offered to every last human being. *Knowledge of the Father,* however, is the exclusive blessing of those who know him through his Son, Jesus Christ.

Those who know Christ, the Word made flesh, have not only a general knowledge of God but a saving knowledge of his reality. However, knowing that God came to earth in the form of man and that all revelation begins in Christ, the living Word — just knowing that, in the same manner as we know the law of gravity, for instance, isn't at all the same phenomenon as knowing it in one's heart. Head knowledge is not the same as heart knowledge. Only those who have been brought near unto God, through his Son, really *know* fully the truth of the gospel's good news.

We're not just hair-splitting here — listen to this. Those who really know God, as fully as human beings can, see God even more clearly in a starry night than those who don't. Our nearness to God himself brings his splendid creation to us in the finest technicolor.

So what? you ask. Here's the goods. Sometimes those who are recently converted find such spiritual ecstasy in his presence that they want to sing forever of his majesty, to concentrate their lives' tasks on basking in the glory of Christ. That's commendable, of course, as long as they don't turn away from the beauty of the world he loves.

When we are brought to God through Christ, we need to let that same light of redemption, that light we know in our inner life, shine gloriously on our outer life as well. "In the beginning was the Word, and the Word was with God and the Word was God." Those familiar words from the Gospel of John insist that Christ shines not only in us, but in his world as well.

Don't run away from the world — that's the idea. Live gloriously in a creation that is immensely brightened by your knowledge of God. What's important to remember is that everything we see around us looks different as a result of our knowledge of the Father through his Son. Our knowing God — in head and heart — unites the life of grace with the life of nature in a glorious harmony, and turns the whole world, all of history and science and art, everything we are and shall be, into — you guessed it — into one mighty revelation of the Father. Wow. Don't miss it.
— James Calvin Schaap, *Near Unto God*

Thank you, Lord, for the beauty of your creation. And thank you for Christ, the light of the world. Through him we see your presence in all you've made. Wow!

July 4

DIVINE SHYNESS

> "O Jerusalem, Jerusalem, you who kill the prophets and stone those sent to you, how often I have longed to gather your children together, as a hen gathers her chicks under her wings, but you were not willing."
> —Matthew 23:37

One more instance of divine restraint comes to mind. It occurred in Jerusalem very near the site of Satan's third challenge. Jesus looked down from a high hill and cried out, "O Jerusalem, Jerusalem, you who kill the prophets and stone those sent to you, how often I have longed to gather your children together, as a hen gathers her chicks under her wings, but you were not willing!" That wail of grief over Jerusalem has about it a quality almost like shyness. Jesus, who could destroy Jerusalem with a word, who could call down legions of angels to force subjection, instead looks over the city and weeps.

God holds back; he hides himself; he weeps. Why? Because he desired what power can never win. He is a king who wants not subservience, but love. Thus, rather than mowing down Jerusalem, Rome, and every other worldly power, he chose the slow, hard way of Incarnation, love, and death. A conquest from within.

George MacDonald, in *Life Essential,* summed up Christ's approach: "Instead of crushing the power of evil by divine force; instead of compelling justice and destroying the wicked; instead of making peace on the earth by the rule of a perfect prince; instead of gathering the children of Jerusalem under his wings whether they would or not, and saving them from the horrors that anguished his prophetic soul—he let evil work its will while it lived; he contented himself with the slow unencouraging ways of help essential; making men good; casting out, not merely controlling Satan.... To love righteousness is to make it grow, not to avenge it.... Throughout his life on earth, he resisted every impulse to work more rapidly for a lower good—strong, perhaps, when he saw old age and innocence and righteousness trodden under foot."

—Philip Yancey, *Disappointment with God*

Lord, I'm in awe of your loving, patient ways. I've found that as a believer, I can see signs of your presence, your power, and your love that I never saw unbelieving! In Jesus' name. Amen.

July 5

MESSAGE IN THE SAND

"Have you journeyed to the springs of the sea or walked in the recesses of the deep?" —Job 38:16

> A shell—how small an empty space,
> a folding out of pink and white,
> a letting in of spiral light.
> How random? and how commonplace?
> (A million shells along the beach
> are just as fine and full of grace
> as this one here within your reach.)
>
> But lift it, hold it to your ear
> and listen. Surely you can hear
> the swish and sigh of all the grey
> and gleaming waters, and the play
> of wind with rain and sun, encased
> in one small jewel box and placed,
> by God and oceans, in your way.
>
> —Luci Shaw, *Horizons*

Maker of heaven and earth, I can never fathom the depths of your creative energy. I know that you are beyond me. But I am grateful that you have given me signs, like shells and poems, that call me to you. Grant me grace and insight that I might see you in all the works in which you choose to make yourself known. Amen.

July 6

THE LIFE OF AN ANT

"A man can do nothing better than to eat and drink and find satisfaction in his work." —Ecclesiastes 2:24

We live in the presence of animals, if not in actuality, then in imagination. "Animals are what men use to wrap ideas into visible form," writes Peter Steinhart in "Dreaming Elands." We are not even subtle about the packaging. One may never see a mountain lion or a big cat in the wild, but one cannot escape seeing a Cougar or a Jaguar on the highway. The names embody sleekness and power, qualities thickening, middle-aged men desire, qualities they imagine they put on as they ease themselves under steering wheels and settle into leather seats. This wishful thinking is, for the most part, harmless.

Sometimes, however, often when it appears to be most beneficial, it is dangerous. Who can forget a childhood exposure to the story of the grasshopper and the ant, that merciless putdown of spontaneity and exuberant celebration in favor of dull, grinding work? Even granting the moral, "All play and no work makes Jack a hungry bug," the story rings false. What sane person would choose the life of the ant? Not even a sweatshop capitalist would endorse it for himself.

"Behold the fowls of the air," Jesus admonished us, "for they sow not, neither do they reap, nor gather into barns; yet your heavenly Father feedeth them." Here is another idea wrapped in an animal story. What it teaches us about work is radically unlike the lesson of the grasshopper and the ant. But note, it does not denigrate work. The fowls of the air labor; they build nests, brood over their eggs, and feed and nurture their young. What they do not do is give themselves up to vanity, to the accumulation of wealth, prestige, and plaque in the arteries.

—John Leax

We come, at last, Good Father, to know our silly work for what it is, an effort to earn what you have given before we've even seen our need. Such grace, showered as freely as the rain, astounds us. Douse us with it. Let us respond as plants in the spring. Amen.

July 7

TO WALK AND NOT FAINT

"But those who hope in the Lord will renew their strength. They will soar on wings like eagles; they will run and not grow weary, they will walk and not be faint." —Isaiah 40:31

There are days when it is all I can do to "walk and not faint." But when I try to understand the phrase, "they who wait for the Lord shall renew their strength," I think about how God intended for men and women to live. And that includes eating right and exercising, which are designed to renew our physical strength.

The basic trouble seems to be in my desires. When I really want something, I can argue my way right past all the reasons it's bad for me and just help myself. The result is that I never seem to reach my weight goal because I am basically unable to curb my desires.

So my prayers have two basic requests. One is for the Lord to change my desires so that it's not so important to me to have unhealthy foods. The other is for him to help me learn that I don't have to gratify every desire that passes through my mind. I can learn to live without every whim being satisfied.

"They who wait for the Lord shall renew their strength," I read. To "wait for" might mean to give up my own ideas about things and to try to understand how and when things should happen from God's perspective. As I try to understand God's timing and how it is different from my own, I find that my desire for doing what God wants me to do is growing and that my other desires are getting smaller. And I have hope that these desires can keep on shrinking until they do not control my life the way that they have before. —Andrea Wells Miller, *BodyCare*

Dear Lord, help me learn to wait for you and understand your way of doing things. Renew my strength when I run out, and help me to walk and not faint. Turn my desires away from impatient thoughts, Lord, and keep me in your way. In Jesus' name. Amen.

July 8

Humility and Service

"Jesus knew that the Father had put all things under his power, and that he had come from God and was returning to God; so he got up from the meal, took off his outer clothing, and wrapped a towel around his waist. After that, he poured water into a basin and began to wash his disciples' feet, drying them with the towel that was wrapped around him." —John 13:3–5

More than any other single way, the grace of humility is worked into our lives through the Discipline of service. Humility, as we all know, is one of those virtues that is never gained by seeking it. The more we pursue it the more distant it becomes. To think we have it is sure evidence that we don't. Therefore, most of us assume there is nothing we can do to gain this prized Christian virtue, and so we do nothing.

But there *is* something we can do. We do not need to go through life faintly hoping that someday humility may fall upon our heads. Of all the classical Spiritual Disciplines, service is the most conducive to the growth of humility. When we set out on a consciously chosen course of action that accents the good of others and is, for the most part, a hidden work, a deep change occurs in our spirits.

—Richard J. Foster, *Celebration of Discipline*

Make Me an Instrument of Thy Peace

Lord, make me an instrument of thy peace;
where there is hatred, let me sow love;
where there is injury, pardon;
where there is doubt, faith;
where there is despair, hope;
where there is darkness, light.
O Divine Master,
grant that I may not so much seek
to be consoled as to console;
to be understood, as to understand;
to be loved, as to love;
for it is in giving that we receive,
it is in pardoning that we are pardoned,
and it is in dying that we are born to eternal life.
— Francis of Assisi

July 9

CHOSEN TO LAY DOWN THE SIGN

"Choose twelve men from among the people, one from each tribe, and tell them to take up twelve stones from the middle of the Jordan from right where the priests stood and to carry them over with you and put them down at the place where you stay tonight."
—Joshua 4:2-3

Joshua bellows your name, you,
among everyone in your tribe the one
to choose the tribe's stone, you!
you, who afterward see nothing but stones
everywhere you go, the different shapes
and sizes, light and shadow
motling each, each shape raising a different
memorial, the sleepless burden of choosing,
leaving out every stone but one,
how you begin to think of yourself as thin,
your arms scrawny, yourself
famous for being slightly gullible,
so how will you lug a thousand pounds
on your mortal shoulder? And then
picking it up, the way it shifts like a planet
grinding across your forearm,

leaving striations of bright blood
and you stagger, no one, now, but the man
who has to bear it all the way
and somehow that's when light spreads —
a fist of weightlessness opening its fingers
from inside the stone,
passing through the baggy skin of granite
into your bones, till they're light
as flutes, and you wonder at how nothing is itself,
at how yesterday the Jordan stopped
and stood in a heap before the holy ark,
at how water and stone and flesh obey like
trained camels, and now, as you thrust it
into its space beside the eleven others,
you can feel the hands of your children's
children's children resting on your back
weightless as spring leaves, and hear their voices,
*he carried this stone? Really! Then I can
pick this up.*

— Jeanne Murray Walker, in *Cortland Review*

Lord, I am the child who remembers your acts in the lives of my ancestors. I dwell in the history of your faithfulness. When trouble comes, gives me a keen mind to remember you and the will to be obedient. Amen.

July 10

Mixed Motives

"I do not understand what I do. For what I want to do I do not do, but what I hate I do.... What a wretched man I am! Who will rescue me from this body of death? Thanks be to God — through Jesus Christ our Lord!" —Romans 7:15, 24-25a

"Mommy, I'm not sure if I am being nice to these people because I like them or because I believe it will make them think I'm a neat kid. And it worries me. Should I quit being so friendly?"

The lady who was showing me this passage from a letter was puzzled. It was from her young teenage daughter who was away at camp for the summer. The mother said that she had not worried about such things when she was a girl and asked me what I thought about the letter.

Smiling a little to myself, I realized that I could have written a similar letter at many different times in my life. The problem — of mixed motives — has given me fits in several different ways. Those of us who have a deep need to be accepted and for whom acceptance as a child was subtly contingent on our "being good" may have more trouble with motivational nit-picking than other people. Sometimes in school, I remember worrying about whether I was thoughtful to other kids because I meant it or because by being friendly to them I would likely be elected to class offices. Although I knew at some level that both motives were there and that both were pretty natural, I wanted to be *sure* my motives were right — like the little girl in the letter.

When I became a Christian, this occasional compulsive need to have pure motives took an especially insidious form, which brought the whole business to a head. Beginning to witness in other churches as a layman, I wondered sometimes if I were going because I wanted to tell people about God... or about me. This worried me, since I really wanted to be God's person and to do his will. On one occasion I almost called a minister and canceled a meeting because I wasn't sure if I were going for God or for Keith. But having put off contacting him until it was very late, I went ahead and drove to the church — knowing that my motives were definitely mixed. Before I spoke that night, I prayed silently that God would use me "if you can use a man as full of himself as I am." After I started speaking, I forgot all about my motives.

Several days later a man who attended the meeting came to my office. He said that he had been desperate and had almost lost hope, but as a result of attending the session that night had decided to give life another try. After he left, I sat thinking about what had happened.

In the first place, my desire to keep my motives spotless and pure had almost kept me from helping a man who was really desperate. I saw how totally self-centered this "keeping myself righteous" is. It constitutes a strange kind of Christian idolatry — I was worshiping clean motives. Keeping them spotless was more important somehow than going ahead with mixed motives and letting God possibly help someone through me.

In the second place, it came crashing home to me that my motives are *always* mixed to some degree — and that most likely they always will be in this life. So that for me the leap of faith in witnessing for Christ is to go, knowing my needs for attention, but taking the risk that I will speak for him instead of for myself. If I go at all, I must go in faith, praying that God will use me in spite of my self-centeredness.

In fact, after all these years, I simply pray that God will free me to point over my shoulder to him. Because when it comes right down to it, all I have to tell about is what I have seen and heard of him — how he is helping me to find freedom, occasionally to love other people, and even to accept myself with my mixed motives.

What can we take with us on this sometimes confusing journey? What we must take is the knowledge of our own unending ambiguous motives.

—J. Keith Miller, *Habitation of Dragons*

The voice that we hear over our shoulders never says, "First be sure that your motives are pure and selfless and then follow me." If it did, then none of us could follow. So when later the voice says, "Take up your cross and follow me," at least part of what is meant by "cross" is our realization that we are seldom any less than nine parts fake. Yet our feet can insist on answering him anyway, and on we go, step after step, mile after mile. How far? How far?
— Frederick Buechner, *The Magnificent Defeat*

Dear Lord, help me not to be a Christian Pharisee who is more interested in "being ethical" than in loving you and your people. Be with the little girl who wrote the letter to her mother, and help her to understand that sometimes she will have to risk her motives in order to do anything good. Give us both the courage to follow you, even if it means taking the risk, as you did, of being misunderstood. I want to resist phoniness — yet without wallowing in the problems of motivation. It all seems very complex, and sometimes I do not even understand my behavior after the fact. So I am offering myself and my subtly mixed motives to you, asking that your will take me beyond such self-centered preoccupations into your loving perspective. Amen.
— J. Keith Miller, *Habitation of Dragons*

July 11

HIS FATHER'S BUSINESS

"But the fruit of the Spirit is love, joy, peace, longsuffering, gentleness, goodness, faith, meekness, temperance: against such there is no law."   —Galatians 5:22–23, KJV

>What is eternity?
>Who was God's mother?
>How many stars are there?
>Do numbers ever come to an end?
>Why is there war?
>How do you know if you're in love?
>What is gravity?

Children are full of questions, wonderful questions, unanswerable questions.

Jesus, too.

And where better to ask questions than in the Temple where the learned doctors were to be found, elders who had spent their entire lives in the study of the holy Jewish Law. Jesus was as curious as any bright twelve-year-old child. So when the family made the annual pilgrimage to Jerusalem, he went to the Temple, where he astonished the teachers with his questions, and also with his answers. And there, at last, his frantic parents found him.

Was he really gone three days as the Bible tells us? Or was it three hours? It really doesn't matter. What matters is that Jesus was an eager questioner, alert, ready to learn. He didn't notice time passing, or realize that his parents might be worried.

Already he was about his father's business.

And that business, he was to learn, was not the law expounded in the Temple. That business was not law — but love.

—Madeleine L'Engle, *The Glorious Impossible*

Heavenly Father, whose business we, too, are learning, help us to better understand and live the life of love to which you have called us. Amen.

July 12

Mustard as a Good Work

"[Jesus] said to them, '... truly, I say to you, if you have faith as a grain of mustard seed, you will say to this mountain, "Move from here to there," and it will move; and nothing will be impossible to you.'"
—Matthew 17:20, RSV

No doubt the seasoned veteran of spirituality will look at C. S. Lewis's spirituality, or my attempt to derive a spirituality from Lewis's own, as amusing, even interesting, but, really, it just doesn't cut the mustard....

And indeed it doesn't cut the mustard; at least in the way that Bernard and Bruno, Dominic and Francis, Ignatius and Alphonsus, Teresa and John, cut it with their own spiritualities. Supposedly, because they've been developed by ordained men and vowed women in the clerical and religious life, they're considered superior, the knife's edge, as it were, on how laymen and laywomen should design their spiritual lives.

But what I'd like to suggest is that, when it comes to spirituality for the Mere Christian, it's not the knife that counts; it's the mustard.

May I explain.

In 1921 Dorothy L. Sayers was hired at Benson's, a London advertising agency, as "an idea man and copywriter," and for the next nine years she contributed enormously to the success of a now-famous campaign for Colman's Mustard. A declining ad budget and the essential dullness of mustard were the problems to be solved. A club was invented, characters concocted, situations devised, and soon members of the Mustard Club and the message of Mustard for the Masses were appearing on posters and billboards, in newspapers and magazines, all over England.

In a like manner she and others revivified Christianity by writing plays, novels, and essays; most notable in this regard is her "The Dogma Is the Drama." And even as Lewis swiped Colman's onto his own meat pies, so he virtually re-metaphorized Christianity in his imaginative, scholarly, and doctrinal works. In a word, he as well as Sayers made believing believable, acceptable, to the masses.

No, it's not the knife that counts when the blade hits the mustard; it's the mustard itself, for the mustard is the masses.

But be it known that Colman's is not a dull mustard; it's a sharp one, a hotter-than-hot one whose rising fumes make the sinus membranes quaver like violas.

Two questions.

Is it just a coincidence that the initials of both Mere Christianity and the Mustard Club are the same?

May Colman's reasonably be considered the official mustard of Mere Christianity? —William Griffin, *C. S. Lewis: Spirituality for Mere Christians*

Dear Lord, sometimes my faith feels smaller than that smallest seed on earth, the mustard seed. Thank you that this tiny seed can become such a spicy condiment. May my life be a living demo of your spicy, radical, truths. Amen.

July 13

THE QUIET HEART

"For I tell you the truth, many prophets and righteous men longed to see what you see but did not see it, and to hear what you hear but did not hear it." —Matthew 13:17

I was searching for a campsite, exploring the wild woods that sloped down to a mountain river in the Canadian Rockies, when I noticed a single deer poised on the bank. She turned her head toward me and "saw" me with her ears. When I think of someone who listens sensitively for God and hears him, I see in my mind this deer, on the alert for the slightest sound or scent.

Sometimes physical seeing becomes impossible, in a blizzard, say, or in the blank blackness of midnight, or when sailing in the middle of a lake, surrounded by fog. We are forced to use our other senses the way blind people learn to do, deprived as they are of the easy, marvelous mechanism of optical vision.

Maybe that was the reason some of the old monastics deliberately practiced sense deprivation. When the mind is no longer distracted and seduced by sounds and smells and sights outside us, it is freed to listen with an inner ear and view the inner landscape of the soul — the baptized imagination. —Luci Shaw, *Horizons*

The world is full of noise, and I move from the din of traffic to the soothing sounds of Mozart. Nowhere, O Lord, can I hear your voice unless you speak in thunder, and even then the pounding rhythms of my anxious striving shut you out. In the few moments of quiet while I utter this prayer, I repent my reluctance to hear your soft calling to me. I hear you now. Hear me when I say, I love you. Amen.

July 14

LETTING GO

"But I trust in you, O Lord; I say, 'You are my God.'"
—Psalm 31:14

After about eighteen months of dating only each other, the man in my life decided he needed to end our relationship. He had some reasons which he explained to me, and I fought hard to "help" him overcome his "reasons" so that we wouldn't need to end our relationship. Finally, I had to accept that it was his decision, and it was not my place to make such a decision for him. I accepted the end of the relationship, although it was very painful for me.

My first reaction was of fright, hurt, and tears. But as the next few days wore on and I couldn't seem to lessen the pain at all, I remembered to try something I had been learning about for the previous two years. I began to pray. I wrote long letters to God in my journal as I tried to sort out the jumble of hostile, angry, frightened, loving, and painful feelings I was having.

In these letters, I asked God to help me see what I needed to learn through this experience. I saw, in a way I never had before, my huge need to control everything, to know what is going on, and to try to influence people to do things my way. I was shocked to realize the extent of this need to control as I now could see example after example of it in my relationship with this man and with other dating relationships I'd had before. I recalled examples of this in my relationships with people at work, with my parents, and with my sisters and brother.

I wanted to eliminate this controlling habit because now I could see how destructive it had been in all my relationships. I realized that I would not be able to find out how a person would handle various situations if I kept *telling* him or her *how* to handle them. I needed to learn to keep my mouth shut and let people go through their own decision-making processes.

So I began to pray that I could learn to give up this control. And I started by giving up my control of this man. It may sound strange to say I tried to give up control of him after he had broken up with me and was out of my life. But it was amazing how much anger was created in me when he didn't do what I wanted him to — keep dating me.

When I was finally able to say out loud to God, "I no longer exert any control over this man's behavior. He can do anything he wants to do without retribution or punishment or reward from me," then part of the pain began to ease. The angry feelings about his going away seemed easier to handle.

"Who am I," I asked myself, "to tell him he has to date me forever? He is free to do as he chooses. If he chooses not to be with me, that hurts, but it's his right. My responsibility is only to myself and to God. I'll just have to ask God how to get through the rest of the pain."

So the anger at his leaving healed first. The sorrow, disappointment and hurt lasted longer.

Time and prayer were two important ingredients in the healing process, along with a real desire to go on and *get over* it, and not wallow in the misery. I had to go to God over and over again with my pride, my anger at being "treated that way," my need to control, my feeling of being misunderstood, my desire to be attractive to a man — my weaknesses one after another.

I believed that God loved me and did not intend for me to lead a sad, angry, hostile life. I felt that God could heal my pain if I would bring it to him and allow him to do so. To seal myself off from this healing and refuse to get over a painful ending to a relationship was to keep myself from being the person he made me to be.

I knew it was my responsibility to care for myself — my mind, my heart, my body — and allow myself to develop and become what God had in mind for me. But it was so hard to let go of my feelings. And I *hated* having to admit my weaknesses, to acknowledge that I had been proud, fearful, manipulative, and selfish. I wanted God to see how "wronged" I was and that I "deserved" some kind of revenge or special reward.

But facing my own part in the deterioration of the relationship was also necessary. Trying to learn to be patient and honest with myself about my pain, pride, fears, and working hard to repeatedly bring these to God were all necessary, for me, in getting over a painful broken relationship.

—Andrea Wells Miller, *The Single Experience*

Dear Lord, having no one to trust led me to take control of everything around me — to keep myself safe and protected. Help me to learn to trust in you — not to be my own god but to say with the Psalmist, "You are my God!" In Jesus' name. Amen.

July 15

Springhouse

"Jesus answered, 'Everyone who drinks this water will be thirsty again, but whoever drinks the water I give him will never thirst. Indeed, the water I give him will become in him a spring of water welling up to eternal life.'" —John 4:13-14

> One summer day, flushed red
> from climbing apple trees,
> I swung the wooden door
> heavy with dampness back
> against the stone wall
> and entered the dark coolness
> flowing from the hill.
>
> Over the square pool
> so clear it seemed to be
> almost not there, I knelt.
> I bent and cupped my hands.
>
> Outside, in the light,
> familial voices rippled
> like water before me.
>
> I drank and drank—
> I rose filled beyond thirst.

—John Leax, *Country Labors*

We have been filled with your living water. Make our lives a spring of grace. Let us bubble over and stream babbling down your hillsides with stone-carving joy. Let us write on the earth the blessing of your thirst-quenching flood. Amen.

July 16

Mining

"For where your treasure is, there your heart will be also."
—Matthew 6:21

In the summer of 1849, my great-grandfather, Hiram White, a red-bearded blacksmith from Maine, invested all his savings to sail around Cape Horn to California. There he staked a gold-mining claim far up the Feather River above the town of Sacramento. He was twenty-seven, single, and full of brawn. For many months he worked the claim, battling grizzly bears, robbers, and lice, finding hardly enough gold to justify his labors. Finally, wasted by dysentery, he sold his claim for a fraction of its cost and took to the sea for a cure, working aboard ship for $10 a day. Back home at last with $1,000 in his pocket, he learned that the two men to whom he had sold the claim had already netted more than half a million dollars and were still going strong. Hiram returned to blacksmithing, got married, and fathered a houseful of children.

That story flies into my mind as I contemplate my history in the church. The odds are not what matter. We try and fail and try again, slowly learning what it means to believe and live the gospel. Where else but in the church of Christ can we practice what the world can't comprehend—the "non-sense" of the Prodigal Son, the Widow's Mite, the Good Samaritan, and the notion of losing our lives to find them. Where else can we learn to apply the standard of love until—to paraphrase Reinhold Niebuhr—the law of love becomes the ultimate measure of justice throughout the world?

It's a preposterous hope. But hope, like responsibility, is what we can't relinquish. We could call it "prospecting." Maybe that word is all I can wrest from my great-grandfather's California adventure, but it seems like enough. It means acting in faith. I like that better than knowing beyond all doubt that the gold is there and easily extracted. This above all is what the world has trouble understanding, that we would be willing to bet our lives on the outrageous treasure of the gospel.

—Shirley Nelson, "Prospecting," in *Rattling Those Dry Bones*

Lord, I didn't win the lottery this week, but I thank you for the riches of the Gospel, that amazing gift which cannot be won, stolen, or taxed. Amen.

July 17

MESSY FAMILY ROOMS

"Up on your feet! Take a deep breath! Maybe there's life in you yet. But I wouldn't know it by looking at your busywork; nothing of God's work has been completed."   —Revelation 3:2, THE MESSAGE

The churches of the Revelation show us that churches are not Victorian parlors where everything is always picked up and ready for guests. They are messy family rooms. Entering a person's house unexpectedly, we are sometimes met with a barrage of apologies. St. John does not apologize. Things are out of order, to be sure, but that is what happens to churches that are lived in. They are not showrooms. They are living rooms, and if the persons living in them are sinners, there are going to be clothes scattered about, handprints on the woodwork, and mud on the carpet.

For as long as Jesus insists on calling sinners and not the righteous to repentance—and there is no indication as yet that he has changed his policy in that regard—churches are going to be an embarrassment to the fastidious and an affront to the upright. St. John sees them simply as *lampstands:* they are places, locations, where the light of Christ is shown. They are not themselves the light. There is nothing particularly glamorous about churches, nor, on the other hand, is there anything particularly shameful about them. They simply are.

—Eugene H. Peterson, *Reversed Thunder*

Dear Lord, thank you that after we are called to repentance there is a place for us to go to find the light of Christ, and to learn to show it. In Jesus' name. Amen.

July 18

SEEING WITHOUT EYES

"Then he turned to his disciples and said privately, 'Blessed are the eyes that see what you see. For I tell you that many prophets and kings wanted to see what you see but did not see it, and to hear what you hear but did not hear it.'"   —Luke 10:23-24

Helen Keller, blind and deaf, found herself in the midst of a ferocious blizzard in Cleveland in the winter of 1913. The winds reached seventy-nine miles an hour, and after two days the city was left under a twenty-one-inch blanket of snow. She could neither see the snow nor hear the screaming wind; yet she experienced the storm of invisible electrical charges that bombarded the earth. She recounts:

"I knew it was storming before I was told. The rooms, the corridors, everywhere within the building vibrated with the power of the storm without — when I knew it was snowing as it never had in this part of the world, I wished to rush out and throw myself into the snow and ride upon the tempest.... I am stirred to the depth of my being by the storm, and my body, mind, and soul are better for this great experience — the greatest of its kind in my life. Few times in my life has it been given me to feel sensations akin to those I have experienced as a captive of the blizzard."

Perhaps it takes the extraordinary configuration of events that make up the life of Helen Keller to reveal to the rest of us, prisoners of our own sight and hearing, the fuller dimension of storm, the minute tactile vibrations, the electrical stimulation that drew her, literally like a magnet, that tempted her "to ride upon the tempest." She, seemingly the most vulnerable of humans, yearned for union with an aspect of Beauty we can scarcely apprehend. —Virginia Stem Owens, *A Taste of Creation*

Lord, I yearn to expand my senses to take in more of the beauty and wonder in the world around me, a world you created for me to inhabit. Draw me like a magnet toward grasping in a fuller dimension the magnitude of who you are! In Jesus' name. Amen.

July 19

SELF-RIGHTEOUS SERVICE VERSUS TRUE SERVICE

"And when you pray, do not be like the hypocrites, for they love to pray standing in the synagogues and on the street corners to be seen by men. I tell you the truth, they have received their reward in full. But when you pray, go into your room, close the door and pray to your Father, who is unseen. Then your Father, who sees what is done in secret, will reward you." —Matthew 6:5-6

Self-righteous service comes through human effort. It expends immense amounts of energy calculating and scheming how to render the service. Sociological charts and surveys are devised so we can "help those people." True service comes from a relationship with the divine Other deep inside. We serve out of whispered promptings, divine urgings. Energy is expended but it is not the frantic energy of the flesh. Thomas

Kelly writes in *A Testament of Devotion*, "I find he never guides us into an intolerable scramble of panting feverishness."

Self-righteous service is impressed with the "big deal." It is concerned to make impressive gains on ecclesiastical scoreboards. It enjoys serving, especially when the service is titanic. True service finds it almost impossible to distinguish the small from the large service. Where a difference is noted, the true servant is often drawn to the small service, not out of false modesty, but because he genuinely sees it as the more important task. He indiscriminately welcomes all opportunities to serve.

—Richard J. Foster, *Celebration of Discipline*

> O fill me with Thy fullness, Lord.
> Until my very heart o'er-flow
> In kindling thought and glowing word,
> Thy love to tell, Thy praise to show.
>
> O use me, Lord, use even me,
> Just as Thou wilt, and when, and where,
> Until Thy blessed face I see —
> Thy rest, Thy joy, Thy glory share.
>
> Amen.

—Frances R. Havergal

July 20

I HIDE ME WITH THEE

"I flee unto thee to hide me."
—Psalm 143:9b, KJV

Let's go to the barnyard. Yellow balls of fluff scurry everywhere, pecking in the dust, while their mother casts a wary eye about, on the lookout for trouble. The moment she sees something, she gathers them under her wings, even if they don't want to go. In fact, only when they see whatever the danger is — maybe a chicken hawk — do they take off to her for protection. But when they do, they throw themselves totally into her care.

Inevitably, times come when all we can do is go to the Lord for protection beneath his motherly wings. Storms rage. Terminal disease comes even to health food addicts. Death strikes wherever humans draw breath. But in every crisis, the Lord holds out his wings lovingly, asking us to seek his protection.

Inevitably in life, we face chicken hawks. We are talking here about extremes, worst-case scenarios. When we're up to our ears in horror, when the flood waters threaten every last thing we own and even our families, then we run. We literally *hide* in God.

When our strength is depleted, we put forth the one last heroic effort, the act which triumphs: we let go of ourselves and let God cover us with his wings. At that moment, no matter how tempest-tossed, the believer hides himself with God, and God binds up our wounds and gently heals.

Hiding in Christ means having listened to his voice; and, having listened, responded in a desperate act of faith. You can bet that right now, somewhere near you, it's happening. —James Calvin Schaap, *Near Unto God*

We carry in our memories the history of your presence in troubled times. You have strengthened us in pain and comforted us in grief. You have protected us in danger and held us in your love in times of stress. You are our refuge and strength. Bless our memories and hold us near you always. Amen.

July 21

The Strange Gift of Free Will

"For we are labourers together with God."
—1 Corinthians 3:9, KJV

The God I believe in is greater than anything I or anybody else can conceive. But part of my faith is that the Creator who made human beings with at least an iota of free will does not diminish that marvelous and terrible gift by manipulating us. God is not a Great Dictator. Every once in a while when life seems nearly unbearable I might long, fleetingly, for such a God who has already, as it were, written the story, but I do not want to be part of a tale that has already been told. God calls us to work with our Maker on the fulfilling of creation. What we do either moves us toward the Second Coming, the reconciliation of all things, or holds us back.

Yes, each of us is that important, and this can be very frightening. With our abuse of free will we have increased the ravages of disease; our polluted planet is causing more people to die of cancer than when the skies and seas and earth were clean. But this does not mean that we have to throw out the idea of a God who loves and cares.

What kind of a God of love can we believe in at this point in the human endeavor? How do we reconcile God's love and the strange gift of free will?
— Madeleine L'Engle, *Sold into Egypt*

Lord, you have given us the dignity and the responsibility of laboring together with you for the completion of our creation. May we honor this partnership by exercising our will in accord with your will that all shall be made well. Amen.

July 22

Is God the Cause?

"'Neither this man nor his parents sinned,' said Jesus, 'but this happened so that the work of God might be displayed in his life.'"
—John 9:3

I once attended a funeral service for a teenage girl killed in a car accident. Her mother wailed, "The Lord took her home. He must have had some purpose.... Thank you, Lord." I have been with sick Christian people who agonize over the question, "What is God trying to teach me?" Or, they may plead, "How can I find enough faith to get rid of this illness? How can I get God to rescue me?"

Maybe such people have it all wrong. Maybe God *isn't trying to tell us anything specific* each time we hurt. Pain and suffering are part and parcel of our planet, and Christians are not exempt. Half the time we know why we get sick: too little exercise, a poor diet, contact with a germ. Do we really expect God to go around protecting us whenever we encounter something dangerous?

As I understand it, the approach Jesus takes corresponds exactly to what I have suggested about "pain, the megaphone of God." Suffering offers a *general* message of warning to all humanity that something is wrong with this planet, and that we need radical outside intervention ("Unless you repent"). But you cannot argue backward and link someone's *specific* pain to a direct act of God.

Another, similar story from the Gospels may clarify this approach even further. In John 9, Jesus refutes the traditional explanation of suffering. His followers point to a man born blind. Clucking with pity, they ask, "Who sinned, this man or his parents?" In other words, why did he deserve blindness? Jesus answers bluntly, "Neither this man nor his parents sinned, but this happened so that the work of God might be displayed in his life."

The disciples wanted to look backward, to find out "Why?" Jesus redirected their attention. Consistently, he points forward, answering a different question: "To what end?" And that, I believe, offers a neat summary of the Bible's approach to the problem of pain. To backward-looking questions of cause, to the "Why?" questions, it gives no definitive answer. But it does hold out hope for the future, that even suffering can be transformed or "redeemed." A human tragedy, like blindness, can be used to display God's work.

Sometimes, as with the man born blind, the work of God is manifest through dramatic miracle. Sometimes it is not. But in every case, suffering offers an opportunity for us to display God's work.

—Philip Yancey, *Where Is God When It Hurts?*

Thank you, Lord for all the ways you offer us hope. In the face of suffering, there is hope for the future — that the suffering can be transformed to display your work. Keep me alert to this expectation as I move through my life. In Jesus' name. Amen.

July 23

THE PARADOX OF HUMANITY

"Teach me your way, O Lord, and I will walk in your truth; give me an undivided heart, that I may fear your name."   —Psalm 86:11

In summer I mow my lawn every week, unconscious of anything but satisfaction as the green velvet unrolls in ribbons behind me. Sometimes, though, as I smell the sweet spice of the cut grass, I hear God's word through his prophet Isaiah, telling me that *I am grass*. As I sniff my way into grass's greenness, its dew-bathed moisture in the early light, I also learn what it means to be as vulnerable as grass is to the scythe or the mower.

Isaiah says: "All people are grass, their constancy is like the flower of the field.... The grass withers, the flower fades; but the word of our God will stand forever." The greenest blades of grass will turn brown in a drying wind or be severed in an instant by a sharp blade and laid in swathes on the stubble to dry. And I bear the same stamp of frailty, weakness, mortality.

So it is a real surprise to read elsewhere in Isaiah's prophecy (Isa. 61:3) that as one of the people of God I am proclaimed an "oak of righteousness, a planting of the Lord." What could show a greater contrast — slender, perishable grass, growing at the foot of a long-lived, stalwart oak tree whose wood is renowned for its toughness? How could the Lord speak of the same person with two such opposite images?

To understand such seeming contradictions, we must learn to think metaphorically — and sometimes it seems that God mixes his metaphors, when he gives us two opposing statements that are both true. It is paradoxical for me to think of my husband, who died of cancer, in terms of the strength and durability of an oak tree (though in his life of service for God he was truly "a planting of the Lord") and yet affirm that in his death he partook of grass's tenderness and transience and vulnerability. Yet both are true.
—Luci Shaw, *Horizons*

It is no simple thing to walk in your truth, O Lord, for your truth is too much for me. I cannot grasp the mystery of your ways. That we are both as vulnerable as the grass and as durable as the oak confounds me. But you have not guaranteed me knowledge. Neither do you require of me explanations. You have, instead, promised me yourself. You ask of me only faithfulness, and for that you give me your grace and strength. Amen.

July 24

PLEASE

"At twilight you will eat meat, and in the morning you will be filled with bread. Then you will know that I am the Lord your God."
—Exodus 16:12b

Give me a bowl
of that soup
you've made with
cabbage, potatoes,
and many carrots.

I'm just back from
Remnant Acres, where
I've been splitting
twisted maple butt.
It ate my wedges
and wore me down.

Give me that good
nourishment your hands
provide. Sit with me
while I ask a blessing
on our day. All
we need is here.

—John Leax, *Country Labors*

Not only through the work of our hands but through the mystery of ways known to you alone you have provided for us, Lord. Though we have often grumbled, all we have ever needed has been ours. Teach us to need less and to give more. Make us, in your image, generous. Amen.

July 25

LOVE OR TERROR?

"Rejoice greatly, O daughter of Zion!...See, your king comes to you...gentle and riding on a donkey, a colt, the foal of a donkey."
—Zechariah 9:9

"Da-a-a-d-dy!" a little girl's voice called out on a cold winter night. I got up, stumbled into my daughter's room and carried her like a limp cotton doll against my chest into the bathroom, where I sat her on her little potty seat. In the red glow of the gas wall heater, I saw the softness of her face, her closed eyes and the long, slightly tousled blond hair. I was filled with the most amazing sense of love and gratitude for that little girl. *Someday* I thought, *we can talk together about this night when she is grown.* But as I tucked her back in bed, it struck me that she would never remember this midnight closeness — because she had been asleep the whole time I was holding her and loving her.

The people in Jesus' day were like my little girl — asleep and unaware of God's love surrounding them. In fact, their view of God was sometimes terrifying. When they asked Jesus how they should pray to this awesome God, Jesus told them to pray, "Father — *Abba* — Daddy." God was a loving Father.

When he entered Jerusalem on a donkey rather than a horse (symbol of war), Jesus was reminding the people again of God's love. It was as if the Hebrew nation had been asleep to the loving, fatherly care they had received from God as he had held them and comforted them through the many long, scary nights in their history. Jesus was trying to wake them up to experience God's love once more.

—J. Keith Miller, *Daily Guideposts,* 1996

Lord, thank you for making your way into the citadel of our frightened, lonely hearts in a way that wouldn't scare off the child part of us — on a little donkey. Amen.

July 26

LEARNING TO SWIM IN LAKE ADLEY

"I will give you the treasures of darkness, riches stored in secret places, so that you may know that I am the Lord...." —Isaiah 45:3a

After church I drive in the rain to Lake Adley.
Here I learn how everything is hooked to
everything else. The waves for instance,
each flashing in like another row of teeth.
From their angle I try to guess the way
the sand bars jut beneath the water.
There is more to this than what it looks like
on the surface. Think of everything the Lake
has caught on its sandy bottom and held there
like a memory: coins, old glasses, seaweed.
Any time we could get back the most important
clues. Today the Lake has tossed up
clam shells, whole clams like dark ears
holding their secrets in, and one big stone, white
and polished as the heart of God.

   I look up
through the drizzle and see Mrs. Sorensen
in her long skirts riding her bicycle toward me.
She stops right here and pulls me up.
We take off our shoes together, unhook our garters,
unroll our stockings till they hang like doughnuts
around our ankles. We shout and shake our hair out,
bright knives. Then we take our black shoes off
and wade in. We bob beside each other,
letting ourselves be carried anywhere, like gifts.

—Jeanne Murray Walker, *Gaining Time*

Lord, teach me to lean on you in total trust — to wade trustingly into life and let you guide me to places where I can find your secrets and your will. Forgive me when I try to run away from the waters of your love and go off in my own directions. Show me the treasures you have in store for me. I want to be yours — help me know the way. Amen.

July 27

ALL CREATURES GREAT AND SMALL

"Oh, the depth of the riches of the wisdom and knowledge of God! How unsearchable his judgements, and his paths beyond tracing out! Who has known the mind of the Lord?" —Romans 11:33-34a

Mayflies: The Hatch
for KS

Still they rise
like stars from the void,
light gone out or not yet kindled.
Each lies flat the pulse of an instant,
then stirs, a small vibrating rose.

At this moment the trout
comes or does not come,
sudden as a trumpet,
blowing a halo of bubbles.

It is no wonder,
lopsided with panic,
each wobbles into flight,
laboring in circles
just above the water.

(Even now a rainbow
may leap after,
rush it back to the deep
like a guilty kindness.)

Then,
straight up,
one after another,
each writes a secret name in the air,
ascending a moth-white sky
to vanish in solid cover.

—Robert Siegel, *In a Pig's Eye*

You have made the world and the smallest creatures in it to give you glory. Though we study, dissect, and analyze, our truest word is silent wonder. Praise to you, Creator Lord, for the smallest things your word has made. Amen.

July 28

Particular Praise

"The creation waits in eager expectation for the sons of God to be revealed." —Romans 8:19

I have a friend, an artist, who says the first thing she notices about a person is the colored splotch on the inner part of the eye socket where it curves upward to become a part of the nose, whether it is blue or purple or maybe slightly green. When she told me this, it startled me, and I was glad I was wearing glasses that hid my own little spot of color until I could go home and check it out for myself. If she had said that the first thing she noticed was the firmness of a person's handshake or the warmth of his smile or any of a dozen other characteristics by which we are admonished to judge people, I would not have felt self-conscious. But the inside of one's eye socket? That suddenly seemed a naked, vulnerable spot.

When my friend speaks of the subtle colors on human faces, it strikes us as extraordinary, a little odd, even faintly amusing, but not of the earthshaking importance it truly is. For how are we to give thanks for something we've never noticed? How shall we praise God for the world we've not paid proper attention to? Our practice of pigeonholing our praise into broad categories — family, friends, country, health, and the like — reminds me of the all-purpose, five-second prayer I devised as a child for use on cold nights: "God bless everybody in the world. Amen." When we pray in terms of everybody-in-the-world, we imagine ourselves to be dealing with a divine, omniscient bureaucracy. But God doesn't love everybody-in-the-world. He loves each of us singly, knowing the hairs of our heads and the shadows of our eye sockets.

One of the chief champions of this way of the senses in the Protestant tradition is, surprisingly, Jonathan Edwards, whose unfortunate reputation as a dour example of asceticism is due to his overly anthologized sermon "Sinners in the Hands of an Angry God." On the contrary, Edwards's early attention was absorbed by the natural sciences, the careful observation of spiders being his specialty. But natural science was not a mere sideline to his theological thought. His scrutiny of creation provided the full heart out of which he wrote his doctrine of creation, with which physics is only now catching up. "God not only created all things, and gave them being at first, but continually...upholds them in being," he says. "It will certainly follow from these things, that God's *preserving* created things in being is perfectly equivalent to a *continued creation,* or to his creating those things out of nothing *at each moment of their existence.*" —Virginia Stem Owens, *A Taste of Creation*

Dear Lord, it amazes me that you love me so individually, knowing the hairs of my head and the shadows of my eye sockets. Help me to pay proper attention to the world around me so that I may praise you in particular. In Jesus' name. Amen.

July 29

I'M TOO SMALL

"Do not be overcome by evil, but overcome evil with good."
—Romans 12:21

My schedule today is disrupted by other duties. So I arrive anxious and annoyed. Cold has returned, and here on the hill, snow is slowly covering the woods' floor. As I walked in, I noted curious patterns on the ground where trees broke the wind-driven snow and created lines free of snow like shadows on the ground. In the cabin the desk puddle was frozen. I set up my heater under the desk and read Psalms out loud until it melted and I regained some equilibrium. Though the Psalms are full of talk about enemies, they do not let the Psalmist/reader off the hook. I read in my anger at circumstances this morning, "Oh Lord my God, if I have done this; if there by iniquity in my hands; if I have rewarded evil unto him that was at peace with me, let the enemy persecute my soul, and take it."

Some days ago, when I began this journal, I said something about not being able to focus long on my sins, about moving directly to grace and being overwhelmed by it and by the restoration taking place. It seems, however, as I've meditated here, I've turned more and more to consciousness of my own sinfulness. What I wonder this morning is where that will take me. How will it lead me to change my life?

The nature of my sin is not flagrant—I needn't stop gambling, boozing, and womanizing. My sins are more subtle, tied to my virtues, are indeed virtues twisted into tools for my own advancement. But I'm not being quite fair to myself. My sin is not jealousy or ambition. It is a concern for good that fails to contain the good of all in its drive for the immediate good of a few. I'm too small. My emotional range isn't large enough to feel all needs. If I had the range to empathize more broadly, I could comprehend the needs that drive others, the needs that make them act unjustly. Then I could act redemptively rather than vindictively to gain a victory—my own way.

—John Leax, *Standing Ground*

Lord, forgive my grandiosity, my tendency to put myself in the center of the picture, to become so agitated at the unjust behavior of others. Help me to realize that there are so many more needs than my own at play in every situation.

Teach me to try to comprehend the needs that drive others to actions that seem unjust to me. Guide me to act redemptively, to find ways of helping to meet the others' need that make their unjust actions unnecessary. When I cannot uncover the need that generates unjust actions, teach me to refrain from cruelty, revenge, or other vindictive actions. Teach me how to be patient and decent as I hold firm to my convictions, trusting that your redemptive action in the world will bring about a resolution — your resolution! In Jesus' name. Amen.

July 30

Dorothy Day as Gardener

> "He said in a parable: 'A sower went out to sow his seed.... Some fell on good soil, and when it grew, it produced a hundredfold.' As he said this, he called out, 'Let anyone who has ears to hear listen!'"
> —Luke 8:4, 8, NRSV

"How can there be no God when there are all these beautiful things?" When the crepe-myrtles are at their most intense, when the caladiums are brimming with raindrops, these words of Dorothy Day come to mind.

Planting, we stick our spades into the soil. We spot the birds nesting under the eaves. We smell how the rain releases some inner fragrance from the earth. There is beauty in things made by people, too. Even in them, as in natural things, we can see the beauty of God. Reason is beside the point. It's the things we love, and the people we love, that are our proofs for the existence of God.

But when I pray with Dorothy I am called to find beauty in unbeautiful places: where people are hopeless and in need. Poverty — spiritual and material — is her way into God's treasure. Can I follow where she leads? From my middle-class perch, can I enter into her Lower East Side circumstances, can I share her vantage point at least for a little while?

Leafing through a biographical treatment of her life, Jim Forest's *Love Is the Measure,* is almost like looking through a family album. In some ways it's hard to identify with that kind, worn face, the white hair and the wispy braids, possibly because I know I will never do such radical and radicalizing things. I identify more easily with the young Dorothy, sitting on the beach at Staten Island with the man she loves. I appreciate the way she experienced God in her pregnancy; for her, having a baby was a metaphor of promise and peace. I know that woman. Also, childbirth was one of her most important learning experiences, which was also true for me. I am moved by the way she turned from unbelief and unmorality...the way an abortion made her dream of motherhood! All this is concrete. And near to me. I can grasp it.

But to go to prison for the Lord's sake? Fearful to the last, my childhood ways come back. I was the one who sat on the grass while others climbed the tree. But even under the tree, God finds me. He is speaking through butterflies, the clover, the grass. His words are quiet, unmistakable. "Follow me, and I will make you a fisher of hearts...." I am called to love, to live, to work, to love God in and through my work. My call is not Dorothy's but my own. The Lord asks something difficult in this very moment. I must live the call of my time, my generation, my city, my poverty, my circumstance.

Following Dorothy, I pass through a narrow door, and the world I have entered is more real than the one I left behind. My companions on the road are a strange lot, and we know the way is dangerous. There are trials ahead. But we are willing pilgrims. We know that to enter in, we must pass through a reversal, a paradox. The hard path is also strewn with roses. Dorothy is leading me in the way of simplicity. It is the Lord's way. Love, as Dorothy tells us, is the measure by which we will be judged.

Suddenly I am sure I don't want to be the good-for-nothing servant, the one who simply stashed his talents and never tried to make them more. I don't want the great door to close against me. I want to follow the Lord, no matter how stony the path, how dangerous the way.

—Emilie Griffin, *Homeward Voyage*

My Lord, I like the image of things that grow and flourish, and I am touched by the creativity of your servant Dorothy Day. She strikes me as an example of one who cultivated your Word, who treasured the seed of it in her heart, until it flowered into a tremendous witness of love. Lord, please give me, in my own way, a touch of Dorothy, her earthiness, her simplicity, her goodness, so I too may serve you worthily. Amen.

July 31

A SECURE PATHWAY

"I will lead the blind by ways they have not known, along unfamiliar paths I will guide them; I will turn darkness into light before them and make the rough places smooth. These are the things I will do; I will not forsake them." —Isaiah 42:16

A verse I read last night — "He will not let your foot be moved" — is working in my consciousness. Lately, walking around the house in leather-soled shoes on wood floors and my mind on other things, my feet *have* moved, slipped from under me, and several times I've landed in an awkward heap on the floor. But on my morning walk in my Reeboks I have no such trouble. I can stride confidently. I progress in a straight line and my mind can move in a hundred directions as I walk because my footing is secure under me. That's *my* part of the process.
—Luci Shaw, *God in the Dark*

Lord, only if you lead me can I walk securely. Be they rough or smooth, I choose to walk in your paths. Be my firm footing all my days. Amen.

AUGUST

August 1

CHOSEN AND LOVED

"The Lord your God has chosen you out of all the peoples on the face of the earth to be his people, his treasured possession.... It was because the Lord loved you." —Deuteronomy 7:6, 8

For all of my life, the effortless, arbitrary beauty of seaside shells and stones has signaled divine generosity. They seem to reflect the richness of God's own mind. Shells and grains of sand remind me of the importance of the microscopic and individual as well as of the vast and collective, like the endless ocean just beyond the line of lace where waves meet beach.

Some shell collectors can sit all day long in one spot on the textured banks of shells, sorting, picking through handfuls of treasures for the perfect specimen, the clearest pattern, the most intense color. The other method, which I prefer, is to walk close to the wave edges. There the wet shells can be seen individually in their tangerine and pink and butter yellow and rainbow iridescence. Their shapes draw my eye to them, as they glint in the sheen of each receding wave. They seem to whisper, "Here I am, waiting just for you." I bend and touch and rinse clean and caress each one with my eyes and my fingers before I store it in the bag I have brought along just for this. Now I can carry it home with me, to the center of a continent where there are no saltwater beaches, no shells like these.

In my home I have shells in every room — in green glass bottles on mantels or windowsills where the light can touch them. I pile shells in clay bowls together with slate pebbles and buttons of driftwood and agates and crab carapaces gleaned from all the beaches I have ever walked. Each of them seems to me to be *a parable of personal choice and significance.* I am amazed when I think of how God values *us,* bending down and raising each of us from among a million others, choosing us with an appreciative glint in his eye, wanting to take us home with him. God searches us out — you and me! —Luci Shaw, *Horizons*

O God, thank you for bending down and lifting me from the waters of anonymity into the fullness of your knowing love. In that love, in being known by you, I am made worthy. Amen.

August 2

LOVE-IN-IDLENESS

"Pharaoh said, 'Lazy, that's what you are — lazy! That is why you keep saying, "Let us go and sacrifice to the Lord." Now get to work.'"
— Exodus 5:17–18

A sign I've seen recently reads something like this: "I was put on this earth to accomplish a certain amount of work. I'm so far behind I'm going to live forever." It reminds me of the Pennsylvania Dutch saying, "The hurrier I go the behinder I get." We all hurry, and we all fall behind. If we are not required by some taskmaster to make bricks without straw, we set ourselves tasks and rush madly to accomplish them. In our frantic effort to do good work we forget we may have been put on this earth with a different purpose in mind. The Westminster Confession I memorized as a child reminds me, "The chief end of man is to glorify God and enjoy him forever." That's strong, counter-cultural stuff to learn as a child.

But what does it mean, particularly that part about enjoying God forever? It seems to imply that he is our pleasure. If so our relationship to him might not be best demonstrated by our acts on his behalf, our doing his work. It may be he prefers to do his own work. It may be our good works that keep us from receiving him as he intends.

It may be that the old saying "Idle hands are the devil's playthings" is entirely false. Idle hands may be the Lord's delight. The Egyptian pharaoh in the Exodus story certainly understood it that way; he makes a direct connection between the alleged idleness of the children of Israel and their desire to worship.

The flower Puck uses to cast his spell in *A Midsummer Night's Dream* is called Love-in-Idleness. Perhaps Shakespeare in choosing that name understood something we have forgotten; love wakens most easily when a lover's eyes can see nothing but the loved, and such singleness of vision occurs rarely in the Egypts of this world where distraction rules and Pharaoh's only end is a splendid tomb. — John Leax

Forgive us, Master, for our busyness, our foolish impulse to mistake you for an Egyptian overseer. Idle us; give us courage to fall sweetly into your grace and rest. Amen.

August 3

SPIRIT, SOUL, AND BODY

"May God himself, the God of peace, sanctify you through and though. May your whole spirit, soul and body be kept blameless at the coming of our Lord Jesus Christ."   —1 Thessalonians 5:23

I first began to realize that God cares about my physical well-being as well as my mind and soul when I came across this verse. This passage means so much to me because it refers to God's ministering to us "wholly"—to our minds, spirits, *and* bodies.

By attending Bible study and prayer groups, I had begun to nurture my soul and grow in my faith by learning more about how to pray and read the Scriptures. I'd also begun to take my emotional concerns to God and pray for the faith to let him help me with my worries and fears. I had begun studying to develop my mind, too, trying to better understand who I am under God and how I can begin to do his will.

But until recently, the idea of seeking God's will concerning my physical fitness and my health never entered my mind. I've always felt that things like how much I weighed and what shape I was in were up to me, and that God was mostly concerned with my spiritual well-being.

And yet, when I read this Scripture verse, I seem to hear Paul asking for a blessing of peace for the Thessalonians "wholly"—for their spirits, souls, *and* bodies. So I'm now beginning to talk to God about my health, too, asking him for the patience, the grace, the discipline, and the desire to make the changes I need to make in order to be healthy.

Resisting the "temptations" of unhealthy foods and getting over being too lazy to exercise have been recurring battles for me. They still are. But trying to develop the *desire* to make these changes has been even more challenging! As Thomas à Kempis pointed out in *The Imitation of Christ,* "He who merely flees the outward occasions of temptation and does not cut away the inordinate desires hidden inwardly in his heart shall gain little; temptation will easily come again and grieve him more than it did at first."

It seems to me that my *desire* for unhealthy foods is what makes it so hard to resist them. If I didn't *want* ice cream so much, I wouldn't care about eating it. I'm certainly never bothered with temptations to eat raw oysters! Ugh! (Pardon me if you're an oyster lover.) So until my desires change, patience, grace, and discipline seem very hard to come by.

So I have decided this time to invite God into my struggle to become fit for him—to be ready to do his will, to see how God might want me to approach this problem in my life. I am learning to pray for help and to try to be specific about the areas which give me the most trouble.

—Andrea Wells Miller, *BodyCare*

Dear Lord, you know I have wanted to keep my body healthy, but I haven't always been willing to pay the price. I want to be sound in spirit, mind, and body. I ask you now to come into my life and to be present as I study how you made my body and what it takes to keep it fit.

When I read Paul's words to the Thessalonians, I am thankful that you are a God of peace and that you care about my health as much as you do about my soul. Help me to remember this as I try to learn what you would have me to learn during this time. In Jesus' name I pray, Amen.

August 4

OF TWO WORLDS

"The Pharisees, who loved money, heard all this and were sneering at Jesus. He said to them, 'You are the ones who justify yourselves in the eyes of men, but God knows your hearts. What is highly valued among men is detestable in God's sight.'" —Luke 16:14-15

A story is told about Rabbi Joseph Schneerson, a Hasidic leader during the early days of the Russian revolution. The rabbi spent much time in jail, persecuted for his faith. One morning in 1927, as he prayed in a Leningrad synagogue, secret police rushed in and arrested him. They took him to a police station and worked him over, demanding that he give up his religious activities. He refused. The interrogator brandished a gun in his face and said, "This little toy has made many a man change his mind." Rabbi Schneerson answered, "This little toy can intimidate only that kind of man who has many gods and but one world. Because I have only one God and two worlds, I am not impressed by this little toy."

The theme of "two worlds," or two kingdoms, emerges often in Jesus' teaching, and two stories in this chapter [Luke 16] draw a sharp distinction between the two worlds. "What is highly valued among men is detestable in God's sight," Jesus said, commenting on the first story. The second story, of the rich man and Lazarus, elaborates on that difference in values between the two worlds. The rich man prospered in this world, yet neglected to make any provision for eternal life and thus suffered the consequences. Meanwhile, a half-starved beggar, who by any standard would be judged a failure in this life, received an eternal reward.

Jesus told such stories to a Jewish audience with a tradition of wealthy patriarchs, strong kings, and victorious heroes. But Jesus kept emphasizing his stunning reversal of values. People who have little value in this world (the poor, the persecuted — people like Lazarus) may, in fact, have great stature in God's kingdom. Consistently he presented the visible world as a place to invest for the future, to store up treasure for the life to come.

Jesus once asked a question that brings the two worlds starkly together: "What good will it be for a man if he gains the whole world, yet forfeits his soul?" (Matt. 16:26).   —Philip Yancey, *A Guided Tour of the Bible*

Dear Lord, keep my focus on the things that will feed and nurture my soul. Help me to grow closer to you and your ways, in Jesus' name. Amen.

August 5

I CRY, BUT THOU HEAREST NOT

"O my God, I cry in the daytime, but thou hearest not."
—Psalm 22:2a, KJV

Half the world away, an earthquake devastates the city of two million people. Newscasts run video of ten-story buildings perfectly flattened, entire communities laid waste, freeways twisted into concrete ribbons. Random fires roam like voracious criminals in the devastation. Everywhere there is looting. People without homes, without shelter, their faces full of the numbing effects of shock, sit and huddle beneath whatever shelter they can find. What we see before us is disaster.

Thirty seconds after the news flashes across the screen, you think of neighbors down the street who have a daughter and a son-in-law in that very city. They're close friends, so you run next door immediately to see how they're doing.

All night, you stay up with your friends as, hour after hour, they sit at the telephone, waiting for some word. Time after time they try, to no avail. The State Department tells them that the moment they get any word, they will call. But your friends keep trying. Every time they hang up the phone, the pain on their faces is more noticeable.

When we get no answers — when we ask, when we beg, when we plead, but no one seems to be there, hope fades effortlessly into despair.

Psalm 83 complains, "O God, keep not thy silence; hold not thy peace as one deaf and be not still, O God!" David begs God to come closer in Psalm 13: "How long wilt thou forget me, O Lord?" for ever? how long wilt thou hide thy face from me?"

Why God chooses at some times to be absent from our misery is a mystery. How, for instance, do we explain what Christ meant when he said, "My God, my God, why hast thou forsaken me?" All we can do is hazard some guesses at why God is away.

Grace is not a habit or an empty ritual. It is a holy thing, not a subject to our whims. God is God, not man. Whatever his reasons for keeping himself afar off, our own experience teaches us that we may well come to value his communion more highly because of those very times when we know, so deeply, that he isn't there.

Perhaps his absence makes our souls search more intensely. We know this: to receive him again, after his withdrawal, bathes our soul in the fullness of his love. Not having him at our side makes his divinity more indisputable. We value his presence more abundantly, having come to know, only too well, the grief of his absence.

—James Calvin Schaap, *Near Unto God*

Lord, we have not always found you in the circumstances of our lives. Whether you have hidden yourself or we have been blind does not change the depth of our loneliness. Thank you for the grace that keeps us searching for you. Thank you for finding us. Amen.

August 6

Bright Upon Your Shoulders

"Have mercy upon me, O Lord; for I am weak: O Lord, heal me; for my bones are vexed." —Psalm 6:2, KJV

"My child," the great warm voice could be formidably stern, "your relationship with the Lord is between him and you. It is not in comparison with one of your Sisters."

Joaquina held out her hand with the gold wedding band on the third finger. "Sometimes I think he doesn't care about me, that he's never wanted me for his bride. While she—"

"Sister Joaquina, these are evil thoughts."

"That is why I confess them."

"Go into the chapel and feel God's love. At first do not attempt to pray. Kneel there and you will feel it as bright upon your shoulders as the rays of the sun coming through the colored glass of the windows. His love for *you*. His love for Sister Joaquina. You are infinitely precious to him."

She responded with obedience but little conviction, "Yes, Father."

—Madeleine L'Engle, *The Love Letters*

> *King of mercy, king of love,*
> *Thou my life, in whom I move,*
> *Perfect what thou hast begun,*
> *Let no night put out this sun.*
> —Henry Vaughan, 1622–95

August 7

MAGIC WORDS

> "Peter said to him, 'You shall never wash my feet.' Jesus answered him, 'If I do not wash you, you have no part in me.' Simon Peter said to him, 'Lord, not my feet only but also my hands and my head!'"
> —John 13:8–9, NKJV

"That was a great job, Keith!" The man who was speaking is a person whom I deeply respect and love. I had just given a talk in our church, and he was enthusiastically and sincerely affirming me.

"Thanks, but I'm afraid I was too direct," I replied. "I was tired and felt a little hostile." He looked at me strangely, and I went into the educational wing to get ready for church school.

While walking away, I realized what I had done. I had very subtly and unintentionally devalued him as a person. He was trying to tell me that I had done a good job, and he had really meant it. But instead of thanking him for his affirmation, I had told him in effect, "Actually, you aren't really very smart. I heard some negative things about my talk that you didn't hear." Although I had not said that, I saw that my negative reply had in some way rejected him and his kindness in complimenting me in the first place.

Thinking about what had happened, I realized how often I turn people off when they try to say something nice to me. If I happened to make a high score on an examination in college, for instance, and someone said, "Congratulations," I might have laughed and come back with something cute like, "As much time as I spent studying for that one, an orangutan would have done well." I seemed to turn attention away from their attempts to affirm me, thinking somehow that I was being humble.

But now I am beginning to see that instead of humility, this inability to accept praise or affirmation is really an insidious form of pride and insecurity. Further, it represents a completely thoughtless attitude toward the needs of the one trying to offer congratulations. If a person is sincere with a compliment, he or she is going out on a limb to identify with me. The person is reaching out to say, "I, too, feel as you do or appreciate life as you do." Or, "In some sense we are related or I would not have responded to what you said." But my reply of supposed humility has turned the attention *away* from the person giving the compliment and toward me and my cleverness. I have devalued the offered love by joking or saying in effect, "No, we are *not* alike, because you misinterpreted my performance." Or, "Your perception is faulty." Or, "If you are like me, you are really a dummy, because any dolt could have done what I have."

It is clear to me now that with all my apparent willingness, as a Christian, to love other people, I fail to love them when I refuse to hear their attempts to love me. I suppose I reject their love because I'm afraid it is unreal and I cannot risk being hurt — in case they do not mean it — or sometimes I evidently want to appear humble, if they do mean it. So I protect myself from being hurt or from looking proud by dismissing as insignificant any attempts people make to say affirming things to me. Never before had I realized fully the negative, squelching effect of refusing to accept another's kind word.

Since making these discoveries, I am going to try to look people in the eye and say simply and warmly, "Thank you," if they try to say something positive to me. At a deep level I know that anything worthwhile I have is from God. And somehow, by letting people express positive feelings to me through a handshake and a few words, I think something is completed in the attempt to communicate the love of God in human terms. —J. Keith Miller, *Habitation of Dragons*

> Words and magic were in the beginning one and the same thing, and even today words retain much of their magical power. By words one of us can give to another the greatest happiness or bring about utter despair.... Words call forth emotions and are universally the means by which we influence our fellow creatures. Therefore let us not despise the use of words.
> —Sigmund Freud, *A General Introduction to Psychoanalysis*

Thank you, God that you are willing to receive my stumbling and often half-sincere attempts to praise you. Since you showed us in Christ that it is important for us to be able to receive, please give us the grace we need to do so. I am grateful that you take these praises of mine seriously rather than rejecting me with a denial or a joke, which would leave me alone and sorry I tried. Help me learn how to love. But, O Lord, give me the security to risk receiving love from other people, love that I fear may not be real. Amen.

August 8

WAIT ON GOD

"Wait for the Lord; be strong and take heart and wait for the Lord."
—Psalm 27:14

I would like to offer counsel to those who find themselves devoid of the presence of God. It is this: wait on God. Wait silent and still. Wait, attentive and responsive. Learn that trust precedes faith. Faith is a little like putting your car into gear, and right now you cannot exercise faith, you cannot move forward. Do not berate yourself for this. But when you are unable to put your spiritual life into drive, do not put it into reverse; put it into neutral. Trust is how you put your spiritual life in neutral. Trust is confidence in the character of God. Firmly and deliberately you say, "I do not understand what God is doing or even where God is, but I know that he is out to do me good." This is trust. This is how to wait.

I do not fully understand the reasons for the wildernesses of God's absence. This I do know: while the wilderness is necessary, it is never meant to be permanent. In God's time and in God's way the desert will give way to a land flowing with milk and honey. And as we wait for that promised land of the soul, we can echo the prayer of Bernard of Clairvaux, "O my God, deep calls unto deep [Ps. 42:7]. The deep of my profound misery calls to the deep of your infinite mercy."

—Richard J. Foster, *Prayer: Finding the Heart's True Home*

GOD, WHERE ARE YOU!? What have I done to make you hide from me? Are you playing cat and mouse with me, or are your purposes larger than my perceptions? I feel alone, lost, forsaken.

You are the God who majors in revealing yourself. You showed yourself to Abraham, Isaac, and Jacob. When Moses wanted to know what you looked like, you obliged him. Why them and not me?

I am tired of praying. I am tired of asking. I am tired of waiting. But I will keep on praying and asking and waiting because I have nowhere else to go.

Jesus, you, too, knew the loneliness of the desert and the isolation of the cross. And it is through your forsaken prayer that I speak these words. Amen.
—Richard J. Foster, *Prayer: Finding the Heart's True Home*

August 9

GOD OF THE ORDINARY

"Listen to this, Job; stop and consider God's wonders. Do you know how God controls the clouds and makes his lightning flash?"
—Job 37:14-15

In the hot noon sun of a summer day I went with two of my daughters, Robin and Kristin, and my granddaughter Lindsay, to a raspberry farm, with acres of bushes in green rows where you can pick your own berries and save some pennies. There we plucked, for eating and for making jam, twelve pounds of raspberries — huge hybrids, sweet, red-velvet pendants ripe enough to drop into our hands and thence into the plastic buckets slung around our necks.

As we slowly passed between the tall green thickets of bushes, starting and stopping, our fingers stained, our mouths tart with the taste of summer, we would be sure we had thoroughly stripped a certain bush. Then, as we crouched lower, we could see from the new angle all the hidden treasures that remained — berries hanging like red hearts, hiding behind the leaves, waiting for our nimble fingers.

I felt sad for the ones that never got picked (no one took the trouble to go slowly enough or search for them carefully enough), for the ones that seemed too small or too hard to reach. All that slow ripening, as the rains fell and the short, cool days turned long and warm — for nothing — fruit without fruitfulness.

Unpicked raspberries are like the ideas we've never discovered because we see and think superficially, like the precious people we ignore, like the images of the holy hinted at in creation, like the glimpses of God we miss because our eyes are half-closed or our attention distracted. Harvesting ideas, loving ordinary people, seeing correspondences between the seen and unseen worlds, and gleaning glimpses of God — such tasks, like berry picking, take time, thoroughness, and the willingness to crouch in the sandy soil, to peer upwards, to lift aside the raspberry leaves, to see deep to the heart of each bush — to penetrate its leafy green reality and value what we find there.

How odd that God humbles himself to be seen in the most ordinary, everyday, taken-for-granted stuff of creation! Yet his image is stamped wherever we turn our eyes. The clues to his reality are under our feet, they brush our hands, they rustle in our ears, they mark our bare legs with their sharpness, and they burn our eyes with their color. We are faced so often with things we know but still need to learn. How marvelous it is that realities as mundane as leaves, sunlight, berries, and the delighted cries of young children, are lenses through which we may find God.
—Luci Shaw, *Horizons*

Creator Father, everywhere about me I sense your wonderful works. How marvelous that you made me to see, to touch and taste. Your world is good. Teach me to love it because it is yours so that my delight might be pure, a return of your extravagant care to you. Amen.

August 10

KNOWING AND BEING KNOWN

"I gave up all that inferior stuff so I could know Christ personally, experience his resurrection power." —Philippians 3:8, THE MESSAGE

The word "know" often has sexual connotations in biblical writings. Adam knew Eve. Joseph did not know Mary. These are not, as so many suppose, timid euphemisms; they are bold metaphors. The best knowledge, the knowledge that is thorough and personal, is not information. It is shared intimacy—a knowing and being known that becomes a creative act. It is analogous to sexual relationship in which two persons are vulnerable and open to each other, the consequence of which is the creation of new life.

Unamuno, a Spanish philosopher, elaborates: "'To know' means in effect to engender, and all vital knowledge in this sense presupposes a penetration, a fusion of the innermost being of a man who knows and of the thing known" (*The Agony of Christianity*). The knowing results in a new being that is different from and more than either partner. No child is a replica of either parent; no child is a mere amalgamation of parents. There are characteristics of both, but the new life is unpredictable, full of surprises, a life of its own.

This sexual knowing that results in newly created life is the everyday experience that is used to show what happens when we pray: withdrawal from commotion, shutting the door against the outside world, insistence on leisurely privacy. This is not an antisocial act. It is not a selfish indulgence. It is no shirking of public responsibility. On the contrary, it is a fulfilling of public responsibility, a contribution to the wholeness of civilization. It is, precisely, creative: You cannot make love in traffic. For all his marvelous creativity, Michelangelo never painted or drew or sculpted anything that compares with any newborn infant. For all his wide-ranging Renaissance inventiveness, Leonardo da Vinci never faintly approximated what any peasant couple brought forth by simply going to bed together. People who pray give themselves to the creative process at this same elemental, world-enriching, self-transcending place of surprise and pleasure.

—Eugene H. Peterson, *Earth and Altar/Where Your Treasure Is*

Dear Lord, thank you that encountering you in prayer is such a world-enriching, self-transcending place of surprise and pleasure. Rekindle in me a desire to enter this creative process, this place of leisurely privacy. And thank you that such a life-giving experience for me will also contribute to the wholeness of civilization. In Jesus' name. Amen.

August 11

THE POOR ON OUR DOORSTEP

> "He has shown strength with his arm;
>   he has scattered the proud in the thoughts of their hearts.
> He has brought down the powerful from their thrones,
>   and lifted up the lowly;
>   he has filled the hungry with good things
>   and sent the rich away empty."
>
> —Luke 1:51–53, NRSV

Let me tell you about Myrtle, who comes to our door every Christmas and holiday, looking for a little something. Because of some of the twists of the social structure in the South I have to believe that even though Myrtle comes to our doorway asking for things, she is not precisely a beggar. Myrtle is a person who believes that the promises made to Israel are true.

Myrtle seems to expect a kind of justice. She supposes that between the people who live on Prytania Street, and the government of the United States, and Kingsley House, and the City of New Orleans, that though she is old and infirm and doesn't have all her own teeth, that everything is going to be all right.

Myrtle is the person the Lord has sent to us to be a vivid reminder of God's presence in our midst. She announces in a somewhat irritating way (she rings the doorbell very noisily, and with high expectations) that the poor who trust in the mercy of God and in the kindness of their neighbors are under his protection. They are his poor; they are my poor; and I am responsible for them.

Now there is another voice in me that cries out, I am powerless. Myrtle better take care of herself, because I have nothing to give her. Myrtle, for me, is that woman bothering the judge in the middle of the night till he got up and gave her justice.

Myrtle is for me, in Hebrew phrase, the *anawim*, the powerless person in the vast, shredding cloth of society, here and everywhere, that reminds me I must care.

Not so many years ago, a number of us were encouraged by the witness of forty-five recording artists who gathered together to accomplish a miracle for the children of Africa.

Yes, we were disillusioned when much of the huge sum raised was siphoned off by graft and double-dealing.

But in our own immediate neighborhoods, when children are in need, and we can see how interwoven the fabric of our society is, we cannot fail to respond to the needs of God's poor. We ourselves, who are powerless, we who are spiritually and materially needy, we who know the pinch of want, we also know the power of the Lord's generosity to us.

—Emilie Griffin, *Homeward Voyage*

Dear God, teach me to embrace your counsels of poverty, and to understand what you are asking of me with regard to your justice. Help me to discern how I can act compassionately, without being overwhelmed by the magnitude and gravity of social concerns. Amen.

August 12

WILD DIVERSITY

"God is exalted in his power. Who is a teacher like him? Who has prescribed his ways or said to him, 'You have done wrong'? Remember to extol his work, which men have praised in song. All mankind has seen it; men gaze on it from afar. How great is God—beyond our understanding!" —Job 36:22-26a

July 23, 199–
(Puget Sound)

I woke about 6:00 a.m. and went off looking for coffee. Since this is Seattle I quickly found a bright, sunny place (yes, a bright, sunny place) open, bought two lattes and brought them back to *Pneuma,* Melissa and Guy's sailboat/home, and woke my wife, Linda. Then I sat in the cockpit, taking the morning sun, and read until about 8:00. Before me, as long as I stayed seated, I saw nothing but seawall and masts. If I stood, I looked across the Sound to the Olympic Mountains, snowy in the mist.

Though this is a place I could get used to, it is a strange place. Looking over the stern, I watched a lion-maned jellyfish about 18 inches across plus tentacles blooming like a flower. It had eight gray fringed petals around a double center. Rust surrounded a bright red middle. The petals were orange, tinged with yellow, before the gray. It opened into a the large disk I first saw; then it closed, collapsing into itself, into a domed circle.

The strangeness of such creatures is compounded by my lack of knowledge. I cannot name the seabirds. The familiar herons, feeding at low tide and perching on the piers and even the tops of masts, comfort me. But how is it such a beautiful bird is endowed with such an awful grating croak of a call and such a foul habit as defecating when it takes flight? God's ways, surely, are not my ways. —John Leax

It is good, O Lord, to travel to new places, for if I travel with open eyes, I discover you anew in the strangeness of your works. I praise you for the wild diversity of what you have made, the revelation of yourself you have spoken in creation. And I give you thanks for the senses you have given me to experience it all — the joyous, the amusing, and the troubling. Teach me to love what you have made with the same love you pour out sustaining it. Amen.

August 13

MARY OF BETHANY

"Then Mary took about a pint of pure nard, an expensive perfume; she poured it on Jesus' feet and wiped his feet with her hair. And the house was filled with the fragrance of the perfume." —John 12:3

Matthew and Mark both place the next Bethany scene at the home of someone called Simon the Leper, while John locates it at the sisters' home. Was Lazarus, like Peter, also called Simon? Had his death in fact been caused by leprosy, a disease that would require him to live outside the city, thus leaving the house in Martha's hands? Now that he was healed and could live at home again, did Matthew and Mark designate the house as his? Whatever the answer to those questions, it is obvious that neither of those two gospel writers was as familiar with the Bethany family as John. As if to clarify Matthew's and Mark's account, John emphasizes that the Mary present at the raising of Lazarus is the same woman who plays a central role in this following scene.

Since Jesus intends to celebrate the Passover this year in Jerusalem, he decides to spend the next week at Martha's house in Bethany, only a few miles from the city. Martha is in the kitchen again, preparing a dinner both to honor her guest and celebrate her brother's restoration. And Mary has once more left her sister to do the work.

But this time she goes to unpack a secret treasure she's squirreled away for some special occasion — an entire pint of an expensive perfume. (Mark prices the contents of the alabaster container at three hundred denarii, almost a year's wages for a working man.) She slips into the dining room where the guests are reclining, assembled to celebrate her brother's new life. Approaching the couch where Jesus reclines, without a word of explanation she opens the vessel and pours it — all of it — over Jesus' feet. As the heavy scent rises, filling the room, the other people turn to stare. Then slowly, deliberately, Mary takes down her long hair and begins to wipe the feet of the man she loves above all others.

Throughout the entire scene, Mary never speaks. In fact, the only time Mary ever speaks is to echo her sister's words at her brother's tomb. Whereas Martha is never at a loss for words, Mary appears reticent in the extreme. She is forced to find other ways to express her devotion.

But Mary is proclaiming something more than simple emotion by this act. Her bizarre exhibition of love is much like the symbolic acts used by earlier Hebrew prophets to deliver their messages. Jeremiah used a rotten linen belt to illustrate his nation's decay; Mary is using her perfume to prophesy what lies ahead for Jesus. She sees what the others do not. Not much more than a week ago her brother came shuffling out of his tomb, grave clothes flapping around him. Another week and there will be another body, another tomb. She alone among Jesus' followers takes to heart his warnings about his approaching death.

Like most prophets, however, Mary and her message go unheeded. The other guests see only a woman with loose hair — something they understand easily enough. In fact, the disciples are outraged by Mary's behavior, finding it immodest, shocking — as well as an extravagant waste of the perfume.

"Shameful," they mutter amongst themselves. Judas, the treasurer of the group, voices what they're all thinking. "We could have done a lot of good with that. If she didn't need it, she could have given it to us. We'd have seen to it that the poor benefited from it at least."

Jesus, unperturbed by her act, speaks up immediately. "Just a minute here," he says. "Leave her alone. Don't you understand what this act of hers signifies? I'm going to die. And she's the only one who sees that. That's why she's used the perfume this way — to prepare me for burial." Then he points out the same thing to them he told Martha when she complained against her sister earlier. "There's nothing to stop you from doing what you want to. It's your choice. You can give to the poor anytime you want to. They're always there, ready and waiting for your charity. Me, on the other hand, you may not have around much longer."

Matthew extends Jesus' defense of Mary: "What she's done for me here is beautiful. Wherever my story is told she'll be a part of it. She'll never be forgotten." And indeed, Mary's story appears in all four gospels.

Jesus never upbraids anyone in the gospels for extravagance. In fact, he applauds it. He's all for generosity, never a utilitarian. In our culture, we tend to side with Judas. "She has done something beautiful for me," Jesus said. But what use is beauty? You can't eat it. It doesn't pay the bills. Yet it points beyond itself, in the direction of all our hungers.

When we grasp at beauty and try to possess it for ourselves, we become like Potiphar's wife, prisoners of sensuality. But when we allow our senses to aim us toward the source of beauty itself, we become like Mary — lavish with love.

Mary remains in the background, except when her passion overwhelms her passivity. Her only means of expressing her inward ardor is aesthetic and symbolic. We *hear* Martha; we *see* Mary, her face veiled by her long hair as she wipes the perfume she's spilled on her Lord's feet. She *enacts* love; our memories are marked with the sight.

—Virginia Stem Owens, *Daughters of Eve*

Help me, O Lord, to allow my senses to aim me toward you, the source of beauty itself. Loosen my frugal hold on my expression, and let me find ways to lavish you with love. In Jesus' name. Amen.

August 14

DYSFUNCTION

"The body is a unit, though it is made up of many parts; and though all its parts are many, they form one body. So it is with Christ."
—1 Corinthians 12:12

I've learned that if I belong to the visible church, then I am also visible, whether or not I'm in the mood. No retreating into a private, none-of-the-world's-business kind of faith. If I call myself a Christian, then I must be one openly, even during the periods of dryness, when there seems no rational or existential justification for such a perspective in the world. Or when I feel only shame and despair at the church's failures, or my own. Even then I can't retreat from confrontation. If I belong to this vast family, I belong, and there is no escape from engagement. All the goofy cousins are mine, the uncles who drink too much and feel you up, the grandpas who rule with their canes, the great-aunts who stuff you with sweets, the sister who bosses you around, and the parents who give and take excessively. I may disagree with them from the bottom of my soul, weep at their tragic decisions, fight them in private and public, and even call the cops, but I can never kid myself into thinking that I'm not connected. They are still my family. "The eye cannot say to the hand, 'I have no need of you'" (1 Cor. 12:21).

And no doubt I'm a nerdy cousin, too, and who else other than my family will tell me so? Who else really worries about me, allows me to sulk and shut myself in my room, kick the door and yell, and still come out for dinner? That may not be everyone's experience in the church, but it's been mine, that I still belong no matter how much at odds I may be with the rest of the family.

—Shirley Nelson, "Prospecting," in *Rattling Those Dry Bones*

Lord, there are not many perfect people in your body, the church. Teach us how to accept and forgive each other's weaknesses and quirks. Amen.

August 15

WITHOUT GOD IN THE WORLD

"At that time ye were without Christ, being aliens from the commonwealth of Israel, and strangers from the covenants of promise, having no hope, and without God in the world." —Ephesians 2:12, KJV

Today atheism is not only commonplace; in some quarters it's fashionable. Those who deny God are far more numerous now than they were years ago, and in many cases no one bugs them for what they preach. Today, believers don't shudder at the atheists' rhetoric as they used to either—and that indifference creates a problem.

Think of it this way. When our political leaders are constantly criticized in the press, in talk shows, on late-night television, we get accustomed to hearing bad things. We stop reacting negatively, and our leaders gradually lose credibility in our eyes. What's more—and what's worse—as the poison works within us, it extinguishes our own aspiration for public service. It's insidious really, isn't it?

Yet it goes on. And so does a relentless campaign against God in our culture.

It is undeniable that a serious menace to public life exists when some of our culture's most prominent figures make religion laughable. Empires leave track records behind them, and many of those histories look identical. A nation and a culture is born and soon grows wealthy. Wealth leads to moral decay, moral decay to religious indifference, religious indifference to atheism—a world without God—and atheism to ruin.

Often those who deny God, love art, practice philanthropy, and promote education enthusiastically. Often they dote on ideals which awaken poetic talent within them. They're nice people. But religion, to them, is superfluous.

How do we preach to those people? As important as are creeds and practices of faith — preaching, baptism, holy communion — the only way to reawaken a thirst for God in these people is the power of love. Love alone can work salvation. Why? In our love, the reality of a life in God is shown clearly. That love thaws frozen hearts.

Look, so much in our lives works against faith: wealth, temptation, our work, our recreation, our troubles and our sorrows. Our busyness distracts us all too often.

In the conflict we all face between our own divided loyalties, only God can equip us with the energy and the armaments to continue to live wholly in his light. We can be real believers only when he equips us to stay near unto God, even though we're in the very center of our busyness.

We can carry his love into all of life, even to the atheists among us, when our nearness to him becomes our own, regenerated, second nature. —James Calvin Schaap, *Near Unto God*

Arm us with your love, O Lord. Let us live wholly in your light that the brightness of your searching beam might reach through us to those among us choosing the darkness of their own ways. Amen.

August 16

BEHIND THE MYSTERY

"...and lo, I am with you always, even unto the end of the world."
—Matthew 28:20, KJV

I do not ever want to be indifferent to the joys and beauties of this life. For through these, as through pain, we are enabled to see purpose in randomness, pattern in chaos. We do not have to understand in order to believe that behind the mystery and the fascination there is love.

In the midst of what we are going through this summer I have to hold on to this, to return to the eternal questions without demanding an answer. The questions worth asking are not answerable. Could we be fascinated by a Maker who was completely explained and understood? The mystery is tremendous, and the fascination that keeps me returning to the questions affirms that they are worth asking and that any God worth believing in is the God not only of the immensities of the galaxies I rejoice in at night when I walk the dogs but also the God of love who cares about the sufferings of us human beings and is here, with us, for us, in our pain and in our joy. — Madeleine L'Engle, *Two-Part Invention*

> *He doth give his joy to all;*
> *He becomes an infant small,*
> *He becomes a man of woe;*
> *He doth feel the sorrow too.*
> *Think not thou canst sigh a sigh,*
> *And thy maker is not by;*
> *Think not thou canst weep a tear,*
> *And thy maker is not near.*
> —William Blake, 1757–1827

August 17

LOVE-MESSAGES FROM HEAVEN

"The heavens declare the glory of God; the skies proclaim the work of his hands. Day after day they pour forth speech; night after night they display knowledge." —Psalm 19:1-2

Humans can't seem to leave the landscape alone, untouched, unmeddled with. What causes us to carve our names or initials on our school desks or on park benches or tree trunks? What impels us to spray paint them on wayside rocks and bridges? We want our identity to be remembered, our love immortalized. We want to leave a message to the next generation: "I was here. Don't forget me!" or "Remember. We two were so much in love."

There are other, less blatant messages to be read, if we open our eyes to decode the clues. Our heavenly Lover's devotion and passion for us are evident in the life of the earth around us, in every natural phenomenon — rounded beach stones, sprouting wheat along the furrows, water running clear over rocks, the spiral shape of a shell, the uncorrupted sky. Everything can speak of God, if we take time to look and listen, to see with the eyes of the heart, which he has promised to enlighten. Can we read his letters to us? "Listen to me. I cherish you. Once I came to live among you so that you could know my love. Now, here in the rain on your windshield, the frost on the stubble, the warm breath of the breeze, is another love note. Read it, and hold it in your heart."

—Luci Shaw, *Horizons*

God, you have given me eyes to see. With them I have read the letters of your creation. Your word is lovely. Make me your linguist. Give me speech to praise your works. Make me holy to honor your name. Amen.

August 18

LEARNED BY HEART

"I have hidden your word in my heart, that I might not sin against you."
—Psalm 119:11

When I was a little girl growing up in Tennessee, I belonged to a Baptist church. I was a member of just about everything there was to join in that congregation. And in the process of attending Sunday School, Girls' Auxiliary meetings, and choir, I learned a lot of Scripture. In choir, we sang anthems that were Scripture verses set to music. I remember with joy an energetic setting of, "If God be for us, who can be against us? Who can separate us from the love of God?" I still am tempted to say it in the musical rhythm of that anthem!

When I was young, however, I thought having to memorize so many Bible verses was rather pointless. I didn't understand the meanings of half of what I learned, and the other half didn't apply to me because I wasn't old enough to know how selfish, lazy, and weak I really am! But now, when I'm really interested in knowing God's will for my life and in trying to put into practice everything I can learn about what his will might be, I find myself repeating fragments of Bible verses I learned as a child. And these fragments are often inspiring, comforting, confronting, educating, and motivating.

I realize that memorizing parts of God's Word has helped me so much today because I can carry promises of God's care and guidance with me wherever I go. These verses sometimes guide me through difficulties or help me celebrate joyful times.

A woman I know told me she uses the time she spends jogging or doing exercises to memorize Scripture verses. She puts a verse or two on an index card and carries it in her hand while she's running. Or she puts the card on the mat beside her and studies it while she works out. Then at some other time, when she doesn't have her card with her, the verse is there to inspire her because it's memorized. Since one of the big problems for some people in exercising regularly is boredom, it seems to me this is a great way to use the time!   —Andrea Wells Miller, *BodyCare*

Dear Lord, thank you that you can communicate with us through the Bible. Help me to want to learn your Word and keep it in my heart so I can know how to be your person all through the day. Guide me to the places in your Word which will speak to me in areas I need to hear. And thank you for my friend, whose example of studying the Bible during exercise has shown me that there is time to do both, if I am willing. In Jesus' name. Amen.

August 19

DESERT RAIN

"The eyes of the blind shall be opened, and the ears of the deaf unstopped; then shall the lame man leap like a hart, and the tongue of the dumb sing for joy. For waters shall break forth in the wilderness, and streams in the desert; the burning sand shall become a pool, and the thirsty ground springs of water; the haunt of jackals shall become a swamp, the grass shall become reeds and rushes. And a highway shall be there, and it shall be called the Holy Way." —Isaiah 35:5-8a, RSV

We prayed for their coming,
Those clouds that moved in.
The heat was condensing;
It stuck to your skin.

The road was white powder
Exploded by wheels.
We breathed it and cursed it.
It flavored our meals.

The cattle were dying.
The crops were all baked;
And into a puzzle
The river had caked.

At first they came slowly,
The drops here and there;
Like bullets they spattered
The dust in the air.

And then they came faster
And swallowed the dust,
And changed the white desert
To colors of rust!

The air was cool water
In silvery sheets.
It deluged the cactus
And thirsty mesquites.

The river was leaping
The torrent came on.
Five days it kept coming—
And then it was gone.

The sun was just setting;
The dripping trees bowed;
The land was all mirrors,
Reflecting the clouds.

And all the year's worry
And fearing and pain
Were lost in that sunset
That followed the rain.

—Keith Miller,
Highway Home through Texas

Lord, it is so true in my experience that into the heat and pain of the seemingly endless desert periods you bring a redeeming rain or beautiful sunset — or both. Thank you that your meanings are hidden for us to discover in the drama of survival. Amen.

August 20

THE HIDDEN REVEALED

"At that time Jesus said, 'I praise you, Father, Lord of heaven and earth, because you have hidden these things from the wise and learned, and revealed them to little children.'" —Matthew 11:25

I carry about in my body, in a single cell, the pattern of the universe. I am pregnant with the cosmos. And in Tasmania, buried in a manioc root, is my body. Select a spot, put your finger down anywhere, and you touch the stars. Pay attention to it, and from your fingerprint, like the rays of an aura photograph, reality radiates, meaning sets out, rippling over the immense ocean of energy until it has fabricated the entire universe.

Gnosticism is still the biggest lie of all. There is no special knowledge squirreled away somewhere from the rest of us. The hiddenness, the mystery, is in plain paradoxical sight. If no one recognizes a messiah or

a saint, it's because he's looking for something else — or has his eyes squeezed shut. I knew that all one had to do to sniff out the secrets was to keep his wits about him. Not go dozing off after dinner, sated and sluggish. The exasperation in Jesus' voice as he demanded eyes to see and ears to hear was not lost on me. My eyes were peeled to the quick. Most children's are.
— Virginia Stem Owens, *God Spy*

Dear Lord, help me keep my wits about me and not go dozing off. Move past any false expectations I may have about how to find you, so that I can better recognize you, and your saints. Help me have eyes that see and ears that hear the reality of you. In Jesus' name. Amen.

August 21

Geographical

"Philip went and found Nathanael and told him, 'We've found the One Moses wrote of in the Law, the One preached by the prophets. It's Jesus, Joseph's son, the one from Nazareth!' Nathanael said, 'Nazareth? You've got to be kidding.' But Philip said, 'Come, see for yourself.'"
— John 1:45-46, THE MESSAGE

The gospel is emphatically geographical. Place names — Sinai, Hebron, Machpelah, Shiloh, Nazareth, Jezreel, Samaria, Bethlehem, Jerusalem, Bethsaida — are embedded in the gospel. All theology is rooted in geology. Pilgrims to biblical lands are sometimes surprised to find that the towns in which David camped and Jesus lived are no better or more beautiful than the home towns they left behind.

If the fallout of our belief in the supernatural is a contempt for these one-horse towns and impatience with their dull-spirited citizens, we had better re-examine what we say we believe in. For supernatural in the biblical sources is not a spectacularly colored hot-air balloon floating free of awkward contingencies but a servant God with basin and towel washing dusty and callused feet.
— Eugene H. Peterson, *Leadership Magazine*, Summer 1991

Here where I live has dust, dirt, and dull-spirited citizens, just as there was during the years about which the Bible was written. Thank you for reminding me that the momentous events in the lives of such people as Abraham, Moses, Mary, Jesus, and the disciples took place in ordinary geographical locations — plagued by the same weather conditions and scenery that I see today. If you can act momentously in those locations, I know you can do so here where I live. Help me to be aware of your power and love. In Jesus' name. Amen.

August 22

LOST SHEEP

"Suppose one of you has a hundred sheep and loses one of them. Does he not leave the ninety-nine in the open country and go after the lost sheep until he finds it?... Then he calls his friends and neighbors together and says, 'rejoice with me; I have found my lost sheep.'"
—Luke 15:4, 6b

Twice a week my church provides a van and driver to chauffeur senior citizens to a county nutrition site for meals and fellowship. Over the summers I enjoy driving the van. Many of the riders are over eighty, a couple are over ninety, and they always enlarge my outlook and enrich my appreciation of life. Sometimes, during breaks in the school year, I fill in if the regular helpers are unavailable. Today was one of those days. The regular helper was available only in the morning. So I went to the nutrition site to make the return trip. Therein was the problem; I did not know who was on the van. I had only a number, and when that number boarded for a ride home, I thought the load was complete and we left.

Forty-five minutes down the road, one of the ladies asked, "Where's Margaret?"

After several phone calls, I went to Margaret's house. One of the site volunteers had driven her home. She met me gruffly, and I could only say, "I'm sorry." It wasn't my fault, but it was my responsibility. How often it is like that in this world. —John Leax, *Standing Ground*

Lord, teach me to recognize my responsibility for what you have given me. May I not be distracted by trying to take on responsibility for what is not mine. May I not be demoralized when I don't have all the facts I need and things turn out wrong.

Instead may I learn to be humbly aware that your love underlies everything else, and you alone have never failed to meet a responsibility. Give me the humility and sensitivity to say "I'm sorry" when I fail, and to be forgiving when others fail. In Jesus' name. Amen.

August 23

INTERRUPTION OF SERVICE

"And Jesus called them to him and said to them, 'You know that those who are supposed to rule over the Gentiles lord it over them, and their great men exercise authority over them. But it shall not be so among you; but whoever would be great among you must be your servant, and whoever would be first among you must be slave of all. For the Son of man also came not to be served but to serve, and to give his life as a ransom for many.'" —Mark 10:42–45, RSV

Last week I was very busy trying to get what seemed like a thousand things done before leaving for a three-day speaking trip on the East Coast. There hadn't been time to prepare my talks, so I was under a lot of pressure when a friend, a fine Christian woman, called. A couple she knew was having marital problems. "They might call you," she said, "because they could not agree on either a minister or a psychiatrist." But my friend thought it crucial that I see them if at all possible.

It seems that the majority of people I've counseled with lately have had marital problems. Even though I was dead tired, I agreed to talk with them, hoping they wouldn't call. But sure enough, at almost midnight, the telephone rang. The man called me "Reverend" Miller (in what I thought was a condescending tone).

"Keith Miller," I said with some definiteness. "I am a layman."

"I'd like to make an appointment to see you," he said without any details or preliminary remarks. Just when I started to ask who was calling, it occurred to me that he must be the husband of the couple having troubles. He proceeded to set up the appointment. I was too tired and off balance to say, "Wait just a minute, friend." Besides I realized the man was under pressure and had probably put off calling all evening. So the appointment was made for one o'clock the following day at our house.

I was irritated, since this meant driving five miles from my writing hideout in the middle of the day. Asking myself, "What kind of Christian are you if you can't help another human being in trouble?" helped some. But it made me mad that this guy was treating me like some sort of a hired hand. I was only seeing him as a friend, with no intention of charging him as a counselor. So I prayed to be open to the man, and I was (at least consciously) by the time I got home the next day at 12:30. The telephone rang at 1:10 and the man said, "Something has come up, and I won't be able to make it to your house." I started to tell him he could just forget it, but then it occurred to me that he might be avoiding the conference purposely. And from what my friend had said, this man could be in serious trouble. So I agreed to see him the following day.

We had a good visit, but it was apparent that their marital problems were severe. By that time my schedule was really pressing. Not long after the husband left, his wife called, and after a long conversation, she asked for an appointment. Knowing how hard it is to wait when things seem to be closing in on you, I agreed to see her at 11:00 the following morning.

I rushed home at 10:55 to find that the woman had just called and left word: something had come up and she was not going to be able to come. I was *furious!* Three days had been fouled up by these people. They didn't even have the courtesy to consider how much inconvenience I was going through for them. I wanted to call and tell them that one of their problems was "self-centeredness." And further I wanted to inform them that I was very busy myself... and then it hit me: how important I must think I am if a thing like this can make me as mad as it did. Here were two people in the agony of struggling to keep their home together — with no telling what other complications — and I was incensed that they were treating me like a common servant... when that is what I have committed my life to be: a servant to Christ and his suffering people. But *my reaction* told me that secretly I must want to be treated like a big-shot writer and counselor. —J. Keith Miller, *Habitation of Dragons*

For the self-flattery of our nature is very subtle and few can discern it. Secretly it pursues only its own ends, though meanwhile its outward conduct is such, that it seems to us we have but the single aim of pleasing God, though in actual fact this is not so.... So if a man does not watch himself well, he may begin some activity with the sole purpose of pleasing the Lord, but later, little by little, introduce into it a self-interest, which makes him find in it also a satisfaction of his own desires, and this to such an extent that the will for God becomes completely forgotten.
—Lorenzo Scupoli, *Unseen Warfare*

In renunciation it is not the comforts, luxuries and pleasures that are hard to give up. Many could forego heavy meals, a full wardrobe, a fine house, et cetera; it is the ego that they cannot forego. The self that is wrapped, suffocated in material things — which include social position, popularity, and power — is the only self they know and they will not abandon it for an illusory new self... which they may never attain. —Louis Fischer, *Gandhi, His Life and Message for the World*

Forgive me, Lord, and help me not to look for the respect and acclaim of people but to be willing to die to my self-concern enough to accept them just as they are. For the good of this couple, I do not think I should be a doormat, and I will be firm in any future contact with them with regard to their keeping appointments if they want help. But I see that the worst problem is mine — not theirs. Change my attitude, Lord, to one of a servant. Amen.
—J. Keith Miller, *Habitation of Dragons*

August 24

SOLITUDE, NOT LONELINESS

"After he had dismissed them [Jesus] went up on a mountainside by himself to pray. When evening came, he was there alone."
—Matthew 14:23

Jesus calls us from loneliness to solitude. The fear of being left alone petrifies people. A new child in the neighborhood sobs to her mother, "No one ever plays with me." A college freshman yearns for his high school days when he was the center of attention: "Now, I'm a nobody." A business executive sits dejected in her office, powerful, yet alone. An old woman lies in a nursing home waiting to go "Home."

Our fear of being alone drives us to noise and crowds. We keep up a constant stream of words even if they are inane. We buy radios that strap to our wrists or fit over our ears so that, if no one else is around, at least we are not condemned to silence. T. S. Eliot analyzes our culture well when he writes, "Where shall the world be found, where will the word resound? Not here, there is not enough silence."[1]

But loneliness or clatter are not our only alternatives. We can cultivate an inner solitude and silence that sets us free from loneliness and fear. Loneliness is inner emptiness. Solitude is inner fulfillment.

—Richard J. Foster, *Celebration of Discipline*

I have, O Lord, a noisy heart. And entering outward silence doesn't stop the inner clamor. In fact, it seems only to make it worse. When I am full of activity, the internal noise is only a distant rumble; but when I get still, the rumble amplifies itself. And it is not like the majestic sound of a symphony rising to a grand crescendo; rather it is the deafening din of clashing pots and clanging pans. What a racket! Worst of all, I feel helpless to hush the interior pandemonium.

Dear Lord Jesus, once you spoke peace to the wind and the waves. Speak your shalom over my heart. I wait silently... patiently. I receive into the very core of my being your loving command, "Peace, be still." Amen.

—Richard J. Foster, "A Prayer for Quiet," in *Prayers from the Heart*

---

1. As cited in Elizabeth O'Connor, *Search for Silence* (Nashville: W Publishing Group, 1971), 132.

August 25

SHORTCHANGING GOD

"Be still, and know that I am God; I will be exalted among the nations, I will be exalted in the earth." —Psalm 46:10

In a letter written by George MacDonald to his daughter Mary, he addresses her concern that she didn't *feel* enough love for God (which so often is exactly my problem). Her father said that there are three requisites for a loving relationship: That the persons involved be capable of loving, that they be themselves lovable, and that they know each other.

For me, it's the last item that is shadowed. How can I know an invisible, inaudible, intangible presence? Through the Word and the Spirit, of course. To my mind steeped in evangelicalism, the orthodox theology springs into place almost automatically. But time is needed, quiet, for the voice of God to be heard, the relationship to be cultivated. And I seem to have none, unless I shortchange the people in my life. I think I hear God saying to me, *"I'm* being shortchanged. Don't you care?"

—Luci Shaw, *God in the Dark*

Dear Lord, draw me toward you. Increase my awareness that I am shortchanging you when I do not cultivate our relationship by spending time with you in prayer and meditation. Help me to know how to create this space without the sense of shortchanging others in my life. In Jesus' name. Amen.

August 26

SPIRIT OF THE AGE

"Brethren, if a man is overtaken in any trespass, you who are spiritual should restore him in a spirit of gentleness. Look to yourself, lest you too be tempted." —Galatians 6:1, RSV

We all confront the Spirit of the Age, when trying to make spiritual sense of the world. When we're young, it often appears attractive, but quickly becomes seductive, swallowing us up like the Vacuum Machine Creature in *The Yellow Submarine,* who when there's nothing left to swallow up, swallows himself. And for those of us who don't flee the confrontation, the Spirit of the Age, which specializes in short-term gains, continues to attract us as we grow older; which is another way of saying, we're never too old to make the wrong choice.

All the commentators on the spiritual life note that one's own life experiences invariably lead to an early crossroad. One may choose to veer to the left or veer to the right. But there's always a third choice. One may turn around and retrace one's tracks to the cloister of the womb.

The fathers and mothers of spiritual direction did just that; from the earliest centuries of the Christian era, they were loners, eremites and stylites. They retreated from the city to the desert, there to await the Second Coming, which, if the Scriptures were worth the parchment they were written on, was sure to come on the morrow; if not on the morrow, then on the morrow thereafter.

When that sacred event didn't come, these loners became cenobites; that is to say, they gathered together in a city of their own; a community, a convent, a monastery. Their bond was, among other things, their hatred of the city and everything in it. When not praying, they wove mats one day and unwove them the next. It was the praying that counted.

When Jesus refused to come on the short schedule, the cenobites extended their frame of reference still further. They no longer undid the mats they wove; they collected them until they had enough to visit the city, where they sold them for as much as the market would bear. Humanism, yes, but with an eschatological tinge.

This return to the marketplace, when they had left in such a huff some decades before, marked the beginning of incarnational humanism, the sort that Jesus personified in his recorded life. He too participated in the city-life of his time. He too approached the crossroad early in his public life. He too was tempted, three times, to accept the apples of this earth for little or no cost, and three times he refused.

—William Griffin, *C. S. Lewis: Spirituality for Mere Christians*

God, all too often the "Spirit of the Age" appears in seductive forms, tempting me to follow. Thank you that — when I make wrong choices — you can restore me to the proper path. Amen.

August 27

To Sing of Meaning

"I will sing unto the Lord as long as I live: I will sing praise to my God while I have my being." —Psalm 104:33, KJV

How can we understand in terms of literalism the glory of the creation of the universe, Jonah in the belly of the large fish, Daniel in the lions' den, or angels coming to unsuspecting, ordinary people and crying out, "Fear Not!"

Literalism is a vain attempt to cope with fear by quelling Scripture, attempting to make it more palatable, less wild and wonderful. Would the angels cry out "Fear not!" if there were nothing to fear?

Story makes us more alive, more human, more courageous, more loving. Why does anybody tell a story? It does indeed have something to do with faith, faith that the universe has meaning, that our little human lives are not irrelevant, that what we choose or say or do matters, matters cosmically. It is we humans who either help bring about, or hinder the coming of the kingdom. We look at the world around us, and it is a complex world, full of incomprehensible greed (why are we continuing to cut down our great forests that supply our planet with so much of its oxygen?), irrationality, brutality, war, terrorism — but also self-sacrifice, honor, dignity — and in all of this we look for, and usually find, pattern, structure, meaning. Our truest response to the irrationality of the world is to paint or sing or write, for only in such response do we find truth.

—Madeleine L'Engle, *The Rock That Is Higher*

Lord God, Source of all creative pattern, structure, and meaning: May the coming of your kingdom be hastened as we look for and find truth in artistic expression, our own and that of others. Amen.

August 28

I WILL WALK AMONG YOU

"And I will walk among you, and will be your God, and ye shall be my people." —Leviticus 26:12, KJV

One's walk with God is not simply personal. It *is* personal, certainly, but it is not *only* personal. If we are to come near unto God, if we are to be strengthened day-by-day, then we need to walk closely with him always, not simply in Sunday worship, morning devotions, or evening prayers.

If you know a deep and abiding communion with God personally, then you are, certainly, a believer. If you know this communion within the context of your family life, your family is certainly blessed. If it's true in your church, then your church is a wonderful place. If it's true in your workplace, then going to work can never be a chore. Knowing God in every area of your life brings peace and only more faith.

But don't ever think that walking with God means you've jettisoned sin from your soul. That doesn't happen, not to the best of us. Sadly, it's possible to walk with God in a way that's still crippled by sin.

It happens like this. We feel this ache for something we shouldn't have — maybe it's someone other than our spouse. But we know terrifyingly well that we can't have that person. Why? Because God's voice — as he walks with us — is a bull horn. So we don't do what we desire, but we grow resentful because we can't. At ourselves, for our sin? Yes, but sometimes at God, too, for restraining us from whatever it is — money, sex, power, whatever.

The command for us to remember is to follow God in all things, for his paths lead to heaven and his glory. What are his ways? How do we distinguish them from our own? Just keep praying the Lord's Prayer: "Hallowed be thy name. Thy kingdom come. Thy will be done." If your repetition of those words is not vain and meaningless, then God's way of life will begin to become yours. You will feel yourself but a drop of water in surf which rises continuously to his glory.

But a drop of water does not a wave make. His will for our lives always includes our lives with others. Only one human being ever had to walk alone. The rest of us can find fellowship, in fact *must* find fellowship to know his way.

Our lives are truly blessed when we walk with God every hour of the day. Then, and only then, will he walk among us.

— James Calvin Schaap, *Near Unto God*

Our Father, hallowed be thy name. We raise our voices, a fellowship of your followers, in praise. We commit our every hour to you. Walk among us, and we will be your people. Amen.

August 29

EVERY GOOD THING

"Through him all things were made; without him nothing was made that has been made." —John 1:3

A Song of Praises

for the gray nudge of dawn at the window
for the chill that hangs around the bed and slips its tongue under
    the covers
for the cat who walks over my face purring murderously
for the warmth of the hip next to mine and sweet lethargy

for the cranking up of the will until it turns me out of bed
for the robe's caress along arm and neck
for the welcome of hot water, the dissolving of the night's stiff
    mask in the soft washcloth
for the light along the white porcelain sink
for the toothbrush's savory invasion of the tomb of the mouth
    and resurrection of the breath
for the warm lather and the clean scrape of the razor and the skin
    smooth and pink that emerges
for the steam of the shower, the apprehensive shiver and then
  its warm enfolding of the shoulders
  its falling on the head like grace
  its anointing of the whole body
  and the soap's absolution
for the rough nap of the towel and its message to each skin cell
for the hairbrush's pulling and pulling, waking the root of each
    hair
for the reassuring snap of elastic
for the hug of the belt that pulls all together
for the smell of coffee rising up the stairs announcing paradise
for the glass of golden juice in which light is condensed and the
    grapefruit's sweet flesh
for the incense of butter on toast
for the eggs like two peaks over which the sun rises and the jam
    for which the strawberries of summer have saved themselves
for the light whose long shaft lifts the kitchen into the realms of
    day
for Mozart elegantly measuring out the gazebos of heaven on the
    radio
and for her face, for whom the kettle sings, the coffee percs, and
    all the yellow birds in the wallpaper spread their wings.

—Robert Siegel, in *Made for Each Other*

Lord, giver of good gifts, we give you thanks for all these good things that you have made for their goodness in themselves and to bring us to yourself. Amen.

August 30

TOO MUCH RELIGION

"You don't make your words true by embellishing them with religious lace. In making your speech sound more religious, it becomes less true. Just say 'yes' and 'no.'" — Matthew 5:36–37, THE MESSAGE

It seems odd to have to say so, but too much religion is a bad thing. We can't get too much of God, can't get too much faith and obedience, can't get too much love and worship. But *religion* — the well-intentioned efforts we make to "get it all together" for God — can very well get in the way of what God is doing for us. The main and central action is everywhere and always *what God has done, is doing, and will do for us.* Jesus is the revelation of that action. Our main and central task is to live in responsive obedience to God's action revealed in Jesus. Our part in the action is the act of faith.

But more often than not we become impatiently self-important along the way and decide to improve matters with our two cents' worth. We add on, we supplement, we embellish. But instead of improving on the purity and simplicity of Jesus, we dilute the purity, clutter the simplicity. We become fussily religious, or anxiously religious. We get in the way.

That's when it's time to read and pray our way through the letter to the Hebrews again, written for "too religious" Christians, for "Jesus-and" Christians. In the letter, it is Jesus-and-angels, or Jesus-and-Moses, or Jesus-and-priesthood. In our time it is more likely to be Jesus-and-politics, or Jesus-and-education, or even Jesus-and-Buddha. This letter deletes the hyphens, the add-ons. The focus becomes clear and sharp again: God's action in Jesus. And we are free once more for the act of faith, the one human action in which we don't get *in* the way but *on* the Way. — Eugene H. Peterson, THE MESSAGE

Dear Lord, How much better my life is when I remember to focus on God's action in Jesus. Help me to turn to you through study and prayer, to improve my focus, and to remember not to get in the way, but on the Way. In Jesus' name. Amen.

August 31

KEEPING THE PLANE UP

"Even to your old age and gray hairs
I am he, I am he who will sustain you.
I have made you and I will carry you;
I will sustain you and I will rescue you."
—Isaiah 46:4

"Sometimes we fill the holes with putty
and paint over them."
—Airline mechanic, *Time*

This time no one can save me,
it's real, the roar, the flames,
and then the sheltering walls of the plane
fly apart like kindling,
the durable seat drops down,
my bag leaps open, turning over,
my calendar flapping like a sparrow,
wires of the headset a black scribble
in the air above me. I plummet,
jackknifed, my bottom down, heavy as gold,
toward the tiny trees, toward
the stippled calm brown hills,
suddenly feeling as fond of
this heavy body as of a dying relative
but I am somersaulting towards
the Minnesota landscape—trees/sky/
trees/sky/over and over
and I try to steady myself
in the eye of God,
a simple act, almost monotonous,
a sound I can not quite remember,
like the quiver of an engine keeping
a plane up, a sound that catches,
stalls, then vibrates in my throat
and pelvis. Could this be
what it feels like, being saved?
I can see the plane's wings level
over the thorny trees,
but I spread my hands above me
like parachutes, just in case.
—Jeanne Murray Walker, in *Gaining Time*

Lord, there are times when I don't think I will survive the circumstances in my life. I can almost see the disintegration of my very soul, the unraveling of my core. Rescue me, O God, from the pictures of my crashing and burning. Sustain me, and create in me the desire to live a healthy balanced life, to find the serenity with which to create a calm space within which I can discover your will for me as I face my problems this day. And thank you that you save me again and again. In Jesus' name. Amen.

SEPTEMBER

September 1

EXCUSES, EXCUSES

"You hypocrites! You are like whitewashed tombs, which look beautiful on the outside but on the inside are full of dead men's bones and everything unclean." —Matthew 23:27a

Many of us run into serious communication difficulties because of unconscious dysfunctional mental habits picked up early in life. These attitudes are like invisible currents that suck us down into deep angry water in our intimate relationships before we know what has happened.

For various reasons many of us develop to a fine art the skill of self-justification. The trouble is that this skill, in its various manifestations, often includes shaming those with whom one is in intimate relationships. Thus it becomes one of the major forces in the destruction of intimacy.

By the time I was eight years old, I was so afraid of failure and criticism that I had an excuse for everything I did that wasn't perfect. When criticized or even questioned about my behavior, I could justify anything I did or said instantly. I remember my mother laughingly saying to me as I was coming home late one day, "Well, here comes Alibi Ike." I was shocked at the time, and I still remember the shame I felt when she said it because I had no idea that I made more excuses than anyone else.

When I got married, my habit of self-justification was neither cute nor joked about. I still wasn't aware that I *had* to be right and would "argue with a post" (another statement I *just this moment* remember my mother saying about me). But the abusing thing about self-justification in my case has been that if I have to be right, then *someone else* usually has to be wrong. For a long time, I didn't know that sometimes being "right" or "wrong" is not the most relevant thing regarding an intimate exchange about something that has happened. But I now know that self-justification in my life is a major destroyer of intimacy. If my "perfection" is at stake and others try to share their differing reality, I will discount it, twist it, or dismiss it as being unimportant. This can happen even in the face of solid evidence that I've made a mistake. I feel very sad as I'm writing this since I have been in touch with just how much misery my self-justification has caused in my intimate male-female relationships and with my adult children.

This habit of "having to be right" seems absolutely normal to many people. After all, we want "the truth" to come out (and the truth is that I'm right and innocent and that we all should agree on that). If you point out my faults or mistakes, for example, I have an instant interior reaction: "That's not right! You don't understand. Here's what really happened." My immediate reaction is to claim your perception is not accurate. I blurt out, "I did *not* say that! What I said was..." and I unconsciously correct my previous statement to say what I *meant,* or wish I'd said (but in reality did not say clearly).

Self-justification is a major character defect that destroys intimacy because self-justifiers *have* to be right or start an argument to support their delusion of being perfect. In most cases they feel sincerely that they are right. To those doing the self-justifying, it seems as if all they are doing is straightening the record.... Many of us have had to learn that healing and growth don't happen until we face our denial, lies, and delusions of perfection, admit them, make amends, and change the behavior of justifying ourselves.

I have a talented, brilliant, and very capable friend who was once late to an important business meeting. When he came in everyone was braced for his smooth excuse. But all he said when he sat down was, "I'm sorry I'm late. I blew it." Period. Suddenly we all saw ourselves. The truth is when we are late, it *is* usually our fault. We have started too late, tried to handle too many things before coming, or did not have good boundaries and let someone "important" derail us. This positive, no-excuse change regarding self-justification often happens to people who are seeking to overcome their habit of self-justification.

It has been *very* difficult for me to face my own self-justification with my close loved ones. But if I want a life of love and intimacy, I believe it is essential that I try. —J. Keith Miller, *Compelled to Control*

Lord, I want more love and intimacy in my life, with you and with the people close to me. Show me any self-justification I may have so that I can begin to eliminate this habit. And thank you that you have indicated that you and your love and grace are with me (Matt. 28:20) through the pain of changing this destructive character defect. In Jesus' name. Amen.

September 2

WE ARE NOT ALONE IN OUR SIN

"Therefore confess your sins to each other and pray for each other so that you may be healed." —James 5:16a

Confession is a difficult Discipline for us because we all too often view the believing community as a fellowship of saints before we see it as a fellowship of sinners. We feel that everyone else has advanced so far into holiness that we are isolated and alone in our sin. We cannot bear to reveal our failures and shortcomings to others. We imagine that we are the only ones who have not stepped onto the high road to heaven. Therefore, we hide ourselves from one another and live in veiled lies and hypocrisy.

But if we know that the people of God are first a fellowship of sinners, we are freed to hear the unconditional call of God's love and to confess our needs openly before our brothers and sisters. We know we are not alone in our sin. The fear and pride that cling to us like barnacles cling to others also. We are sinners together. In acts of mutual confession we release the power that heals. Our humanity is no longer denied, but transformed. —Richard J. Foster, *Celebration of Discipline*

A Prayer of Cleansing

Clean out, O God, the inner stream of my life:
 all the duplicity,
 all the avarice,
 all the falsity.
Search out, O Lord, the hidden motives of my life:
 all the conceit,
 all the anger,
 all the fear.
Root out, divine Master, the destructive actions of my life:
 all the manipulation,
 all the scheming,
 all the guile.
May the operations of faith, hope, and love increase
in everything I am and in everything I do.
 Amen. —Richard J. Foster, in *Prayers from the Heart*

September 3

BLESSED ARE THE SOMEBODIES

> "Ah, you who make iniquitous decrees,
> who write oppressive statutes,
> to turn aside the needy from justice
> and to rob the poor of my people of their right,
> that widows may be your spoil,
> and that you may make the orphans your prey!
> What will you do on the day of punishment,
> in the calamity that will come from far away?"
> —Isaiah 10:1-3, NRSV

Martin Luther King Jr. was *somebody*. Very few people would disagree with that. Born in Atlanta in 1929, he whizzed through school. His talent was such that he skipped both ninth and twelfth grades. His college entrance exam score was so high that he entered Morehouse College at fifteen, without having formally graduated from Booker T. Washington High.

King earned a B.A. from Morehouse and entered Crozer Theological seminary in Chester, Pennsylvania. Concurrently he studied at the University of Pennsylvania. He was president of the senior class, valedictorian, won the Pearl Plafker Award for most outstanding student; a fellowship for graduate study; a Bachelor of Divinity degree. Then he earned his doctorate in systematic theology at Boston University, while also studying at Harvard.

King's life achievements skyrocketed. He became a brilliant Baptist preacher, like others in his family before him. He headed the Southern Christian Leadership Conference. Spearheaded the Civil Rights Movement. Led the Montgomery boycott. Led the March on Washington. Received some twenty honorary degrees and hundreds of awards. Received the Nobel Peace Prize. King was assassinated in April 1968, a martyr to his cause. Later a national holiday was established in his name.

Were these things what made him *somebody?*

In his preaching, King said that being somebody is a gift of God.

He spoke often about the worth of every person: "The woman or man who goes in (to the hospital) to sweep the floor is just as significant as the doctor.... Whoever cooks in your house, whoever sweeps the floor in your house is just as significant as anybody who lives in that house. And everybody that we call a maid is serving God in a significant way. I love the maids. I love the people who have been ignored. I want to see them get the kind of wages that they need. And their job is no longer a menial job, for you come to see its worth and its dignity" (*The American Dream*, 1965).

For his notion of *somebodiness*, King relied on Scripture and on the founding documents of the United States of America. He emphasized the nonviolent teachings of Jesus and what he called "the creative weapon of love." Some hated him for his eloquence. But many hearts were changed.

King was afraid of self-importance and self-righteousness. Yet he had a profound sense of calling. "And when God's word gets upon me, I've got to say it. I've got to tell it all over everywhere! And God has called me to deliver those that are in captivity" (*Guidelines for a Constructive Church*, 1966).

But most of all, he recognized, and preached, what Jesus meant by greatness. "Everybody can be great, because everybody can serve. You don't have to have a college degree to serve. You don't have to make your subject and your verb agree to serve. You don't have to know Plato and Aristotle.... Einstein's theory... the second law of thermodynamics.... You only need a heart full of grace; a soul generated by love" (*The Drum Major Instinct*, 1968).

Whatever his flaws (there were some), King was a prophet and a hero.

He showed us something about courage, and listening to God's voice. He lived the high calling of his daily work.

—Emilie Griffin, *The High Calling of Our Daily Work*

Dear God of just decrees, teach me how I may serve you with a right conscience and by an honorable use of the gifts of skill and persuasion that you have given me. Allow me to see your image in everyone, and to act with liberty and justice for all. Amen.

September 4

LIGHT IN THE EYE

"The eye is the lamp of the body. If your eyes are good, your whole body will be full of light." —Matthew 6:22

Why do we seek out trails over rocks and through snowdrifts that do not accommodate for comfort? Why do we, at great difficulty and expense, search out experiences that provide totally intangible satisfaction? Because beauty is in our eye, itching like a curious conjunctivitis that refuses to be soothed until proper material is supplied it to sort, arrange, pattern, proportion.

Perception, especially visual perception, has been counted as one of the most passive occupations of human intelligence. Supposedly one simply opens one's eyes and takes it all in. But the research of physiologists has shown the whole process to be one of continual interaction with the environment. The eyeball itself is undergoing small, steady, rapid vibrations, shifting the image received on the retina by the microscopic distance that lies between its adjacent cells. Added to that rapid oscillation is a slow drift of the image across the retina, continually corrected by a flick, like a typewriter carriage being flung back to its starting point. When these normal movements of vision are impeded in an experiment using a series of mirrors, sight first becomes distorted and finally fails altogether. The researchers discovered that the nerves must constantly participate in an interchange with light, must probe and feel the image presented to it. If the stimulus supplied to each retinal cell is kept constant, the nerves learn to accommodate the stimulus, and it soon falls below the level of perception. The eye, in other words, must toss light about as if it were winnowing wheat from chaff, sifting, sliding, flicking it, in order to garner shape, distinction, color, form.

—Virginia Stem Owens, *God Spy*

Dear Lord, just as the physical eye must constantly toss light about as if winnowing wheat from chaff, so must the eye of my soul constantly search for your truth. If the movements of the soul's eye, are impeded, my spiritual sight eventually fails. I will strive to sharpen the movement of my soul's eye, so that I can keep my sight on you and your will for my life. In Jesus' name. Amen.

September 5

THE CURSE AND GRACE OF LABOR

"By the sweat of your brow you will eat your food until you return to the ground, since from it you were taken; for dust you are and to dust you will return." —Genesis 3:19

Thoreau, being no more a respecter of Scripture than he was of persons, once quipped, "No man need live by the sweat of his brow unless he sweats easier than I do." Even if his quip accurately represented his abilities, his truth provides us little comfort. We must remember he also claimed that the digging of his cellar "was but two hours work." Most of us, figuratively at least, sweat. But what is it we sweat at, and to what end?

The poets have long questioned this and exclaimed at our propensity to engage in foolish labor. Wordsworth for example wrote:

> The world is too much with us; late and soon,
> Getting and spending, we lay waste our powers...

I wonder what he would have written if he had walked, as I have, through an upscale mall on the first day of the Christmas shopping season. So many laboring to sell what so many have made! So many laboring to buy to offer as a little sign of ill-defined affection what no one really wants!

How far we have come from the straightforward expending of our energy to feed and cloth and house ourselves upon being cast out of Eden. How much farther we have come from the pleasure of dressing and keeping the garden provided for us. Do we even remember, as we speak our perfunctory graces, that we eat in sorrow? That our labor, however profitable it might be, is now a reminder that we were meant to live in the abundance of God's extraordinary generosity toward us? That we, even in our fallenness, continue to live in that generosity? For what else is all that we have — our designer clothes, our waxed fruits, our air conditioned houses — but sad remnants, vain elaborations, of the coats of skins God gave our rebellious parents to cover their nakedness and keep them warm in the fierce world they made?

How changed our lives might be if we could see that even the curse of labor is a grace, that it is given to us as a way to find what we have lost, to anticipate what Christ recovers for us.   —John Leax

All that we have lost you give back to us. Give us the sense to know our real work: to walk about shouting your name. Let our every word praise you for you are generous beyond imagining. Amen.

September 6

OWNERSHIP

"And if you have not been trustworthy with someone else's property, who will give you property of your own?"   —Luke 16:12

Stewardship, that poor manipulated word, relegated to the Sunday when it's time to ask for money. Yet stewardship is only incidentally about money. In the biblical sense a steward is a manager of goods and resources of all kinds, responsible for conserving, investing, and distributing. A good steward must be found faithful, said Paul, for precisely one reason: The steward is not the owner of the assets, but in charge of someone else's belongings.

The appointment to steward belongs to everyone in Christ's church, as all the really important calls do, acting as a great leveler between the ordained and the unvalidated, the rich and the poor, the intelligentsia, the rest of us. Stewardship carries its own authorization.

So if I belong to God then all that I am is God's and I am the steward of my body and my brain, my health, my talent and education, my capacity for hard work and my ability to play. If we really believe that everything we own belongs to God, that knocks the pride out of sacrificial giving. It knocks the martyrdom out of service, the ego out of heroism, the self-congratulation out of success, and the self-pity out of failure. There's no possible confusion between what we own and what we are.

—Shirley Nelson, meditation, First Presbyterian Church, Albany, N.Y.

O, most loving Father, who willest us to give thanks for all things, to dread nothing but the loss of thee, ... Preserve us from faithless fears and worldly anxieties. Amen. —Book of Common Prayer

September 7

THE AMPHIBIOUS CHRISTIAN

"Here we have no continuing city, but we look for one to come."
—Hebrews 13:14, author's paraphrase

In my search for metaphors by which to see and shape my life, I spent a year viewing myself in the skin of a green frog. It seemed to me a perfect image for the dilemma of the person linked to God by personal relationship, drawn toward heaven, but of necessity still human, "of the earth, earthy," tied to a physical body with all its needs and impulses.

Most frogs, amphibious, designed to breathe air but swim water, cannot exist for long in either element. Frog (as I named myself) must pivot continually between the upper-air level and the underwater level. In air, she will dehydrate and wither; submerged too long in water, her lungs will be deprived of oxygen and she will drown.

I, too, am restless, shifting up and down, pulled in two directions. I have already breathed the air of heaven, by virtue of the Spirit now resident in me, but I'm not yet ready for heaven, ill-equipped for its fierce air; it is too bright, too sharp, too clean, too intense for my fleshly frailty. Having emerged from the sludge at the bottom of the pond, I am sucked down into it again by my humanity, only to be dragged up again by my need to breathe.

What, on earth, is the job of a frog — her reason for existing? To replicate herself? To keep the insect population in check? To look decorative on a lily pad? To inspire poets? I think she is meant to exhibit the attributes of *frogness* for which she was created.

I ask myself the same question — what am I here for? If I read my own nature and my Bible aright, I am to be a link between earth and heaven, to be in relationship with both persons and the Person. I am to be poised for upward movement, with one foot in heaven, one on earth. And I am to fulfill the true humanity I was created for, which suggests an earthiness discontented with mere earth. —Luci Shaw, *Horizons*

Lord Jesus, you have entered my life and begun a new work. But even while you are in me and I am in you, your work is not done. I long for that day when all that you have been sent to do is accomplished, when all of us will be free entirely of the bondage to sin. Come quickly! Amen.

September 8

STRANGE GODS

"After the earthquake came a fire, but the Lord was not in the fire. And after the fire came a gentle whisper." —1 Kings 19:12

Four prominent poets sat on the panel, three of them associated with the environmental movement, the fourth with justice issues. The topic was: poetry and the earth. Almost as an aside, one tossed off a remark, "We realize, of course, that monotheism is one of those mistakes humans make." The other three nodded. The audience tittered. No one protested. Time may have been a factor; the panel disbanded without taking questions. But it would have taken an Elijah to stand before the power of Jezebel governing that discussion. It was just such pressure the author of the biblical creation account challenged with the astounding cosmology revealed in the opening chapters of Genesis: one God created it all.

In the midst of that account, however, the reader encounters this puzzling statement, "And God said, Let us make man in our image, after our likeness." The statement is not a crack in the argument. It is an anticipation of a truth to be revealed in the life of Christ and explicated by the New Testament writers: God is three in one. Inherent in his person is communion.

Humanity, made in God's image, is made for communion. Human history, however, is a litany of broken relationships. Separated by ignorance or by deliberate choices not only from the single source of being, but from all else that he has made, many succumb to the same temptation as the Canaanites; they invent gods. Christians, like Elijah, are called to risk all that they have to say the truth. It is a frightening call, but all who receive it have the promise of Christ: "I will pray the father, and he shall give you another Comforter, that he may abide with you forever."

— John Leax

Creator of all that is, we give ourselves to you. No other god shall command our interest, our resources, or our work. There is none like you. You alone, Father, Son, and Holy Spirit, are worthy of praise, adoration, and love. Amen.

September 9

THE LAST ENEMY

"Listen, I tell you a mystery: We will not all sleep, but we will all be changed — in a flash, in the twinkling of an eye, at the last trumpet. For the trumpet will sound, the dead will be raised imperishable, and we will be changed."   —1 Corinthians 15:51-52

Some people in Paul's day were challenging the Christian belief in an afterlife. Death, they said, is the end. Throughout history, many people have taken such a position. In Jesus' day, a Jewish sect called Sadducees denied the resurrection from the dead. Doubters persist today, among them are Black Muslims, Buddhists, Marxists, and most atheists. Some New Age advocates present death as a natural part of the cycle of life. Why consider it bad at all?

The Corinthian church soon learned not to voice such an attitude around the apostle Paul. Belief in an afterlife to him was no fairy tale; it was the fulcrum of his entire faith. If there's no future life, he thundered, the Christian message would be a lie. He, Paul, would have no reason to continue as a minister; Christ's death would have merely wasted blood; and Christians would be the most pitiable of all people on earth.

The Bible presents a gradually developing emphasis on the afterlife. Old Testament Jews had only the vaguest conception of life after death. But as Paul points out, Jesus' resurrection from the dead changed all that. Suddenly the world had primary proof that God had the power and the will to overcome death. Chapter 15 brings together the threads of Christian belief about death. With no hesitation, Paul brands death "the enemy," the last enemy to be destroyed.

This chapter often gets read at funerals, and with good reason. As people gather around a casket, they sense as if by instinct the *unnaturalness*, the horror, of death. To such people, to all of us, this passage offers soaring words of hope. Death is not an end, but a beginning.

—Philip Yancey, *A Guided Tour of the Bible*

Your promise of life after death is wonderful! When I remember people I love who have died, when I think of my own death or the coming deaths of people I love, I take comfort and hope in this—that they, and I, will live forever with you in heaven. In Jesus' name. Amen.

September 10

A Way Out

"No temptation has seized you except what is common to man. And God is faithful; he will not let you be tempted beyond what you can bear. But when you are tempted, he will also provide a way out so that you can stand up under it."   —1 Corinthians 10:13

I woke up this morning and weighed myself. I had gained a pound! In my head I know that gaining a pound even when I've stuck to my diet is a common thing, possibly due to water retention or extra muscle weight. But my heart sank anyway. I could hear the taunting voice of this beast in my head, a fat women with scraggly hair and puffy cheeks. She tries to convince me I will never reach my goal.

"See, you're wasting your time with all this health business," she taunts me. "You're never going to make it!" And this morning I believed her. I was so tempted to throw the whole plan out the window and treat myself to a day off, a week off—maybe even the rest of my life off! Wild thoughts crashed around inside me as I headed for my quiet time.

Then I read this Scripture verse. The promise God has made to us leaped off the page: "But when you are tempted, he will also provide a way out." I asked him, "Really, Lord? You promise? Then why do I feel so discouraged because of one itty-bitty pound?!"

I thought of many other times when I've felt helpless in the face of the pressures of my world. The times when special friends were coming over for dinner and I felt obliged to serve "standard" foods such as desserts and creamy casseroles, that I knew were not healthy. The times when I was out of town in a strange city and didn't have the courage to put on shorts and jog around the streets for fear of what might happen to me.

But with God's promise that there would always be a way out, I pushed my thinking further and asked myself, "What could I do in those cases?" With this new attitude, the answers seemed to pop up like the numbers on an old-fashioned cash register. "When those guests come you could search harder for delicious ways of fixing standard foods without the unhealthy ingredients. If dessert is a must, you could not eat yours, or serve yourself dessert and only take a bite or two, throwing the rest in the garbage."

When that last thought came, the voice of the beast laughed at me and insisted, "But that's too hard for you." I wondered, "Could I really find the discipline to serve myself a dessert and then not eat much of it?" Well, reluctantly I admitted, "Yes. It *is* an escape, and God has promised to help me. Maybe I could try it."

Then the beast spoke up: "But what about the danger of jogging in a strange town?" With my newfound confidence in God's promise, I responded, "I could stay in my hotel room and jog in place. I could take a small tape recorder and do an aerobic tape in my room. I could jog with someone else at a safe time of day. If the hotel has a swimming pool, I could go swim some laps." Wow! I couldn't believe how these answers came to me when I kept God's promise in front of me, and I was shocked when I realized that no answers had come before when I was really faced with those situations.

I got the message. As long as I am convinced there is no solution to the situation, the answers eluded me. I resolved to remember that, when that helpless feeling comes up, I am *not* helpless. I'm going to try to make an extra effort to look at the situation with God's promise in mind, and to pray for his answers to my "impossible' situations.

—Andrea Wells Miller, *BodyCare*

Dear Lord, your promises for help are so good, and I have seen that without your help I am really helpless. Thank you for showing this promise to me again today, and help me to remember it whenever I feel helpless. Arranging my schedule, disciplining my will, and adjusting to changes are all things I struggle with. Keep me in your care and remind me often that you will not let me be tempted beyond what I can bear, and that you will provide a way out. In Jesus' name. Amen.

September 11

UNINTENDED CONSEQUENCES

"We know that in everything God works for good with those who love him, who are called according to his purpose." —Romans 8:28, RSV

Mohamed Atta and his friends had a plan and, on 09/11/01, against all odds, they managed to carry it off. We all know the impact on us, and indeed on the rest of the world. But there were a few unintended consequences....

Patriotism

Flags came quick as dandelions from Ground Zero. America's anthems were whipped out of the piano bench. We sang, and we wept as we sang, and the television cameras caught us not knowing the words. Crime statistics went down; Scripture sales went up. And wonder of wonders! Clergy of all religions and denominations within religions fell over each other to appear at the Yankee Stadium prayer service.

What general councils of the Church and general goodwill across the religions had been unable to do for millennia, you, dear Atta, did with one swift gesture. But was that what you originally intended? Even your beloved Islam linked arms and joined voices with the Hindu and the Sikh, the Catholic and the Protestant, the Jew and the Orthodox. All of which is to say that, at the very least, in public discourse, the words "and mosque" would be forever added to the words "church and synagogue."

And as if that weren't blasphemy enough, dear Atta, joining the clergy to intone a patriotic hymn was Bette Midler, the sort of basal American babe you've so often railed against. And there was that other babe at the mouth of the harbor, the one with the torch! How much you missed and how far you missed it by!

Mercy

Where was the mercifulness of Yahweh, Allah, God, in all of this? Right where its always been — in the thick of it. Death was swift, yes, but not unkind, what with the Divinity sweeping up to its bosom all the chosen souls before the final blows fell.

"Cut down in their prime," the headlines would proclaim. But were they? The Divinity, or so it seemed to me, had harvested them in the fullness of his own time; that's to say, 9/11 proved to be their perfect day, perfect moment, perfect circumstance.

As for the rest of us, however, Death was unkind, unmerciful, unbecoming a Divinity whose Scriptures occasionally boast his omnipotence.

On the ground, though, mercy was everywhere. Instantly, everyone was a beloved of everyone else. Accidentally, Moses, Jesus, Mohammed were scrambling all over the rubbled landscape.

Was this what Atta and friends intended as the result of their heroic, patriotic acts?

"Well, not really," they'd say. "These were unintended consequences, yes, but they have no meaning whatsoever. Ours is the only meaning."

Ah, my dear Atta, what could you have been thinking of? You wounded us, yes, you wounded us grievously, but at the same time, with the very same stroke, you healed us, brought us together.

May the Final Judge who awaits us all tender you all the mercies you need! —William Griffin, *Image: A Journal of the Arts and Religion,* Fall 2001

Dear God, when it seems impossible to see anything good about an experience, thank you that you are at work anyway. Amen.

September 12

THE FOOLISHNESS OF CONGREGATIONS

"Take a good look, friends, at who you were when you got called into this life. I don't see many of 'the brightest and the best' among you, not many influential, not many from high-society families. Isn't it obvious that God deliberately chose men and women that the culture overlooks and exploits and abuses, chose these 'nobodies' to expose the hollow pretensions of the 'somebodies'?"
—1 Corinthians 1:26-28, THE MESSAGE

St. Paul talked about the foolishness of preaching; I would like to carry on about the foolishness of congregation. Of all the ways in which to engage in the enterprise of church, this has to be the most absurd — this haphazard collection of people who somehow get assembled into pews on Sundays, half-heartedly sing a few songs most of them don't like, tune in and out of a sermon according to the state of their digestion and the preacher's decibels, awkward in their commitments and jerky in their prayers.

But the people in these pews are also people who suffer deeply and find God in their suffering. These are men and women who make love commitments, are faithful to them through trial and temptation, and bear fruits of righteousness, spirit-fruits that bless the people around them. Babies, surrounded by hopeful and rejoicing parents and friends, are baptized in the name of the Father and the Son and the Holy Ghost.

Adults, converted by the gospel, surprised and surprising all who have known them, are likewise baptized. The dead are offered up to God in funerals that give solemn and joyful witness to the resurrection in the midst of tears and grief. Sinners honestly repent and believingly take the body and blood of Jesus and receive new life.

But these are mixed in with the others and are, more often than not, indistinguishable from them. I can find, biblically, no other form of church.
— Eugene H. Peterson, *Under the Predictable Plant*

Dear Lord, the life of the church is full and rich. I thank you for your patience, your forgiveness, and even your sense of humor about the way we go about being your people in the church. Help me to be who you would have me to be as I participate in the life of the church. In Jesus' name. Amen.

September 13

GOD'S HOUSE

"Mine house shall be called an house of prayer for all people."
— Isaiah 56:7, KJV

Being in church with Frank was being much closer to God in the house of God than I had ever been before. We sat there for quite a while and I began to unfreeze and to be happy again. I don't know what Frank was thinking, but I was thinking about what he had said about going on to different planets and learning and growing and improving, and it seemed terribly right to me, and I felt, too, oh, yes, God is here, this is God's house.

I looked around. Although there was no service going on, there was somehow a lingering smell of incense in the musty air, and the light came through the stained-glass windows warm and beautiful and unlike the gray air outside.... We got up to leave and just as we got to the outside doors a gray-haired lady in expensive furs came in and she looked at me and said, "Oh dear, you didn't go into the church without a hat, did you?"

"Yes," I said, remembering my red beret drowning in New York Harbor.

"But you know you mustn't ever go into a church without covering your head, dear," the lady said. "Didn't your mother teach you that?"

"Yes," I said. I felt Frank stiffen with rage beside me.

"I am so sorry," Frank said, his voice soaring and then cracking down onto a deep note, "that you object to Miss Dickinson's going into a church without her hat. However, I'm sure that God doesn't object, and after all, that's all that matters." And he swept me out.

— Madeleine L'Engle, *Camilla*

Lord, help us to see beyond outward appearances and look as you do, on the heart, with a welcoming heart. Amen.

September 14

BJORN LARSEN AND AUNT JOE AT THE DUMP

> "If I rise on the wings of the dawn...."
> —Psalm 139:9a

> For whatever is hidden is meant to be disclosed, and whatever is concealed is meant to be brought out in the open. —Mark 4:22

How can a man know which minute the sun
will perch on the shoulder of the dump?
But Bjorn could tell you. We rattle out of town
in his Chevy truck on the dirt road
that picks its careful way through the swamp
—leaves that grow even while we sleep,
whose flowers we beat back twice a year
before they swallow up the town.

At the swamp's mouth, Bjorn pulls the truck
inside a wire fence. This is where everything ends up,
like that old wringer washer, once someone's tubby angel.
We sit on the ripped cloth seats and watch the sun
open its heart. It sends light rolling
like mercy across old boots and tires and bedsprings.
I can hear the whole dump breathing.

It would be easier to lay my future on the butcher's block
and have its head severed with a clean chop.
A decent funeral and afterwards, silence.
But the dump is coming to life. It is pure gold.
Those boots are getting up to walk away.
Any minute the tire might spin above us
like a new planet. Bjorn's hand reaches out for mine.
Against his, I can feel my hand's thick heel,
its bones, and its nails like little stars
that are going to shine forever.

—Jeanne Murray Walker, in *Gaining Time*

Lord, the miracle of your love is like the sun lighting up the dump with pure golden light. It shines everywhere, on all the broken pieces of my life, in all the neglected spaces in my soul. Thank you for your warming touch, your steady presence always nearby. Amen.

September 15

Squeezing through the Needle's Eye

"Indeed, it is easier for a camel to go through the eye of a needle than for a rich man to enter the kingdom of God." —Luke 18:25

Only a nun can afford the luxury of loving mankind in general. The rest of us are stuck with particular specimens. A mendicant may wander the byways and backwaters without anxiety; no one is ever waiting for him at home, vexed or anxious over his lingering. Anne Morrow Lindbergh declares that there are so many women in church because it is the one hour of the week when no one can call "Mother!" The respite most women taste in the sanctuary for only an hour is the continual reward of the wise virgins on the far side of the door. That hour, out of the week's one hundred sixty-eight, is their needle's eye.

Thoreau, that Concord nun, threw away the pretty piece of limestone he had on his mantelpiece because it distracted him by requiring dusting. He had no doubt taken warning from his friend and mentor Emerson concerning the heart held hostage by family ties. When Emerson's firstborn son died at six, darkness such as the celibate can never know descended on him. It was a man pinned and wriggling in the needle's eye who wrote, not long after his son's death,

> There are moods in which we court suffering, in the hope that here at least we shall bind reality, sharp peaks and edges of truth. But it turns out to be scene-painting and counterfeit. The only thing grief has taught me is to know how shallow it is. That, like all the rest, plays about the surface, and never introduces me into the reality, the contact with which we would even pay the costly price of sons and lovers.

Those of us who, one way or another, have ended up with a life that demands taking thought for the morrow must be grateful even for the escape offered in the needle's eye. And for its tag-end promise without which we might lose heart: with God, nothing is impossible. Not even

the necessary shrinking to a single filament that will fit through that aperture. If the door is shut, then we must somehow struggle through the keyhole.
— Virginia Stem Owens, *God Spy*

In times of busyness, Lord, help me to know that I, too, can find a way to penetrate this needle's eye, this place where distraction tempts me to disown my faith. In Jesus' name. Amen.

September 16

KEEPING THE FOCUS ON GOD AND LOVE

"No one can serve two masters. Either he will hate the one and love the other, or he will be devoted to the one and despise the other. You cannot serve both God and Money." —Matthew 6:24

The Bible is not against money. Jesus didn't say money was evil. It was, in fact, something to be desired. For instance, in the story of the ten talents (Matt. 25:14–30), the guy who had ten talents went out, invested them, and made ten more. And *he* was the one who got the reward, not the man who protected what he'd been given. Money couldn't have been evil, or Jesus wouldn't have talked about it like that, even in an illustration.

As I see it, the problem with money is that it does provide certain securities. It will help us avoid certain calamities. But the difficulties come when we look to money as our *ultimate* security, so that it becomes a substitute for God who can provide the only security that really does transcend our problems. And if we put our confidence in God and his kingdom, Jesus said, then the material things will be taken care of. But in our panic and insecurity, we forget about God and drive for money with all we're worth. And when we do, money becomes like a totally demanding master that takes God's place as the hope for the meaning of our lives.

Jesus said no one can serve two masters because when we try we'll always wind up loving one and hating the other. "You cannot serve both God and Money," he said.

The subtle strength of money as a competing security to God is so great that the author of First Timothy says that the "love of money is the root of all evil" (6:10, KJV). It's not *money* that's evil but the *love of it*. Gertrude Behanna used to say, "Money is like bricks. You can either build hospitals with them or slug people." Money *in itself* is not evil, then, for a Christian. But it becomes bad when one attempts to use it as an ultimate security instead of depending on the living god.

When I start going after money as the most important thing in my life, something very bad happens to me. I start calculating all the time about how I'm going to make more money or get more power or control. And all of a sudden all my relationships suffer. I trample over the people close to me to get out and make things happen financially. And the things I believe God considers of value — peace, long suffering, patience, the kind of love that Christ had — I don't have time for. I seal them off because of a love for material things which I feel I must have beyond basic needs (i.e., luxuries, investments, etc.).

I'm always scared to turn loose of any controls, but I have found myself needing to do this again and again in my Christian life, and I'm always glad when I do. Some people seem to risk easily. But when I have to give up something that's really important to me, I just sweat blood, struggle against it, and say, "I don't want to risk it, God!" But finally if I do risk it for him and for the truth, life looks good again, and I feel much safer and ironically much more at home in the world.

Money represents a strange paradox. If you have a lot of it, it can get in the way of your growth and faith. But if you don't have enough, life can be an absolute terror. The only approach I've found is to go to God with the problem.

I just say, "God, I want you to be first in my life. Will you become my security? Because I can't seem to turn loose of the idea of how much money I need." And then I begin to face the question of what I actually *need* to take care of my obligations and basic retirement planning. Then I form an action plan to take care of those basic needs, believing that God will handle the ultimate results of my life as I try to keep him as my center and ultimate security. —J. Keith Miller, *The Single Experience*

Lord, forgive me for forgetting that you are my ultimate security, and not money or possessions. Today I renew my commitment to you as my security. Everything I have really belongs to you. Keep me ever mindful that my job is to take care of what you have given me and use it for your purposes in the world of responsibilities you have put me in. Amen.

September 17

THE FOOLISHNESS OF GOD

"The foolishness of God is wiser than man's wisdom."
—1 Corinthians 1:25

The sermon was about a fig tree. The story, as told in the Gospel of Mark, describes how Jesus, hungry, went up to a leafy fig tree to find some fruit to eat. When he saw that it was barren of figs, he cursed it.

By the next day it had withered from the roots up. The surprising thing is that Jesus' demand for figs seems so unreasonable. As the gospel narrative makes clear, "It was not the season for figs." How, then, could Jesus *expect* to find fruit on it?

Sometimes God's demands on us seem unreasonable. "After all," we protest, "we're only human." Where can we find the faith to move mountains? How can he ask us to "hate" our parents? Must we actually love our enemies? Or forgive and forgive and forgive, more than four hundred ninety times? Or give the shirt off our backs to some panhandler? Does God really expect us to pluck out our eyeballs or hack off our hands if they "offend" us?

These and other divine requirements are sometimes known as "the hard sayings of Jesus." But our response to God's desire for our perfection is too often based on human logic. No. We cannot possibly live up to his standards; we are flawed, foolish, inadequate. Only as we plunge into the supernatural realms of the Spirit, forsaking the weedy shallows of our human wisdom, can we see that God's "foolishness" is really his super-wisdom. "My ways are not your ways," he tells us, "nor are your thoughts my thoughts." If we are to see from God's perspective, we must allow the Holy Spirit to "lead us into truth." Only then will we be able to "perform impossibilities."
—Luci Shaw, *Horizons*

Lead me, O Holy Spirit, into the truth of Christ. Become the strength of my weakness that in him I might perform impossibilities I'd never, on my own, imagine. Amen.

September 18

LOVING OTHERS THROUGH PRAYER

"I urge, then, first of all, that requests, prayers, intercession and thanksgiving be made for everyone."
—1 Timothy 2:1

If we truly love people, we will desire for them far more than it is within our power to give them, and this will lead us to prayer. Intercession is a way of loving others.

When we move from petition to intercession we are shifting our center of gravity from our own needs to the needs and concerns of others. Intercessory Prayer is selfless prayer, even self-giving prayer.

In the ongoing work of the kingdom of God, nothing is more important than Intercessory Prayer. People today desperately need the help that we can give them. Marriages are being shattered. Children are being destroyed. Individuals are living lives of quiet desperation, without purpose or future. And we can make a difference — if we will learn to pray on their behalf.

Intercessory Prayer is priestly ministry, and one of the most challenging teachings in the New Testament is the universal priesthood of all Christians. As priests, appointed and anointed by God, we have the honor of going before the Most High on behalf of others. This is not optional; it is a sacred obligation — and a precious privilege — of all who take up the yoke of Christ.

—Richard J. Foster, *Prayer: Finding the Heart's True Home*

Gracious Holy Spirit, so much of my life seems to revolve around my interests and my welfare. I would like to live just one day in which everything I did benefited someone besides myself. Perhaps prayer for others is a starting point. Help me to do so without any need for praise or reward. In Jesus' name. Amen. —Richard J. Foster, *Prayer: Finding the Heart's True Home*

September 19

MIRACULOUS STRENGTH

"By my God I have leaped over a wall."
—Psalm 18:29b, KJV

All our woes and miseries come from one of three sources — from nature (storm and sickness), from our fellow man (bickering, even war), or from the powers of Satan (all kinds of temptations). Don't let anyone tell you — sentimental believers or television commercials — that life is a breeze. It isn't. It's a battle. Many face behemoth struggles that demand heroism, whether it be against a drought that threatens the farm or cancer that threatens our lives; whether it be vicious rumors created in animosity, or war itself; whether it be temptation in a thousand forms, or even martyrdom. This world can be and is a vale of tears.

Formidable walls arise against us throughout our lives, stand there monster-like, impregnable, unmovable. Injustice, for one — we'll know it in our gut and see it in our own backyard, feel powerless in its grisly shadow. Sickness or death can prompt a despair so deep it becomes suicidal. Friends turn into enemies for reasons we don't understand. Our own sinful desires arise again and again despite our best efforts to hold them down.

Heroic courage is needed all through life, courage from the strength of the Almighty. When the Psalmist says, "By my God I leap over a wall," he does not mean to imply that his action is some out-of-body phenomenon. What he means to say is that with God in his heart, the greatest of inspirations the Holy Spirit can deliver, he knows that he can take on the width and breadth of any barrier, any wall before him.

What's miraculous is not so much the action, but the strength given us to take it on, for we couldn't lift ourselves off the ground without God.

Think for a moment about someone you know as a real hero of faith. Isn't this true? — Once they're up and over whatever wall presents itself before them, those heroes who know the real source of their strength will actually fall to their knees. You know why.

— James Calvin Schaap, *Near Unto God*

Lord Christ, by your strength we can accomplish all things. Take our weaknesses and glorifying yourself. Amen.

September 20

AT HOME IN CHRIST

"He is like a tree planted by streams of water, which yields its fruit in season and whose leaf does not wither." —Psalm 1:3a

In his life and in his writing Thomas Merton affirmed that the Christian has only one place to be: in Christ. Having that one place to be — which is no place and every place — frees the Christian from having to be going anywhere but where he is. As I understand this, by choosing to stay where I am, where Christ has placed me, I act out in my life my resting in him.

None of this is easy. But when I drive up to the house at 19 Torpey Street, I feel sort of joy. I look at the massive white front rising nearly three stories above me. I look past the house to the trees I have planted. I look past them to the woodpile and to the garden. I hear the voices of my wife and daughter. I know all of this has come to me by grace that someday I might become a man worthy of what I have been given.

— John Leax, *In Season and Out*

O Christ, our rock and resting place in a world suffering storms of ambition, anger, and pride, we thank you for the opening in your love made for us. Give us sense to relish the haven of your stone. Keep us safely in you. Amen.

September 21

A New Name

"To him that overcometh will I give to eat of the hidden manna, and will give him a white stone, and in the stone a new name written, which no man knoweth saving he that receiveth it."
—Revelation 2:17, KJV

Voice of Many Waters

for Clyde Kilby

The night is cluttered with stars.
    The drift of the earth
is dark, enormous
       bulking shoulder of the undersea whale
in the Atlantic's winking canyons.
    Trees wait
for the slow stain of day
       walking now over the water
west of England.

    I put two sticks on the fire
on the ghost of logs
       that fade into the red eye
drawing the circle of my campsite
       about which hang
my all-weather tent, glinting axe
       myself, like planets
inching the swarm of stars.

    Twelve o'clock:
The beast startles first with his foot
       broad as unbearable moon,
his leg the shank of stars
       his mane the black roar of space
turning to the white heart of fire
       in which begin to move
thick and uncertain
       the rivery shapes of trees
bending over water
       cradling a platinum light
running to gold
       and pebbles
each speckled with suns
       each turned and lapped by the water.

> Green steals over me:
>   I am swung in a net of leaves.
> Birds wrap me tight in their songs:
>   drunk with the trauma of flowers
> I am and I hear a voice calling
>   within the voices of water.
> A shadow brightens the ground.
>   A hand darkens all but itself.
>
> Somewhere in the face of the trees
>   a large clumsy beast is singing
> the brood of pain and music
>   played on the stops of the worlds
> the flute of starlight and vacuum
>   the unending theme of Abyss
> and the trees are growing before me
>   translating all to flowers.
>
> Now the voice is within a white stone
>   round in my hand like water
> that speaks one word running through fingers
>   to shred in my mouth like the moon.
> Outside the sun is rising. Blue,
>   the sky is blue
> and the far forest neighing.
>
> I wake in the orange flower of my tent.
>
>   —Robert Siegel, *The Beasts and the Elders*

By your word you made the world. Each morning you speak it new, filling it with your life. Each morning you speak our new name waking us to your presence. Let our words respond to yours. Let our words be your words. Amen.

September 22

Progress

"Although he was a son, he learned obedience from what he suffered and, once made perfect, he became the source of eternal salvation for all who obey him."   —Hebrews 5:8–9

From the Old Testament we can gain much insight into what it "feels like" to be God. But the New Testament records what happened when God learned what it feels like to be a human being. Whatever we felt,

God felt. Instinctively, we want a God who not only knows about pain but shares in it; we want a God who is affected by our own pain. As the young theologian Dietrich Bonhoeffer scribbled on a note in a Nazi prison camp, "Only the Suffering God can help." Because of Jesus, we have such a God. Hebrews reports that God can now sympathize with our weaknesses. The very work expressed how it was done: "sympathy" comes from two Greek words, *sym pathos*, meaning "suffer with."

Would it be too much to say that, because of Jesus, God understands our feelings of disappointment with him? How else can we interpret Jesus' tears, or his cry from the cross? One could almost pour the three questions of this book into that dreadful cry. "My God, my God, why have you forsaken me?" God's Son "learned obedience" from his suffering, says Hebrews. A person can learn obedience only when tempted to disobey, can learn courage only when tempted to flee.

Why didn't Jesus brandish a sword in Gethsemane, or call on his legions of angels? Why did he decline Satan's challenge to dazzle the world? For this reason: if he had done so, he would have failed in his most important mission — to become one of us, to live and die as one of us. It was the only way God could work "within the rules" he had set up at creation.

All through the Bible, especially in the Prophets, we see a conflict raging within God. On the one hand he passionately loved the people he had made; on the other hand, he had a terrible urge to destroy the Evil that enslaved them. On the cross, God resolved that inner conflict, for there his Son absorbed the destructive force and transformed it into love. —Philip Yancey, *Disappointment with God*

Dear Lord, your example of the use of your power — to identify with us and absorb the destructive forces of evil, transforming it into love — is incredible! I can feel the power behind that kind of love reaching out to me, and I yearn to respond. Here is my heart, teach me to love and live as you would have me to. In Jesus' name. Amen.

September 23

TRUTH AND LOVE

"Jesus answered...To this end was I born, and for this cause came I into the world, that I should bear witness unto the truth. Every one that is of the truth heareth my voice." —John 18:37, KJV

I do not want to romanticize about Mother's senility. I know that there is no turning back the clogging of the arteries, and that there is nothing to look forward to but further decline. But if I stop here I am blocked in my loving, just as her thinking is blocked by atherosclerosis.

I try to accept the bare factual truth of Mother's condition, as Mado accepted loss and death; and yet I remember Tallis saying once that "we are not interested in the love of truth *as against* the truth of love." This does not mean that we are not interested in the love of truth; his statement is one which I have to try to understand with all of me, not just my conscious mind. The love of truth without the truth of love is usually cold and cruel, I have found. The truth of love can sometimes be irrational, absurd, and yet it is what makes us grow toward maturity, opens us to joy. Mado, holding a dying soldier in her arms, was witness to the irrationality of the truth of love. This kind of truth is often painful; it must have been so for her, and I am certainly finding it true in this household this summer. But it is all that gets me through each day.
—Madeleine L'Engle, *The Summer of the Great-Grandmother*

Lord of truth and love, may we be true to love, that we may know and bear witness to the truth of love. Amen.

September 24

THE SHAPE OF TRUTH

"If you hold to my teaching, you are really my disciples. Then you will know the truth, and the truth will set you free."   —John 8:31-32

Of course, this Scripture verse has a general application to more than just getting in shape, but when I think of it in relation to health, my thinking goes something like this. This verse says to me that when I know the truth it can set me free. But this is apparently hard for me to accept, because I'd rather *not* know the truth — so that I can keep enjoying my favorite, though unhealthy, foods.

The truth about health and fitness seems to include the fact that there are certain foods and ways of living that nurture and improve our health, and others that do not. And I must admit that most of the time I've been studying about this I've wished that what I was learning weren't true.

I believe that when I really know the truth, the next step is to be able to allow it to make me free to lose the weight. In the meantime, as I behave in ways that are the opposite of the truth I'm learning, I will not be free of this weight.

So this passage, as I've related it to my health, is a message of hope, and yet of responsibility. I have the means with which to become healthy, but I have the responsibility to learn the truth, believe it, and act upon it. And it is only through a relationship with Jesus Christ that I can begin to do this. That seems to be the *only* way it works for me.

—Andrea Wells Miller, *BodyCare*

Dear Lord, thank you for your willingness to let me choose how I will live my life. I know that you make truth available to me, if only I will look at it, believe it, and act upon it. Forgive me when I behave as if I don't believe what is true, or as if I don't respect the truth enough to do the things I know I should do. Help me want to begin to try harder to learn about my body and about the foods you provided for its care.

I want to be free, Lord, free to do your will and to live as long as you want me to. I shall try hard to learn the truth, with your help, and to believe that eventually it will really make me free. In Jesus' name. Amen.

September 25

THE SOUND OF LOVE AND THE FRAGRANCE OF CHRIST

"...speaking truth in love, we will in all things grow up into him who is the Head, that is, Christ. From him the whole body, joined and held together by every supporting ligament, grows and builds itself up in love, as each part does its work." —Ephesians 4:15-16

[After committing one's life to Christ], a person is faced with a paradox. Although he or she may now be free to actualize that unique potential God has given him or her, the person's *hope* is that he or she will become more *like Christ* as he or she matures. And a strange thing seems to emerge—the more of the person's life that he or she commits to God, the more *creative* and *unique* that person may *appear* to be to others. People feel the Christ-like love of God coming through such a person, but *the person* doesn't feel "like Jesus." He or she feels and looks free and interested in others.

At a conference for ministers several years ago we were talking about Christian loving concern. One young man said, "I wonder how it would feel to love people *the way Jesus* did?" A silence followed. Then a white-haired minister said thoughtfully, "A Christian would probably never know. If you were loving people the way Jesus did, you'd be concentrating totally on the *other person and his problems*... and not on how you were feeling."

What this says to me is that an authentic Christian — becoming that person he or she was most nearly "designed" to be — does not wind up being an imitator when he or she becomes more mature. Of course at first we must imitate other Christians as Paul suggested in Philippians 3:17. We have to pick up the openness and life-style of the Christian family way. But as a person becomes more committed to Christ and more transparent in being who he or she is, such a person does less posturing and imitating. This might mean, for instance, that the more totally and transparently I am being Keith Miller with you, *living for God*, the *more nearly* you will see *Jesus Christ through* me. And the Scriptures indicate that although we all receive the same Spirit and are to imitate God *in being loving, each* of us will be given the grace and the specific gifts we particularly need to grow up in Christ's perspective (see Ephesians 4).

What all this means to me is that God is not making *imitations* of anything — even Jesus. He is creating authentic, original human beings who have the sound of Love in their lives and who unconsciously leave the fragrance of Christ behind them wherever they go.

—Keith Miller, *The Becomers*

Dear Jesus, grant me the grace to grow up, to let go of imitating some idea of how to be like you and, instead, become transparently myself, free to focus my loving interest on others. Amen.

September 26

UP OR DOWN?

"I wait for the Lord, my soul waits, and in his word I put my hope."
—Psalm 130:5

Psalm 130, a psalm of Ascent, emphasizes the inevitability of human struggle — depression, bankruptcy, shame, disillusionment, loneliness, despair, ill health, financial need — all conditions which we can label "the depths" and in which we need to hear two messages: *Wait* on the Lord, *hope* in his Word.

When we're *up* we tend to talk to God from the top of our hearts — complacently. Only when we are *down*, suffocating like Jonah inside the whale, do we engage in real prayer — the kind that changes us profoundly. I keep thinking of our own realities — my husband's couch of pain, our fears — and know this to be true. We cry to God out of extremity, not from the easy couch of comfort.

The theme of this morning's sermon was hunger and bread. In the Lord's Prayer we ask for "daily bread"; we take into our mouths the bread and wine and "feed on them in our hearts by faith"; after Communion we thank God for feeding us with spiritual food and drink. But like physical nourishment, our spiritual food must be taken often, or we faint with hunger and grow spiritually anorexic.

I've been thinking more about hunger for God. I find it sharpest, most tantalizingly close to being satisfied, at Communion. As I am on my knees at the altar, cupped hands held up, mouth open, being fed like a baby bird, I want to stay there and feel what it is like to go on being fed. I want to prolong *the real something* that happens there.

—Luci Shaw, *God in the Dark*

Dear Lord, I hunger for you, like a fledgling who needs to be fed. Thank you that you feed us through prayer, Communion, and in a thousand other ways! In Jesus' name. Amen.

September 27

MANIPULATIVE WOMEN

"Here is my servant whom I have chosen,
the one I love, in whom I delight;
I will put my Spirit on him,
and he will proclaim justice to the nations."
—Matthew 12:18

"Manipulative" isn't a word we like to be called. We may admire the intelligence it implies, but we dislike the suggestion of meanness it carries. Owning up to deceit and stratagems shows us the worst side of women. Recently, I was disturbed to read the advice a Christian mother gave her daughter: "You have to know when to stop submitting and start outwitting." Only the servile need to manipulate others, we think.

True enough. But most of the world's women have indeed led lives of virtual, if not actual, servitude. Many women around the world today still do. Does that make their lives unimportant, their stories of no interest? Decidedly not. The Old Testament, in particular, seems unencumbered by our own culture's disdain for manipulation. The Hebrew tales present the shrewd maneuverings of their characters — both men and women — as cleverness, a way of outsmarting a more powerful adversary, rather than as a sign of weakness or servility.

In the New Testament we see a different attitude toward manipulation, however. In these stories, candor becomes the ideal way of dealing with conflict. Jesus himself is never manipulative — though his friends and followers sometimes wish he were a little less direct. In his dealings with the religious establishment, in particular, he is downright confrontational. Nor does he ever allow himself to be manipulated. He often requires people to state exactly what they want. And at his trial, he doesn't try to plea-bargain.

Which is not to say he doesn't practice indirection. His parables ambush us with the truth of human life. And in his conversations with individuals, many of them women, he patiently directs the discussion toward their deepest concern. Even with Salome, the mother of James and John, he strikes precisely the right note, neither trivializing her request nor patronizing her concern.

Servanthood, not servility, is the New Testament ideal. And manipulation a worn-out tool. —Virginia Stem Owens, *Daughters of Eve*

Let me learn servanthood, O Lord, as I let go of manipulative ways. In Jesus' name. Amen.

September 28

YESTERDAY, TODAY, AND TOMORROW

"Jesus Christ is the same yesterday and today and forever."
—Hebrews 13:8

I discover what I have to say as I write. This is crucial to my thinking. It is also crucial to my becoming. But it is not what I am speaking of now. The discovery of what I have to say, of what my poem or essay means is, like the poem or essay itself, the product of my work. It is not my work.

As I write, the poem I am writing is always in the future. When I have finished writing, it is behind me. It is in the past. Only as I am writing it, as it is in the process of becoming, is it in the present. And only as it is in the present is it my concern. Compare this to salvation. Salvation is a process occurring in all three tenses. It is future because it will not be complete until Christ returns. It is past because Christ accomplished it on the cross. It is present as I give myself to Christ. Here as in the writing of a poem, my concern is with my present action. What is past is related to the present only as the present brings its meaning into being. What is future is related to the present only as it is imagined and desired in the present, that is, as it is part of present.

Holiness and craft come together at this point: the moment of the poem is also the moment of salvation. Both occur in the present. I make my way as a poet and as a Christian by giving my attention to being in Christ, and in doing in him the work before me. Quoting Thomas Merton, "It is in the ordinary duties and labors of life that the Christian can and should develop his spiritual union with God."

—John Leax, *Grace Is Where I Live*

Lord, today as I give my attention to being and doing in you all these ordinary duties and work I will undertake, may I experience moments of spiritual union with you. Keep my mind and heart sensitive to your presence in all that I think, do, or say. In Jesus' name. Amen.

September 29

Constant Communion

"Mine eyes are ever toward the Lord."
—Psalm 25:15a, KJV

No scriptural command is particularly easy to follow, but some seem downright impossible. "Pray without ceasing," for example. Not even time off to sleep? Who can possibly pray without ceasing? The Bible offers testimonies that are just as forbidding. The Psalmist says, "I set the Lord *always* before me" (16:8); "Nevertheless, I am *continually* with thee" (73:23); and again, "Mine eyes are *ever* toward the Lord" (25:15).

The intent here is not "now and then." The lines say *always, continually, without ceasing*—ALL THE TIME. Maybe it's simply poetic license, like the young and in love who gush poetically that they will love each other "till all the seas run dry."

Wrong. What Scripture testifies to is continual commitment, every day, every hour. It doesn't intend to infer that we can draw God to us, but instead that we allow God to draw us up, *all the time,* into the eternal. Our personal fellowship with God here in his world is the verifying prospect of what is perfectly heavenly in essence.

And that's not impossible, even though it seems terribly unlikely amid the zany and frantic lives we live. Neither David nor Paul were spiritual aesthetes, after all. Both know our lives are more than endless devotional moments, and the world is no monastic cell.

Everyone has spiritual highs, times when, in some secluded spot, one's soul is not only alone with God but lost in him. We all seek those moments to escape from the world's busyness to seek solitude which will fortify us for our return. But if that's all we know of spiritual life, then our lives are schizoid — one without God, one with.

We don't exist to take vacations. People who require retreats for spiritual renewal often drug themselves against their own denial. When the retreats don't inspire, such people are inclined to give up, having missed the highs they so urgently need.

Uninterrupted, ceaseless continuation of fellowship with God doesn't depend on our thinking or planning, and can't be willed.

It must spring up from the inner motion of a heart in which the Holy Spirit has put down roots. If you know the Holy Spirit's indwelling, then you understand that intimacy with God happens whether or not we will it to happen. Like a mother tending her baby, the Holy Spirit is ever vigilant, even though the child sleeps.

The more deeply God comes to indwell, the more we see him in the busyness of our lives — and the more others see him in us. Then, our lives continually sing his praise. — James Calvin Schaap, *Near Unto God*

Holy Spirit, root deep in the soil of our lives. Let the mind of Christ grow in us that our communion with the Father might be true and constant. Amen.

September 30

DELIVERED FROM AN IMMENSE CLUTTER

"Every part of Scripture is God-breathed and useful, one way or another — showing us truth, exposing our rebellion, correcting our mistakes, training us to live God's way. Through the Word we are put together and shaped up for the tasks God has for us."
—2 Timothy 3:16–17, THE MESSAGE

The image of the stones, waiting to be selected from the brook by David as he prepares for his meeting with Goliath, holds my attention. David has just discarded King Saul's armor as ill-fitting. The offer of bronze helmet and coat of mail was well intentioned. But to accept it would have been disastrous. David needed what was authentic to him. Even as I do. For even though the weaponry urged upon me by my culture in the form of science and knowledge is formidable I cannot work effectively with what is imposed from the outside. Metallic forms hung on my frame will give me, perhaps, an imposing aspect but will not help me do my proper work.

And so I kneel at the brook of Scripture, selecting there what God has long been preparing for the work at hand and I find smooth stones. The rough edges have been knocked off. The soft parts have been eroded away. They are bare and hard. Nothing superfluous. Nothing decorative. Clean and spare. Scripture has that quality for me — of essentiality, of the necessary. I feel that I am, again, traveling light, delivered from an immense clutter. —Eugene H. Peterson, *Five Smooth Stones for Pastoral Work*

Dear Lord, help me to trust that the qualities you have given to me are just what I need to do your will. Help me to recognize and eliminate any unnecessary clutter that has been imposed from outside and to rely on your love, patience, guidance, and empowerment to do my proper work. In Jesus' name. Amen.

OCTOBER

October 1

SOLOMON IN ALL HIS SPLENDOR

"And why do you worry about clothes? See how the lilies of the field grow. They do not labor or spin. Yet I tell you that not even Solomon in all his splendor was dressed like one of these." —Matthew 6:28-29

Dandelions

My yard is solid yellow with dandelions.
They gather there for a convention,
arriving from all over, forming a carpet
too brilliant to look upon.
My white house blushes gold
as their fuzzy heads press against its clapboards.

Each of my neighbors snickers out his window
as the last squatters run, bright heads tossing,
to my place — leaving their lawns green and flat.
I open my window and breathe in the wine
of their fragrance, gold under me like Solomon.
All day they give the sun up to the sun.

All night pollen thickens around me.
I carefully gather and press it between pages
until I am empty and drained. The next morning
all have gone silver in a cloud, a mist
that you see a loved face through in a wet October.
I breathe out the window slowly upon them:

The white seeds shake, twinkle to be gone.
In a swirl they rise, weightless as gossamer,
obscuring windows, dissolving walls:
Houses, neighbors, blow into the sky,
lawns falling away like tiny emeralds,
as a thousand suns falter, vanish into light.

—Robert Siegel, *In a Pig's Eye*

The extravagance of your glory surrounds me, O Lord. The gold of your love covers the field of my morning. There is no end to the wild seed of your word. Let me be soil to receive your presence. Amen.

October 2

Soul Surgery

"Whoever does not love does not know God, because God is love."
—1 John 4:8, KJV

A chill sets into the church when people begin to claim that only a sturdy set of doctrines will bring us to a knowledge of God. Our knowing God has its source in our very identity; we are, after all, his image-bearers. What's more, our knowledge of him matures in often surprising revelations. As if he were a clown, he often startles us in the middle of our deepest and even most dreary distractions.

On the other hand, if we think that knowing God has nothing to do with creeds, we're wrong. Without a foundation, we're bound for silly mysticism and bizarre New Age–like fantasies.

To grow in our knowledge of God requires our spiritual experiences *and* our doctrines — *and* more. We come to know God by loving others. "Whoever does not love does not know God," says John, "because God is love" (1 John 4:8).

Consider forgiveness. There's an angle in the Lord's Prayer that's helpful here: "Forgive us our debts as we forgive our debtors." A command is suggested in Jesus' words: we must love as we want to be loved; we must forgive as we want to be forgiven.

But don't overestimate yourself. The forgiveness here described is no trifle, and certainly not the action of some overworked police officer for a two-bit cook. To forgive petty wrongs is no more difficult that shooing off flies.

Real forgiveness is more than simply excusing someone, because real forgiveness requires soul surgery. We need to be opened up, painfully, and, as if with a scalpel, have that which is diseased cut out. God is that surgeon, and what he cuts away is our sin. Our growing in knowledge through forgiveness is not something we set out to accomplish on our own. God is the source of our ability to forgive others — let that never be forgotten.

That person who learns to love — and to forgive — his fellow human travelers comes to know something of the eternal, something of God Almighty.

—James Calvin Schaap, *Near Unto God*

Be my surgeon, Lord. Cut from me the disease of my sin. Make me whole that I might forgive those who have wronged me and in forgiving learn to love with your love. Amen.

October 3

PARADOXES

"By honour and dishonour, by evil report and good report: as deceivers, and yet true; as unknown, and yet well known; as dying, and, behold, we live; as chastened, and not killed; as sorrowful, yet alway rejoicing; as poor, yet making many rich; as having nothing, and yet possessing all things." —2 Corinthians 6:8-10, KJV

Chapel began at 8:15. Dr. Peckham was the speaker.

It was the shortest chapel message they had yet heard. He began by saying he had been getting a lot of questions lately about something called the "victorious life" or "the life that wins." It went by many names and involved some special act of God which would bring power and blessing. He had been asked if he believed in such an experience, and his answer was yes, he did, but if he must name it he would rather call it "the life that loses."

"As I get the picture," he went on, his funny cross face just over the top of the pulpit, "the life that wins is a shining life in which we are endowed moment by moment with unquenchable joy and a new strength of character. We want to be like Christ, we say. We want to have his heart—to be courageous, serene in the face of adversity, powerful in soul-winning, steady and unmovable in faith, all in our places, with sunshiny faces.

"But friends, it may not go that way. If you ask for the heart of Christ, yours may be broken. If you ask for the eyes of Christ, you may be horrified at what you see. If you try to embrace all mankind, as Christ did, you may be consumed by that love. If we fight injustice, we are identified with the condemned. We will bear about in our bodies the paradoxes of mankind, the yeas and the nays.

"What we have then is a flat contradiction. Dead in him. Alive in him. 'as dying, and, behold, we live; as chastened, and not killed; as sorrowful, yet alway rejoicing; as poor, yet making many rich; as having nothing, and yet possessing all things.' That's the life that wins.

"But how will I know? How can I tell when I've got it, when I'm filled with the Holy Spirit? I don't think we will know. I don't think we'll even ask, or give it much thought. We won't say, 'I've got it!' or 'Ah, now I am like Christ,' or 'At last, I am godly.' That will never occur to us, because we will only seem to be more human."

—Shirley Nelson, *The Last Year of the War*

Christ, make me like yourself, open to the contradictions of this unpredictable life. Amen.

October 4

THE GOD WHO IS THERE

"How long, O Lord? Will you hide yourself forever?"
—Psalm 89:46

Perhaps it's a matter of perspective. Perhaps it's having eyes to pierce fog or dark or whatever walls us off from God. More likely, it's patience.

Disappointment is a large part of our experience with God. We live one day at a time, not knowing what will happen tomorrow. But we hope. We ache to have "the eyes of our hearts enlightened" so that we can see God, who is a Spirit. But our own efforts can never achieve it.

In the autumn of 1988, I was writer in residence at Regent College in Vancouver, Canada, while living sixty-five miles south in the U.S. In practical terms, this meant a drive north along the coast on the days I had office hours or a class to teach. The Pacific Northwest is known for rains that fall gently but steadily for days and for clouds that hug the earth and shroud the landscape. Just a few miles in from the coast rise the Cascade Mountains and, spectacular among them, Mount Baker, when we're fortunate enough to see it!

I wrote in my journal: "For weeks I drive my highway, north in the morning, then south again at the end of the day. The mountains are on the map, but they might as well not exist, lost as they are in drizzle, fog, haze — atmospheric conditions that interfere with clear vision. Then some strong air from the Pacific sweeps away the mask, the sun shines cleanly, and Mt. Baker, towering beyond the foothills, is seen to be what it has been all along — strong, serene, unmoving, its profile cut clear against a sky of deepest blue.

"The mountains are getting whiter these days as the nights chill and snow covers their gray blue peaks. Today I kept turning my eyes from the road to glance once more at Mt. Baker, wanting to be overwhelmed again and again by the spectacular view. It is heart stopping; I can't get enough of the sight. And I can never take it for granted — I may not see it again for weeks.

"For me it's another picture of God. I mean — he's *there*, whether I see him or not. It's almost as if he's lying in wait to surprise me. And the wind is like the Spirit, sweeping away the fogs of doubt or discouragement, opening my eyes to the truth of the mountain's pure perfection, its heartbreaking beauty." —Luci Shaw, *Horizons*

Lord, you are not like the mountain, passively hidden from our view. But neither are you aggressively present, overwhelming me with your glory. You wait for me to see, and you move to be seen by me. What joy it is to know, when I seek you, that you are there, eager to be found. Motivated by your Spirit, may I be always seeking you. Amen.

October 5

Gift of Words

"The right word at the right time is like a custom-made piece of jewelry, and a wise friend's timely reprimand is like a gold ring slipped on your finger." —Proverbs 25:11-12, THE MESSAGE

The gift of words is for communion. We need to learn the nature of communion. This requires the risk of revelation — letting a piece of myself be exposed, this mystery of who I am. If I stand here mute, you have no idea what is going on with me. You can look at me, measure me, weigh me, test me, but until I start to talk you do not know what is going on inside, who I really am.

If you listen and I am telling the truth, something marvelous starts to take place — a new event. Something comes into being that was not there before. God does this for us. We learn to do it because God does it. New things happen then. Salvation comes into being; love comes into being. Communion.

Words used this way do not define as much as deepen mystery — entering into the ambiguities, pushing past the safely known into the risky unknown. The Christian Eucharist uses words, the simplest of words, "this is my body, this is my blood," that plunge us into an act of revelation which staggers the imagination, which we never figure out, but we enter into. These words do not describe; they point, they reach, they embrace.

Every time I go to the ill, the dying, the lonely, it becomes obvious after a few moments that the only words that matter are words of communion. What is distressing is to find out how infrequently they are used. Sometimes we find we are the only ones who bother using words this way on these occasions. Not the least of the trials of the sick, the lonely, and the dying is the endless stream of cliches and platitudes to which they have to listen. Doctors enter their rooms to communicate the diagnosis, family members to communicate their anxieties, friends to communicate the gossip of the day. Not all of them do this, of course, and not always, but the sad reality is that there is not a great deal of communion that goes on in these places with these ill and lonely and dying people, on street corners, in offices, in work places, in schools. That makes it urgent that the Christian becomes a specialist in words of communion. —Eugene H. Peterson, *Subversive Spirituality*

Dear Lord, help me to take the risk of talking about what is going on inside of me with someone today. Guide me to that person, and nurture in me an ability to offer words of communion where needed. In Jesus' name. Amen.

October 6

TOO GOOD TO BE TRUE

"'For a brief moment I abandoned you, but with deep compassion I will bring you back. In a surge of anger I hid my face from you for a moment, but with everlasting kindness I will have compassion on you,' says the Lord your Redeemer." —Isaiah 54:7-8

One day when George MacDonald, the great Scottish preacher and writer, was talking with his son, the conversation turned to heaven and the prophets' version of the end of all things. "It seems too good to be true," the son said at one point. A smile crossed MacDonald's whiskered face. "Nay," he replied, "it is just so good it must be true!"

Does any human emotion run as deep as hope? Fairy tales pass on through the centuries a stubborn hope in a happy ending, a belief that in the end the wicked witch will die and the brave and innocent children will somehow find a way of escape. A dozen cartoons in a row on Saturday morning television crank out a similar message to children who sit enthralled, too young to sneer at impossibly cheery endings. In real life, a mother caught in a war zone holds her infant son tight against her breast, pats his head, and whispers, illogically, "It'll be all right," even as the percussive blasts grow closer.

Where does such hope come from? Searching for words to explain the ageless attraction of fairy tales, Tolkien said:

[Fairy tale] does not deny the existence of...sorrow and failure: the possibility of these is necessary to the joy of the deliverance;

it denies (in the fact of much evidence, if you will) universal final defeat... giving a fleeting glimpse of Joy, Joy beyond the walls of the world, poignant as grief.

No summary of the prophets would be complete apart from one last message: their loud insistence that the world will not end in "universal final defeat," but in Joy. They spoke in foreboding times to audiences filled with fear, and often their dire predictions of droughts and locust plagues and enemy sieges fueled that fear. But always, in every one of their seventeen books, the prophets of the Old Testament got around to a word of hope. The wounded lover will recover from his pain, Isaiah promises: "For a brief moment I abandoned you, but with deep compassion I will bring you back."

—Philip Yancey, *Disappointment with God*

Dear Lord, the promise of hope and joy means so much to me. Thank you that you are true to your word, and let me be the same. In Jesus' name. Amen.

October 7

A Voice for Creation

"You will go out in joy and be led forth in peace; the mountains and hills will burst into song before you, and all the trees of the field will clap their hands." —Isaiah 55:12

This is one of those annoying questions science thought it had left behind: how important is matter? The Manichean contempt for matter that early infected the church still plagues it today, and indeed undermines all areas of human endeavor. We continue to imagine that we can exist as disembodied intelligences. The resurrection of the body has only the dimmest possible meaning for us. Such contempt for creation lays the groundwork for an unwitting alliance between religious spiritualizers, whether of the demythologizing or the supposedly literalist school, and a science that would have us believe that matter itself is dead and thus would strip everything "merely" material of significance. Even, ultimately, ourselves.

In a secular society such as ours, devoted to de-sacramentalizing and de-carnating the world, the very concept of "holy" becomes an empty category. Yet this vacuum cannot now be replenished by going back to a dualistic understanding of a "spiritual" world over against a "physical" world. It is not a case of mind over matter because mind *is* matter, and no less allowed for that. As Owen Barfield has insisted, we can no longer be satisfied with a "religious" truth that fails to implicate matter — and vice versa.

An explication of the new physics that is only discursive, however, fails to give any indication of the urgency, elegance, and richness of the subject. It cannot show how all of life must incandesce and pulsate with this understanding of the universe that is groaning in travail. We live a cosmic drama just by opening our eyes and metabolizing carbohydrates, and it is imperative to engage matter on those terms. Therefore, what follows is no philosophical discussion of propositions, but an attempt to find the flesh from which the propositions were extracted.

I declare that the prophet's figures of trees clapping their hands is a living reality and that Christ's life is simultaneously symbol and fact. This is the reality of matter we have not dared to dream. To declare this reality one must allow one's own life to flow into this tributary of testimony. —Virginia Stem Owens, *God Spy*

Dear Lord, I want my life to flow into this tributary of testimony, this cosmic drama, so that my life in this world becomes united with Paul's image of living Christ's life. Guide me as I journey toward this living reality. In Jesus' name. Amen.

October 8

STEWARDSHIP OF THE EARTH

"God saw all that he had made and it was very good.... The Lord God took the man and put him in the Garden of Eden to work it and take care of it." —Genesis 1:31a, 2:15

The message from all quarters is the same: *our undisciplined consumption must end.* If we continue to gobble up our resources without any regard to stewardship and to spew out our deadly wastes over land, sea, and air, we may well be drawing down the final curtain upon ourselves.

I need to add a reason for curbing our gluttonous consumption that Christians should consider very seriously. Overconsumption is a "cancer eating away at our spiritual vitals" (Wayne Rieman). It cuts the heart out of our compassion. It distances us from the great masses of broken bleeding humanity. It converts us into materialists. We become less able to ask the moral questions. For example, just because we have the economic muscle to buy up vast amounts of the world's oil, does that give us the right to do so? When the poor farmer of India is unable to buy a gallon of gasoline to run his simple water pump because the world's demand has priced him out of the market, who is to blame? You see, our sensitivities have been dulled by our overconsumption. Our undisciplined squandering is destroying us spiritually. Walter Harrelson, professor of Old Testament at Vanderbilt University, says in *Lifeboat Ethics*: "Overeating and overconsumption, gross inequity in the control of wealth, and a desire to maintain one's own style of life irrespective of world famine clearly constitutes sin in the biblical perspective.

Christians can make, I think, a unique contribution to this issue, because biblically and theologically we have a vital interest in both stewardship of the earth and economic justice for the poor. And because our allegiance to God is higher than to any nation-state, we have a commitment to global citizenship that can help us transcend the provincial claims of national interest.   —Richard J. Foster, *Freedom of Simplicity*

I pray, O Lord, for the earth. Forgive us for the waste, the destruction, the disrespect. Heal the earth, O God. Heal the earth. Amen.
—Richard J. Foster, "The Creation Wails," in *Prayers from the Heart*

October 9

Keep Walking

"And he awoke and rebuked the wind, and said to the sea, "Peace! Be still!" And the wind ceased, and there was a great calm."
—Mark 4:39, RSV

It seemed strange to be back at the coast again. The light pre-dawn breeze coming in from the Gulf had only a tinge of the salt marsh smell of the sea. The atmosphere was heavy, another hot June day coming. As I walked the block from where I was staying to the water, in the grayness I passed our old beach house crouched sleeping on top of the big dune. A family from Canada owned the house now. A hundred ghosts of the past seemed to come out and dance around on the long front deck — the ghosts of children laughing and playing tag, and a big white dog, a white Siberian Husky, smiling through the railing at me with his tongue lolling out from running. They all seemed to be beckoning to me to go back in time with them. As I stopped for a moment and watched them in my imagination, I felt a real tugging from the past. But then shaking my head I turned and started on toward the beach. And I saw a horizontal slit of light, high above the gray rolling surf. I was startled to realize that the sun had already risen, but it had come up behind the clouds and I had not seen it.

By the time I'd walked in the water's edge barefooted on the slick wet, gray-tan sand left by the sliding waves, all the way to the old wooden pier where I'd shouted so many of my questions at God, the sun had split the clouds in a dozen places, creating in the leaden sky a towering pink and white castle coming out of its gray cocoon. From all around the castle came shafts of gold and silver pointing down to the sea in front of me.

I stood on the end of the pier and let the spray hit my face as I heard and felt the thud and boom of the waves crashing into the huge pilings below. Then I felt hot tears of hope, and happiness, mingled with the fine salt mist on my face.

Years ago, after the divorce, I'd screamed my questions to God in the roar of the surf.

"What kind of a person am I, really?"

"Is there any hope for me?"

"How can I risk relating intimately to you and to people — and just be myself?"

No answer.

But now above in the sunrise, a deep Voice seemed to whisper in my ear, "Don't run away any more. Keep walking *right through* the loneliness and fear with me to the place where I will break through the clouds and bring the light you need. I've already risen behind your gray clouds and am about to show you a new day! Your next step will put you in your new life."

Almost involuntarily I stepped forward.

"Good," the Voice seemed to say, "you've begun!"

—Keith Miller

Lord, thank you that when we shatter our grandiose crystalline plans against your immutable laws, you save the colorful broken pieces to create mosaics from the pain. Amen.

October 10

Ears to Hear

"Blessed are...your ears, for they hear."
—Matthew 13:16, KJV

Have you ever walked in the woods on a windless autumn day when, as if by inaudible command, a scatter of golden leaves let go above you and begin to float down from their parent branches, whispering their obedience, their "yes" to God, as they land on the forest floor and gild it seamlessly with "gold leaf"?

The trees in the forest listen to their Creator. With every season he whispers his old/new words; thy hear him attentively and obey him instantly. But we humans are different; a separate created order infinitely more complex and clever, we have been given some risky gifts — self-consciousness, reflective intelligence, imagination, and a free will that makes wide-reaching choices and decisions. Yet in spite of these advantages we have been rendered tone-deaf by sin, and although we ought gratefully to return our gifts to God, we choose often to serve our own petty purposes and ignore his voice.

Unlike the trees, people aren't rooted in one place; we are constantly pulled off course by life's distractions. The small, interior voice of God is drowned out in human hubbub. When I read Jesus' urgent plea for followers who have "ears to hear," I feel his longing for listening ears. He wants his Word to be made flesh again in each one of us.

—Luci Shaw, *Horizons*

Lord, even as we're thinking about this process and how it should happen, can we hear your voice with our inner ears? Yes. And as we walk among the trees and realize suddenly why autumn is called Fall (the leaves in the still air begin to float down as if by your secret command), we know you are telling us about our own need to listen and obey. Our inner ears are open toward you. Widen and fill them with your messages. Amen.

—Luci Shaw, *Horizons*

October 11

GROWING TOWARD PURITY

"Blessed are the pure in heart: for they shall see God."
—Matthew 5:8

When Christ laid out the Beatitudes, he was describing a single state of mind and heart, not necessarily a variety of believers. All of the descriptions — to be meek, to be peacemakers, to mourn — are meant to describe the same kind of person: those who place themselves under the guardianship of Jesus and want to enter his kingdom. To be pure in heart should not be misunderstood to mean sinless. If Jesus meant this beatitude only for those who had never entertained a miserable thought or done some regrettable sin, we should all despair. To the moment of death, we all fight iniquity.

Which is not to say that the Christian does not make progress toward righteousness. The more we grow in faith, the more keen our eye becomes in understanding faith and fleeing evil. Even though the world is befuddled by a truly saintly person who pleads passionately to be free from sin, those who know their sinful condition inside and out know only too well that sin often lurks even in their most virtuous acts.

In some ways, we might consider that we have two selves — one of which is, by the nature of our fallen humanity, sullied by sin. But another self is capable of understanding that condition and arming itself against giving in to its baseness.

We cannot be pure as long as we live on earth, but we can grow toward purity in our attitude toward the poisonous inclinations of the heart. When we begin to hate the evil that is within us, battle against sin with every strength the Lord gives, then we say with Christ, "Deliver us from evil."

If, with God's help, we struggle against our own darkness, we can be pure in our attempts to fight it, even though our hearts will never be without sin. With God as ally, Satan cannot bully. This struggle will bring us ever closer and closer to God, and in that position — and that position only — will we see God with the eye of a soul dedicated to him.

—James Calvin Schaap, *Near Unto God*

Lord, in our struggle against the darkness of our sin only your light can bring clarity. We invite you to illumine our hearts that we might see those areas of sin we have not yet perceived. Give us grace to repent and persistence in our journey toward you. Amen.

October 12

THE CHURCH COLLECTS SINNERS

"If we claim that we're free of sin, we're only fooling ourselves. A claim like that is errant nonsense. On the other hand, if we admit our sins — make a clean breast of them — he won't let us down; he'll be true to himself. He'll forgive our sins and purge us of all wrongdoing."

—1 John 1:8-9, THE MESSAGE

When Christian believers gather in churches, everything that can go wrong sooner or later does. Outsiders, on observing this, conclude that there is nothing to the religion business except, perhaps, business —

and dishonest business at that. Insiders see it differently. Just as a hospital collects the sick under one roof and labels them as such, the church collects sinners. Many of the people outside the hospital are every bit as sick as the ones inside, but their illnesses are either undiagnosed or disguised. It's similar with sinners outside the church.
—Eugene H. Peterson, THE MESSAGE

Dear Lord, thank you that there is a place to go for healing for our souls. Help me to try to be part of the solution when things go wrong in the church. And when I have been part of the problem, help me to know how to acknowledge it and return to the solution side of things. In Jesus' name. Amen.

October 13

THE WORK OF PRAYER

"Rejoice in your hope, be patient in tribulation, be constant in prayer."
—Romans 12:12, RSV

Not to put too fine a point on it, C. S. Lewis's life, although rich in wit and love and prayer, was nonetheless a trudge. In a poem entitled "As One Oldster to Another," written in his fifty-second year to an American of approximately the same age, he likened the Christian path through life to a night train, screaming through the stations toward the ultimate terminus, and he not knowing yet when to take down his case from the overhead rack.

What with fatigue of body and spirit, rudeness, rejection, deadly sins everywhere he put his feet, pains physical and spiritual, debilitating illness, and eventually death, the emotion Lewis felt most in life was drudge. Prayer helped, but just. In the end he too suffered, died, and was buried; in his case, under a larch in the graveyard surrounding Holy Trinity Church, Headington.

And so it is with the Mere Christian (MC). Discovering the Christian path comes first. Faithfulness to the pathway comes next, even if the fog rolls in and one can't see much beyond one's nose. An Ordnance Survey map would help — its palette of pale colors always pleasing to the bleary eye — but where the Christian is ultimately heading, the crown surveyors have yet to map. Weariness dogs the MC's tracks. And if it weren't for moments of prayer and acts of belief — echoing the name of Jesus in the wilderness seemed to help — the MC would end up in a ditch, there to await the merciful arrival of death. Without religion life on this earth can be made bearable. With religion life is acceptable. With Christianity life is hopeful. Keeping hope alive is the work of prayer.

— William Griffin, *C. S. Lewis: Spirituality for Mere Christians*

God, at times like C. S. Lewis, I am dragged down by fatigue of body and spirit, rudeness, rejection, deadly sins everywhere, pains physical and spiritual, debilitating illness. Help me to be patient in tribulation and constant in prayer, so to continually rekindle my faith and hope. Amen.

October 14

IT'S THE SHIRTS!

"Let your attitude to life be that of Christ Jesus himself. For he, who had always been God by nature, did not cling to his privileges as God's equal, but stripped himself of every advantage by consenting to be a slave...and...he humbled himself by living a life of utter obedience, to the point of death." —Philippians 2:5-8, PHILLIPS

The longer I am involved in the Christian life, the more clearly I see that the beginnings of significant lifelong changes often hinge on seemingly insignificant discoveries and decisions in the intimate arena of personal relationships.

Some time ago about twelve of us got together to form a small group. We were trying to find out how we could learn to be God's people away from the church during the week. This was a new adventure that was exciting for most of the group. We decided that we would not tell anyone outside the group what we were doing. The idea was to attempt various experiments in our lives during the week and then report to the group what happened to us.

Our plan was to begin in our families and work outward into the world. During the first week we were to look around, listen in our homes and see what *we* were doing to bug the people we live with, and then pray about our behavior to see if we could change it. Usually in prayer groups we had looked for those things *other people* were doing to bother *us* and then pray for *them* to change. This is a very different approach.

The next week was an interesting one. One member of our group was a lovely, pleasingly plump, white-haired woman, who was very attractive. At the first meeting I remember thinking that Lillian looked almost angelic...with a slight twinkle in her eye. She didn't seem to have any problems and prayed sweet, sincere prayers. Frankly, I wondered how she got in our group. Lillian had not said much so far, but she came into the next meeting like a rodeo rider out of chute four. She was so excited she was practically bubbling over. When I asked the group about the experiment, all Lillian could way was, "You all, it's the *shirts!*"

All I could think of to say was, "Would you like to talk about it?"

She went on, "I'm from the old South. And when I got married, my mother told me, 'Don't you ever iron any man's shirts. That's not wives' work.' So after the honeymoon, twenty-five years ago, I told my husband I was not going to iron his shirts. He was a struggling student at that time, and we didn't have very much money, but he had to send his shirts out. After a few years, he developed a rash on his neck and had to wear shirts that required hand ironing. So for sixteen years Bill has been getting up on Saturday mornings and ironing his own shirts — right in front of me — while I fixed breakfast. We were both Christians, but about that time we started going to different churches."

She stopped talking and put her fist against her mouth, and her bosom shook with an involuntary sob. In a moment she went on with tears in her eyes: "This week I discovered that all my guilt and self-hate as a woman, all of the wrangling and separation I've caused in our marriage, stem from the fact that I wouldn't iron Bill's shirts. I've prayed all week, and I don't know if I can do anything this late to change things for Bill — but I'd like for you to pray for me that I will." And we did.

Well, I don't know what Lillian did at home those next few days, but the following week Bill showed up at the meeting, smiling from ear to ear. And they came to the group together regularly, like two happy kids, until Lillian died suddenly of a stroke a year later. But you know, that couple found each other, found a new kind of life together after twenty-five years.

What is that experience worth in terms of changing the world? I don't know, but watching it happen changed the rest of us in that group somehow. We began to see that the closed doors in our lives and relationships which we had been trying to batter down with argument and reason all these years, that those doors often stuck on small rusty hinges, on little things — like the shirts.   — J. Keith Miller, *Habitation of Dragons*

> Indeed, this need of individuals to be right is so great that they are willing to sacrifice themselves, their relationships, and even love for it. This need to be right is also one which produces hostility and cruelty and causes people to say things that shut them off from communication with both God and man.
>
> —Reuel Howe, *The Miracle of Dialogue*

Lord, help me to have the courage to look for the little inner walls and fortresses in my relationships, behind which I protect my pride. Forgive me for camouflaging these defenses and calling them "matters of principle" when so often they are only means to keep from having to admit that I have been wrong and wanted to be number one. I guess this is what has always made you so threatening to me. When you expose my self-justifying defenses, I either have to confess them or put you down — which is what I guess we tried to do on the cross. And I still try to put you down when you get close to revealing the motives I have hidden. Help me, Lord, not to cling to my "rights" but to unclench my spiritual fist so that I can be free to follow you. Amen. —J. Keith Miller, *Habitation of Dragons*

October 15

ONE VICE A YEAR

The point is this: the one who sows sparingly will also reap sparingly, and the one who sows bountifully will also reap bountifully. Each of you must give as you have made up your mind, not reluctantly or under compulsion, for God loves a cheerful giver."
—2 Corinthians 9:6-7, NRSV

These Scripture verses have two different messages for me when I think of them in relation to getting in shape. The first sentence, "The one who sows sparingly will also reap sparingly, and the one who sows bountifully will also reap bountifully," says to me that I can become fit only in proportion to the amount of effort I'm willing to put into it. I've seen that the amount of work I need to do to learn about exercise, dieting, and cooking is a lot. How faithfully and vigorously I'm willing to exercise will also determine how fit I can become. So, being a very competitive person who is anxious to jump right in and get busy, I started pushing myself to learn quickly and exercise hard in a hurry!

After a few weeks, I was feeling burned out and ready to quit. About that time I reread Paul's words from 2 Corinthians. And this time the second sentence jumped out at me in a new way: "Each of you must give as you have made up your mind, not *reluctantly or under compulsion,* for God loves a *cheerful giver*" (italics mine). I saw then that my enthusiastic attack was mostly due to my *compulsion* for doing the most, the best, and the fastest. And part of my compulsion was due to my desire to get it all over with faster so I could forget about it and go back to my familiar, though unhealthy, habits. And I was definitely not feeling *cheerful* about what I was doing!

I reevaluated my approach. I thought about some of the pleasurable things I had squeezed out of my schedule so I could begin this massive reeducation process. And I decided I really wanted to become the "cheerful giver" God wants me to be, not to fake it any more. I needed to take a new look at the way I was going about making these changes. Instead of rushing, like I had to get it all done immediately, I needed to develop a realistic, gradual plan.

My thinking began to go like this, "I've got the rest of my life to live, which is plenty of time (unless I have an unusual accident along the way). I've spent years learning these old habits, so why do I need to relearn everything in three months, six months, or even a year? And why the hurry to get it over with if I've decided I'm not going back to my old, unhealthy habits? As long as I've made a commitment inside myself to change, and do something every day — however small it may be — toward making that change, then eventually I'll make it. Over the years, I *can* improve my health — rather than continue to make it worse." And I won't be so constantly frustrated. After all, as a doctor pointed out to me, we don't usually gain weight at a rate of twenty pounds a month, so there's no point in trying to lose it that fast.

Again, I was reading *The Imitation of Christ* by Thomas à Kempis. I noticed that he spent a lot of time writing about changing habits. One paragraph stuck in my mind as I was wrestling with the problem of compulsion and how it led me to be unhappy and resentful. The paragraph was, "If we would every year overcome one vice, we should soon come to perfection, but I fear rather to the contrary, that we were better and more pure at the beginning of our conversion than we were many years after we were converted." I realized I had been much more enthusiastic and optimistic about getting in shape when I had first gotten started than I was now after weeks of knocking myself out trying to do it all at once.

So I made up my mind to back up and try to do what Thomas à Kempis recommended — to overcome one vice each year. It seems like this has left me more time to have a balanced life. Having room for friendships, recreation, meaningful work, and prayer time gives me a more cheerful and less impatient attitude.

Four years later, I find that not everything I need to change is changed. But when I look back over that time, I can see some major changes that are now a part of my routine life. And I feel genuinely cheerful a lot more of the time.   —Andrea Wells Miller, *BodyCare*

Dear Lord, I realize that the effort I'm willing to put into making the changes to become your person directly affects the results I can expect. But I also know that these changes must become a part of my life — as much a part as breathing is or as sleeping at night.

Help me to make these changes one by one, and to learn how to give you more and more control over this area of my life, without losing my cheerful attitude which I know you love so much. And help me to learn balance as I develop a plan for growth. I see so much I need to change. Lead me one step at a time through this learning and adjusting period. In Jesus' name. Amen.

October 16

DREAM OR REALITY?

"He who gets wisdom loves his own soul; he who cherishes understanding prospers."
— Proverbs 19:8

Our skull is like a cup holding this heady decoction of mingled memories, saved from decaying into chaos by the preservative of reason and kept brimming by continually new distillations from the senses. Few, I think, choose to bear such a cup, to stand under such a load.

For the load is just this: the creation, the fabrication of phenomena. Without perception, not only is there no crash as the tree falls in the forest, but there is no tree, no forest, no sound of any kind. Not the clicking of chitin-shelled insects in the quivering summer heat, not the call of birds stitching through the branches, not the tensile creak of the tree's raised column of water and minerals sprouting like a fountain in the wind. Not even silence.

Not that I doubt the world or think I'm dreaming. This is no Descartes who confides only in consciousness, who would cut the carnal cords that bind him to the earth and float free of phenomena. However one digs at the roots of the world — with quantum bundles of energy, with molecular galactic systems, with undulating fields of electromagnetism — the world is still out there waiting — pure movement, pure being. But in here, and only in here, sucked up by the senses into the nervous system and delivered crackling and popping to consciousness, it takes shape as tree, leaf, resin, root.   —Virginia Stem Owens, *God Spy*

Dear Lord, I praise you for the wonder of all you have created, especially the process of taking things in through my senses and sifting these sensations in this fabulous brain, where perception is born. Help me to filter my perceptions through your truth and to enlarge my consciousness even more as I take in the sensations from your marvelous world! In Jesus' name. Amen.

October 17

LANDMARKS

"No one lights a lamp and hides it in a jar or puts it under a bed. Instead, he puts it on a stand, so that those who come in can see the light."
— Luke 8:16

I am fifty miles into Iowa, driving to a speaking engagement. Here and there the flat prairie landscape is enlivened by spring plowing. Between long, uncultivated stretches I see disking machines, like ships plowing the waves of the fields, trailing clouds of dust thick as sea-mist and wakes of turf folded back, rounded and shining as waves, but solid. Small clumps of trees lie like islands around which the bare ocean of landscape stretches, cut in sharp relief against the simple immensity of the sky. Now and then a single tree breaks the flatness of a plowed field.

This has been a day of solitude on almost deserted highways with no towns for twenty or thirty miles at a stretch. Only the plows and a now-and-then barn glimpsed on the horizon give me a clue that this land is inhabited. The earth is bare and dun-colored. The cool weather of this past week has put spring on hold until today, and the south sides of banks and ditches are still mottled with rags of snow. The tree islands are innocent of leaves, though I can see the fattening buds. Their fringed tops let light through, and their nakedness makes for a clarity, a straightforwardness, a disclosure that the lush growth of summer obscures.

Later, in the home of my hosts I voice a question: "Why do farmers sometimes leave one lone tree standing in the middle of a field?" I get an eminently practical answer from the man who grew up on a farm: "So that when they're plowing, they have something to rest the eye on. It helps them keep the furrows straight."

So. Since then, whenever I drive the prairie, I look for the lone trees — the plowman's navigational buoys set in seas of soil. I ask myself, can I be for someone else an interruption in the horizon, a landmark, a directional signal, a simplicity on which they can rest the eye and know they're going straight?
— Luci Shaw, *Horizons*

Jesus, you have called me to yourself and filled me with your Spirit. You have made me upright. Now let me stand, as a tree on the horizon or a lamp on the hill, that others, seeing me, might see you. Amen.

October 18

The Scent of Hay

"Then make my joy complete by being like-minded, having the same love, being one in spirit and purpose. Do nothing out of selfish ambition or vain conceit, but in humility consider others better than yourselves."
—Philippians 2:2-3

The dusty light above
the rabbit hutch
shapes a circle
of cheerfulness
in the scent of hay.

My hands, offering lettuce,
chill and redden,
but from the fresh water
steam rises,
and in its rising I know
a kind of order
in the world.

May I, by faithfulness
in such small chores,
be found in grace
and come one day
to waken,
my labor complete
in love.

—John Leax, *The Task of Adam*

Son of Man, born in the scent of hay, obedient unto death, all we enjoy comes from your humility. Walk with us that we might learn to walk in faithfulness with you. Amen.

October 19

THE BIG PICTURE

"I looked up and there before me was a man dressed in linen, with a belt of the finest gold around his waist....I, Daniel, was the only one who saw the vision; the men with me did not see it, but such terror overwhelmed them that they fled and hid themselves. So I was left alone, gazing at this great vision; I had no strength left, my face turned deathly pale and I was helpless." —Daniel 10:5, 7-8

In the supernatural realm, our vision is even more limited, and we get only occasional glimpses of that unseen world.

An incident in the life of another famous Bible character makes this same point in a very different way. The prophet Daniel had a mild — mild in comparison with Job's — encounter with the hiddenness of God.

Daniel puzzled over an everyday problem of unanswered prayer: why was God ignoring his repeated requests? For twenty-one days Daniel devoted himself to prayer. He mourned. He gave up choice foods. He swore off meat and wine, and used no lotions on his body. All the while he called out to God, but received no answer.

Then one day Daniel got far more than he bargained for. A supernatural being, with eyes like flaming torches and a face like lightning, suddenly showed up on a riverbank beside him. Daniel's companions all fled in terror. As for Daniel, "I had no strength left. My face turned deathly pale and I was helpless." When he tried talking to the dazzling being, he could hardly breathe.

The visitor proceeded to explain the reason for the long delay. He had been dispatched to answer Daniel's very first prayer, but had run into strong resistance from "the prince of the Persian kingdom." Finally, after a three-week standoff, reinforcements arrived and Michael, one of the chief angels, helped him break through the opposition.

I will not attempt to interpret this amazing scene of the universe of war, except to point out a parallel to Job. Like Job, Daniel played a decisive role in the warfare between cosmic forces of good and evil, though much of the action took place beyond his range of vision. To him prayer may have seemed futile, and God indifferent; but a glimpse "behind the curtain" reveals exactly the opposite. Daniel's limited perspective, like Job's, distorted reality.

What are we to make of Daniel's angelic being who needed reinforcements, not to mention the cosmic wager in Job? Simply this: the big picture, with the whole universe as a backdrop, includes much activity that we never see. When we stubbornly cling to God in a time of hardship, or when we simply pray, more — much more — may be involved than we ever dream. It requires faith to believe that, and faith to trust that we are never abandoned, no matter how distant God seems.

—Philip Yancey, *Disappointment with God*

Dear Lord, my faith is small compared to Daniel's and Job's. So much more is involved in how things operate, more than I could ever dream. Help me grow in faith and trust that I am never abandoned by you, no matter how distant you seem. In Jesus' name. Amen.

October 20

LOVE WILL START

"...Being confident of this very thing, that he which hath begun a good work in you will perform it until the day of Jesus Christ."
—Philippians 1:6, KJV

Siri had a nice voice, I thought, but not really a gorgeous one. What Benjy was reacting to was the whole experience of Siri and the music and the penguins, and yes, that was gorgeous. And maybe he was reacting to Siri herself. I walked along between Benjy and Sam. Cook and Leilia were behind us, chatting away. When we got back to the beach and the Zodiacs, Siri had her harp slung on her back again and was walking with Greta. They seemed to get along very well, despite Greta's musical lacks.

In my head I began to write a poem, sort of inspired by what Siri had sung and remembering what Aunt Serena had said about penguins and intimacy. While we were waiting to get in the Zodiacs, I sat on the beach and scribbled, and waited for the last Zodiac, so I had something more or less finished.

> High lifts my heart in warmth and cold,
> Moonlight and starlight, cloud and sun,
> Sea spray and salt and the land's fold,
> Lamb and fledgling, and love begun
> In the heart that dares not warm
> But cannot chill. Stars! Stay my heart
> And keep my burning love from harm,
> For love will start, oh, love will start.
>
> —Madeleine L'Engle, *Troubling a Star*

Lord, feed and fan the starting sparks to glow and grow into your unquenchable flame of divine love. Amen.

October 21

O GOD, MY GOD!

"Then will I go unto the altar of God, unto God my exceeding joy: yea, upon the harp will I praise thee, O God my God."
—Psalm 43:4, KJV

For years a child's prayer, no matter how deeply meant and felt, is limited by the range of his understanding and experience. We can be tickled by kids' prayers, but they are "kiddish," childish.

But sometime along the line, the child begins to take the practice of prayer — the folded hands, the closed eyes, the silence — and appropriate it for him or herself. At some moment in their lives, all believing kids pray on their own. When they do, they know prayer and fellowship in a way that they never had experienced before. For many kids, this begins to happen somewhere around the age of ten or twelve, when the world starts to look a bit bigger and more formidable than it did from their limited and egocentric childish perspectives. Prayer becomes more than custom or quaint behavior. It becomes real.

But from a parent's standpoint that's a risky time in the life of a child. The protective idealism of childhood — even the idealism of prayer and faith — gets tested by what children begin to see as a more and more hazardous world facing them. The difference between appearance and reality suddenly stands front and center. For some kids, the radical difference between the dark world and the joy of childish faith makes them abandon prayer as silly idealism, as an infantile escape from the real world. For others, more fearful, the idealism of faith is so attractive that they hide in piety and practice a sickly mysticism that can easily master the soul.

But in the ordinary pilgrimage to mature faith, spiritual stability emerges from that period of struggle. The mature Christian begins more and more to understand the relation between the life of the soul and life in the world. Heroic devotion to one's task in life goes hand in hand with a life of prayer that develops ever more richly. Our work and our prayer become almost one as prayer becomes more instantaneous and regular, less patterned by obligation or public necessity. We begin to understand the command to pray without ceasing. We begin to understand that we live in God's presence every minute of the day.

The Psalmist's resounding testimony, "O God, my God!" is the avowal of the believer who knows his Father's eternal love. And when we can say those words because we know that love, it is the soul's booming affirmation of being known intimately by the Creator.

—James Calvin Schaap, *Near Unto God*

Lord, we have left our childhoods behind. Still we are troubled by the complexity of living in you and in the world. We seek to pray without ceasing, to offer our work as a sacrifice, to become mature in faith. Continue to call us to yourself. Know us that we might know you. Amen.

October 22

RECALLED TO FREEDOM

"Let me be blunt: If one of us—even if an angel from heaven!—were to preach something other than what we preached originally, let him be cursed." —Galatians 1:8, THE MESSAGE

God is cosmic and sovereign. God has the first word and the last. "The kingdom of God is at hand." "Do not fear." History shows that people who believe and live in response to the good news are not naive innocents, but the most clear-sighted realists. We are recalled to freedom. We will not abandon the free life of the gospel. Let the people who tell us those lies about God be cursed! —Eugene H. Peterson, *Traveling Light*

Dear Lord, inspire in me the will to love you and your ways and to live my life by them. Help me to surround myself with sources of support for this life, through study, prayer, association with other believers, and bold action. In Jesus' name. Amen.

October 23

HUMILITY: POWER UNDER CONTROL

"He guides the humble in what is right
and teaches them his way."
 —Psalm 25:9

Humility is power under control. Nothing is more dangerous than power in the service of arrogance. Power under the discipline of humility is teachable. Apollos was a powerful preacher, but he was also willing to learn from others (Acts 18:24–26). In the course of his powerful ministry, Peter made some serious mistakes, but when confronted with his errors he had the humility to change (e.g., Acts 10:1–35; Gal. 2:11–21).

Believe me, this is no small matter. Many have been destroyed in their walk with God simply because their exercise of power was not controlled by humility. Power without humility is anything but a blessing.

James Nayler was one of the greatest of the early Quaker preachers. But he got carried away by his exercise of power, and in 1656 some of his wilder followers persuaded him to re-enact at Bristol Jesus' Palm

Sunday ride into Jerusalem. This act proved to be his undoing. He was tried and convicted of blasphemy. The story does have a happy ending, for in time Nayler repented of his presumption, but he had lost his effectiveness in the service of Christ. Power destroys when it is not coupled with the spirit of humility.

To really know the power of God is to be keenly aware that we have done nothing more than to receive a gift. Gratitude, not pride, is our only appropriate response. The power is not ours, though we are given the freedom to use it. But when we truly walk with God, our only desire is to use power in the service of Christ and his kingdom.

—Richard J. Foster, *The Challenge of the Disciplined Life*

Loving God, I choose this day to be a servant. I yield my right to command and demand. I give up my need to manage and control. I relinquish all schemes of manipulation and exploitation. For Jesus' sake, Amen.

—Richard J. Foster, "A Prayer of Self-Emptying," in *Prayers from the Heart*

October 24

In the Desert

"Jesus was led by the Spirit into the desert to be tempted by the devil."
—Matthew 4:1

The word of God "came upon" John the Baptist. The Greek word *epi* (upon), gives the sense of "pouncing upon, with pressure and intensity."

The word *rhema* is to *logos* as laser is to floodlight. This sharp splinter of light from God pierced John the Baptist (not Tiberius Caesar, or Pontius Pilate, or Herod, or Philip, or Annas, or Caiaphas — the powerful professionals). And it happened in the wilderness, the desert place (not in Rome or Jerusalem). No one likes the desert — sterile and lonely, a rocky barrenness — but it was there, in space and silence, that God was heard and obeyed.

I think of past desert years of mine, not of my choosing. Maybe if it had been all smooth and comfortable, if my pride and professionalism were defining life for me, God's steel-quiet, penetrating word would have been lost in the babble and sheen of success.

—Luci Shaw, *God in the Dark*

God, pierce me with your voice. You pierced Mary's heart with misgiving before her Son's death and grief afterwards. But her sorrow and struggle were redemptive — the result, like John the Baptist's, of humility and obedience.

If I am destined for the desert, programmed for pain, may my pilgrimage signify something, resolve the impasse between us, produce some lasting result. Amen.
—Luci Shaw, *God in the Dark*

October 25

ROOM FOR TRUE RELATIONSHIPS WITH GOD AND OTHERS

"A crowd was sitting around [Jesus], and they told him, 'Your mother and brothers are outside looking for you.'

"'Who are my mother and my brothers?' he asked. Then he looked at those seated in a circle around him and said, 'Here are my mother and my brothers! Whoever does God's will is my brother and sister and mother.'"
—Mark 3:32-35

My father had died several months before. And because my brother had been killed, I was the only remaining child, and I was newly married.

Mother didn't have to work. She was an intelligent, capable, strong and loving person. But when she came to visit my wife and me, she very subtly tried to run things — from the kitchen to my "weight and general health." She would say, upon entering our front door, "Oh, Keith, you look so *thin!* I'll have to fatten you up!" My wife was furious, but helpless. After all, my mother was a sweet woman and had lost her husband. The conflict was terrible for me — in the middle.

Finally, I realized how wrong all this was. I went to see my mother alone. As I pulled in the driveway at her house, I knew this was going to be an agonizing encounter and almost decided to put if off again. But I realized it had to be done. I opened the back door. "Hi, Mom! Anybody here?"

When we'd had dinner I told her my concern and how hard it was to talk about. Finally I said, "You've always been a wonderful mother, but I'm married now and you're not first in my life anymore." She just looked at me. I didn't know much about Christianity at that time, but I reminded her that the Bible said to "leave your father and mother and cling to your wife," and that I was going to do that.

She wept and I felt terrible. I thought she would never speak to me. I told her again that I loved her, but I didn't apologize or try to back down as I always had when she'd cried and been hurt. I just sat there. It was an awful time. Finally I left.

A week later she called to tell us happily that she had gotten a position as a hostess in a sorority house. And she got up from her bed of grief over my dad's death and became an effective and productive person the rest of her life, because she needed to make the break too. And I could then relate to her as an adult — at least most of the time.

Even Jesus broke with his mother publicly in what must have been a very painful experience for her. When Jesus was in a meeting, his mother and brothers arrived outside and sent word to him to come out to them. Pointing to his peers and fellow adventurers for God, he said in effect, "Tell my mother I'm not coming out. This is my family" (see Mark 3:31–35). He was making a definite break with his own mother and did not let her control his actions.

I am of course *not* saying that we should be cruel to our mothers and fathers. But I do believe that if we do not break the dependent parent-child relation with them, then sooner or later, our lovers, mates, friends, and God will miss a true relationship with us.

— J. Keith Miller, *The Single Experience*

Lord, may I discover the way to an appropriate relationship with my parents, so that I may be more available for a true relationship with you. Show me any places where I am still too attached to them.

And may I release my adult children into your care, to live their life stories and learn from their experiences, coming to rely on you rather than earthly caregivers, for their ultimate guidance. Help me to refrain from promoting dependency on me, and instead, by my own behaviors, to point the way to a relationship with you through which they may find their own independence as they learn to depend on you. In Jesus' name. Amen.

October 26

Tongue-Tied

"Moses agreed to stay with the man, who gave his daughter Zipporah to Moses in marriage. Zipporah gave birth to a son, and Moses named him Gershom, saying, 'I have become an alien in a foreign land.'"

— Exodus 2:21-22

David has come here to die, just as I have. The death he desires is the refining of his vocation, a certain purification of purpose. He needs pruning, he feels, of the irrelevant undergrowth that is leaching away the fruits of his life.

He remembers with longing his liturgical chores: being a spearhead for the ascending songs and prayers of a congregation, aimed toward God with the people like the shaft of a spear at his back. But turning to face them — their expectations, questions, assessments — he becomes distracted, embroiled, forgets what he was about.

He feels like Moses, fled to the wilderness of Midian. He has killed a man back in Egypt, a man he found scathing God's people. A man who was himself. He has buried that self in the sand, the self that strikes out of grief and rage. Now he lives here in the Wyoming wilderness, keeping a wary eye on every bush that might suddenly burst into flames of speech. As they were for Moses, God's people are both his bane and blessing.

And like Moses he stumbles, forgets words, is overwhelmed with a sense of stupidity and shame. Dyslocution sweeps over him at odd moments like waves of nausea. In midsentence his voice will suddenly falter and fail, like a candle guttering out.

He is all too familiar with the story of Moses. He knows he is not really safe here in Midian. Sooner or later, you have to go back to Egypt. It is only a matter of time until some bush speaks. And when it does, it will be to give him impossible instructions such as Moses received.

Can you really imagine going to strangers and, with a straight face, telling them I AM sent you? If they have any sense at all, they'll laugh you out of town.

Arnold Schoenberg, the twentieth-century Jewish composer, wrote an opera, *Moses und Aron,* which he was never able to complete to his satisfaction. It is about Moses, who is entrusted with the impossible task of verbalizing in human language to the people of Israel the name of God, the Word, the I AM. Being true to the content of that message necessarily ties up his tongue and tears apart any form that tries to contain it.

Therefore, Moses must rely on Aaron, the silver-tongued accommodator willing to build a golden calf to relieve the people's intolerable anguish over an invisible God, a people who wanted to "see" what that Word meant.

"O my Lord, I am not an eloquent man, neither heretofore, nor since thou hast spoken unto thy servant: but I am slow of speech, and of a slow tongue." Is there any tongue fleet enough to say what God is? I don't blame Moses for balking. Only a fool would willingly take up the task of speaking God's unspeakable name. Unless, like Aaron, he hasn't really understood the impossibility of the task. God and his people are always at odds. The one in the middle, like Moses, gets caught in the squeeze.

If you say yes, however reluctantly, to I AM, the effort will kill you, and more than once. To get from Midian back to Egypt was in fact another death for Moses. "At an inn on the way I AM met him and sought to kill him." And it will be no different, I'm afraid, for us. Here we are at our wayside inn in the wilderness. I feel like Zipporah now, Moses' Midianite wife. "Surely," she told him, "you are a bridegroom of blood to me."

—Virginia Stem Owens, *Wind River Winter*

Whenever I am in wilderness places, O Lord, keep me close to you. Help me with life's process of death and rebirth as I face the changes that life with you requires of me. Remind me that I am not the only one who has journeyed through the wilderness, and that you have brought the others through — every one of them! In Jesus' name. Amen.

October 27

GOD IN THE MARKETPLACE

"Love is patient; love is kind; love is not envious or boastful or arrogant or rude. It does not insist on its own way; it is not irritable or resentful; it does not rejoice in wrongdoing, but rejoices in the truth."
—1 Corinthians 13:4-6, NRSV

Once I spent a morning of prayer in lower Manhattan, taking time to reflect on the economic power of the United States. I prayed in St. Paul's, the church where George Washington once worshiped, in an effort to connect American faith and American enterprise. In a book I wrote on business and spiritual life, I suggested praying in the down and out sections of our cities, where God might speak to us more deeply about the healing of society. If we are truly following Christ we will also find him in the marketplace.

What about virtuous living then, that notion so unfashionable we hardly dare to mention it? Perhaps it is best pursued as an underground movement, kept close to the vest, closer still to the heart. Even so I can commend two ancient methods for seeking Virtue, methods lately being revived as part of good spiritual living. One of these is the practice of *examen,* and a second is the discipline of confession.

No doubt everyone understands what is meant by confession, a practice engaged in one way or another by all Christians, but according to different formal procedures. But perhaps a few words can be said about the usefulness of the practice of *examen. Examen* (it is a Latin word) is an ancient prayer-form by which we may specifically review a given portion of the day, or the week, in order to determine where we may have fallen from grace; or more broadly, how God was specifically with us. Plan to use the prayer of *examen* daily or weekly, before or after lunch, or in the evening. Begin by giving thanks to God for all the graces you have received. Try to name them: a telephone call from a friend, chrysanthemums on the reception-desk that caught your eye as you passed; a joke told in the elevator, at which everyone laughed; a funny e-mail from a colleague; something achieved in your work.

What does this have to do with an increase in Virtue? To do this often brings a sense of balance or consolation. Instead of reflecting on what we haven't received we recollect and gather in the blessings of the day. Only then do we set ourselves to noticing where we fell short of the grace of God. Surrounded by God's love, we turn constructively to self-criticism. Now we may be able to pinpoint a challenge or notice a bad tendency that needs correction. Did I lash out at a fellow employee? Did I "stir the pot" in the office lunchroom? Is gossip becoming a way of life for me, one that I justify as "just reporting the news"? Was I the first one on the phone when I found out the gory details of Margie's divorce? How will God lift these burdens from my soul until I am willing to admit them to myself and ask God to take them from me?

Perhaps the questions are grander in scale. Were my aspirations to leadership tinged with arrogance, spitefulness, self-preoccupation? Can I handle fair criticism without defensiveness? Was I cowed by someone's strong disagreement? Or was I willing to stand up for what I believe in?

Whether or not we call it the prayer of *examen,* there is a real value in reflecting on the day's activities and seeing how God was present to us in any given time. Now our prayers can touch on very specific needs. "Lord, let me temper my criticism with fair-mindedness. Allow me to see the merit in Jack's recommendations before I start to trash them. Make me a better colleague. Give me an easygoing collaborative style." All these, in one way or another, may be prayers for an increase of prudence, temperance, justice, and fortitude.

Take heart, fellow professionals. Holiness, then, despite its antique vocabulary, is not out of the question.

—Emilie Griffin, "Confessions of a Virtue-Loving Professional," *Radix Magazine* (Spring 2002).

Dear Jesus, I want you to be my mentor and role model in the difficulties of the marketplace. I see you as a man of the marketplace, one who spent time with sinners and less than perfect people. I want some of your tolerance, your inspiration, your perseverance. Teach me to work well in the abrasive situations of the real world. Help me to live out the will of God in the midst of everything. Amen.

October 28

SOLACE FOR THE WORRIED AND ANXIOUS

"I will both lay me down in peace, and sleep: for thou, Lord, only makest me dwell in safety." —Psalm 4:8, KJV

I've been reading Eugene H. Peterson's new book on the Psalms, *Answering God.* Last evening his words directed me to Psalm 4, an evening prayer. I read first Peterson's words, "What is wrong with the world is God's business. It is a business in which you will have a part, come morning when you get your assignment. Meanwhile, God is giving help at a far deeper level than any of your meddling will ever reach."

Then I read from the psalm, "I will both lay me down in peace, and sleep: for thou, Lord, only makest me dwell in safety." I went to bed, I prayed, on my back staring into the darkness, and I slept for the first time in many nights without dreaming of an agonizing decision I had made.

This morning, as I sit here in the quiet of Remnant Acres, I am conscious that I live not only in this world, but in Christ. He is my dwelling place. And I think on what that means. It does not mean that my anxiousness doesn't matter. Christ is in his creation, and I dwell in him here, in this world. Here I act out the terms of my salvation. I work it out with fear and trembling. But it is Christ working in me that sanctifies my actions. It is indeed Christ acting when I set my obtrusive, self-conscious self aside. And that changes everything.

I have nothing to do but to choose to be faithful, to offer myself, prepared for whatever Christ desires. To place my body on the arrest line. To write these words. To withdraw. To be silent. To discern the moment when it comes. To refuse to worry until then.

—John Leax, *Standing Ground*

Lord, as I go to bed tonight, help me find your peace, and a restful sleep. I offer you my specific worries today, the people or situations that occupy my mind and heart. Keep them in your care as I withdraw, be silent, and try to discern my assignment — the part that is mine to play — and to leave the rest alone. Amen.

October 29

SO FAR, SO GOOD

"Keep me safe, O God, for in you I take refuge."
—Psalm 16:1

I'm peering through my son's telescope
to see whether the universe has shrunk
overnight, as the *Times* claims. I don't doubt it.
If Jack plunks down his milk glass
these days, it entirely blots out Europe.
Yesterday I had to make him uncross
his arms and stop leaning on the world.

Have a little heart, I said,
wiping spaghetti off the teal face of Hungary
on his place mat. Now as he digs into
his mashed potatoes, I pray for him,
for all kids who'll soon be cut loose
into contracting space, where I could
fax you this in minutes, where the Concorde
swims through our miniature sky like a minnow.
What keeps us, against all odds,
in a universe we know nothing about?
Jack's made it to the age of ten. So far,
so good. But the facts! My neighbor tells me
potatoes, if they're dug too green,
are poison. And how green is too green?
We could keel over from green potatoes
any day, from mother love, from a truckload
of bananas that neglects to swerve. Every morning
I wake up like a hypochondriac who's cured,
to the shock that we're still safe.
Peer through the telescope. Can you see
the hocus-pocus stars out there?
And scanning across the sky, what's that?
A blue eye blinking — God, it might be —
way out at the edge, so far,
so good.
— Jeanne Murray Walker, in *Gaining Time*

Lord, it's so good, so comforting and strengthening, to think of your calm presence watching over our world. You are my refuge. I give you my anxieties and worries for today and breathe a deep sigh of relief. Amen.

October 30

SHARED SUFFERING

"Finally, be ye all of one mind, having compassion one of another."
—1 Peter 3:8, KJV

Reality is something we participate in making, as co-creators with God. Making reality is part of our vocation and one of the chief concerns of prayer. And it is an affirmation of interdependence.

When I turn to the piano and a Bach fugue, I compose it along with Bach as I hear it and attempt to play it. A writer, alone and with great struggle, writes a book. That book becomes real only as someone reads it and creates it along with the author. Each one of us, reading Genesis, will begin to create a new reality. The important thing is that our realities intersect and overlap.

One way of overlapping is to identify with someone else, for instance, in intercessory prayer. To have compassion (com = with; passion = suffering) means to share with another whatever it is that circumstances are bringing to bear on that other. It does not mean to coerce or to manipulate or to dictate. ("Of *course* you must sell your house first thing. After that there is nothing for you to do but leave him. What you *really* need is a new wardrobe.") When we coerce or manipulate or dictate we don't have to be involved with the one we are hoping to help. Compassion means to be with, to share, to overlap, no matter how difficult or painful it may be.

And compassion is indeed painful, for it means to share in the suffering of those we pray for; to love is to be vulnerable, and to be vulnerable is to be hurt, inevitably, yet without vulnerability we are not alive, and God showed us this when he came to live with us, in utter vulnerability, as Jesus of Nazareth.   —Madeleine L'Engle, *And It Was Good*

Emmanuel, God With Us: melt away our self-protective walls that we may be with others as you are with us. Amen.

October 31

IT DIDN'T HAPPEN

"But Jonah was greatly displeased and became angry. He prayed to the Lord.... 'Now, O Lord, take away my life, for it is better for me to die than to live.'"   —Jonah 4:1–3

How unreasonable is Jonah's anger with God? He has endured more than a little inconvenience and put himself at some risk to announce a judgment on Nineveh, a judgment complete with a timetable: "Forty days and Nineveh shall be overthrown." And it hasn't happened.

The people of Nineveh have repented. God has repented. And life is good for everyone except Jonah. He has promised a doomsday that did not come. Being anything but stupid, he is sensitive to the irony. He is sure that in a very short time the people of Nineveh will forget their repentance and remember only their escape. He fears he will live in their stories as a comic figure — a prophet who got it wrong.

These thoughts about Jonah come to me because I happened upon a chorus of the frogs in a ditch near the Washington Beltway. Enviroprophets tell me they shouldn't be there, that acid rain threatens their survival, but there they were, happily croaking. Remembering them forces me to think about all the dire predictions I've read about the "fragile earth."

Gregg Easterbrook, writing in *Newsweek* about an anniversary edition of Rachel Carson's *Silent Spring,* observes, "Few books have fallen so wide of the mark — because none of the environmental calamities predicted...has happened." But Easterbrook is not denigrating Carson. He is, in fact praising her. He concludes his essay, "That the predictions in Rachel Carson's masterpiece did not come true should be seen as the greatest aspect of her legacy."

Jonah and Rachel Carson. Prophets who predicted dooms that did not come. Did the people of Nineveh eventually forget their repentance and laugh? We'll never know. When we look back at the predictions of the prophets who have come to us, will we forget and laugh? Before we yield to that temptation, before we sneer, "It didn't happen," let us remember, apart from their voices crying in the wilderness of shopping malls and eight-lane interstates we might not have made it.

—John Leax

Holy Spirit, Comforter, discomfort us. Remind us our good fortune comes not by our effort, but by our yielding to the Word spoken in the desert. Amen.

NOVEMBER

November 1

MY CHOICE

"Who are you to judge someone else's servant? To his own master he stands or falls. And he will stand, for the Lord is able to make him stand." —Romans 14:4

One of the unexpected miracles in my life took place when my wife quit monitoring what I was eating and reminding me of my dietary decisions. Some strange and unexpected things began to happen. At first I was a little hurt and angry, even though I had resented her reminders. The thought crossed my mind that maybe she didn't love me any more and didn't care if I let my cholesterol get too high and died of a heart attack. But then I realized that she wasn't going to remind me any more because she'd learned that it was my job to take care of myself. I realized that my cholesterol *might* get too high and I *might* die of a heart attack. I got on a food plan and exercise program, which I have no trouble keeping and actually enjoy! Before, I hated the diet because I felt controlled. This may not be true for anyone else, but it has been for me. If she hadn't quit judging that I was too forgetful to take care of myself and decided to let me live or die as an adult, I might never have grown up and taken responsibility for my physical health. This may sound strange and very abhorrent to some of you, but only when we quit trying to control each other do we give (and get) the chance to grow up and be responsible for our lives.

People have said to me, "But what if you *hadn't* changed and decided to take care of yourself?" Well, that would have been my decision. Even though I might be dead by now, it would have been my choice. Recently my wife told me that she had to accept that possibility when she made her decision. Making a healthy break from controlling others can involve serious risks, but spirituality and authentic intimacy demand that neither party control the other and take away his or her choice.

—J. Keith Miller, *Compelled to Control*

Dear Lord, help me to remember that it is the responsibility of each person to make his or her own choices. Instead of giving warnings, criticizing, or ridiculing the choices of others, I need only to share my own experience, strength, and hope; to love them; and to trust that person (and his or her relationship to God) to you, and then wait to see what happens as a result of their choices. At the same time, increase my sensitivity to your will for me, so that I may be more attentive to making the right choices about my own life. In Jesus' name. Amen.

November 2

REMEMBERING

"If only for this life we have hope in Christ, we are to be pitied more than all men." —1 Corinthians 15:19

There have been many days for publicly remembering the dead in the divisions of the Roman Church over the centuries. A delightful body of ritual has grown up around All Souls' Day, more festive than sorrowful — long processions to cemeteries, bells tolling, the blessing and decoration of graves, hundred of candles left flickering through the night. And in parts of Austria, the story goes, children are instructed to pray out loud as they take shortcuts through the church grounds on All Souls' Day — not to protect themselves so much as to assure the suffering ones who hover there that they are not forgotten.

Prayer for the dead is not a traditional Protestant practice. I grew up in a family not only Protestant but stoic. Things that mattered in life were inherently private. You took things on the chin, kept your mouth shut, and went on with life. I don't defend that strategy (and it was a strategy); I simply recognize it as how we were. We'd have felt silly lighting candles for our dead. A candle was only a candle (we thought), while the person it represented — ah so alive, so bone of our bone, registering in our voices, seeing through our eyes. A candle would seem like a mockery.

But I don't kid myself. All the solemn processions I have not followed in the street, the wreaths I have not laid, the bugles I have not blown, have found their way onto the page, my dead commemorating themselves, you might say (though they'd be embarrassed at the thought), in re-created life. Lighting a candle is one way, and poetry is another. It's for each of us to do what we find natural and true, children (as we are) praying out loud as we walk through the cemetery.

—Shirley Nelson, "All Souls," in *Stories for the Christian Year*

Lord, as we race through the cemetery, we shout the names of your saints who have gone before us. Their lives are alive in ours. And we shout your name. Be alive in us also. Let the oneness of your body in eternity be present now in the dailiness of time. Amen.

November 3

SIMPLICITY

"People are slaves to whatever mastered them."
—2 Peter 2:19b, NRSV

Contemporary culture is plagued by the passion to possess. The unreasoned boast abounds that the good life is found in accumulation, that "more is better." Indeed, we often accept this notion without question, with the result that the lust for affluence in contemporary society has become psychotic: it has completely lost touch with reality. Furthermore, the pace of the modern world accentuates our sense of being fractured and fragmented. We feel strained, hurried, breathless. The complexity of rushing to achieve and accumulate more and more frequently threatens to overwhelm us; it seems there is no escape from the rat race.

Christian simplicity frees us from this modern mania. It brings sanity to our compulsive extravagance and peace to our frantic spirit. It liberates us from what William Penn called "cumber." It allows us to see material things for what they are — goods to enhance life, not to oppress life. People once again become more important than possessions. Simplicity enables us to live lives of integrity in the face of the terrible realities of our global village.

Christian simplicity is not just a faddish attempt to respond to the ecological holocaust that threatens to engulf us, nor is it born out of a frustration with technocratic obesity. It is a call given to every Christian. The witness to simplicity is profoundly rooted in the biblical tradition, and most perfectly exemplified in the life of Jesus Christ. In one form or another, all the devotional masters have stressed its essential nature. It is a natural and necessary outflow of the Good News of the Gospel having taken root in our lives. —Richard J. Foster, *Freedom of Simplicity*

Suffer us, O father, to come to Thee.
Lay Thy hands on us and bless us.
Take away from us forever our own spirit and replace it by the
    instinct of Thy divine grace.

Take away from us our own will and leave us only the desire of doing Thy will.
Give us that beautiful, that lovable, that sublime simplicity which is the first and greatest of Thy gifts.
Amen.

—J. N. Grou, "Give Us That Sublime Simplicity"
in *The Ways of the Spirit*

November 4

TAKING THE HEAT

"The Lord is thy keeper:
the Lord is thy shade upon thy right hand."
—Psalm 121:5, KJV

In some coastal regions especially, it's hard to imagine that anyone might want shelter from the sun. Some of us see it so infrequently, we celebrate its appearance. But in the desert the sun is an oppressor. People wear white to avoid it, build thick walls to insulate themselves from its heavy hand. Where the temperature hovers at the unbearable for weeks and months, every living thing seeks the shade.

Against what? Against the sun. None of us — not even the boldest, the most powerful, the smartest — can take the constant heat, figuratively or literally. Stress — and distress — comes into our lives, as all of us know, in many forms. What is assumed here is a force that is constant in its advance, wilting in its pressure. Like desert heat, it parches our throat, makes us speechless. In the methodical assault of that kind of debilitating force, God is our shade. This is not a macho image — no flexed biceps. Shade is our relief. When the only posture is prostration, God offers us shelter.

The medium is a cloud, which removes us from the heat. A father can, by his own size, become a shadow for his child on a walk through the desert sun. This is the picture the Psalmist beings to mind in "thy shade upon thy right hand," a father, taking the heat.

Here is our comfort: God does not, and mercifully will not, leave us alone. And the fact is, everyone walks in a desert. Nobody was ever promised a rose garden. But the Lord follows us through the heat, hovers over us, cloud-like, bringing us shelter — enabling us to go on and even pick up the pace.

We know this kind of biblical poetry well. But it's no fiction. That God is our shade is the honest-to-God truth. When the assault of the sun threatens to wilt us to parched tomato vines, his shadow comes over us and stands at our right hand, stands near unto us, taking the heat.

—James Calvin Schaap, *Near Unto God*

Father, walk near us. Shade us from the punishing heat of our daily temptations with your presence. Preserve us for yourself. Amen.

November 5

AM I REALLY READY?

"And the foundations of the threshold shook at the voice of him who called, and the house was filled with smoke. And I said, "Woe is me! For I am lost; for I am a man of unclean lips, and I dwell in the midst of a people of unclean lips for my eyes have seen the king, the Lord of Hosts!... And I heard the voice of the Lord saying, 'Whom shall I send, and who will go for us?' Then I said, 'Here I am! Send me.' And he said, 'Go, and say to the people....'" —Isaiah 6:4-5, 8-10, RSV

The darkness was pitch black. I was up on my elbows in bed, alone because my wife, Andrea, was out of town. The wind was still howling from a storm which had come in from the Gulf of Mexico the evening before.

Suddenly I heard a voice, a voice deeper than Tennessee Ernie Ford's. It resounded from the upper right-hand corner of the room in the darkness, and it spoke my name: "Keith."

I couldn't say anything. I was paralyzed with fear. I had no idea to whom the voice belonged. And then it spoke again: "KEITH, I'm talking to you; can you hear Me?"

All of a sudden I realized Who it was that was paying me a visit. Now I was really afraid. There was no way this could be happening. My heart was pounding so loudly I could hardly hear the words. I answered in a voice that was husky with sleep... and fear. "Yes, Sir, ah..."

My eyes were straining in the dark toward the part of the room from which the voice was coming. I could see only a kind of blur, like a gray shadow moving and shifting, lighter than the rest of the blackness. Or was it my imagination?

Before I had time to think, I could hear it speaking again, "Keith, are you ready to follow Me?"

"Yes, Sir, I... am." I managed to say without moving in the bed.

"I mean *right now!*" the Presence demanded.

Terror. Then I heard a very small childlike voice come out of me. "Where are we going?"

There was a pause. Then, "Keith, my heart is about to break. I've been frustrated for years about what's going on in My church, and lately I've been getting very angry! I want to take you with Me and show you what's happening."

"Why?" I asked, still frightened.

"Because I want you to tell My people what you will see," He answered.

I shrank back. "Oh no, you've got the wrong person. I've had lots of problems — still do — and the church is not looking for a direct message from You through me."

"But I've *chosen* you to tell them," He said, sounding a little impatient.

"Why me?" I persisted. (I didn't want any part of this assignment.)

"Well," the Presence answered slowly, "because the other people I thought of are all engaged in important ministries for Me. And since you're not exactly exhausting yourself loving other people, you're the one."

I lay there for about thirty seconds, thinking about what He'd said. Then suddenly the house was filled with the loudest voice I'd ever heard — almost a roar.

"GET UP!" His voice shook the room.

—Keith Miller, *The Dream*

Lord, I keep praying, "I commit my life to thee, use me and build with me as thou wilt." But how would I feel if you came tonight and said, "Okay, I am here. Let's go!" What would I say? Help me either to mean what I am praying every day or to look for and be ready to respond to your call. Amen.

November 6

LIGHT IN THE DARK

"And we, who with unveiled faces all reflect the Lord's glory, are being transformed into his likeness with ever-increasing glory, which comes from the Lord, who is the spirit." —2 Corinthians 3:18

The strong imagery of darkness and light pervades the biblical text. Again and again we see the dark night representing ignorance, evil, calamity, death, and damnation, characteristics of a kingdom over which Satan rules. In contrast, light stand for spiritual illumination, clarity, purity, life, all of which thrive in God's domain.

Jesus gave his friends the picture of a city on a hill that "cannot be hidden." Why not? Because a city is full of dwellings where people try to prolong the day with lanterns, oil lamps, candles, or (today) with electric light. Such light is almost impossible to contain. It glints through cracks and crevices, from behind closed doors. And the darker the night, the more brilliantly the light shows.

But no lantern, no modern searchlight or beacon, can hold a candle to the sun! Christians today are more like small signal mirrors that flash messages from the desert by reflecting the solar beams. Perhaps Jesus, had he lived today, would have used such an image.

—Luci Shaw, *Horizons*

Lord Jesus, be in me the light of the world. Shine from me so that all who see me might see, not my face, but your presence dwelling in me. Amen.

November 7

COOPERATION WITH CREATION

"Therefore, my dear brothers, stand firm. Let nothing move you. Always give yourselves fully to the work of the Lord, because you know that your labor in the Lord is not in vain."

—1 Corinthians 15:58

"That which is too serious for tragedy is the subject of comedy," my theater professor told me in college. His statement explains the unrelenting birthday jokes typified by the T-shirt or coffee mug inscribed, "Forty isn't old if you're a tree." The joke, however light it intends to be, opens upon reflection. What in us causes us to measure our human three score and ten against the mayfly's brief moment, the turtle's hundred years or more, and the bristlecone pine's millenniums? One possibility is resentment, an unresolved anger. That leads to despair. And despair results in war — hatred of our limitations, the destruction of creation, and separation from God.

Another, brighter possibility, is that it is nothing less than the need to feel ourselves a part of something larger than ourselves, an innate suspicion of our age's dominant anthropocentricism. This longing to be related to the other leads to joy. Joy results in good work — acceptance of our mortality, cooperation with creation, and trust in God.

—John Leax

We long, O Lord, to escape the loneliness of our isolation. We want to see you in your creation and join with the trees that clap their hands to give you praise. Free us to know joy in the work our hands were made to do. Amen.

November 8

ABSOLUTION IN THE ABSOLUTE

"And the Lord God commanded the man, saying, Of every tree of the garden thou mayest freely eat: But of the tree of the knowledge of good and evil, thou shalt not eat of it: for in the day that thou eatest thereof thou shalt surely die." —Genesis 2:16–17, KJV

It is a criterion of love. In moments of decision we are to try to make what seems to be the most loving, the most creative decision. We are not to play safe, to draw back out of fear. Love may well lead us into danger. It may lead us to die for our friend. In a day when we are taught to look for easy solutions, it is not always easy to hold on to that most difficult one of all, love.

During a summer session at Wheaton, one of the students asked, "Do you think there are any absolutes?"

I thought for a second and then said, off the top of my head, "Yes, I think the ten commandments are absolutes." Later, as I set them against the great works of literature, they seemed to hold fast. When we break one of the commandments, we are doing something we would not want the children to see. We are being destructive, rather than creative. We are taking things into our own hands and playing God. Playing God, hubris, presumption, the tragic flaw of all the great Greek heroes. But having broken the first commandment, it is almost inevitable that the breaking of others will follow. Oedipus dishonors both his parents. Anna Karenina commits adultery. Macbeth is covetous. Dorian Gray makes a graven image of himself. Iago bears false witness against his neighbor. And so it goes. Whenever the first commandment is broken, more breakage follows. We are, as a consequence, unable to love ourselves, and so we are not able to love our neighbor.

—Madeleine L'Engle, *Walking on Water*

O God, when we are tempted to prove ourselves, we pray that by remembering that absolution is in the absolute, we will choose our True Life Source and act in Love. Amen.

November 9

WIND AND FIRE

"In speaking of the angels he says, 'He makes his angels winds, his servants flames of fire.'" —Hebrews 1:7

Raphael

Raphael's wings are gold, an airy gold that thins
to transparency like sun falling on a wall
and yet are deep and wide as sun taking
a field full in the morning or
leaving wheat in the eve-
ning. When he flies
away, they are a
streak of salmon or
carmine along the curve of
the sea, and where his feet touch
last, whitecaps rise to rollers and throw
themselves in ecstatic, bright hosannas
over and over against the eroding shore.
—Robert Siegel, *Cresset*

As you have made the angels wings beautiful to bear your messengers to us, fill us with the fire of your Holy Spirit that we might live as sacrifices, holy and acceptable to you. Amen.

November 10

SEEING TO BELIEVE

"Though you have not seen him, you love him; and even though you do not see him now, you believe in him and are filled with an inexpressible and glorious joy, for you are receiving the goal of your faith, the salvation of your souls." —1 Peter 1:8-9

It took thirty-eight thousand Levites to give thanks to God in David's day; every morning and every evening the shifts changed. Four thousand were needed just to carry the hacked carcasses of cattle, and another four thousand were needed to sing about it. The place reeked of blood, was soaked in blood. The priests stood around gnawing and chewing and giving thanks. They did not cross-stitch their gratitude on samplers to frame and hang on the wall. They wrote their thanks in blood on the doorposts every year.

Thanksgiving is not a task to be undertaken lightly. It is not for dilettantes or aesthetes. One does not dabble in praise for one's own amusement, nor train the intellect and develop perceptual skills in order to add to his repertoire. We're not talking about the world as a free course in art appreciation. No. Thanksgiving is not a *result* of perception; thanksgiving is the *access* to perception. Or, as Laurel Lee wrote, some things have to be believed to be seen. Only the open heart, the open eye, the open throat can take in the world.

—Virginia Stem Owens, *God Spy*

Lord, I thank you for my very being and the miracle of consciousness and perception. Open my heart, eye, and throat that I may take in more and more of your world, and help me to perceive my place in it — how you would have me to live and be. In Jesus' name. Amen.

November 11

SUBVERSIVE

"The disciples came up and asked, 'Why do you tell stories?' He replied, 'You've been given insight into God's kingdom. You know how it works. Not everybody has this gift, this insight; it hasn't been given to them. Whenever someone has a ready heart for this, the insights and understandings flow freely. But if there is no readiness, any trace of receptivity soon disappears. That's why I tell stories: to create readiness, to nudge the people toward receptive insight.'"

—Matthew 13:10-13, THE MESSAGE

Jesus was a master at subversion. Until the very end, everyone, including his disciples, called him Rabbi. Rabbis were important, but they didn't make anything happen. On the occasions when suspicions were aroused that there might be more to him than that title accounted for, Jesus tried to keep it quiet — "tell no one."

Jesus' favorite speech form, the parable, was subversive. Parables sound absolutely ordinary: casual stories about soil and seeds, meals and coins and sheep, bandits and victims, farmers and merchants. And they are wholly secular: of his forty or so parables recorded in the Gospels, only one has its setting in church, and only a couple mention the name God. As people heard Jesus tell these stories, they saw at once that they weren't about God, so there was nothing in them threatening their own sovereignty. They relaxed their defenses. They walked away perplexed, wondering what they meant, the stories lodged in their imagination. And then, like a time bomb, they would explode in their unprotected hearts. An abyss opened up at their very feet. He was talking about God; they had been invaded!

Jesus continually threw odd stories down alongside ordinary lives (*para*, "alongside"; *bole*, "thrown") and walked away without explanation or altar call. Then listeners started seeing connections: God connections, life connections, eternity connections. The very lack of obviousness, the unlikeness, was the stimulus to perceiving likeness: God likeness, life likeness, eternity likeness. But the parable didn't do the work — it put the listener's imagination to work. Parables aren't illustrations that make things easier; they make things harder by requiring the exercise of our imagination, which if we aren't careful becomes the exercise of our faith. —Eugene H. Peterson, *The Contemplative Pastor*

Exercise my imagination, O Lord, that I may know you better. Strengthen my faith as I seek to strengthen my connections to you in eternity. Show me these connections in the odd stories thrown down in the path of my life — the stories of my experiences, not obvious, unlikely, yet full of your truth and love. In Jesus' name. Amen.

November 12

WHO IS A MERE CHRISTIAN?

> "Only take heed, and keep your soul diligently, lest you forget the things which your eyes have seen, and lest they depart from your heart all the days of your life...." —Deuteronomy 4:9a, RSV

Is there such a thing as Mere Christianity? If Mere Christianity isn't a denomination, then can there be such a thing as a Mere Christian? I've yet to meet one. I presume there are many, but there's no way to count them or indeed no reason to hold them to account. There's no sacrament to mark them as MCs (if I may so abbreviate), no membership card, no sacred certificate declaring baptism or marriage, no profane piece of paper stating birth or death. Hence, the MC, if he or she exists, is an invisible, mysterious, perhaps even mystical, being.

I suppose a case could be made that one who buys a copy of *Mere Christianity* is an MC, in potency if not already in act, but even here there's a fallacy. One is not what one reads. One may approach the cash register or cash point with a book plainly entitled *Homosexuality*, and not be a homosexual, no matter what the snoops in the line may think; and the same holds true for the homosexual. After all, Democrats buy books by Republicans, and Tories buy books by Laborites. The obese buy diet books, and the obtuse buy how-to books. Hence, it's not much of a hop, skip, and jump to Christians who buy copies of Bertrand Russell's *Why I Am Not a Christian* or A. N. Wilson's *Against Religion: Why We Should Try to Live Without It.* All readers buy books in order to know, not necessarily to follow. Which is another way of saying that buying a copy of *Mere Christianity* however ostentatiously, and reading it however surreptitiously, and stashing it under one's pillow however superstitiously, doesn't make one an MC.

But if one takes the contents of *Mere Christianity* to heart and tries to put into practice some of its prescriptions, then one may be well on his or her way to becoming a bona fide MC. But who would know? Not many, if any. How, then, would one MC know another? There's no secret handshake, no variation in the Sign of the Cross. But Jesus Christ would know and, if that's the case, no one else need ever know.

—William Griffin, *C. S. Lewis: Spirituality for Mere Christians*

O God, help me to practice your prescriptions, that my life may be a reflection of your love. Amen.

November 13

RENUNCIATION

"Keep your lives free from the love of money and be content with what you have, because God has said, 'Never will I leave you; never will I forsake you.'" —Hebrews 13:5

For the Desert Fathers, the flight to the desert was a way of escaping conformity to the world. The world, including the church, had become so dominated by secular materialism that, for them, the only way to witness against it was to withdraw from it. Thomas Merton writes in the introduction to his *Wisdom of the Desert,* "Society... was regarded by the Desert Fathers as a shipwreck from which each single individual man had to swim for his life."

They were seeking to revive true Christian devotion and simplicity of life by intense renunciation. Their experience has particular relevance, because modern society is uncomfortably like the world that they attacked so vigorously. Their world asked, "How can I get more?" The Desert Fathers asked, "What can I do without?" Their world asked, "How can I find myself?" The Desert Fathers asked, "How can I lose myself?"

Their world asked, "How can I win friends and influence people?" The Desert Fathers asked, "How can I love God?"

The Desert Fathers renounced things in order to know what it meant to have the single eye of simplicity toward God. They were the *Athletae Dei,* the athletes of God, who sought to strip away all hindrances. There is no question that there were excesses in the monasticism of the Desert Fathers, but no more so than the excesses evidenced in the church of today in the opposite direction.

The renunciation of the Desert Fathers had great transforming power. They renounced possessions in order to learn detachment. These men and women of the desert gained a great freedom when they surrendered the need to possess. Among the sayings of the Fathers is the story of an important dignitary who gave a basket of gold pieces to a priest in the desert, asking him to disperse it among the brethren. "They have no need of it," replied the priest. The wealthy benefactor insisted and set the basket of coins at the doorway of the church, asking the priest to tell the brethren, "Whoso hath need, let him take it."

No one touched it, or even cared enough to look at it. Edified, and no doubt astonished, the man left with his basket of gold.

Detachment frees us from the control of others. No longer can we be manipulated by people who hold our livelihoods in their hands. Things do not entice our imaginations, people do not dominate our destinies.

—Richard J. Foster, *Freedom of Simplicity*

God, of your goodness give me yourself, for you are enough for me. And only in you do I have everything. Amen.
—Lady Julian of Norwich, "Give Me Yourself," in *Showings*

November 14

PAIN AND HOPE

"We also rejoice in our sufferings, because we know that suffering produces perseverance; perseverance, character; and character, hope. And hope does not disappoint us, because God has poured out his love into our hearts by the Holy Spirit, whom he has given us."
—Romans 5:3–5

When I wake up in the mornings after a really hard day's exercise and feel the aches and pains in my muscles, I try to remember these words. To me, my sore muscles indicate several things.

First of all, the soreness means I have been lazy for too long. Just doing a normal workout was too much for me, and I'm now suffering for it.

But then I realize that I'm suffering because I'm going to stop being lazy. In three or four days, depending on how bad the sore muscles are, I'll feel fine again. And after I'm over the pain, I'll be stronger and have more endurance.

When I think of endurance, I think of being able to walk up a flight of stairs more easily, carry two bags of groceries at a time without almost dropping them, sit and write longer without getting a backache. I'll also be able to do more of the exercises instead of dropping out so often to rest. So I begin to feel that the sore muscles are "worth it," especially since I know they're only temporary.

Being aware of the good things exercise is doing for my health inspires me to keep on exercising, in spite of the pain. That's a form of building character. I learn, too, that I can endure pain and still perform, which gives me courage in other painful areas of my life.

The *hope* of becoming fit begins to enter my mind, and every time I move a sore muscle I am reminded that I'm getting closer to my goal. The soreness is a source of both pain and hope at the same time!

So I come full circle, lying there in the bed dreading the pain that will come when I try to sit up and swing my legs over to the side. I suffer, I rejoice, I endure, I grow, and I have hope.... Most of the time.

—Andrea Wells Miller, *BodyCare*

Dear Lord, sometimes it hurts to grow. I don't like to hurt, and so avoiding pain becomes an excuse that keeps me from doing what I know I must do to grow as you would have me to. Your caring Spirit helps me face the pain. Forgive me when I duck out of my responsibilities because of pain — or my fear of it. Help me to trust in you when the going gets rough. In Jesus' name. Amen.

November 15

A Gift from Uncle Windy

"Then those 'sheep' are going to say, 'Master, what are you talking about? When did we ever see you hungry and feed you, thirsty and give you a drink?'...Then the king will say, 'I'm telling you the solemn truth. Whenever you did one of these things to someone overlooked or ignored, that was me — you did it to me.'"

—Matthew 25:37-40, THE MESSAGE

One morning not too long ago I was washing my face in the bathroom and I saw my hands — saw them as I never had. I realized with a shock that they were the hands of an old man — my father's hands. Quickly I made fists out of them and pulled them out of sight into my chest. I looked at my face, and saw that the same frightening thing had happened: at age sixty-eight I was no longer "ruby-lipped and twenty-two." Where had the years gone?

I sat down in my big chair to have a quiet time with God. Sadness came. And then out of nowhere I remembered that my last Miller relative, my uncle Windy, had died over five years ago. In my mind's eye I saw Windy alive and us picking Windy up at the retirement home and taking him to a movie, or shopping, or out to our house for dinner — or to the Mexican food place — he loved Mexican food. Every week as we began our outing, he made the same remarks and asked the same questions about us and how we were doing, before we settled into a quiet companionship and spent time together. If my wife, Andrea, was with me, he was always gracious to her and asked what she'd "been up to."

As I replayed the scenes of our weekly visits with Windy, I began to remember how he chose to act as his growing old forced him to give up all that brought him pleasure and security: First his wife — through "the Big C," as Windy called cancer, then his little two-person airplane, then his home, then the small trailer in the retirement park, and at last his choice of where to live, as the time came when he couldn't remember things — like turning off the burners on the stove, or where he parked his car in front of Sears. He had always been the most independent person I had ever known. And because I knew how independent he was, I felt a lot of sadness about the fact that he had to be moved to our city so that I, his nephew, could take care of him.

I was the only close family he had. Now he carried all his security and potential for happiness with him. And he did not give up these remaining freedoms easily.

Most of the old people around him spent a great deal of time complaining about the nurses, the food, the temperature, and their uncaring families. But Windy was different from the rest. Although he was alert, he only complained once, and that was when they moved a roommate in with him. The man was bedridden and seemed to be spoiled about getting his own way. He insisted on playing the television late at night after Windy had gone to bed. After several nights of not sleeping well, Windy confronted his roommate — and almost got thrown out of the retirement home.

I asked Windy what in the world had happened. He pursed his lips and said thoughtfully, "After I'd asked him politely three nights in a row to turn the TV down and he wouldn't, I walked over to his bed last night and got down close enough to be certain he couldn't miss what I was saying, and I said, 'If you don't turn that thing down, I'm going to rip it off that pedestal and stick it up your nose! And if you don't believe I'm absolutely serious, just try me!' "

The man requested another room, and in order to stay, Windy had to promise not to threaten people. After that he had no power at all. But — and this is the point I want to make that has given me a peace about how I can grow old more gracefully: With no immediate family, no home, no living friends, no independence of movement or choice, and no hope of ever getting out again, Windy had every reason to be angry and bitter, but he wasn't.

In fact, I saw a miracle in that old man. Every time I came to visit or take him out, he would light up with a smile and say, "I'm glad you're here." He never fussed because I was late, or badgered me because I didn't come more often — as many of the other residents did their families. And when I asked how he liked the food — which was pretty gray — he would say with a smile, "It's okay, certainly better than the alternatives," and then he'd laugh that charming open Texas laugh of his.

As we would drive away from the place each week to go on our outing, Windy never complained about anything that had happened since our last visit. And when we'd get back after our time together, he always said, "I appreciate your coming more than I can say." Even when I had to skip a week because of being out of town.

The evening before he died at eighty-nine (although no one knew he was dying) I sat on the side of his bed as he lay sick. And though he was still managing a spoon awkwardly, I asked him if he wanted me to feed him. And this man who had never let anyone help him nodded, like a little boy, and whispered "yes," an amazing act of humility for him.

After his death, we went to get his things the next day. The room was soon filled with old men and women milling in a shuffle dance around us and the staff members, all wanting to tell us stories about what a friendly, good-natured person Windy had been to them. And as they spoke, I saw that his constant attitude of gratefulness about what he did have, and his never complaining about what he'd lost, made other people not want to be so negative.

So this morning I thanked God for Windy. Sometimes I'd thought I was doing a big favor by being with him, but I saw now with great clarity that by his continual gratitude, and without ever preaching at me, Winfield Lewis Miller was teaching me a great lesson I needed very much to learn: how to accept life and grow old with gratitude to God and to the people around me.

I just now stopped typing, went into the bathroom, and put some lotion on my hands, to get ready to drive to work. And I thanked God that these hands can still type on a word processor — so I can tell you about Windy's profound gift to me (to be used in the event I should ever grow old... now where did I park my car?)

—J. Keith Miller, *CrossPoint Magazine,* Fall 1995

Lord, grant me a thankful heart, and to remember that you are good, all the time. Give me the grace to learn from the people you have put in my life and to keep my focus on gratitude to you and to the people around me. In Jesus' name. Amen.

November 16

GOD OF SMALL THINGS

"Four things on earth are small, yet they are extremely wise: Ants are creatures of little strength, yet they store up their food in summer; coneys are creatures of little power, yet they make their homes in the crags; locusts have no king, yet they advance together in ranks; a lizard can be caught with the hand, yet it is found in kings' palaces."
—Proverbs 30:24-28

In our astonishingly loud, verbal world, where achievements are arrogantly proclaimed and every new enterprise is ushered in with a blast and a clatter, it is tranquilizing to see how some small creatures, whose intelligence is mere instinct, who aren't concerned with reputation or credibility, perform their beautiful, ordinary tasks in perfect silence. Yet though spiders, for instance, perform in a kind of private obedience to their calling, they seem to give as much attention to detail and form as if their work were to be exhibited to the whole world.

Another thing. The spider is not easily discouraged. Wipe away her work of art with a clumsy sweep of your elbow and next night she'll do it over for you. This is her vocation—to spin, to weave, to wait, to entangle. She is wholly committed to it; nothing but death will interrupt her persistence.

With my camera as companion, I stalked through the early mist this morning, with the milky light of the sun pressing down, its silver tracing the edges of every wet branch and bud. I noticed how the moisture had condensed along the spider threads in pendant half-circles between the twigs, turning the silk, which I might otherwise have passed without a glance, into star-shaped snares and glistening necklaces of crystal.

An asterisk (that twinkling, star-shaped typographical symbol whose name springs from the same root as "star") calls attention to something, or footnotes it for our enlightenment. Highlighted for me this morning by the moisture of mist is the invisible web of the spider. It tells me to be spider-like, creating in unself-consciousness what I have been called to create—some footnote to the work of my Creator.

—Luci Shaw, *Horizons*

You have given me talents, Lord, and called me to use them. My vanity would have me do something big to bring you honor. But you need nothing I can accomplish. I give you, instead of great works, my ambition and faithfulness. In Jesus' name. Amen.

November 17

BIRDSONG

"I am like a pelican of the wilderness: I am like an owl of the desert. I watch, and am as a sparrow alone upon the housetop. Mine enemies reproacheth me all the day." —Psalm 102:6-8a, KJV

> We do not know when
> the sparrow fell,
> but when I opened
> the stove to build
> autumn's fire,
> he lay on the ashes
> of spring's burning.
>
> I wanted flight and song
> to break from the door,
> to fill the room,
> but he lay still.
>
> Through the long winter
> I listened to the wind
> drawing smoke like song
> up the chimney.
> —John Leax,
> *The Task of Adam*

Sometimes, Lord, we feel abandoned. Our enemies, those sins that beset us, strive to bring us down. You know us even when we fall. Lift us from our brokenness. Restore us to flight and song. Amen.

November 18

TRIAL BY FIRE

"Beloved, think it not strange concerning the fiery trial which is to try you, as though some strange thing happened to you."
—1 Peter 4:12, NKJV

When I returned to my room, wrapped in a great white towel, Honoria had unpacked for me. On the bed table were my books, the ones I had brought to read on the ship: the latest French translation of Tolstoy, *Anna Karenina* (the Oblonskys, I thought, were simple in comparison to the Reniers); one of my father's marked volumes of Plato; some poems. Under these was a book which was not mine: Pascal's *Pensées*. I opened it. On the flyleaf, in firm but delicate hand, was written *Marguerite Dominique de la Valeur*. My husband's grandmother, his dearly loved Mado. Marking one of the pages was a slip of paper with some verses carefully copied out:

> In this parched place of desert wilderness,
> This war-torn, hate-split world, oh, who will bless,
> Bless and redeem the blood-stained, tear-drenched ground
> So once again the healing sun will blaze,
> The small birds sing, the flowers be found,
> And lion and lamb in loving joy may graze?
>
> Who is there left the truth of love to guess?
> How shall we stand the violence of the sun?
> How hate redeem, how brother's love confess?
> What will be left when wind and fire are done?
> Only on love's terrible other side
> Is found the place where lion and lamb abide.

"...Listen to Mado's words. Love's terrible other side. Terrible. She knew it was terrible all right, old Mado. But you, Mrs. Renier? Do you have any idea of the enormity of the fiery darkness of the sun we have to go through before there can be any other side?"
—Madeleine L'Engle, *The Other Side of the Sun*

Lord, as gold tried by fire is made malleable in your hands, lead me, take me, push me, through the fiery darkness to the other side where peace abides. Amen.

November 19

The Plot Thickens

"They arranged to meet Paul on a certain day, and came in even larger numbers to the place where he was staying. From morning till evening he explained and declared to them the kingdom of God and tried to convince them about Jesus from the Law of Moses and from the Prophets. Some were convinced by what he said, but others would not believe."
— Acts 28:23-24

Why wasn't God more obvious? I wanted him to conduct well orchestrated, televised miracles so that I could invite my skeptical friends to see an act of God they could never deny. The problem, as I saw it, was that the Christian acts — praying, loving each other, sharing faith with others, worshiping — just weren't supernatural enough to convince anyone that Christianity is true. "What we really need," I thought, "is a giant, world-wide awesome display of God's power." Naturalism would topple to the ground.

Even as I thought that, I realized it wouldn't work. The Bible records scores of instances when God really shocked the world. The ten plagues of Egypt, for example. Cecil B. DeMille spent millions to imitate them, and his film sequences still look phony. What of the resurrection of Jesus? More than five hundred people attested that he had come back from the dead, but most people refused to believe them. God himself walked on earth for thirty-three years, teaching and performing astounding miracles. Yet, of those who heard him, only a minority believed.

Miracles — the wide open, fireworks, supernatural sort — will always be an exception. Oh, I believe they occur. Many of my friends tell me of some miraculous healing, or a dramatic change God worked in a drug addict. But those miracles which suspend the laws of nature for an instant — I must admit I have never seen one personally.

I don't need miracles to believe; God has lovingly proved himself to me. It only bothers me when I think about my skeptical friends. If God really did a miracle, right in front of their eyes, would they believe? I don't know.

Instead I am left with the simple, sometimes tedious Christian acts of praying, sharing, loving, serving. As I know too well from my early contacts with weird Christians, those acts fall short of convincing a skeptic. They can even be expertly duplicated as a joke or as a sociology experiment.

I never did come up with a good strategy for convincing skeptics. Some came to believe, some didn't. Some were attracted to God by Christians' love; some fled to him when their world was crumbling. Many others, though, are far from God today.

—Philip Yancey, *What They Never Told Me When I Became a Christian*

Dear Lord, sometimes it bothers me that I cannot convince someone that you love him or her and your grace is freely given. Your love is so vital to me that it is frustrating that I can't get through to that person. I give that person to you, Lord, trusting that in your wisdom you will lead him or her to a place in life in which your grace and love can be revealed. In Jesus' name. Amen.

November 20

ACQUAINT NOW THYSELF WITH HIM

"Acquaint now thyself with him, and be at peace: thereby good shall come unto thee."
—Job 22:21, KJV

It's an odd admonition, isn't it? — "acquaint yourself with God." It implies estrangement or distance. If someone were to tell any one of us to "acquaint yourself with God," we'd likely take offense.

Kids from broken homes can be told to acquaint themselves to a stepdad or stepmother. That makes some sense. And we can all be advised to acquaint ourselves with new people — in the office, in the church, in the school. It's good advice. In fact, it's necessary. If we want to get along with new relatives or friends, we've got to accustom ourselves to their ways — maybe they're hard of hearing, or talk too much, or they let the kids get away with murder. Hey, if we want to get along, we've got to adjust, to hold something back in ourselves — sometimes, the desire to scream. Acquainting ourselves with others almost always means putting on some restraints for the sake of getting along.

Not so with God. If something strikes us strange in the Lord's ways, it's our perceptions that are badly wired. If we were what we should be, we'd never consider his ways odd. But sin scrambles everything. The problem is our unbelief.

Unbelief, you see, is quite reasonable, and it happens in understandable steps. First, we look at life and speak almost reverently of impenetrable mysteries and problems which defy human understanding. Then, we begin to doubt whether what is revealed to us is accurate, or instead merely conditioned by time and, by modern standards, eccentric. We question the Word first, then God. And here's where unbelief ends, always: we begin to understand and interpret life by our standards, not God's. Our belief about God becomes so completely changed that he appears only where our ideas allow him.

What we've done thereby is completely reverse the order of creation. In essence, we've become atheists because God is no more than our own construction.

We all need to acquaint ourselves with God, to break our ties to the wisdom of the world and enter again with all the senses and ponderings of the heart into his most holy thoughts.

—James Calvin Schaap, *Near Unto God*

Lord, throw down the idol that I have raised trying to know you. Show yourself through your word, your world, and your Spirit that I might acquaint myself once more with you. Amen.

November 21

A Series of Broken Relationships

"Christ came and preached peace to you outsiders and peace to us insiders. He treated us as equals, and so made us equals. Through him we both share the same Spirit and have equal access to the Father."
—Ephesians 2:17-18, THE MESSAGE

The biblical material consistently portrays the family not as a Norman Rockwell group, beaming in gratitude around a Thanksgiving turkey, but as a series of broken relationships in need of redemption, after the manner of William Faulkner's plots in Yoknapatawpha County.

At the very least, this means that no one needs to carry a burden of guilt because his or her family is deficient in the sweetness and light that Christian families are supposed to exhibit. Since models for harmonious families are missing in Scripture (and for that omission I am repeatedly grateful to the Holy Spirit), we are free to pay attention to what is there — a promise of new community which experiences life as the household of faith, a family in Christ. Life together consists of relationships that are created not by blood (at least not by our blood) but by grace. We get along not because we are good but because we are forgiven.
—Eugene H. Peterson, *Like Dew Your Youth*

Dear Lord, thank you that having a Norman Rockwellian perfect family is not a prerequisite to living my life in faithfulness to you. Help me to pay attention to the family I have and to contribute to it as a person of faith, seeking to build a household of faith. Help me to forgive others in my family as you have forgiven me — and them. In Jesus' name. Amen.

November 22

RAISED UP TOGETHER

"God, who is rich in mercy, made us alive with Christ even when we were dead in transgressions — it is by grace you have been saved. And God raised us up with Christ and seated us with him in the heavenly realms in Christ Jesus, in order that in the coming ages he might show the incomparable riches of his grace, expressed in his kindness to us in Christ Jesus." —Ephesians 2:4b-7

Nothing cleans a skunked dog, or person for that matter. Whatever it is that carries that lovely odor is absorbed by the hair, so not even tomato juice, the standby folk remedy, can cut it.

A curious thing happens to humans who tangle with skunks. Their nose hairs absorb the odor, so they sneak around trying to keep their distance from their friends because they think they stink. And indeed, to themselves, they do.

An analogy comes to mind. The same thing occurs when we sin. Long after the noticeable consequences have passed from our lives, long after those around us have ceased to be offended by our reek, we live in the stench of our actions, for they have become a part of us. And like the skunk, it takes more than tomato juice to restore us to an acceptable state. —John Leax, *In Season and Out*

What laughter, Lord, we share, for you have plunged us in the bath of Christ's suffering, and lifted us dripping, all odors gone, wrapped us in the towel of forgiveness, and dressed us in the softness of cotton. Now we gather before you. Our joy is uncontrollable. Your laughter is our salvation; our laughter is your joy. Amen.

November 23

A SPIRIT OF THANKSGIVING

"Enter his gates with thanksgiving
and his courts with praise;
give thanks to him and praise his name."
—Psalm 100:4

It seems that thanksgiving does not come naturally to human beings. (Anyone who has children needs no further elaboration on that point.)

However, we do need ways to help each other grow in gratitude. Often we miss the lavish provision of God — the air, the sunshine, the rain, the magnificent colors that delight our eyes, the many friendships that enrich our lives. The very rhythms of the earth are gracious gifts from the hand of the Creator.

Can we learn to wake up in the morning rejoicing in the miracle of sleep? Anyone who suffers from insomnia knows what a great gift sleep is. Perhaps at night we could go to the rooms of our sleeping children and sit down and watch them, all the time giving thanks. We can also look at our possessions and, without treasuring them, give thanks for them.

When we have a spirit of thanksgiving we can hold all things lightly. We receive; we do not grab. And when it is time to let go, we do so freely. We are not owners, only stewards. Our lives do not consist of the things that we have, for we live and move and breathe in God, not things. And may I add that this includes those intangible "things" that are often our greatest treasures — status, reputation, position. These are things that come and go in life, and we can learn to be thankful when they come and thankful when they go.

—Richard J. Foster, *The Challenge of a Disciplined Life*

We thank Thee, then, O Father, / For all things bright and good—
The seed-time and the harvest, / Our life, our health, our food;
Accept the gifts we offer / For all Thy love imparts,
And, what Thou most desirest, / Our humble, thankful hearts.
All good gifts around us / Are sent from heaven above:
Then thank the Lord, O thank the Lord / For all his love. Amen.

—Mathias Claudius (Tr. Jane M. Campbell)

November 24

WHAT TO DO?

"Surely God is my salvation; I will trust and not be afraid. The Lord, the Lord, is my strength and my song; he has become my salvation."

—Isaiah 12:2

It was morning and I lay in bed, eyes wide open, realizing that I was alone in the house. It was raining outside and still dark. My husband had left early and would not be back until late that evening. It was a Saturday, and I didn't have to go to work or get out of bed or do anything. So, as I lay there staring at the ceiling, I started imagining what I would do if I didn't have to do what anybody else expected me to do — my mother, my husband, my boss. I expanded the fantasy in my mind to include more questions like: What if I had all the money I needed or could go anywhere I wanted to go, then what would I do?

There was absolutely no answer. I couldn't even make a list to choose from. My mind went blank and I panicked. There I was, with a whole long day ahead of me and I couldn't think of anything I wanted to do, either on a grand scale or a small scale, like brush my teeth or make a cup of coffee.

I finally got up, automatically got into my robe and made coffee. I walked around the living room holding a cup of hot coffee and thinking about that blank in my mind. All I could think of doing was to fantasize asking my mother or husband or boss what to do, imagine an answer from one of them, and then do it. I was stunned that morning to realize that I'd never dared to think of what I was really like and what I might want to do or be as a person apart from my family's expectations.

—Andrea Wells Miller, *The Single Experience*

Dear Lord, finding out who you made me to be — and daring to be her — is a huge part of my salvation! Thank you that you are trustworthy, and that when my mind goes blank and I panic about what to do next, you are there to guide me. In Jesus' name. Amen.

November 25

Unlikely Images

"So God created man in his own image, in the image of God he created him; male and female he created them." —Genesis 1:27

I look around at the people gathered unwittingly with me for this sacrament at Sambo's. A couple of postmen who came in from the cold are warming themselves over their coffee. A businessman in baggy polyester makes bad jokes for the benefit of the thin waitress. I think a mountain might be easier to move, to lift up, than the man at the end of the counter slumped on his stool in spider-like torpor. In the booth next to mine is a lady in yellow-gray coronet braids, and behind her a cowboy with his girlfriend and weekend custody baby. There is nothing very remarkable about any of us except the image of God shining from and sunk into our faces, the mark of which, according to Hasidic legend, even the demons beg to be allowed to behold.

—Virginia Stem Owens, *God Spy*

Dear Lord, in your image are all people made. Keep me mindful of this as I move among the people who occupy my world. How remarkable that we, such unremarkable, everyday people, have your image shining and sunk into our faces. In Jesus' name. Amen.

November 26

RADIANCE OF GOD

"The Lord is God, and he has made his light shine upon us."
—Psalm 118:27

My recent frost slides are back. They were taken during below-zero temperatures when the frost seems to form faster, in a flash of spreading baroque flourishes across the glass. What heightens the effect of the ice curls and feathers and spears is the brilliant orange of the sun-lightened sky behind them, the color caught and intensified by the crystals, highlighted against the darker, blurred arboreal foreground. Somehow there's an attention-getting incongruity—the remote, enormous incandescence of the sun in service to these small, pale, cold fragments of frost, the permanent illuminating the transient, power caressing fragility, the interplay of far and near kissing on the window before my eyes. This could be a metaphor for God's reaching to humankind to bathe them in brightness...or to take them home to heaven. —Luci Shaw, *God in the Dark*

Incandescent Other, Bright Maker of Heaven and Earth, bathe me in your brightness. Make me shine with your indwelling presence. Amen.

November 27

PRAYER OF A WALLPAPER STRIPPER

"Bless all his skills, O Lord, and be pleased with the work of his hands."
—Deuteronomy 33:11

> For the swish of alyssum which grazed
> like spume the gangplank of this walk
> in the long pull of hot wind,
> for the clouds which rolled this morning
> on the hot sky like cool water,

for this house which hovers in the neighborhoods
of mimosa trees and tar,
for the door, for the walls
which will confess slowly the stripes and secret roses
of seven families in the halls,

for the black handle of the putty knife
which winks in my hand like a tiller,
sure as the star
that rode last night over the city
in the clean hands of the air,

for the knife's deep glide,
for the good path my scarred hands find,
I give thanks now
and for the contagion of wallpaper
which foams beneath its prow.
— Jeanne Murray Walker, in *Fugitive Angels*

O God, you humbled yourself in human form and bent your back to physical labor. Draw my thoughts to you as I labor with my hands and body. When my mind is free, keep me focused on you and away from criticism, complaining, worrying, or obsessing. Amen.

November 28

THE STEEL OF SPIRITUAL FRIENDSHIP

"Jonathan's soul became closely bound to David's and Jonathan came to love him as his own soul.... He took off the cloak he was wearing and gave it to David, and his armor too, even his bow and his belt."
—1 Samuel 18:1, 4, JB

"Night and day, I thank God...and always I remember you in my prayers; I remember your tears and long to see you again to complete my happiness.... This is why I am reminding you now to fan into a flame the gift that God gave you when I laid my hands on you.
—2 Timothy 1:3-4, 6-7, JB

How amazing it is to love and be loved. How unlike what we supposed it to be! How astonishing that this capacity grows more so with each love, so that we feel, even in the pain of a declining love, the deepening possibilities of loving again. All the while we resist and draw back from love — mindful of the mingled pleasure and pain of it, the vulnerability, the surrender, the helplessness in the hands of another person — we also run headlong into it with joy, careless as children who experience intense affection for the first time.

Amazing, too, that the life of the spirit in us makes it possible to love God first in himself, and then in another person, and that he definitely and without question sends himself to us in a person he has made. What a sharp sense of grace there is in discovering a person so made for us, so shaped that it seems that person was destined for us from birth, whose mind is open to us as though we together were thinking the same thoughts at the same moment, so that the very fact of this person is for us a proof of the existence of God.

And at the same time, how much, in the like-mindedness of the other person we also sense a difference. The very kindredness of the person is also a reminder of otherness, the exquisiteness of that person's being entirely herself or himself so that in all creation there is no one else like this.... This is the adventure of having a partner in prayer.... Don't ask me where such a friend can be found. It is hardly a question of finding at all, for nothing we do can ever accomplish it. To "find" a spiritual friend is truly to be found, to be chased down, smoked out of one's hiding place in the corner of existence and brought into the center, swept into the blazing presence of God.

There is a hush in it, a stillness, a wonder, that drives us to prayer and into prayer, drives us deeper into God and towards heaven. This is a friendship that is never consummated or possessed, fully, except in the context of God, with a consciousness of God dwelling in the other person, and in ourselves, and in the space between us, a space that seems to be continually dwindling because it soon becomes impossible to know where I leave off and the other person begins.... And because of prayer, it somehow becomes possible to take up every friendship into ourselves and make it part of our own way of loving.

Because we love this new person, we love more intensely, and more freshly, and with a new immediacy those whom we already love. Love squares and cubes in us. It is the overflowing pitcher, the bottomless cup.

—Emilie Griffin, *Clinging: The Experience of Prayer*

Dear Lord, help me to recognize and cherish the spiritual friends you send to me, and to discern your hand in these relationships. Help me to draw strength from such friends, but never to burden them, or cling to them unduly; help me to encourage others in the mutuality of godly love. Amen.

November 29

THE MERCY OF GOD

"For the Lord is good; his mercy is everlasting; and his truth endureth to all generations." —Psalm 100:5, KJV

"What Mac saw was not an act of love but an act of abuse, and abuse stretches across all sexuality." I must have looked as though I were about to faint, because he handed me a glass of water.

Finally I whispered, "How did you know?"

"We live in a very small world," he said, and Mac's behavior in school had made him wonder. It took a while and some general questioning for him to put two and two together, and I know that he didn't tell me everything. There was compassion in his voice, and no trace of fear for the consequences to himself. I found myself talking, telling him what he had only guessed. Promising silence.

He reached across his desk to me and took my hands. He told me that people make mistakes, but we are not bound by them. He told me that Art and I would love each other more, not less. I sat there and wept because I thought I had lost Art forever, that he might as well be dead. Young Edward handed me his handkerchief, a clean white square, and quoted to me something written around fourteen hundred, by William Langland. Olivia closed her eyes, remembering, reciting. "*But all the wickedness in the world which man may do or think is no more to the mercy of God than a live coal dropped in the sea.*"

Camilla shuddered. Mercy? If she accepted mercy for Olivia and Art, for Mac, she had to accept it for herself, for Rose, for whoever had fathered the baby. —Madeleine L'Engle, *A Live Coal in the Sea*

> *These mercies which thy Mary found,*
> *And who thy Cross confessed and crowned,*
> *Hope tells my heart, the same loves be*
> *Still alive, and still for me.*
> —Richard Crashaw, 1613–1649

November 30

HOLDING WHOLENESS IN IMAGINATION'S EYE

"I will weep and wail for the mountains and take up a lament concerning the desert pastures. They are desolate and untraveled, and the lowing of cattle is not heard. The birds of the air have fled and the animals are gone." —Jeremiah 9:10

What once was here, O Lord,
I hold in my imagination's eye —
the forest grown to climax,
the elk, the bear, the wolf
at home, part of your
intention
for this place.

Though I cannot by my labor
change for good the way
this valley yields to willfulness,
one man alone
against devouring man,
I give to you the world
that you have given me.

That the constancy
of my labor might be
my unceasing prayer,

that the fragrance
of humus held to my nose
might rise
an acceptable sacrifice,
that my heart and mind
might incline to no profit
other than your joy.

that my work might be
at last, your work,
bring wholeness to your earth,
the trees I plant
grown to praise the Christ
incarnate in the wood,
the Maker of
elk, and bear, and wolf.

—John Leax, *Standing Ground*

Lord, you have said that what we keep in our minds and hearts is who we are. Help me to keep the vision of a healthy earth in mind and heart, that I might contribute toward its restoration rather than its destruction. In Jesus' name. Amen.

DECEMBER

December 1

ADVENT PRAYER

"Now there was a man in Jerusalem called Simeon, who was righteous and devout. He was waiting for the consolation of Israel, and the Holy Spirit was upon him. It had been revealed to him by the Holy Spirit that he would not die before he had seen the Lord's Christ."
—Luke 2:25-26

Lord of Time, teach us to wait.

Deliver us from the glamour of speed.

Help us to renounce our constant motion which moves us nowhere.

Into the darkness of our anxiety,
   into our fear of being left behind,
   into our apprehension that we are meaningless
   introduce your light.

We will try to wait,
   we will try to hold still,
   we will try to remember what we are waiting for.

Oh God Who is Timeless, whose son invaded our history,
May we see that we were made not only for history.
May we see that we were made to live in eternity, even now.
May we see that you have given us a universe of time
   and more
   if that's what it takes
   to hear your still, small voice.

—Jeanne Murray Walker

December 2

BREAKOUT

"And Mary said: 'My soul glorifies the Lord and my spirit rejoices in God my Saviour, for he has been mindful of the humble state of his servant.'" —Luke 1:46-48

For the Jews in Palestine two thousand years ago, all hope seemed like a fairy tale. As Middle Eastern empires rose and fell, the tiny nation of Israel could never break free from the domination of greater powers. No prophet had spoken to them in four hundred years. At the end of the Old Testament, God was in hiding. He had long threatened to hide his face, and as he did so a dark shadow fell across the planet. This is how one Jewish poet expressed the mood of the times:

> We are given no miraculous signs;
> no prophets are left,
> and none of us knows how long this will be.
> How long will the enemy mock you, O God?
> —Ps. 74:9-10

For four centuries, the four hundred years of God's silence, the Jews waited and wondered. God seemed passive, unconcerned, and deaf to their prayers. Only one hope remained, the ancient promise of a Messiah; on that promise the Jews staked everything. And then something momentous happened. The birth of a baby was announced — a birth unlike any that had come before.

You can catch the excitement just by watching the reactions of people in this chapter. The way Luke tells it, events surrounding Jesus' birth resembled a joy-filled musical. Characters crowded into the scene: a white-haired great uncle, an astonished virgin, a tottery old prophetess. They all smiled broadly and, as likely as not, burst into song. Once Mary overcame the shock from seeing an angel, she let loose with a beautiful hymn. Even an unborn cousin kicked for joy inside his mother's womb.

Luke takes care to make direct connections to Old Testament promises of a Messiah; the angel Gabriel even called John the Baptist an "Elijah" sent to prepare the way for the Lord. Clearly, something was brewing on planet earth. Among dreary, defeated villagers in a remote corner of the Roman Empire, something climactically good was breaking out. —Philip Yancey, *A Guided Tour of the Bible*

As I read about the various reactions to the angels' appearances in the opening acts of the story of your birth, I try to imagine how I would react. Fear and doubt like Zechariah, Elizabeth's husband? Obedience, singing and rejoicing like Mary? I'll probably never know unless it happens to me. Help me to be open to your surprises in the world. In Jesus' name. Amen.

December 3

WHATEVER IS EXCELLENT

"Finally, brothers, whatever is true, whatever is noble, whatever is right, whatever is pure, whatever is lovely, whatever is admirable — if anything is excellent or praiseworthy — think about these things."
—Philippians 4:8

I believe that if I'm going to get healthy I've got to improve not only my body, but also my mind and spirit. And I also believe that what I think about while I'm going through the physical motions of exercise can affect my overall health as much as whether I do the exercises correctly or incorrectly.

So while I'm exercising, I sometimes to through the parts of the passage and try to think of an example of each thing mentioned. For example, when I think, "whatever is true and noble," a person I'm going to meet that day may come to mind. Will I be able to behave in a noble way with her? If she shares a problem with me, will I find myself trying to straighten her out, to talk her into doing something my way, or will I be able to listen, try to understand it from her perspective, and be a friend who cares?

Am I doing right or being fair? My mind takes quick review of my relationships. Is there a situation in which I'm not being fair? Do I need to forgive anyone? Have I done everything I promised to do?

Things that are pure and lovely are a joy — when I can find them! So often I get caught up in thinking thoughts about myself that I forget about anything else. But admiring a friend's beautiful hair and telling her so or noticing the way God put together a wildflower or a sunset and telling him so seem to have a good effect on me, too.

When I think about things that are admirable, I ask myself, "Can I look for God's grace in the good things which happen, the forgiveness and hope his love brings into my life, and the touches of concern and caring that come my way?" When I can do this, I can see that my life is full of the signs of his grace.

And finally, "If anything is excellent or praiseworthy, think on these things." A lot of the time when I start out running, my body seems to resist me. I feel out of breath, my legs are stiff, my calves ache. But as I go along, my system perks up and I feel better. Sometimes my mind tries to imagine what I could see if my skin were transparent — the intricate way my muscles are put together to hold the bones in place, the way the blood flows around my body, taking oxygen to the muscles and going back to the lungs to get more, the way the kidneys and liver and intestines process waste materials. It's amazing to me! And I feel like praying, "Thanks, God, for creating all this."

The more I can keep my mind on the things that are true and noble, right, pure, lovely, excellent, and praiseworthy, the more I can live with the aches and pains, problems and failures, and not let them get me down quite so much.　　　　　　—Andrea Wells Miller, *BodyCare*

Dear Lord, thank you that, in a world so full of problems and frightening things, there are still things worthy of praise. Your excellence alone amazes me, and I am grateful to you for all you've given me. I ask you to come into my mind and fill it with true and noble thoughts, so that I can learn to love other people with your kind of love. In Jesus' name. Amen.

December 4

How to Knit a Life

"He who began a good work in you will carry it on to completion."
　　　　　　—Philippians 1:6

I'm making some progress on my new project—the sweater I promised to knit for my friend Candace. The pattern is a continental one translated, very badly, from Italian into English, which makes it ambiguous and confusing. The photo of the sweater helps; what sounds impossible in the printed instructions comes clearer when I can see the pictured shape and the patterned textures, knit without seams, all in one piece.

I am feeling, in the roughness of the yarn as the garment grown in my hands, what it is like, also to knit a life. How experimental it is; how the instructions are not always intelligible and often make no sense until I knit them into reality, doing it over and over until it's right and finally something interesting and warm and beautiful takes shape under my fingers. A slow process, stitch added to stitch, row to row, the work picked up and put down at odd moments, the way one adds to one's own life by fits and starts.

I am both knitter and knitted one. In God's hands I can see myself taking shape, all my yarns and fibers looped in rows that hold together and capture within them the tiny pockets of air that insulate and comfort the body—the air is part of the pattern, plained and purled into the pieces. Knitted stitch by stitch, hour by hour, it will take all of the years of my life to finish.　　　　　　—Luci Shaw, *God in the Dark*

Lord, I hope it looks good when it's done—a seamless garment. Amen.

December 5

THE LIGHT IN THE DARK

"This is the message we have heard from him and declare to you: God is light, and in him there is no darkness at all." —1 John 1:5

When I walked Poon last night the darkness seemed greater than usual. Stars were out, but haze diminished them so their light seemed far away and powerless. I felt vaguely restless, at loose ends, and spiritually cold. Sometimes the immanence of God in the things of this world is hard to perceive. His transcendence seems so great I despair of ever knowing him. He seems wholly other, as apart from me as I am apart from the dog I was walking. He seems apart in the same way too — not uncaring, simply beyond.

A quarter mile down the road I realized I'd walked further into darkness than I usually go. Then over Snyder Hill, just above the woodlot, I saw a thin slice of orange. Poon and I stood still and watched the moon rise until it broke free of earth and floated in the sky.

I can't say my spirits rose with the moon. But I learned a long time ago to trust God's character and not my momentary feelings about his presence. —John Leax, *In Season and Out*

Light of the World, though we cannot see you, we walk enclosed in your glory. Though we close our eyes, you remain about us. Though we turn away, you do not turn. Thank you for shining when we would put you out. Amen.

December 6

VESSELS OF CLAY

"But we have this treasure in earthen vessels." —2 Corinthians 4:7, KJV

The root word of "humility" is *humus*, earth; to be *human*, too, comes from the same word; and the parables of Jesus which show the kind of humility he is seeking in us are often earthy, such as the parable of the workers in the vineyard, the parable of the seed and the sower and the parable of the prodigal son. We all have within us that same lack of humility as the workers who worked in the heat of the day and resented those who got equal pay for shorter hours of work; and we all understand the lack of humility in the elder son who was offended by his father's humble forgiveness.

King Lear's humbleness at the end of his play is all the more moving because it has been born of the pain caused by his arrogance.

And another lovely paradox: we can be humble only when we know that we are God's children, of infinite value, and eternally loved.

—Madeleine L'Engle, *Walking on Water*

Lord, you are the potter, we are the clay; you are forming us of the earth and breathing into us the breath of life so that we may bear your everlasting love in our mortal bodies.

Be it unto us according to your word. Amen.

December 7

ONE KIND OF LONELINESS

"The King will reply, 'I tell you the truth, whatever you did for one of the least of these brothers of mine, you did for me.'"

—Matthew 25:40

There is a loneliness which is strictly social, just a need to have someone to talk to. I would sometimes find myself lonely and just want to reach out and touch someone or talk to a friend. And when this happened I realized that I just needed to get out of my chair and call someone I knew. But often I've been strangely shy about calling people when I've been lonely. I've felt that my friends probably didn't want to be with me (or I didn't want to risk that they might not). When I felt that way, someone suggested that I could go see someone else who might be very lonely and whom I might have neglected.

At first, I rejected this idea because when I am down and feel like a misfit, the last thing I want to do is visit with another "loser." I'd rather see someone who is going to make *me* happy. But I decided to give "visiting" a try. The first time I tried going to see someone when I was feeling lonely, I went on raw faith. I didn't feel this person would reject me because I knew he was in worse shape than I was, and probably just as lonely. Finally I drove to his house.

As I walked up the front steps, I dreaded the next half hour. What would I say to a man who had always appeared to me to be sort of arrogant and defensive when I'd seen him at church? I'd pegged Bart as a "know it all" type who felt superior to the rest of the members of the church. He was not attractive to me in any way.

But I'd heard that Bart was hurting and he'd said he'd like to see me some time. He smiled in surprise as he opened the door — even though he'd known I was coming. It was an awkward moment as we both realized what he'd done. But when we sat down and began talking — after reviewing the weather that day — I began to feel a change in the atmosphere. The arrogance melted, and there sitting before me was a man just like me, afraid he really wasn't much good at relationships and yet not knowing what to do. He began to tell me about his life and what had happened to him.

Sometimes he would pause for thirty seconds and stare at the floor as his story unfolded.

Although he was a respected community and church leader, his marriage had been bad for years. Recently he'd had an affair and fallen in love with the other woman. Bart was really open in admitting his problems, mistakes, and sins. And I found myself caring very much about him. An hour flew by. And when it was time to leave, I hated to go. I had gotten outside myself and really become involved in Bart's life. And as I had, he became more animated and interesting — whereas before I'd showed interest in him, he had been drab and boring. And I realized that my being bored sometimes when I had gone to see people before must have communicated itself at some level, and they had *become* passive and boring. But my listening and asking questions changed the experience for Bart and for me. We prayed together. And when I left, I found that my loneliness had evaporated for the rest of the evening.

—J. Keith Miller, *The Single Experience*

Lord, you reached out to us in our aloneness to show us more about who God is, so that we might enter a deeper relationship with him through you. Help me to remember that my reaching out to one of your lonely brothers or sisters is not only healing for both of us, but is a way of reaching out in gratitude to you in that brother or sister. Give me strength and courage to get through the awkwardness of moving out of my lonely but safe cocoon into the presence of someone. In Jesus' name, Amen.

December 8

THE POWER OF SILENCE

"My soul finds rest in God alone; my salvation comes from him."
—Psalm 62:1

Contemplative Prayer immerses us into the silence of God. How desperately we in the modern world need this wordless baptism! We have become, as the early church father Clement of Alexandria says, like old shoes — all worn out except for the tongue. We live in a wordy world with our sophisticated high-tech telecommunication systems. We now have the dubious distinction of being able to communicate more and say less than any civilization in history.

Isaac of Nineveh, a Syrian monk, once observed, "Those who delight in a multitude of words, even though they say admirable things, are empty within."[1] We today stand under the rebuke of this observation.

Contemplative Prayer is the one discipline that can free us from our addiction to words. Progress in intimacy with God means progress toward silence. "For God alone my soul waits in silence," declares the Psalmist (Ps. 62:1). The desert father Ammonas, a disciple of St. Anthony, writes, "I have shown you the power of silence, how thoroughly it heals and how fully pleasing it is to God.... Know that it is by silence that the saints grew, that it was because of silence that the power of God dwelt in them, because of silence that the mysteries of God were known to them"[2] It is this recreating silence to which we are called in Contemplative Prayer.

—Richard J. Foster, *Prayer: Finding the Heart's True Home*

My Lord and my God, listening is hard for me. I do not exactly mean hard, for I understand that this is a matter of receiving rather than trying. What I mean is that I am so action-oriented, so product-driven, that doing is easier for me than being. I need your help if I am to be still and listen. I would like to try. I would like to learn how to sink down into the light of your presence until I can become comfortable in that posture. Help me to try now.

Thank you. Amen.

—Richard J. Foster, *Prayer: Finding the Heart's True Home*

December 9

LORD, TEACH US TO PRAY

"One of his disciples said unto him, 'Lord, teach us to pray, as John also taught his disciples.'" —Luke 11:1b

Even though at times we do it poorly, there's no escaping the fact that every believer *must* pray. One cannot come near to God without it. Prayer requires clarity, urgency, and readiness of soul — and it's never simply crafted. If it's artifice, it's not prayer.

---

1. As quoted in Thomas Merton, *Contemplative Prayer* (Garden City, N.Y.: Doubleday/Image, 1971), 30.
2. As quoted in Merton, *Contemplative Prayer*, 42.

And yet prayer is something learned. Even the disciples, who followed Jesus every day, didn't know exactly how to do it. "Lord, teach us to pray," they asked. When he answered, Christ didn't say, "Do it after this fashion." What he told them was this: "When you pray, say..." He gave them the very words in a form that seems specially designed for groups. The pronoun *our* is used throughout: *our* Father, *our* daily bread, *our* sins. For centuries, that prayer has been used in worship.

Some reformers, fervent about ridding the church of its formalism, stopped using the Lord's Prayer in worship. To them, the Lord's Prayer seemed canned — ritualistic, meaningless repetition. Prayer reaches its highest form when, free from every bit of formality, it rises from the depths of the soul on the wings of the Spirit and comes before God the Father in holy and consecrated language. When we offer that kind of prayer, the words of the Lord's Prayer may not be adequately specific for our needs.

Most of us know that kind of intense prayer because in our own lives, those prayers are memorable to us. But few of us experience that kind of fervency every day. It's equally unlikely that every single Sunday of the year someone from the congregation can reach that level of intensity. While such vigor may be the mountaintop, above the tree line there's not much life, really. In public worship at least, extemporaneous prayer isn't *always* preferable to the Lord's Prayer — or fixed forms in general.

Besides, as everyone knows, certain repetitions feed spirituality — a treasured verse of Scripture, the chorus of "Jesus Loves Me," the hymn sung at a grandma's funeral.

Most preachers don't write individual benedictions for the close of the service. Does their repetition of those same words numb and freeze? In many ways, for us to hear them time and time again as we leave the sanctuary is to know that we have been part of God's greater and larger family, hearers of certain words repeated throughout the world and for as long as his people have come together to worship him.

Sometimes the words of the Lord's Prayer, like so many fixed forms, are the gentle dew of grace that comes only from God Almighty. That prayer is not designed for a showcase. It's given to us for our use. It is the very model for our coming near unto God.

—James Calvin Schaap, *Near Unto God*

Lord Jesus, we cannot always say what we feel. We sometimes fail either to praise or to articulate our needs. Thank you for the words that give voice to our deepest need, our need to confess, to trust, and to hallow the Father's name. Amen.

December 10

C. S. Lewis on Laughter

"Vanity of vanities, says the Preacher, vanity of vanities! All is vanity."
— Ecclesiastes 1:2, RSV

What Screwtape is talking about here,[3] at least philosophically, is not causes (Joy, Fun, Joke Proper, Flippancy) or effects (laughter is but one of many possible effects) but comedy itself, of which Lewis was both critic and practitioner. Sad to say, nowhere, in any of his works, does he — or indeed any other spiritual writer in the history of the western world — define comedy in relation to the spiritual life. In Lewis's life and works, however, such an application is supremely possible.

Before making the grand attempt, I think I must make several distinctions based on my own reading of Lewis and my own personal experience with comedy in a variety of forms, dramatic as well as literary.

First, comedy is conservative in nature. It scourges the assumed inanity of the present by contrasting it with the presumed sanity of the past.

Second, comedy is always in bad taste. The comedian can't peek under a lady's hem or tweak a gentleman's hairpiece, then make a caustic if correct observation, and still expect to remain in good taste or good odor. The result on the one hand is disgust; on the other, laughter.

Third, comedy is always cruel. We laugh at the caustic comment because it's all too true, but there'll always be someone else within earshot to whom it's almost too true. It's like a feathery shaft to the heart. There's a whoosh, a thunk, and a slump to the floor, the glassy eyes having that But-why-me? I-wasn't-doing-anything-to-hurt-you sort of stare.

Fourth, comedy is a mirror, not of our perfections, but of our imperfections. We live in an age of comedy, what with more comic novels and plays and films and television series than we know what to do with. We're constantly being bombarded by comic images of humankind on the hoof. We laugh outwardly, sometimes loudly, when the images are of other people, but we cry inwardly, uncontrollably, when the images are of ourselves.

In Letter XI and indeed in the entire correspondence, Lewis seems to be saying, look to the comic, for therein one will see oneself. It's instantaneous recognition, a Polaroidal caught-in-the-act portrait of oneself. First thing we notice, however, is that the image in the polished mirror with the wavy surface is distorted. That's the imperfection. That's what needs improvement in one's spiritual life. "Vanity of vanities," saith Ecclesiastes, "all is vanity," and nowhere is this vanity better shown than

---

3. C. S. Lewis, *The Screwtape Letters* (New York: Macmillan, 1961), 57.

in comedy. Madam Eglantyne, the Prioress in *The Canterbury Tales,* is vain about her table manners, ever applying the napkin to her upper lip. Malvolio, the gangly steward in *Twelfth Night,* is vain about his yellow stockings and crossed garters. The Rev. Mr. Collins in *Pride and Prejudice* is vain about his marriageability, believing that a young woman's polite but public refusal is really a mask for her acceptance.

Laugh at others, then. That's what Lewis would have us do, for doing so is to laugh at oneself.

—William Griffin, *C. S. Lewis: Spirituality for Mere Christians*

Dear God, help me to lighten up about my flaws and foibles, and always to keep in mind that you love me just as I am. Amen.

December 11

THE MYSTERY OF PRAYER

"Likewise the Spirit also helpeth our infirmities: for we know not what we should pray for as we ought: but the Spirit itself maketh intercession for us with groanings which cannot be uttered."

—Romans 8:26, KJV

In Hugh's hospital room, where I spend seven or more hours a day, I am always on the alert toward my husband, even when he is sleeping. My quiet time comes in the evening, when we sit out on the terrace and wait for the stars. Most evenings I go upstairs early, at nine o'clock, to read, to think, to be quiet for a couple of hours. To unwind enough for sleep, which I need if I am to keep up my strength.

Piano time is very slim. I don't get home from the hospital in time to have the usual treasured hour at the piano before dinner. Writing, too, has been difficult. I have been drafting a novel, but the work has gone slowly. Although I am encouraged to use my little six-pound electronic typewriter in the hospital, I am constantly yearning toward Hugh in inner prayer. Not demanding prayer. Just a small giving of love flowing steadily to him. Most of what I have written this summer is this journal, and it, too, is a form of prayer and a source of strength.

Prayer. What about prayer? A friend wrote to me in genuine concern about Hugh, saying that she didn't understand much about intercessory prayer. I don't, either. Perhaps the greatest saints do. Most of us don't, and that is all right. We don't have to understand to know that prayer is love, and love is never wasted. —Madeleine L'Engle, *Two-Part Invention*

Though earth and man be gone,
And sun and universes cease to be,
And Thou wert left alone,
Every existence would exist in Thee.

There is not room for Death,
Nor atom that his might could render void:
Thou — Thou art Being and Breath,
And what Thou art may never be destroyed.

—Emily Brontë

December 12

A NEW HEART

"I will give them an undivided heart and put a new spirit in them; I will remove from them their heart of stone and give them a heart of flesh. Then they will follow my decrees and be careful to keep my laws."
—Ezekiel 11:19-20

I am listening to a phrase from the Collect: "Grant that all who have been reborn into the fellowship of Christ's Body may show forth in their lives what they profess by their faith." It's a message for "professional Christians," those who know it all, yet whose testimony has expired from lack of reality. The new birth transformation is so radical. Why is it not existentially active in so many of us? I feel my heart quicken. God is speaking to me! He is using the vision of the Wadi of Dry Bones, needing not only flesh and skin to cover them (the true teachings of the gospel) but breath to fill them, to activate the mechanism (the moving Spirit). I think, again, of Ezekiel 11:19: "I will...put a new spirit in them; I will remove from them their heart of stone and give them a heart of flesh." The paradoxical people — body of flesh, heart of stone — God wants to integrate, to unify by the Spirit's power until they are *alive clear through*, the cold, dead, hard core replaced by a warm pulsing heart that is a part of the rest of their flesh.   —Luci Shaw, *God in the Dark*

Transfuse me, re-oxygenate my spirit. By the electricity of your life in me, you have been nudging me across the frontier. My faith has not been one grand leap, but a series of small, halting steps toward you. It's like a dance between us; I wanted you to do the work, the revelation, but passive waiting was not enough to get the dancing going. I must step out on the floor and trust you to step toward me. Amen.   —Luci Shaw, *God in the Dark*

December 13

THE CHRISTMAS AX

"The ax is already at the root of the trees, and every tree that does not produce good fruit will be cut down and thrown into the fire."
—Matthew 3:10

a new ax
> to cleave oak
to split it clean
> to open my mind
like heartwood

a new ax
> to fit my hands
to wear callouses
> on my palms
and make them shine

a new ax
> to wield with care
to loose from the tree
> the new man
born in fire

—John Leax, *Country Labors*

Christ, be the ax that splits us from our sin, the presence in our lives that makes us shine, the one triumphant from the cross, risen in glory, to walk us through the cleansing fire and stand us restored before the Loving Father. Amen.

December 14

FORGETTING THE MISSION

"He took a little child and had him stand among them. Taking him in his arms, he said to them,....'I tell you the truth, anyone who will not receive the kingdom of God like a little child will never enter it.'"
—Mark 9:36, 10:15

The child, newborn, is a natural spy. Only his inherent limitations impede him from consuming all the clues of the universe fitted to his perceiving capacities. Sent here with the mission of finding the meaning buried in matter, of locating the central intelligence, he goes about his business briskly, devouring every detail within his developing grasp. He is devoted to discovery, resists sleep in order to absorb more data. Never again will he seek to unearth the treasure buried in the field with such single-mindedness. He has to learn the world from scratch, but the task seems nothing but a joy. Yet gradually, over time, something goes wrong.

The spy slowly begins to forget his mission. He spends so much time and effort learning the language, adopting the habits and customs, internalizing the thought patterns flawlessly, that somehow, gradually, imperceptibly, he becomes his cover. He forgets what he's about. He goes to school, grows up. He gets a job, collects his pay, buys a house, waters the lawn. He settles down and settles in. He wakes up each morning with the shape of his mission, what brought him here in the first place, grown hazier, like a dream that slides quickly away. He frowns and makes an effort to remember. But the phone rings or the baby cries, and he is distracted for the rest of the day. Perhaps he forms a resolution to remember; still he seems helpless to keep the shape, the color of his mission clear in his mind. Then one morning he wakes up and only yawns. It must be there somewhere, buried in the brain cells, but at least superficially the memory is erased. The spy goes native.

—Virginia Stem Owens, *God Spy*

Dear Lord, I've forgotten my mission and gone native. Now I'm longing for that hazily remembered childlike fascination I once had about my relationship with you. Awaken my yawning soul, and sharpen my dulling senses to absorb once again the life-giving data you send my way. In Jesus' name. Amen.

December 15

SEEN AND UNSEEN WORLDS

"All these people were still living by faith when they died. They did not receive the things promised; they only saw them and welcomed them from a distance. And they admitted that they were aliens and strangers on earth." —Hebrews 11:13

Richard lay prone on the wooden floor of his apartment, pleading for God to "reveal" himself, gambling all his faith on God's willingness to step into a seen world as he had done for Job. And Richard lost that gamble. Frankly, I doubt whether God feels any "obligation" to prove himself in such a manner. He did so many times in the Old Testament, and with finality in the person of Jesus. What further incarnations do we require of him?

I say this with great care, but I wonder if a fierce, insistent desire for a miracle — even a physical healing — sometimes betrays a lack of faith rather than an abundance of it. Such prayers may, like Richard's, set conditions for God. When yearning for a miraculous resolution to a problem, do we make our loyalty to God contingent on whether he reveals himself yet again in the seen world?

If we insist on visible proofs from God, we may well prepare the way for a permanent state of disappointment. True faith does not so much attempt to manipulate God to do our will as it does to position us to do his will. As I searched through the Bible for models of great faith, I was struck by how few saints experienced anything like Job's dramatic encounter with God. The rest responded to God's hiddenness not by demanding that he show himself, but by going ahead and believing him though he stayed hidden. Hebrews 11 pointedly notes that the giants of faith "did not receive the things promised; they only saw them and welcomed them from a distance."

We human beings instinctively regard the seen world as the "real" world and the unseen world as the "unreal" world, but the Bible calls for almost the opposite. Through faith, the unseen world increasingly takes shape as the real world and sets the course for how we live in the seen world. Live for God, who is invisible, and not for other people, said Jesus in his words about the unseen world, or "the kingdom of heaven."

Once the apostle Paul directly addressed the question of disappointment with God. He told the Corinthians that, in spite of incredible hardships, he did not "lose heart": "Though outwardly we are wasting away, yet inwardly we are being renewed day by day. For our light and momentary [!] troubles are achieving for us an eternal glory that far outweighs them all. So we fix our eyes not on what is seen, but on what is unseen. For what is seen is temporary, but what is unseen is eternal" (2 Cor. 4:16–18).

—Philip Yancy, *Disappointment with God*

Dear Lord, help me to begin to see the "unseen world," the kingdom of heaven, as more real, to set the course for how I live in the seen world. In Jesus' name. Amen.

December 16

HOLY NIGHT

"When King Herod heard this he was disturbed, and all Jerusalem with him. When he had called together all the people's chief priests and teachers of the law, he asked them where the Christ was to be born."
—Matthew 2:3-4

Chicago. This place may yet be Bethlehem.
Wheels unlace the streets all night,
silent on the strict ice. Listen. The hymn
of a drummer boy glistens and guts the neat
air. The shattered poor dream of God's clean
coming. The lake, shocked with cold
is torn. The ragged moon turns tired, old.

Yet briefly this place may be Bethlehem.
Chicago, two thousand years broken to peace,
waiting, wreathed and torn to be the home
of Christ. Christmas preys on this tired place.
Father, be with us in the ripping dark.
Send splints of angels, send the child, and mark
the place we cheat the centuries, where we, weary,
kneel down in praise, arise in mended fury.

—Jeanne Murray Walker, in the *Christian Century*

May my Chicago heart become Bethlehem. Christ be born in me this day and every day. Amen.

December 17

THE BREATH OF GOD

"For since the creation of the world God's invisible qualities — his eternal power and divine nature — have been clearly seen, being understood from what has been made, so that we are without excuse."
—Romans 1:20

I stood at our window Saturday afternoon and looked west. The sun was low, shining along the surface of the deep snow. A strong wind flowed over the icy crust and carried snow particles along in its eddies. It made the wind visible in a curious and beautiful way, like a fast-moving river of light, the snow-dust catching and holding the glints from the sun. I think the Spirit (wind) of God is made visible in the individuals in our lifestream. God shines on them, and shows us in their lives the way the wind is moving. —Luci Shaw, *God in the Dark*

Father of all things, you have made your nature visible in all you have made. The works of creation declare you. And each individual I meet, created particularly in your image, bears yourself to me. Open my eyes and let me see, I have never been without you. Amen.

December 18

WALKING ON ICE

"Then the Lord answered Job out of the storm. 'He said, Who is this that darkens my counsel with words without knowledge?'"
—Job 38:1–2

> This river runs beneath
> the surface of my thought;
> I know it once reached
> out an arm and wrapped
> my house in its embrace.
>
> I walk
> one side of sliding
> upon a will
> I can't by strength or words
> stay.

—John Leax, *The Task of Adam*

Dumbfounded by your otherness, Lord, we confess we have tried to make you in our image. We have tried to fit you into our world and have diminished you accordingly. You are beyond the formulations of our words. Forgive us. Let your Spirit make intercession for us for we are silenced by your greatness. Amen.

December 19

RIGHT HERE IN THIS ROOM

"I will not leave you comfortless: I will come to you."
—John 14:18, KJV

I woke up in the middle of the night terribly afraid. It was pitch black in my room, and my body was covered with cold sweat. I'd had a dream about going broke and winding up as an old man in shabby clothes on a tenement step, with no family or friends. The dream still seemed very real. I flipped on the light and glanced at the clock. It was 4:02 a.m.

Although we're not rich, we're certainly not bankrupt. Why, then, was I thinking, *there will soon be a total financial disaster!* If God was in my life, why was I fearful?

I thought about Jesus and his promises about fear. And in my half-asleep state, I began to dream about two little girls who reminded me of two of my daughters when they were little. In the dream, the older one, Rachel, was consoling her three-year-old sister, Janie, who had awakened scared and howling in the middle of the night after a Christmas play in which they both had been angels. In my dream, I heard Rachel say, "Janie, fear not! For I come to bring good tidings." And then she added, in a loud stage voice, "Jesus is right here in this room!"

"Oh," a tiny, tearful voice said, "okay," and Janie went back to sleep.

I smiled. What I needed there in the dark was not an answer to my financial problems but a Counselor, a Comforter to be with me through the long night. And, grateful that Jesus *was* right there in that room, I went back to sleep. —Keith Miller, *Daily Guideposts*, 1998

Thank you, Lord, for your promise that the Comforter will be with us always. Amen.

December 20

CLINGING TO GOD

"When I found him whom my soul loves,
I held him, and would not let him go
until I brought him into my mother's house,
into the chamber of her that conceived me."
—Song of Solomon 3:4, NRSV

We must depend on God. We must rely on him, embrace him. We must cling.

We must cling to the one reality that does not crumple. The one rock that will not be washed loose in the tide and onslaught of anything. We must cling to the one reality that will hold firm, though the earth be destroyed and the mountains flung into the sea and the sun put out. We must cling to the One who holds eternity in his hand, who will not perish in the end, and has the power to save us, too. The One who knew us before we existed, in whose thought and by whose hand we exist from moment to moment. He chose and shaped us from our mother's womb to be intimate with him.

This clinging will no doubt make us foolish in the eyes of the world. Even among our fellow Christians, it can make us a little conspicuous. ...When we speak of it, we are likely to hear talk of neurosis and escape from reality.

But the more we cling, the more we experience strength not as what we do, but what God does in us. The more we understand that when we ask, he will give us the words to say. Like Stephen, we ask for the spirit of God to give us the words we lack — and when the time comes, we have the courage and the words. When the high hillsides loom before us, we are afraid. But by clinging and knowing that God is our strength, we find, one step at a time, that we are ascending, not by any doing of our own, but purely by his grace.

—Emilie Griffin, *Clinging: The Experience of Prayer*

Dear Lord, may I become detached from all the distractions and burdens of this world, and rest entirely in your care. May I cherish the intimacy of your unique friendship, your everlasting and extravagant love. Sustain me in your grace, and let me never be parted from you. Amen.

December 21

PRAYER IS ELEMENTAL

"When I call, give me answers. God, take my side!
Once, in a tight place, you gave me room;
Now I'm in trouble again: grace me! hear me!"
—Psalm 4:1, THE MESSAGE

Untutored, we tend to think that prayer is what good people do when they are doing their best. It is not. Inexperienced, we suppose that there must be an "insider" language that must be acquired before God takes us seriously in our prayer. There is not. Prayer is elemental, not advanced language. It is the means by which our language becomes honest, true, and personal in response to God. It is the means by which we get everything out in the open before God.

—Eugene H. Peterson, THE MESSAGE

Dear Lord, my heart speaks without language, my soul longs for you without words. My mind sees images and tries to form them into words of prayer. I want to get everything out in the open before you. Help me as I try. In Jesus' name. Amen.

December 22

THE WAY UP

"This will be a sign to you: You will find a baby wrapped in cloths and lying in a manger." —Luke 2:12

Like everything Mac initiated, the excursion to go caroling on Beacon Hill in Boston was a mixture of pleasure and confusion. It was indeed bitterly cold, and we girls were too short to see into many of the windows, but I loved the dignified houses and the clusters of carolers with their voices mingling and colliding up and down the block.

Mac lifted us one by one up to the best windows, with an elaborate running commentary on the scenes laid out on the sills. When it was my turn to look at a particular crèche, he exclaimed in my ear, "There it is, Annie! There it is!"

"You mean the baby?" I asked. A baby was all I could see. The entire display consisted of an exquisite life-size china doll lying in the straw, holding his toes and laughing.

"That's the secret stair," said Mac. Stair? I saw no stair.

" 'Thou com'st down Thine own secret stair,' " Mac said, dramatically, in his poetry-reciting voice. 'Com'st down to answer all my need.' I think that's how it goes."

"Stair?" I asked, completely baffled.

" 'They all were looking for a king... To slay their foes and lift them high' " Mac went on, reciting again. " 'Thou cam'st a little baby thing... to make a woman cry.' "

I glanced into the room behind the baby, still looking for a stair. None was in sight. A family sat around a table, drinking something from steaming cups. Cocoa, I thought. A deep hunger and thirst seemed to rise out of my toes. I wanted that cocoa, that bright, warm house, and something else I could feel but not name.

"That's George MacDonald," said Mac.

"Where?" I asked. But he didn't answer. He set me down. It was Peggy's turn to see.

—Shirley Nelson, "The Secret Stair," in *Once Upon a Christmas*

O God of infinite surprises, help us to recognize your ways in the unexpected places of our lives. Amen.

December 23

Pain and Meaning

"I tell you the truth, you will weep and mourn while the world rejoices. You will grieve, but your grief will turn to joy.... Now is your time of grief, but I will see you again and you will rejoice. And no one will take away your joy." —John 16:20, 22

We often think of Jesus' suffering on this earth. Sometimes we forget that most of what we know about Mary, Jesus' mother, is also in the context of pain. Even her name means "bitter."

Her role was a difficult one from the start. Young and inexperienced, she was called by the Lord's angel to a pregnancy that owned no human father and opened her to charges of promiscuity. Her vocation was to be the mother of a paradox—God in a man's body, a man who would be considered a failed rebel by the leaders in his day, and finally a criminal.

Early on, she felt dismay at having to travel to Bethlehem in her ninth month, of giving birth in the most primitive and comfortless of conditions, of knowing later that her own little one survived at the life cost of Bethlehem's baby boys who were slaughtered by Herod in Jesus' place.

On the eighth day after Jesus' birth a prophecy laced with further torment was spoken to Mary: "A sword will pierce your own soul"—a pain for her to ponder and dread for over thirty years. During that waiting time, Jesus directed some of his hardest sayings to his gentle mother—words that must have wounded. But the culmination of all her anguish was at the cross, under its very arm, as she watched her beloved son die a slow and brutal death.

But hers was not the kind of dead-end pain that has no meaning. She was privileged to be caught up in the life of the One who fought the fierce battle between light and darkness. We can understand that mix of pain and joy only as we carry Christ in our hearts, birthing him into a hostile world. That may mean suffering; we may be as misunderstood as Mary. But there is a reward: *Because eternity was closeted in time, he is our open door to forever.* —Luci Shaw, *Horizons*

Thank you, Lord, for giving me your whole story, for not calling me, like Mary, to suffer the agony of the unfolding truth of your redemption. Still, I suffer the anguish of partial knowledge, for I do not know what you will call upon me to endure for the sake of my salvation or for the sake of your work in the world. In all things, I know, your grace is sufficient. I would be your willing servant. Use me as you wish. Amen.

December 24

IN THE WOODS
THE WILD ONES GATHER

"For the creation was subjected to frustration, not by its own choice, but by the will of the one who subjected it, in hope that the creation itself will be liberated from its bondage to decay and brought into the glorious freedom of the children of God." —Romans 8:20-21

Christmas Eve

While cattle stupidly stare
over straw damp from their breathing
and the horse lazily stirs
over his trough, and the lantern
licks at shadows in corners,

in the woods the wild ones gather,
the rabbit twitching with care,
sooty shrew, and imperial mole
with the hands of a lost politician,
to shine in the branch-broken light

of a moon which in mid-career
lights up a church of snow.
Now one paw after another
about the bones of weeds
in a soft worrying circle

the helpless ones dance out their fear,
watching the glittering air
where he shines in the eyes of the others
naked, with nothing to wear.
Long before he comes to the stable

to the shrew's moving smudge on the snow
to the mole's ineffectual gesture
to the soft hide of the hare
he comes, warming each creature
naked in the fangs of the year.

— Robert Siegel, *In a Pig's Eye*

Incarnate Christ, wherever there is something, you are there, naked in your love, moving to bring about the terrible goodness of this world. Praise be to you! Amen.

December 25

SHE DID

"And she gave birth to her firstborn, a son. She wrapped him in cloths and placed him in a manger, because there was no room for them in the inn." — Luke 2:7-8

scheme of terrible softness
sleepier than her sandals, her home's rafters,
Joseph's beard, any rough child's bed
she had heard of.
. . . .

She did scheme. But some king
blew the bugle that started her down the road
to Bethlehem, and no dream
bore up under that brutal ride.

When she came to the time
where she thought softness waited
the place of her dream had changed, and she laid
her child in the clash and scratch of dirt

but knew what she forgot to scheme
when she looked at that night's humpbacked moon and crazy star:
    that no old dream, no rafters, no ruin matters much when
God needs you to hold his hand. — Jeanne Murray Walker

Incarnate son, who did empty yourself to become a dependent child, you wait for us still to raise you in the world, to be mother and father to your life in the lives of those you seek. Amen.

December 26

THE STORY OF A BEGINNING

"Commit your way to the Lord; trust in him."
—Psalm 37:5

I will put my trust in him.
—Hebrews 2:13

After helping John lie down on the examination table, they waited outside while Dr. Magie listened to John's heart with a cold stethoscope. John opened his eyes to a bright glare from the bulb in the ceiling and heard the clock on the little church's tower chime: 4:00 a.m. The old doctor began to ask him questions in English with only a slight French accent. His voice was calm and assuring. John closed his eyes and suddenly felt more at peace than he had in years. There was something about this doctor that made him feel hopeful and safe. John had no way of knowing that Dr. Magie traveled all over the world lecturing to groups about the emotional and spiritual aspects of physical illness.

The next morning when John woke, the sun was shining brightly through a large window in the white-walled room. For a few minutes he lay still and peacefully listened to the distinctive tick-tocking of a large clock from another part of the house. Then he became aware that Dr. Magie was sitting in a chair by the window, reading. "Ah," the doctor said, "You feel better?"

After they had visited for a few moments, Dr. Magie explained his findings to John. "I can detect nothing wrong with your heart physically.... It seems to me that your problem is not about physical lesions, but perhaps your life—a bigger problem? I have other patients to see now. But if you would like, you can come to my house after supper. We can talk before the fireplace in my study."

That evening as they sat and looked into the dancing flames in the old stone fireplace, John felt that same cozy, safe feeling he'd felt in the doctor's clinic. They now sat in the book-lined study. There was an Oriental rug in front of the hearth, and over the mantel an oil painting of the sun rising over Lake Geneva far below. Dr. Magie was answering John's questions.

They talked for some time about John's life. Finally, Dr. Magie looked up with a kind smile. "You seem to be an intelligent man with great abilities, but you don't appear to have any concrete dreams or goals for your own personal life. When you talk about yourself, I sense a great sadness, as if your heart is breaking because you haven't heard it calling to you to wake up and live for your own dreams."

John nodded his head in agreement. "That's right. When you say that, I know it's true, but I don't even know where to begin to find out what I want to do with my life — even tomorrow."

Dr. Magie looked at John thoughtfully for a few seconds. "For a few moments, John, I want you to play a game with me. We are not talking about your vocation, or your relationships, but what overall state or personal experience you'd like to have as a result of all your efforts. Do you have any idea what that overall hoped-for state is for your personal life?"

John thought for a few seconds, and then said very definitely, "No question — serenity, peace of mind." He laughed. "But I don't have a clue as to how to get it."

"I think I can help you find out," Dr. Magie said quietly. "But you will have to trust. He paused for a few seconds and looked directly at John. "Are you willing to do that?"

—J. Keith Miller, *What to Do with the Rest of Your Life*

Dear Lord, please help me to learn really to trust you — especially when I'm faced with a change, the outcome of which I neither know nor can control. My head wants to commit my way to you, but my fear of failure and of being exposed as inadequate make my heart resist the trusting that I know is the beginning of all new life. Amen.

December 27

JOY IS THE END RESULT

> "The Lord is my strength and my shield,
> my heart trusts in him, and I am helped.
> My heart leaps for joy
> and I will give thanks to him in song."
> —Psalm 28:7

There is something sad in people running from church to church trying to get an injection of "the joy of the Lord." Joy is not found in singing a particular kind of music or in getting with the right kind of group or even in exercising the charismatic gifts of the Spirit, good as all these may be. Joy is found in obedience. When the power that is in Jesus reaches into our work and play and redeems them, there will be joy where once there was mourning. To overlook this is to miss the meaning of the Incarnation.

Joy is the end result of the Spiritual Disciplines' functioning in our lives. God brings about the transformation of our lives through the Disciplines, and we will not know genuine joy until there is a transforming work within us. Many people try to come into joy far too soon. Often we try to pump up people with joy when in reality nothing has happened in their lives. God has not broken into the routine experiences of their daily existence. Celebration comes when the common ventures of life are redeemed. —Richard J. Foster, *Celebration of Discipline*

> *Today, O Lord, I accept your acceptance of me.*
> *I confess that you are always with me and always for me.*
> *I receive into my spirit your grace, your mercy, your care.*
> *I rest in your love, O Lord. I rest in your love.*
> *Amen.*
> —Richard J. Foster, "A Prayer of Accepted Tenderness,"
> in *Prayers from the Heart*

December 28

STAYING TRUE

"We don't take God's Word, water it down, and then take it to the streets to sell cheap. We stand in Christ's presence when we speak; God looks us in the face. We get what we say straight from God and say it as honestly as we can." —2 Corinthians 2:17, THE MESSAGE

Great crowds of people have entered into a grand conspiracy to eliminate prayer, Scripture, and spiritual direction from our lives. They are concerned with our image and standing, with what they can measure, with what produces successful church-building programs and impressive attendance charts, with sociological impact and economic viability. They do their best to fill our schedules with meetings and appointments so that there is time for neither solitude nor leisure to be before God, to ponder Scripture, to be unhurried with another person.

We get both ecclesiastical and community support in conducting a ministry that is inattentive to God and therefore without foundations. Still, that is no excuse. A professional, by some definitions, is someone who is committed to standards of integrity and performance that cannot

be altered to suit people's tastes or what they are willing to pay for. Professionalism is in decline these days on all fronts — in medicine, in law, in politics, as well as among pastors — but it has not yet been repudiated. There are still a considerable number of professionals in all areas of life who do the hard work of staying true to what they were called to do, stubbornly refusing to do the easy work that the age asks of them.
—Eugene H. Peterson, *Working the Angles*

Dear Lord, I seek to be professional in my standards of integrity and performance with regard to my daily work, and my relationship to you. Help me protect my prayer time and Scripture study from the demands for my time that are all around me. In Jesus' name. Amen.

December 29

SPENDING IT ALL

"A bruised reed he will not break,
and a smoldering wick he will not snuff out."
—Isaiah 42:3

On Epiphany Sunday we sing about myrrh, one of the gifts the three kings brought to the infant Messiah. It symbolizes, so the song says, the death to come, hanging over the cradle. A shadow falling around the radiance of the angle chorus.

Mary, the Scripture reading for the day says, kept all these things and pondered them in her heart. The heart, you will remember, that was to be pierced by a sword. Did she tuck away this treasure of the magi with a doubtful smile, keeping it as an heirloom to give her son, along with the strange story, when he grew up and had a home of his own one day? Was this Christmas-present myrrh one of the spices she took to the tomb to anoint her son's body?

Primitive tribes sometimes startle Western missionaries at Christmas by enacting, not the manager scene, but the Crucifixion. In their remarkable capacity for nonlinear thinking, they perceive the entire rondure of the story simultaneously, the end inherent in the beginning. They don't miss the point of the myrrh.

How are we weak-kneed Westerners, who have not the courage to recognize the death impending in the birth, who want to celebrate Christmas and Epiphany as one long season of unrelieved if artificial light, who delete the last verse of Simeon's song and ignore Herod's slaughter of the innocents — how are we ever to face the shadows that aborigines accept so easily? We have no forty-percent mortality rate.

Disease does not bring premature darkness to our eyes. Our crops do not fail. We have never seen anyone starve except in pictures. Our lack of experience puts us at a disadvantage when finally we must face certain stark realities. We do not sleep in our coffins like the Capuchins. And we try to forget the myrrh, sitting there among the gifts like a time bomb. The myrrh is a reproach, a reminder of why the child is there at all, a hostage to death.

How can we bear it? How can we possibly bear it, the dramatic irony of the wise men presenting the gift of death to the newborn God? Why, when we pour from the church, the taste of his blood still in our mouths, why do we love the sound of the bell ringing, long and loud, announcing all over the little town, to the drugstore on the corner, the gas station doing a desultory Sabbath business, the stale odors of the Rustic Pine bar, the steamy interior of the Grub and Tub Washateria, why do our own hearts fly up and out also, like pigeons disturbed from the belfry by sudden joy, flapping and wild with victory?

The Lord is gracious, even to us. I cling to the promise of today's Old Testament lesson; I intend to remind the Lord of it often. "A bruised reed he will not break, and a smoldering wick he will not snuff out." Bruised and smoldering, we need to give thanks while we can. We need to grab the moment with the bell rope and spend it wildly. Quickly.

Do not worry that joy is not now our perpetual state. Be greedy. Snatch it and stuff it away before the dark descends again. It is no less real for being transitory. Feed on it in your heart through the long night when no bell rings. Give thanks while you still have the strength.

—Virginia Stem Owens, *Wind River Winter*

Lord, my heart has been swept away at times by sudden joy, flapping and wild with victory! Thank you for those times. Help me to remember them when I get too serious about my life. I will savor these moments, grabbing them up, and relishing them, for they are gifts from you! In Jesus' name. Amen.

December 30

PRAYERS OF THE PEOPLE FOR EPIPHANY

"On coming to the house, they saw the child with his mother Mary, and they bowed down and worshipped him. Then they opened their treasures and presented him with gifts of gold and of incense and of myrrh. And having been warned in a dream not to go back to Herod, they returned to their country by another route." —Matthew 2:11-12

Dear Christ, who is the great gift,
see us kneeling beside our Lady Mary.
Teach us how to give ourselves back to you.

May we keep this day as keep the saints in heaven,
nimbly remembering, as they remember,
That we were made not for time but for eternity.

Teach us to see beyond the surface,
teach us to touch beyond the tangible,
Teach us to love beyond the body.

Like the wise men broke open the box of myrrh,
Break open this world to your peace.

Give integrity to those who rule,
And give rule to your ministers.

Give joy to those who suffer,
give light to those who blunder,
give patience to those who search,
give us back our sense of surprise at this gentle world.

And may we, like the three wise men,
having made Christ the king of our hearts,
go home by a different way.

—Jeanne Murray Walker

December 31

THE COURSES OF THE AGE ARE HIS

"His ways are eternal."
—Habakkuk 3:6b

Old Years Eve and New Years Day are peculiar, aren't they? Because we come to the end of the calendar, we quite naturally pause and reflect on both what's behind and what we believe is to come. Every year 365 rotations of the earth occur, but only once do we step out of ourselves and take note of time.

The Creator inhabits a whole different world than we do. His ways are eternal. He feels the need for no New Years' resolutions, no "Auld Lang Syne." The I AM bathes himself in eternity. Even though none of us can quite understand what *eternity* means, it's fatal for us to forget that fundamental difference between ourselves and God.

The fact is, he sets the clocks of our lives. He gave us seconds and minutes and hours; he puts the calendars on our walls. The rotation of the earth, the pulse of blood through our arteries, the aging process of our skin — all of it is God-designed. We didn't invent time, but it is our milieu, and it's a whole lot different world than eternity.

And it's a blessing. Even if, however clumsily, only once a year we grab the opportunity to look back and forward through time, that ability to step outside ourselves is a privilege, isn't it? We aren't just creatures of the clock; we can, at least, watch it turn.

But time itself is only a convenience. It isn't real. Time is God-chopped eternity — little divisible chunks, diced up for us. God didn't need it. It's a gimmick he invented for us, and it's not real, not at all.

What is real is eternity — really. What matters, finally, is not time but our destiny; and our destiny is eternal. It's incredibly easy to forget that, isn't it?

Those who judge happiness on the basis of what they have, or get, or can control, are going to discover that what they're after is unadulterated dust. One of his greatest gifts to us is explained in Ecclesiastes 3: "He has set eternity in our hearts." He created us — now listen to this! — with the capacity to lift ourselves up from what's around us and latch onto the eternal. We can do it.

There is a destiny for our lives, and it's a plan designed exclusively for us by none other than God Almighty.

— James Calvin Schaap, *Near Unto God*

We grab at time, Lord. We watch the clock and worry that the best days of our lives will escape us. How foolish we are! Stuck in time, we forget you have made us for eternity. Forgive us and awaken in our hearts the truth that there is no clock we need to fear. Amen.

PERMISSIONS

Jan. 3, Feb. 1, Mar. 17, June 7, June 23, July 8, July 19, Aug. 24, Sept. 2, Dec. 27 excerpts from *Celebration of Discipline: The Path to Spiritual Growth* by Richard J. Foster. Copyright © 1978, 1988, 1998 by Richard J. Foster, LLC. Reprinted by permission of HarperCollins Publishers Inc.

Apr. 22, May 20, Oct. 23, Nov. 23 excerpts from *The Challenge of the Disciplined Life: Christian Reflections on Money, Sex, and Power* by Richard J. Foster. Copyright © 1985 by Richard J. Foster, LLC. Reprinted by permission of HarperCollins Publishers Inc.

Apr. 26, Oct. 8, Nov. 3, Nov. 13 excerpts from *Freedom of Simplicity* by Richard J. Foster, LLC. Copyright © 1981 by Richard J. Foster, LLC. Reprinted by permission of HarperCollins Publishers Inc.

Jan. 16, Feb. 21, Mar. 23, May 6, Aug. 8, Sept. 18, Dec. 8 excerpts from *Prayer: Finding the Heart's True Home* by Richard J. Foster. Copyright © 1992 by Richard J. Foster, LLC. Reprinted by permission of HarperCollins Publishers Inc.

Feb. 1, May 6, June 7, June 23, July 8, Aug. 24, Sept. 2, Oct. 8, Oct. 23, Dec. 27 excerpts from *Prayers from the Heart* by Richard J. Foster. Copyright © 1994 by Richard J. Foster, LLC. Reprinted by permission of HarperCollins Publishers Inc.

Nov. 13 excerpt from *Showings* by Julian of Norwich, copyright © 1978 by Paulist Press, Inc., New York/Mahwah, N.J. Used with permission of Paulist Press.

Nov. 3 excerpt by J. N. Grou as quoted in *The Ways of the Spirit* by Evelyn Underhill. Copyright © 1990 by Evelyn Underhill Trust; used by permission of The Crossroad Publishing Company.

Nov. 28, Dec. 20 excerpts from *Clinging: The Experience of Prayer* by Emilie Griffin. Copyright © 2003 by Emilie Griffin. Reprinted by permission of Emilie Griffin.

Jan. 29, Apr. 30, May 24, June 30, July 30, Aug. 11 excerpts from *Homeward Voyage: Reflections on Life's Changes* by Emilie Griffin. Copyright © 1994 by Emilie Griffin. Reprinted by permission of Emilie Griffin.

Feb. 24 excerpt reprinted by permission of Emilie Griffin.

Oct. 27 excerpt from *Radix Magazine* 27, no. 2 (Spring 2002). Copyright © 2002 by Emilie Griffin. Reprinted by permission of Emilie Griffin.

Mar. 19, Sept. 3 excerpts from *The High Calling of Our Daily Work* (www.thehighcalling.org). Copyright © 2002 by Emilie Griffin. Reprinted by permission of Emilie Griffin.

Apr. 10, June 14, July 12, Aug. 26, Oct. 13, Nov. 12, Dec. 10 excerpts from *C. S. Lewis: Spirituality for Mere Christians* by H. William Griffin. Copyright © 1998 by Henry William Griffin. Reprinted by permission of H. William Griffin.

Sept. 11 excerpt from *Image: A Journal of the Arts & Religion* 32 (Fall 2001). Copyright © 2001 by Henry William Griffin. Reprinted by permission of H. William Griffin.

Jan. 13 excerpt from *The High Calling of Our Daily Work* (www.thehighcalling.org). Copyright © 2002 by Henry William Griffin. Reprinted by permission of H. William Griffin.

May 7 excerpt from *The High Calling of Our Daily Work* (www.thehighcalling.org). Copyright © 2003 by Henry William Griffin. Reprinted by permission of H. William Griffin.

Feb. 11, Mar. 10 excerpts printed by permission of H. William Griffin.

Apr. 7, May 12, July 15, July 24, Dec. 13 excerpts from *Country Labors* by John Leax. Copyright © 1991 by John Leax. Reprinted by permission of John Leax.

Jan. 28, June 16, June 27, Sept. 28 excerpts from *Grace Is Where I Live: Writing As a Christian Vocation* by John Leax. Copyright © 1993 by John Leax. Reprinted by permission of John Leax.

Jan. 1, Feb. 20, Mar. 7, Apr. 4, May 22, Sept. 20, Nov. 22, Dec. 5 excerpts from *In Season and Out* by John Leax. Copyright © 1985 by John R. Leax. Reprinted by permission of John Leax.

Jan. 15, Feb. 28, Mar. 20, Mar. 24, July 29, Aug. 22, Oct. 28, Nov. 30 excerpts from *Standing Ground: A Story of Faith and Environmentalism* by John Leax. Copyright © 1991 by John Leax. Reprinted by permission of John Leax.

Jan. 22, Feb. 10, May 8, Oct. 18, Nov. 17, Dec. 18 excerpts from *The Task of Adam* by John Leax. Copyright © 1985 by John R. Leax. Reprinted by permission of John Leax.

Mar. 31, Apr. 12, May 1, June 4, July 6, Aug. 2, Aug. 12, Sept. 5, Sept. 8, Oct. 31, Nov. 7 excerpts printed by permission of John Leax.

Jan. 27 excerpt from *A House Like a Lotus* by Madeleine L'Engle. Copyright © 1984 by Madeleine L'Engle. Reprinted by permission of Farrar, Straus and Giroux, LLC.

Nov. 29 excerpt from *A Live Coal in the Sea* by Madeleine L'Engle. Copyright © 1996 by Crosswicks, Ltd. Reprinted by permission of Farrar, Straus and Giroux, LLC.

Feb. 12 excerpt from *A Ring of Endless Light* by Madeleine L'Engle. Copyright © 1980 by Crosswicks, Ltd. Reprinted by permission of Farrar, Straus and Giroux, LLC.

Feb. 2 excerpt from *A Severed Wasp* by Madeleine L'Engle. Copyright © 1983 by Crosswicks. Ltd. Reprinted by permission of Farrar, Straus and Giroux, LLC.

Mar. 4 excerpt reprinted from *A Stone for a Pillow* by Madeleine L'Engle. Copyright © 1986 by Crosswicks, Ltd. Used by permission of WaterBrook Press, Colorado Springs, Colo. All rights reserved.

Mar. 15 excerpt from *A Wind In the Door* by Madeleine L'Engle. Copyright © 1973 by Crosswicks, Ltd. Reprinted by permission of Farrar, Straus and Giroux, LLC.

Mar. 25 excerpt from *A Wrinkle in Time* by Madeleine L'Engle. Copyright © 1962, renewed 1990 by Madeleine L'Engle Franklin. Reprinted by permission of Farrar, Straus and Giroux, LLC.

Apr. 25 excerpt from *An Acceptable Time* by Madeleine L'Engle. Copyright © 1989 by Crosswicks, Ltd. Reprinted by permission of Farrar, Straus and Giroux, LLC.

Oct. 30 excerpt reprinted from *And It Was Good* by Madeleine L'Engle. Copyright © 1983 by Crosswicks, Ltd. Used by permission of WaterBrook Press, Colorado Springs, Colo. All rights reserved.

Sept. 13 excerpt from *Camilla* by Madeleine L'Engle, copyright © 1965 by Crosswicks Ltd. Used by permission of Dell Publishing, a division of Random House, Inc.

Apr. 6 excerpt from *Certain Women* by Madeleine L'Engle. Copyright © 1992 by Madeleine L'Engle. Reprinted by permission of Farrar, Straus and Giroux, LLC.

May 4 excerpt from *Dance In the Desert* by Madeleine L'Engle. Copyright © 1969 by Madeleine L'Engle. Reprinted by permission of Farrar, Straus and Giroux, LLC.

May 25 excerpt from *Dragons In the Waters* by Madeleine L'Engle. Copyright © 1976 by Crosswicks, Ltd. Reprinted by permission of Farrar, Straus and Giroux, LLC.

June 28 excerpt from *Many Waters* by Madeleine L'Engle. Copyright © 1986 by Crosswicks, Ltd. Reprinted by permission of Farrar, Straus and Giroux, LLC.

Jan. 6 excerpt from *Meet the Austins* by Madeleine L'Engle. Copyright © 1997 by Crosswicks, Ltd. Reprinted by permission of Farrar, Straus and Giroux, LLC.

May 14, June 13 excerpts reprinted from *Penguins and Golden Calves* by Madeleine L'Engle. Copyright © 1996 and 2003 by Crosswicks, Ltd. Used by permission of WaterBrook Press, Colorado Springs, Colo. All rights reserved.

July 21 excerpt reprinted from *Sold into Egypt* by Madeleine L'Engle. Copyright © 1989 by Crosswicks, Ltd. Used by permission of WaterBrook Press, Colorado Springs, Colo. All rights reserved.

July 11 excerpt reprinted with the permission of Simon & Schuster Books for Young Readers, an imprint of Simon & Schuster Children's Publishing Division from *The Glorious Impossible* by Madeleine L'Engle. Copyright © 1990 Crosswicks Ltd.

July 1 excerpt from *The Irrational Season* by Madeleine L'Engle. Copyright © 1977 by Crosswicks, Ltd. Reprinted by permission of HarperCollins Publishers Inc.

Aug. 6 excerpt from *The Love Letters* by Madeleine L'Engle. Copyright © 1966, renewed 1994 by Madeleine L'Engle. Reprinted by permission of Farrar, Straus and Giroux, LLC.

Nov. 18 excerpt from *The Other Side of the Sun* by Madeleine L'Engle. Copyright © 1971 by Madeleine L'Engle. Reprinted by permission of Farrar, Straus and Giroux, LLC.

Aug. 27 excerpt reprinted from *The Rock That Is Higher* by Madeleine L'Engle. Copyright © 1993 by Crosswicks, Ltd. Used by permission of WaterBrook Press, Colorado Springs, Colo. All rights reserved.

Sept. 23 excerpt from *The Summer of the Great-Grandmother* by Madeleine L'Engle. Copyright © 1974 by Crosswicks, Ltd. Reprinted by permission of Farrar, Straus and Giroux, LLC.

Apr. 16 excerpt from *The Young Unicorns* by Madeleine L'Engle. Copyright © 1968 by Madeleine L'Engle. Reprinted by permission of Farrar, Straus and Giroux, LLC.

Oct. 20 excerpt from *Troubling a Star* by Madeleine L'Engle. Copyright © 1994 by Crosswicks, Ltd. Reprinted by permission of Farrar, Straus and Giroux, LLC.

Aug. 16, Dec. 11 excerpts from *Two-Part Invention* by Madeleine L'Engle. Copyright © 1988 by Crosswicks, Ltd. Reprinted by permission of Farrar, Straus and Giroux, LLC.

June 2, Nov. 8, Dec. 6 excerpts reprinted from *Walking on Water* by Madeleine L'Engle. Copyright © 1980, 1998, and 2001 by Crosswicks, Ltd. Used by permission of WaterBrook Press, Colorado Springs, Colo. All rights reserved.

Feb. 23 excerpt from *With the Angels in Lent*. Copyright © 1996 by Madeleine L'Engle. Reprinted by permission of Madeleine L'Engle.

Jan. 26, Feb. 29, Mar. 12, Apr. 28, May 10, May 30, June 18, July 7, Aug. 3, Aug. 18, Sept. 10, Sept. 24, Oct. 15, Nov. 14, Dec. 3 excerpts from *BodyCare* by Andrea Wells Miller. Copyright © 1984 by Andrea Wells Miller. Reprinted by permission of Andrea Wells Miller.

Mar. 27, July 14, Nov. 24 excerpts from *The Single Experience* by Andrea Wells Miller and Keith Miller. Copyright © 1981 by Andrea Wells Miller and Keith Miller. Reprinted by permission of Andrea Wells Miller and Keith Miller.

Mar. 29, May 02, May 13 excerpts from *A Second Touch* by Keith Miller. Copyright © 1967 by Keith Miller. Reprinted by permission of Keith Miller.

Feb. 15, June 8, June 26, Sept. 1, Nov. 1 excerpts from *Compelled to Control* by J. Keith Miller. Copyright © 1992, 1997 by J. Keith Miller. Reprint permission from Health Communications, Inc.

Jan. 20, Nov. 15 excerpts from *CrossPoint Magazine* (Fall 1995 and Fall 1996). Copyright © 1995, 1996 by J. Keith Miller. Reprinted by permission of Cross Point.

Mar. 5, Apr. 13, Apr. 23, May 26, July 25 excerpts from *Daily Guideposts*. Copyright © 1996 by J. Keith Miller. Reprinted by permission of J. Keith Miller.

Dec. 19 excerpt from *Daily Guideposts*. Copyright © 1998 by J. Keith Miller. Reprinted by permission of J. Keith Miller.

Mar. 13, July 10, Aug. 7, Aug. 23, Oct. 14, Dec. 26 excerpts from *Habitation of Dragons* by Keith Miller. Copyright © 1992 by Keith Miller. Reprinted by permission of Keith Miller.

Jan. 5, Aug. 19 excerpts from *Highway Home Through Texas* by Keith Miller. Copyright © 1993 by Keith Miller. Reprinted by permission of Keith Miller.

Jan. 17, Sept. 25 excerpts from *The Becomers* by Keith Miller. Copyright © 1973 by Keith Miller. Reprinted by permission of Keith Miller.

Nov. 5 excerpt from *The Dream* by Keith Miller. Copyright © 1985 by Keith Miller. Reprinted by permission of Keith Miller.

Sept. 16, Oct. 25, Dec. 7 excerpts from *The Single Experience* by Andrea Wells Miller and Keith Miller. Copyright © 1981 by Andrea Wells Miller and Keith Miller. Reprinted by permission of the Andrea Wells Miller and Keith Miller.

Feb. 8 excerpt from *Witness* (Sum. 1985). Copyright © 1985 by Keith Miller. Reprinted by permission of Keith Miller.

Oct. 9 excerpt printed by permission of J. Keith Miller.

June 10 excerpt from *Fair, Clear and Terrible: The Story of Shiloh, Maine* by Shirley Nelson. Copyright © 1989 by Shirley Nelson. Reprinted by permission of Shirley Nelson.

Dec. 22 excerpt from *Once Upon a Christmas*, "The Secret Stair" by Shirley Nelson. Copyright © 1993 by The Chrysostom Society. Reprinted by permission of The Chrysostom Society.

July 16, Aug. 14 excerpts with minor alterations from *Rattling Those Dry Bones: Women Changing the Church,* compiled by June Steffensen Hagen, "Prospecting" by Shirley Nelson. Copyright © 1995 by June Hagen. Reprinted by permission of Shirley Nelson.

Nov. 2 excerpt from *Stories for the Christian Year*, "All Souls" by Shirley Nelson. Copyright © 1992 by The Chrysostom Society. Reprinted by permission of The Chrysostom Society.

Oct. 3 excerpt from *The Last Year of the War* by Shirley Nelson. Copyright © 1989 by Shirley Nelson. Reprinted by permission of Shirley Nelson.

Jan. 23, Feb. 14, Mar. 21, Apr. 30, May 31, Sept. 6 excerpts printed by permission of Shirley Nelson.

Apr. 3, July 18, July 28 reprinted from *A Taste of Creation* by Virginia Stem Owens, copyright © 1980 by Judson Press. Used by permission of Judson Press, 800-4-JUDSON, www.judsonpress.com.

Mar. 30, May 5, June 9, Aug. 13, Sept. 27 copied from *Daughters of Eve* by Virginia Stem Owens, copyright © 1995. Used by permission of NavPress – www.navpress.com. All rights reserved.

Jan. 10, Jan. 25, Feb. 3, Mar. 2, Mar. 16, May 17, June 19, Aug. 20, Sept. 4, Sept. 15, Oct. 7, Oct. 16, Nov. 10, Nov. 25, Dec. 14 excerpts from *God Spy* by Virginia Stem Owens. Copyright © 1988 by Virginia Stem Owens. Reprinted by permission of Virginia Stem Owens.

Feb. 18, Apr. 17, May 28, Oct. 26, Dec. 29 excerpts from *Wind River Winter* by Virginia Stem Owens. Copyright © 2001 by Virginia Stem Owens. Used by permission of Virginia Stem Owens.

Jan. 11, June 6 excerpts from *A Long Obedience in the Same Direction* by Eugene H. Peterson. Copyright © 2000 by Eugene H. Peterson. Reprinted by permission of InterVarsity Press.

Feb. 22 excerpt from *Answering God: The Psalms as Tools for Prayer* by Eugene H. Peterson. Copyright © 1989 by Eugene H. Peterson. Reprinted by permission of HarperCollins Publishers Inc.

June 15 excerpt from *Christianity Today* (Oct. 1977). Copyright © by Eugene H. Peterson. Reprinted by permission of Eugene H. Peterson.

Apr. 1, May 15, Aug. 10 excerpts from *Earth & Altar/Where Your Treasure Is* by Eugene H. Peterson. Copyright © 1993 by Eugene H. Peterson. Reprinted by permission of Wm. B. Eerdmans Publishing Company.

Mar. 28, Sept. 30 excerpts from *Five Smooth Stones for Pastoral Work* by Eugene H. Peterson. Copyright © 1992 by Eugene H. Peterson. Reprinted by permission of Wm. B. Eerdmans Publishing Company.

Aug. 21 excerpt from *Leadership Magazine* (Sum. 1991). Copyright © 1991 by Eugene H. Peterson. Reprinted by permission of Eugene H. Peterson.

Nov. 21 excerpt from *Like Dew Your Youth* by Eugene H. Peterson. Copyright © 1994 by Eugene H. Peterson. Reprinted by permission of Wm. B. Eerdmans Publishing Company.

May 29 excerpt from *Praying with Jesus* by Eugene H. Peterson. Copyright © 1993 by Eugene H. Peterson. Reprinted by permission of HarperCollins Publishers Inc.

July 2 excerpt from *Psalms: Prayers of the Heart* by Eugene H. Peterson. Copyright © 2000 by Eugene H. Peterson. Reprinted by permission of InterVarsity Press.

Feb. 6, July 17 excerpts from *Reversed Thunder* by Eugene H. Peterson. Copyright © 1988 by Eugene H. Peterson. Reprinted by permission of HarperCollins Publishers Inc.

Mar. 14 excerpt from *Run with the Horses* by Eugene H. Peterson. Copyright © 1983 by Eugene H. Peterson. Reprinted by permission of InterVarsity Press.

Apr. 19, Oct. 5 excerpts from *Subversive Spirituality* by Eugene H. Peterson. Copyright © 1997 by Eugene H. Peterson. Reprinted by permission of Wm. B. Eerdmans Publishing Company.

Nov. 11 excerpt from *The Contemplative Pastor* by Eugene H. Peterson. Copyright © 1993 by Eugene H. Peterson. Reprinted by permission of Wm. B. Eerdmans Publishing Company.

Feb. 27, Apr. 24, June 25, Aug. 30, Oct. 12, Dec. 21 excerpts from *The Message*. Copyright © 1993, 1994, 1995, 1996, 2000, 2001, 2002 by Eugene H. Peterson. Used by permission of NavPress Publishing Group.

Oct. 22 excerpt from *Traveling Light* by Eugene H. Peterson. Copyright © 1989 by Eugene H. Peterson. Reprinted by permission of Helmers & Howard.

Jan. 2, Jan. 21, Sept. 12 excerpt from *Under the Unpredictable Planet* by Eugene H. Peterson. Copyright © 1994 by Eugene H. Peterson. Reprinted by permission of Wm. B. Eerdmans Publishing Company.

Dec. 28 excerpt from *Working the Angles* by Eugene H. Peterson. Copyright © 1990 by Eugene H. Peterson. Reprinted by permission of Wm. B. Eerdmans Publishing Company.

Jan. 8, Jan. 19, Jan. 30, Feb. 5, Feb. 16, Feb. 25, Mar. 9, Mar. 22, Apr. 18, Apr. 27, Apr. 29, May 9, May 27, June 1, June 11, June 21, July 3, July 20, Aug. 5, Aug. 15, Aug. 28, Sept. 19, Sept. 29, Oct. 2, Oct. 11, Oct. 21, Nov. 4, Nov. 20, Dec. 9, Dec. 31 excerpts from *Near Unto God* by James Calvin Schaap. Copyright © 1997 by James Calvin Schaap. Reprinted by permission of CRC Publications.

Jan. 14, Feb. 13, Mar. 3, May 23, June 29, July 31, Aug. 25, Sept. 26, Oct. 24, Nov. 26, Dec. 4, Dec. 12, Dec. 17 excerpts from *God in the Dark* by Luci Shaw. Copyright © 2000 by Luci Shaw. Reprinted by permission of Luci Shaw.

Jan. 9, Jan. 24, Jan. 31, Feb. 4, Mar. 11, Mar. 18, Mar. 26, Apr. 2, Apr. 8, Apr. 11, Apr. 15, May 3, May 11, May 19, June 3, June 12, June 20, July 5, July 13, July 23, Aug. 1, Aug. 9,

Aug. 17, Sept. 7, Sept. 17, Oct. 4, Oct. 10, Oct. 17, Nov. 6, Nov. 16, Dec. 23 excerpts from *Horizons: Exploring Creation* by Luci Shaw. Copyright © 1992 by Luci Shaw. Reprinted by permission of Luci Shaw.

Feb. 26 excerpt printed by permission of Luci Shaw.

Jan. 12, Mar. 8, Apr. 20, May 21, July 27, Oct. 1, Dec. 24 excerpts from *In a Pig's Eye* by Robert Siegel. Copyright © 1985 by Robert Siegel. Reprinted by permission of Robert Siegel.

Aug. 29 excerpt from *Made for Each Other: Reflections on the Opposite Sex* compiled by Michele Guiness. Copyright © 1996 by Robert Siegel. Reprinted by permission of Robert Siegel.

Sept. 21 excerpt from *The Beasts and the Elders* by Robert Siegel. Copyright © 1973 by Robert Siegel. Reprinted by permission of Robert Siegel.

Nov. 9 excerpt from *The Cresset: A Review of Literature, Art and Public Affairs.* Copyright © 1993 by Robert Siegel. Reprinted by permission of Robert Siegel.

Feb. 9 excerpt from *Whalesong* by Robert Siegel. Copyright © 1981 by Robert Siegel. Reprinted by permission of HarperCollins Publishers Inc.

June 17 excerpt printed by permission of Robert Siegel.

Dec. 16 excerpt from *Christian Century.* Copyright © by Jeanne Murray Walker. Reprinted by permission of Jeanne Murray Walker.

July 9 excerpt from *Cortland Review* (www.cortlandreview.com) no. 16. Copyright © Jeanne Murray Walker. Reprinted by permission of Jeanne Murray Walker.

Apr. 9, Nov. 27 excerpts from *Fugitive Angels* by Jeanne Murray Walker. Copyright © 1985 by Jeanne Murray Walker. Reprinted by permission of Dragon Gate Press.

Mar. 6, May 18, July 26, Aug. 31, Sept. 14, Oct. 29 excerpts from *Gaining Time* by Jeanne Murray Walker. Copyright © 1997 by Jeanne Murray Walker. Reprinted by permission of Copper Beech Press.

Jan. 7, Feb. 19, June 24, Dec. 1, Dec. 25, Dec. 30 excerpts printed by permission of Jeanne Murray Walker.

Jan. 18, Apr. 5, May 16, July 4, Sept. 22, Oct. 6, Oct. 19, Dec. 15 excerpts from *Disappointment with God* – softcover by Philip Yancey. Copyright © 1988 by Philip Yancey. Used by permission of The Zondervan Corporation.

Apr. 14, June 5, Aug. 4, Sept. 9, Dec. 2 excerpts from *A Guided Tour of the Bible* by Philip D. Yancey. Copyright © 1989 by Philip Yancey. Used by permission of The Zondervan Corporation.

Feb. 7 excerpt from *The Student Bible – NIV* by The Zondervan Corporation. Copyright © 1986 by The Zondervan Corporation. Used by permission of The Zondervan Corporation.

Feb. 17, Nov. 19 excerpts from *What They Never Told Me When I Became a Christian* by Verne Becker, Tim Stafford, and Philip Yancey. Copyright © 1986, 1991 by Campus Life Books, a Division of CTi. Reprinted by permission of The Zondervan Corporation.

Jan. 4, Mar. 1, June 22, July 22 excerpts from *Where Is God When It Hurts?* – Hardcover by Philip D. Yancey. Copyright © 1977, 1990 by Philip Yancey. Used by permission of The Zondervan Corporation.

ABOUT THE CONTRIBUTORS

RICHARD J. FOSTER is the founder and president of Renovaré (an effort working for the renewal of the Church of Jesus Christ in all its multifaceted expressions) based in Denver, Colorado, where he and Carolynn live. He is the author of *Celebration of Discipline, Prayer: Finding the Heart's True Home,* and *Streams of Living Water.*

EMILIE GRIFFIN, after working in New York as an advertising executive, returned to her home state, Louisiana, with her husband, William. Her books on conversion and prayer include *Turning: Reflections on the Experience of Conversion, Clinging: The Experience of Prayer,* and *Doors into Prayer: An Invitation.*

WILLIAM GRIFFIN worked as an editor for Macmillan and Harcourt in New York City before moving to Louisiana with his wife, Emilie. As a free-lance writer he has worked on biographies of C. S. Lewis, Billy Graham, and G. K. Chesterton and has translated Latin works by Thomas à Kempis and Augustine of Hippo.

JOHN LEAX finds time to write poetry and prose in addition to teaching at Houghton College, Houghton, New York, and participating in environmental issues. *Country Labors, Standing Ground: A Story of Faith and Environmentalism, Grace is Where I Live,* and *The Task of Adam* are among his titles.

MADELEINE L'ENGLE, a long-time resident of New York City and Connecticut, has written more than fifty books that cover many genres: fantasy (*A Swiftly Tilting Planet*), poetry (*A Cry Like a Bell*), essays (*Walking on Water*), and biography (*Two-Part Invention*). She received the Newbery Award for *A Wrinkle in Time.*

ANDREA WELLS MILLER worked for Word Music, Inc., in Waco, Texas, for many years and now lives with her husband, J. Keith Miller, in Austin. She has collaborated with Pia Mellody, Richard D. Grant, Jr., and J. Keith Miller on books and is the author of *BodyCare: A Proven Program for Successful Diet, Fitness, and Health.*

J. KEITH MILLER's resume lists basketball player, businessman, founding director of Laity Lodge, poet, and speaker along with authorship of over twenty books. Keith is a graduate of Oklahoma University and holds graduate degrees from Earlham School of Religion (Theology) and the University of Texas (Psychology) in Austin, Texas, where he lives with his wife, Andrea Wells Miller. *The Taste of New Wine* and *The Edge of Adventure* (with Bruce Larson) are his best-known books.

SHIRLEY NELSON wrote the novel *The Last Year of the War* and the narrative history of a nineteenth-century cult, *Fair, Clear, and Terrible: The Story of Shiloh, Maine.* Rudy and Shirley live in Albany, New York, where they recently produced a video entitled *Precarious Peace* on the peace movement in Guatemala.

VIRGINIA STEM OWENS, a native of Texas, writes fiction and nonfiction. She received an award for a book about her father, *If You Do Love Old Men,* while her latest work, *Living Next Door to the Death House,* focuses on capital punishment at a Texas Department of Criminal Justice Prison in Huntsville, which is near her and David's home.

EUGENE H. PETERSON was the pastor of a Maryland church for three decades and is professor emeritus of spiritual theology at Regent College, Vancouver, British Columbia. His writing projects include *The Message,* a translation/paraphrase of the Bible, and books on spiritual formation. Eugene and Jan live near Lakeside, Montana.

JAMES CALVIN SCHAAP is the author of short story collections, novels (the most recent being *Touches the Sky*), devotional books, and a variety of nonfiction works. Living in Sioux Center, Iowa, with his wife, Barbara, Jim has received awards from the Evangelical Press Association and Associated Religious Press.

LUCI SHAW is writer-in-residence at Regent College, Vancouver, British Columbia. A poet, essayist, and author of twenty-five books, she is a frequent speaker, retreat facilitator, and writing workshop leader in church and university settings. She and her husband, John Hoyte, live in Bellingham, Washington.

ROBERT SIEGEL's book of poems, *In a Pig's Eye,* is a fitting follow-up to his well-known prose piece, *Whale Song.* His poems have won *Poetry*'s Glatstine Prize and fellowships from Bread Loaf, the Ingram Merrill Foundation, and the National Endowment for the Arts. Robert and Anne live in South Berwick, Maine.

JEANNE MURRAY WALKER teaches at the University of Delaware and writes poetry, prose, and plays. Her plays have been produced in Boston, Washington, Chicago, and London. Among her awards Jeanne lists National Endowment for the Arts and Pew Fellowships. She lives in Merion, Pennsylvania, with her husband, Dan Larkin.

PHILIP YANCEY, former editor of *Campus Life,* now writes regularly for *Christianity Today* as editor-at-large. His numerous books include *Where Is God When It Hurts?* which was reprinted immediately after 9/11, and *Fearfully and Wonderfully Made.* Residing in Evergreen, Colorado, Janet and Philip love to ski and explore.

ACKNOWLEDGMENTS

Assembling this astonishing sampler of inspired writings by such exceptional and committed communicators has been a life-changing experience. The process of choosing selections, writing many prayers, providing accompanying scriptures, and arranging them all within the calendar year enfolded me in a warm, soul-satisfying quilt of spiritual companionship.

Although I did not fully understand the enormity of the project when I began, God provided an outstanding team of people to help me put it together. The unstinting generosity of the other fourteen contributors, not only with their writing, but with their responsiveness to my endless questions, and their caring, prayerful encouragement, has made the complexity of the project bearable.

A new level of respect and affection was born in me toward Lynda Graybeal as we worked our way through the many details involved in this project. I am particularly grateful for her patience, knowledge, expertise, and stamina—all of which were needed to organize and gather the permissions.

The significance of the steady support and confidence I received from Roy M. Carlisle, Senior Editor of Crossroad Carlisle Books, cannot be measured. I pulled back from the precipice of panic more than once because of his support. The careful attention to detail and encouragement from John Eagleson, editor, designer, and typesetter, has been a joy to experience. His watchfulness allowed many imperfections to come to my attention for correction. Any that remain are my responsibility, not his.

The loving support, patience, counsel, and praise from my husband, Keith, carried me through days and nights of intense focus. My heart overflows with joy and gratitude that he is in my life.

ANDREA WELLS MILLER

SCRIPTURE INDEX

Genesis
1:26a	February 16
1:27	May 19
	November 25
1:31a, 2:15	October 8
2:16–17	November 8
2:21–23	June 24
3:19	September 5
9:2	April 12
9:13, 15	January 9

Exodus
2:21–22	October 26
3:14–15	February 19
5:17–18	August 2
16:2–3	June 30
16:12b	July 24

Leviticus
17:11	April 15
26:12	August 28

Deuteronomy
4:9a	November 12
4:29	June 7
6:5a	April 27
6:5b	May 27
7:6, 8	August 1
8:13–14	February 7
30:19	January 27
33:11	November 27

Joshua
4:2–3	July 9

1 Samuel
2:1	February 24
18:1, 4	November 28

1 Kings
19:12	September 8

1 Chronicles
16:33–34	March 7
29:18b	February 14

Job
10:12	June 21
22:21	November 20
36:22–26a	August 12
37:14–15	August 9
38:1–2	December 18
38:16	July 5
39:10	May 4
40:6–9	June 22
42:1–6	January 18

Psalms
1:3a	September 20
3:4	January 13
4:1	December 21
4:8	October 28
5:4–6	March 20
6:2	August 6
8:3–5	January 31
8:4–6a	May 22
12	April 24
16:1	October 29
17:6–7	May 15
18:29b	September 19
19:1–2	August 17
22:2a	August 5
22:20	February 5
23:1–2	June 17
23:2b	April 18
25:9	October 23
25:15a	September 29
27:14	August 8
28:7	December 27
31:14	July 14
32:8	February 26
34:8	May 1
36:9	March 25
37:5	December 26
43:4	October 21
46:10	August 25
51:10–11	May 28
51:17	January 24
62:1	December 8
73:28a	January 19

Psalms (continued)

84:11a	February 25
86:11	July 23
89:46	October 4
91:11–12	March 19
100:1–2	April 20
100:4	November 23
100:5	November 29
102:6–8a	November 17
103:1	March 16
103:11–12	July 2
104:33	August 27
113:5–6	June 11
116:1a	April 29
116:12–14	February 22
118:27	November 26
119:11	August 18
119:103	May 5
119:176	March 22
121:5	November 4
124:1–3	June 6
126:4–6	January 11
130:5	September 26
130:5–6	March 24
135:3–4	June 29
136:24	May 25
139:1–3, 13–15	May 10
139:11–12	January 14
139:16	March 14
145:17	January 1
139:9a	September 14
143:9b	July 20
145:9	July 1

Proverbs

3:5–8	March 12
18:9	March 21
18:21	January 2
19:8	October 16
25:11–12	October 5
29:18	May 8
30:24–28	November 16

Ecclesiastes

1:2	December 10
2:24	July 6
3:1, 10–11	February 13

Song of Solomon

3:4	December 20

Isaiah

6:4–5, 8–10	November 5
10:1–3	September 3

Isaiah (continued)

12:2	April 16
	November 24
30:21	May 6
35:5–8a	August 19
40:28	March 2
40:31	January 12
	July 7
42:3	December 29
42:16	July 31
43:1–2	March 4
45:3a	July 26
45:12	January 6
45:18	February 3
46:4	August 31
52:7a	January 23
52:10	May 3
53:4	March 28
54:7–8	October 6
55:12	October 7
56:7	September 13
66:2	February 1

Jeremiah

9:10	November 30

Ezekiel

11:19–20	December 12
37:5	May 18

Daniel

10:5, 7–8	October 19

Jonah

4:1–3	October 31

Habakkuk

3:6b	December 31

Zechariah

4:6b	March 18
9:9	July 25

Malachi

3:17–18	June 5

Matthew

2:3–4	December 16
2:11–12	December 30
3:10	December 13
4:1	October 24
4:4	June 18
4:16	February 9
5:1–11	February 27
5:8	October 11

Matthew (continued)

5:36–37	August 30
5:45b	May 7
5:48	May 31
6:5–6	July 19
6:6	February 17
6:9b	June 1
6:21	July 16
6:22	September 4
6:24	September 16
6:28–29	October 1
6:34	June 16
7:1, 3	June 26
11:2–3	April 17
11:25	August 20
11:27	July 3
11:28–29	February 21
12:18	September 27
13:2–3, 9	June 4
13:10–13	November 11
13:16	October 10
13:17	July 13
13:45–46	April 30
14:23	August 24
14:29b–30	January 5
15:28	February 23
16:24	January 29
17:20	July 12
18:3	June 12
18:21–22	January 20
21:12	April 23
21:28–31	February 11
23:27a	September 1
23:37	May 12
	July 4
25:37–40	November 15
25:40	December 7
25:45	May 26
26:31–32	April 2
26:39	March 5
26:40	February 11
26:42b	May 9
28:20	June 20
	August 16

Mark

1:6–8	February 10
1:35–38	April 1
3:32–35	October 25
4:22	September 14
4:39	October 9
9:24	January 17
9:36, 10:15	December 14
9:37	March 29
10:6–9	June 15

Mark (continued)

10:42–45	August 23
14:22–24	April 11
15:33–34	April 14

Luke

1:46–48	December 2
1:51–53	August 11
2:7–8	December 25
2:12	December 22
2:25–26	December 1
8:4, 8	July 30
8:16	October 17
10:23–24	July 18
10:38–42	March 30
11:1	March 27
11:1b	December 9
15:4, 6b	August 22
16:12	September 6
16:14–15	August 4
18:16	February 8
18:25	September 15
19:37, 39–40	May 21
20:38	January 7
21:2–4	May 20
23:42–43	April 4
23:49	April 13
24:28b–31a	April 7
24:39	May 18

John

1:3	August 29
1:3–4	April 8
1:45–46	August 21
3:8	February 18
4:13–14	July 15
8:6b–7	March 10
8:31–32	September 24
9:3	July 22
10:3	March 8
11:31	June 9
12:3	August 13
13:3–5	July 8
13:8–9	August 7
13:34	June 13
14:18	December 19
14:18–19	March 13
16:13	May 23
16:20, 22	December 23
17:3a	March 9
17:9	May 29
12:3	August 13
18:2	March 31
18:37	April 3
	September 23

Acts
6:4	June 2
28:23–24	November 19

Romans
1:20	December 17
5:3–5	April 5
	November 14
5:8	March 28
7:15, 24–25a	July 10
8:19	July 28
8:20–21	December 24
8:24–25	January 22
8:26	June 14
	December 11
8:28	September 11
11:33–34a	July 27
12:1	April 28
12:2	March 17
12:12	October 13
12:21	July 29
13:12a	January 8
14:4	November 1

1 Corinthians
1:25	September 17
1:26–28	September 12
2:12	March 3
3:9	July 21
6:19–20	May 30
7:7	January 30
10:13	September 10
12:12	August 14
13:4–6	October 27
15:17–19	April 9
15:19	November 2
15:42	February 20
15:51–52	June 3
	September 9
15:58	November 7

2 Corinthians
1:5–7	March 23
1:21–22	May 16
2:17	December 28
3:17	June 3
3:18	May 14
	November 6
4:7	December 6
6:8–10	October 3
9:6–7	October 15
9:7	April 22
10:12	May 13
12:9	February 29
12:9a	June 8

Galatians
1:8	October 22
2:20	June 19
5:22–23	July 11
6:1	August 26
6:2	February 2

Ephesians
2:4b–7	November 22
2:8	January 1
2:12	August 15
2:13–14	May 2
2:17–18	November 21
3:16–19	March 26
4:15, 26a	February 15
4:15–16	September 25
5:2	March 15
5:13–17	January 10

Philippians
1:6	October 20
	December 4
1:21	January 25
2:2–3	October 18
2:3	January 16
	April 21
2:5–8	October 14
3:8	August 10
4:8	December 3
4:13	January 26
	June 8

Colossians
1:9	June 23
1:15, 19	May 11
1:17	April 25
2:2	February 12
3:13	June 28
4:3–4	January 15
4:6	April 19

1 Thessalonians
4:17	June 3
5:23	August 3

1 Timothy
2:1	September 18
2:5–6	March 11

2 Timothy
1:3–4, 6–7	November 28
2:15	January 28
	June 10
3:16–17	September 30

Hebrews

1:7	November 9
2:13	December 26
5:8–9	September 22
11:13	December 15
12:14	June 27
13:5	November 13
13:8	September 28
13:14	September 7

James

1:23–25	April 26
5:16a	September 2

1 Peter

1:8–9	November 10
1:8–10	May 24
3:4	March 6
3:8	April 10
	October 30
4:9–10a	January 21
4:12	November 18

1 Peter (*continued*)

5:7	February 4
5:10	February 28

2 Peter

1:19	May 17
2:13b	March 1
2:19b	November 3

1 John

1:5	December 5
1:8–9	October 12
3:16–18	January 4
4:7–8	June 25
4:8	October 2

Revelation

2:17	September 21
3:2	July 17
3:20	January 3
3:22	February 6
22:2	April 6

AUTHOR INDEX

Foster, Richard J.

January 3	April 26	August 8	November 13
January 16	May 6	August 24	November 23
February 1	May 20	September 2	December 8
February 21	June 7	September 18	December 27
March 17	June 23	October 8	
March 23	July 8	October 23	
April 22	July 19	November 3	

Griffin, Emilie

January 29	April 30	July 30	October 27
February 24	May 24	August 11	November 28
March 19	June 30	September 3	December 20

Griffin, William

January 13	April 10	July 12	October 13
February 11	May 7	August 26	November 12
March 10	June 14	September 11	December 10

Leax, John

January 1	April 4	July 15	October 28
January 15	April 7	July 24	October 31
January 22	April 12	July 29	November 7
January 28	May 1	August 2	November 17
February 10	May 8	August 12	November 22
February 20	May 12	August 22	November 30
February 28	May 22	September 5	December 5
March 7	June 4	September 8	December 13
March 20	June 16	September 20	December 18
March 24	June 27	September 28	
March 31	July 6	October 18	

L'Engle, Madeleine

January 6	April 6	June 28	September 23
January 27	April 16	July 1	October 20
February 2	April 25	July 11	October 30
February 12	May 4	July 21	November 8
February 23	May 14	August 6	November 18
March 4	May 25	August 16	November 29
March 15	June 2	August 27	December 6
March 25	June 13	September 13	December 11

Miller, Andrea Wells

January 26	May 10	August 3	November 14
February 29	May 30	August 18	November 24
March 12	June 18	September 10	December 3
March 27	July 7	September 24	
April 28	July 14	October 15	

Miller, J. Keith

January 5	April 13	July 25	October 14
January 17	April 23	August 7	October 25
January 20	May 2	August 19	November 1
February 8	May 13	August 23	November 5
February 15	May 26	September 1	November 15
March 5	June 8	September 16	December 7
March 13	June 26	September 25	December 19
March 29	July 10	October 9	December 26

Nelson, Shirley

January 23	April 21	July 16	October 3
February 14	May 31	August 14	November 2
March 21	June 10	September 6	December 22

Owens, Virginia Stem

January 10	April 3	July 18	October 7
January 25	April 17	July 28	October 16
February 3	May 5	August 13	October 26
February 18	May 17	August 20	November 10
March 2	May 28	September 4	November 25
March 16	June 9	September 15	December 14
March 30	June 19	September 27	December 29

Peterson, Eugene H.

January 2	April 1	July 2	October 12
January 11	April 19	July 17	October 22
January 21	April 24	August 10	November 11
February 6	May 15	August 21	November 21
February 22	May 29	August 30	December 21
February 27	June 6	September 12	December 28
March 14	June 15	September 30	
March 28	June 25	October 5	

Schaap, James Calvin

January 8	April 18	July 3	October 11
January 19	April 27	July 20	October 21
January 30	April 29	August 5	November 4
February 5	May 9	August 15	November 20
February 16	May 27	August 28	December 9
February 25	June 1	September 19	December 31
March 9	June 11	September 29	
March 22	June 21	October 2	

Shaw, Luci

January 9	April 8	July 13	October 17
January 14	April 11	July 23	October 24
January 24	April 15	July 31	November 6
January 31	May 3	August 1	November 16
February 4	May 11	August 9	November 26
February 13	May 19	August 17	December 4
February 26	May 23	August 25	December 12
March 3	June 3	September 7	December 17
March 11	June 12	September 17	December 23
March 18	June 20	September 26	
March 26	June 29	October 4	
April 2	July 5	October 10	

Siegel, Robert

January 12	April 20	July 27	October 1
February 9	May 21	August 29	November 9
March 8	June 17	September 21	December 24

Walker, Jeanne Murray

January 7	May 18	August 31	December 1
February 19	June 24	September 14	December 16
March 6	July 9	October 39	December 25
April 9	July 26	November 27	December 30

Yancey, Philip

January 4	April 5	July 4	October 6
January 18	April 14	July 22	October 19
February 7	May 16	August 4	November 19
February 17	June 5	September 9	December 2
March 1	June 22	September 22	December 15

OF RELATED INTEREST
by HENRI J. M. NOUWEN

LIFE OF THE BELOVED
Spiritual Living in a Secular World

Now available in paperback!   Over 200,000 copies in print!

"One day while walking on Columbus Avenue in New York City, Fred turned to me and said, 'Why don't you write something about the spiritual life for me and my friends?'

"Fred's question became more than the intriguing suggestion of a young New York intellectual. It became the plea that arose on all sides — wherever I was open to hear it. And, in the end, it became for me the most pertinent and the most urgent of all demands: 'Speak to us about God.'"   *— from the prologue*

This personal witness to a God who calls us the Beloved is the fruit of a long friendship between journalist-writer Fred Bratman and Henri Nouwen. Henri is trying to respond to Fred's concern to live a spiritual life in the midst of a very secular world. A remarkable aspect of this book is that while Henri writes to a personal friend, he in fact found a language that speaks clearly and convincingly to all who search for the Spirit of God in the world. This work is a ringing affirmation that everyone is loved by God and can enjoy "the life of the beloved." It reveals the wonders of the spiritual journey and renews the fire of faith.

Paperback, 160 pages, 978-0-8245-1986-5

THE ONLY NECESSARY THING
Living a Prayerful Life
Compiled and Edited by Wendy Greer

Prayer is the dominant theme of Nouwen's books, talks, and life. This rich, deeply inspiring book will surely become the authoritative edition of Nouwen's writings on prayer.

Paperback, 224 pages, 978-0-8245-2493-7

crossroad

OF RELATED INTEREST
by HENRI J. M. NOUWEN

THE HEART OF HENRI NOUWEN
His Words of Blessing
Edited by Rebecca Laird and Michael J. Cristensen

In commemoration of the 70th anniversary of Nouwen's birth, Crossroad has issued this anthology of the best of Henri Nouwen from our list: *Life of the Beloved, Here and Now, Beyond the Mirror, Finding My Way Home,* and *Sabbatical Journey.* This collection focuses on the three themes that were closest to his own heart: hope in suffering, a personal relationship with God, and living for others.

Paperback, 978-0-8245-2220-9

Support your local bookstore,
or order directly from the publisher at www.crossroadpublishing.com

To request a catalog or inquire about quantity orders, contact
sales@crossroadpublishing.com

crossroad

www.ingramcontent.com/pod-product-compliance
Lightning Source LLC
Chambersburg PA
CBHW022056150426
43195CB00008B/164